THE GENTLE AMERICANS

BOOKS BY HELEN HOWE

The Gentle Americans
The Fires of Autumn
The Success
The Circle of the Day
We Happy Few
The Whole Heart

ONE GENTLE AMERICAN
M. A. DeWolfe Howe in 1955 at ninety-one

The Gentle Americans

1864-1960

Biography of a Breed

HELEN HOWE

HARPER & ROW, PUBLISHERS

New York

Sonnet XXIX by George Santayana is published in *Poems* by George Santayana, Charles Scribner's Sons, 1901.

Quotations from *A Venture in Remembrance* by M. A. DeWolfe Howe, copyright 1941 by M. A. DeWolfe Howe, reprinted with the permission of Little, Brown, and Company, publishers.

Quotations from *History of the Saturday Club* by M. A. DeWolfe Howe, reprinted with permission of Houghton Mifflin Company, publishers.

Quotation on page 60 from *Copey of Harvard* by J. Donald Adams, reprinted with the permission of Houghton Mifflin Company, publishers.

"For One Without Fear," pages 216–217, © 1961 by Abbie Huston Evans. Reprinted from her volume *Fact of Crystal* by permission of Harcourt, Brace & World, Inc.

Quotation on pages 291–292 from *Beatrice Webb's American Diary*, 1898, David Shannon, ed. University of Wisconsin Press, 1963, reprinted with the permission of the Passfield Trust, London School of Economics, London, England.

Quotation from "Provide, Provide" on page 432 from *Complete Poems by Robert Frost*, copyright 1936 by Robert Frost, © 1964 by Lesley Frost Ballantine, reprinted by permission of Holt, Rinehart and Winston, Inc.

The lines on page 435 are from Emily Dickinson's poem "This quiet Dust was Gentlemen and Ladies." Copyright 1914, 1942 by Martha Dickinson Bianchi. Reprinted by permission of the Belknap Press of Harvard University Press and of Little, Brown, and Company, publishers.

LIBRARY OF CONGRESS CATALOG CARD NUMBER: 65-20431

A-Q

For my father's grandchildren

CONTENTS

IV
Old Age Is Like Another Country

ILLUSTRATIONS

Frontispiece: One Gentle American

These illustrations follow page 140

Captain "Nor'west" John DeWolf
Weetamoe
"A little boy our man was then"
Light and fantastic
The Lehigh tennis team of 1886
The Bishop in a see of family
The Boosey Club
Codman on "The Shoulder"—Aunt Katy's
Mother and Father as engaged couple
The young Copeland
Aunt Mabel and admirer
Putnam Camp group in the 1880's
Mrs. Fields's drawing room in Charles Street
Uncle Wal
Robert Savage Chase
Arthur Dehon Hill
Naushon house party
The bell-ringing Shurcliffs of Beacon Hill

These illustrations follow page 332

Four Josiah Quincys (1772–1919)
The young Frances G. Curtis
The Curtis champions
Alice Bache Gould
Mary Cabot Wheelwright

ACKNOWLEDGMENTS

First, I wish to thank my friend Leo Lerman, without whose greathearted and inspiriting encouragement I might never have struggled beyond the amorphous first draft of these pages. Then, to my friend Jacques Barzun, for his incisive criticism of them at an early stage, my grateful thanks.

I am also greatly indebted to Norbert Slepyan, for his painstaking editorial counsel, and to Walter Muir Whitehill, Director of the Boston Athenaeum, for his careful reading of my final text for accuracy of its Boston detail.

I deeply appreciate the cooperation and helpfulness of Mr. William Bond and Miss Carolyn Jakeman of the Houghton Library at Harvard, of Miss Margaret Hackett of the Boston Athenaeum, of Mr. Stephen Riley, Director of the Massachusetts Historical Society, and the staff of the New York Society Library.

One friend in particular must receive grateful special mention, *post mortem:* It was the persistent and affectionate interest in my father's correspondence over many years on the part of Mr. William A. Jackson, Librarian of the Houghton Library of the Harvard College Library, that led Father, in his own lifetime, to arrange for this archive to be permanently deposited at Harvard. I lament that Bill Jackson did not live to see his imaginative foresight put to its first research use.

Only my two brothers and my husband can know how heavily I have leaned on their patience in the face of my persistent badgering of them with questions, as well as on their concrete assistance in countless details.

And finally, without the many friends of my father's, and the families of those friends, who not only have supplied personal recollections and anecdotes but have been so generous in granting me permission to quote from letters and to reproduce photographs,

[xi]

there would have been no book at all. These friends are too numerous to mention individually, but I am grateful to each and all.

H. H.

I wish to express my gratitude to:

Mr. Samuel Chamberlain for generously allowing me to reproduce his photograph of Nos. 20 and 22 Louisburg Square, from *Boston Landmarks* by M. A. DeWolfe Howe, New York, 1946.

Mr. Ogden Nash for allowing me to use his verses.

Mr. Verner Reed for generously allowing me to reproduce as the frontispiece for this book his photograph published in *Time*, August 29, 1955.

The Boston Athenaeum for allowing me to reproduce the photograph of Mrs. Fields and Miss Jewett in the drawing room at 148 Charles Street.

The Massachusetts Historical Society for allowing me to reproduce the photograph of Gamaliel Bradford.

Foreword

"PAPA'S PAPERS"

FROM MY BOSTON CHILDHOOD there remains for me a clear memory of two older ladies—faded beauties both. Each, with a wisp of graying hair falling against her rather distraught face, carried a green baize bag so heavy that her frail figure bent under its weight. The bulge in the bottom of that bag—and one knew that it represented a very small fraction of a larger burden—she referred to with a mingled sweetness and despair as "Papa's papers." It was in the hope of obtaining counsel concerning these papers that the daughter of William Dean Howells and the daughter of Professor Charles Eliot Norton used to pursue my father with majestic instancy, either into the Boston Athenaeum or into his own library at home. He was known to both these ladies as biographer and historian of literary New England.

Witnessing the spectacle of a maiden life laid down on the altar of a father's memory, as it had been laid down on the altar of that same father's demands during his lifetime, I shuddered—and vowed that the fate of such a Boston daughter would never overtake *me*. I knew, of course, that my father was less eminent than either of the two distinguished progenitors I have mentioned, but still there was a hazard all the same in living under the same roof with any man of letters who showed a tendency to becoming engulfed in "papers." In his old age, as he contemplated this tide which was rising around him, he used to say a little wistfully, "I suppose no one will ever want to write my biography." I was apt to answer with what I flattered myself was a far more realistic and "modern" attitude than that assumed by those daughters of the earlier generation, "No, Father. I should think it unlikely." "I suppose, however," he would continue, "that some of my correspondence might be of interest to historians who are curious about my 'period.' I think they might find a good deal of material in my papers." And, with this thought in mind, he bequeathed them to the Harvard College Library.

When, five years ago, Father died at the age of ninety-six I was moved to sit down and put something on paper of my memories of him. I felt at that time with particular poignancy the fact that I, unlike my two brothers, had no children of my own. To twist the Scripture which says, "Whoso honoreth his father shall have joy of his own children," I say that whoso shall have joy of his own children honoreth his father. Because I could not offer him the future, through flesh and blood, I could offer my own memories of the past—through a sort of daughter's "documentary." And though this act of picking up my pencil was prompted originally by no more complicated reason than that I enjoy remembering him, I thought it possible that I might be able to put those recollections into the space of a few pages, which would serve as a modest memoir. I had no intention of attempting a scholar's approach to that Pandora's box of "papers." But, as I wrote my own recollections, I could feel the magnetic pull growing stronger. Perhaps one peek would serve to help me to remember more. And so, for all the world like a serious sociological student, I applied for permission to sit down in the reading room of the Houghton Library and turn over the letters (now so beautifully catalogued) which had collected dust and bulged out of drawers at home, and had always stood for the past, when my own thoughts and dreams were centered on a present and a future. And thus, though my destiny—which has included many years of travel over the country in monologue recitals, appearances in New York nightclubs, and three years of living in Hollywood with my husband—has seemed so different from that of Miss Mildred Howells and Miss Sara Norton, now it is I who trail in and out of the Boston Athenaeum, as my own graying hair grows disheveled, and it is I who stoppeth one of three, to ask how I should treat "Papa's papers." This book which has grown so far past my original scheme for it is the result. My selection of letters written to Father has been dictated by my own interest only, and the ways of random sampling. Many, many more letters remain for the serious researcher.

In its issue of December 19, 1960, *Time* announced Father's
death: *Died, Mark Antony DeWolfe Howe, 96, biographer, historian
and poet, whose warmth and urbanity led his fellow Harvardman
Alfred North Whitehead to nominate him as the ideal man to represent the human race on a mission to Mars.* . . . Actually it is my
own recollection that Professor Whitehead was quoted as saying, at
a meeting of Boston's Saturday Club, "If I were asked to choose a
representative of Homo sapiens to send to Mars, I believe I should
choose Mark Howe." It is the life, the family, and friends of this
particular American example of Homo sapiens, by profession a
writer, which I have been interested in re-creating. In spite of his
having won one Pulitzer Prize Father's books were known, even in
his lifetime, to a limited number of readers; today they must be
known, if at all, to a mere handful. I do not come to praise him
as one of the famous men of Scripture. Indeed his own best hope
for himself as a biographer and historian was for "the survival
of my labors through the pale immortality of footnotes." Believing
Father's dear friend Van Wyck Brooks to have been right when he
wrote that "It is the minor books and writers that bring forth a
culture, creating the living chain that we call tradition," I offer
this record in remembrance of one link in that chain.

The pinpoint of space occupied by this minor writer for most
of his adult life was Boston, Massachusetts; the pinpoint of time,
1864–1960. The same setting, the same period, the same tastes and
talents as Father's have afforded the stuff out of which more than
one fictional Bostonian has been created by more than one satirical
novelist. (Indeed I hope that past writings of my own bear witness
to the fact that I myself have never been prone to take Boston
"straight.") The man I offer here differs from the Bostonian of
fiction in that he was neither born nor bred in Boston.

And yet it is there, returning in the flesh or in fancy, that—as the
taste of the *madeleine* dipped in tea performed the magic for
Proust—the quintessential flavor of Father comes alive again—for
me. This is not because he grew up in Boston—because he didn't—
but because I did. Even as I flew through the starry night sky on a
cold December evening in 1960 (children of the very old learn to

harden themselves to hurried trips, made under a succession of false alarms), knowing that this time, after ninety-six years of life, Father was dying, I also knew that the journey for me was not only one through space; it was one through time as well. It landed me away from my present and future in New York, back in the past, back in Boston. So, in this study subject and object reverse the roles they have played in works of fiction dug from the same pit: the man under scrutiny is not drawn by the hand of an outsider, looking in, but is recollected by a mind and heart shaped on the inside—looking back.

My hope is that the reader may find some of the same interest concerning a way of life that he would find in any other "documentary." I have tried to make my account as honest as any daughter can, consciously, make it. I have tried not so much to show him as the product of a time and place as to show that even that time and that place could contain not only a Homo sapiens, but an Everyman who lived and worked, who loved and was loved.

In looking back at my father, his family, and his friends I have written only of the dead—and in so doing am aware, for the first time, of something of the freedom known to the poet on his "Arrival in Edinburgh," and finding none of his old friends living.

> All have grown fictional, and thus complete,
> While in suspense, breathing the lively air,
> I step for the first time unguarded here.

Even my parents' three children of these pages are dead today. It is to be hoped that, fatherless at last, they are no longer recognizable as the unformed lumps of clay that appear here. Inevitably, there is more of myself than of my brothers, but I am sure they cannot regret that it is my lumpiness more than theirs which is on display. We children figure at all only in so far as we represent what my parents bequeathed to the future; just as their forebears figure as representing the forces in the background that went toward shaping *them*. And both the past and the future that bracketed my parents' generation are here limned to drive home, in one family chronicle, the brevity of American history.

In his later years Father used often to say, "I am not only an old man. I am a very old man." *How* old is borne in upon me in the realization that this month in which I write is the one hundredth anniversary of his birth. Though he remembered being held up as a child in Philadelphia to see the lines of blue-coated soldiers of the Northern Army of Occupation returning from the Civil War, he lived to see his son Quincy acting as moderator on the last pre-election television debate between John F. Kennedy and Richard Nixon—and, indeed, to vote himself for Kennedy. Father's temperament was uncomplicated and his life uneventful—as outer complications and outer events are measured. His nature had the clarity of a smoothly flowing stream, and it has been my pleasure to see in that stream, as it meandered pleasantly through so many years of American history, other faces reflected in it, returning to me along with his own. Although he and his friends lived during those years in American life which have come to be thought of as "The Good Years," associated with new money and new power, they moved in a world entirely removed from the manifestations of their more flamboyant contemporaries, involved with muckraking and trust busting. Although the outlines of my father's life and the use of many of "Papa's papers" are contained in these pages, this is not the biography of one man, but a picture of a circle. I have called them, on my title page, the Gentle Americans. I do not know how else to describe them!

In another context it was the same philosopher Whitehead who observed that "the immediacy of some mortal circumstance is only valuable because it shares in the immortality of some value." The "mortal circumstance" of the better part of a long life lived in Boston would not alone attract me as a subject, although, with Henry James I have found Boston's "local look" to be "full . . . after the appraisable fashion of some composed town-face in one of Balzac's *villes de province*." The provincial men and women under whose shadow I grew up all had individuality; I can testify that I have known no two alike. But it is the larger implication suggested by Whitehead—the universal "value" to be derived from the local and particular—which has deepened for me the meaning of my

return journey. My sardonically inclined brother Quincy recalls
with amusement watching Father settle back with a happy smile on
his face to read a review of one of his own books, which started with
the words, "Mark Howe is a Christian gentleman." As he read
further the smile slowly faded, as the realization grew that both
words were used as terms of opprobrium. I can add two more, applicable to him and most of his friends, which convey either satisfaction or distaste, according to the slant in the eye of the beholder.
For one, Father called himself an "unrepentant liberal." For the
other, he, who so loved people, called himself a "personist"—
though I should choose the broader, if more usual nomenclature
"humanist." One of his marked limitations—and it was shared by
most of his contemporaries—was a bland unawareness of the giant
strides science was making toward changing the world in which they
were exclusively preoccupied with human beings and the humanities. How would it have been possible for a writer grounded in the
classics to communicate with one of today's adventurers in space,
airborne on the language (and the grammar) of John Glenn's discipline? "I thought it would be just a matter of maybe a minute
after the sun went down, but apparently there's quite a bit of light
curving around through the atmosphere and that keeps the horizon
very visible for a period of five minutes or so. And this would bring
us around to a sunrise. This turned into a pretty interesting area
each time around, I think, as most of you are aware. At this
first light of sunrise—the first sunrise I came to—I was still faced
back toward the direction in which I had come from with normal
orbit attitude." Two cultures indeed!—when Eos, the rosy-
fingered Dawn has become a "pretty interesting area."

If today we smile at men whose "mode, or attitude of thought or
action [is] centered upon distinctively human interests or ideals"
(the dictionary definition of Humanism) we would do well to remember that Science itself has prophesied that Man in outer space
must ultimately confront merely—Man. Just as no stream can rise
higher than its source, so man cannot travel farther afield among
the stars than his own life span can take him, and no matter what
instruments he may devise for recording whatever may be shimmer-

ing or lurking at the edges of comprehension, that comprehension, which is to interpret the findings of the instruments, must not extend beyond that of—Man. If, then, the Man we send and the Man we find are to be one and the same it may be pertinent to consider again Professor Whitehead's choice of an archetypical ambassador. Our envoy cannot now be a Gentle American. The breed is.already extinct. We have already been catapulted into the world of C. P. Snow's "new men," and have lightheartedly jettisoned the values of the old men behind us. "Facing backward in the direction in which [we have] come," I invite my contemporary Americans to take one more look at the gentle generation that has just dropped below our national horizon. Our look may at least give us one last laugh. And when we hear it, let us be very sure that it is our own.

H.H.

New York City
March 15, 1965

What riches have you that you deem me poor,
Or what large comfort that you call me sad?
Tell me what makes you so exceeding glad:
Is your earth happy or your heaven sure?
I hope for heaven, since the stars endure
And bring such tidings as our fathers had.
I know no deeper doubt to make me mad,
I need no brighter love to keep me pure.

To me the faiths of old are daily bread;
I bless their hope, I bless their will to save,
And my deep heart still meaneth what they said.
It makes me happy that the soul is brave,
And, being so much kinsman to the dead,
I walk contented to the peopled grave.

Sonnet XXIX, GEORGE SANTAYANA

I

That Most Engaging Youth—
the Gallant and Genial DeWolfe

1

MARK HOWE OF BOSTON

"GET UP OFF YOUR STEAMER CHAIR, young lady, and walk around the deck with me. My companion here is tired. He's just had a baby, and it's done him in no end."

The young lady so addressed lived to be an old lady, and pass the story on to me. The scene, a ship on its way to the Azores. The year, 1905. The speaker, Professor William James. The "companion" who had been done in by having a baby, my father. The baby, me.

It was many years later that Father used to point out to me the little house—number 114—on Lower Mt. Vernon Street, Boston, in which he had flung himself weeping, face downward, on a sofa in the corner of the same room in which I was born. The new father, in those days, was not insulated from witnessing the birth pangs of his wife. My brother accompanied the event, I was also told, by singing in his nursery upstairs, in the falsetto voice of five and a half years, "Hark! the herald angels sing." The fact that Christmas was only two weeks past explains his choice of selection. (It was many years later that that same voice was to become familiar to radio listeners when it pronounced in unmistakable Yankee accents the most superfluous words on the air, his own announcement of his identity, "This is Quincy Howe.") Only a few weeks later Mother, always cynical about the lack of stamina in the *sexe faible*, urged Father to accept an invitation from a friend to join him on a trip to the Azores. The trip afforded just the recuperation needed, part of it hastened, no doubt, by the kindness of Professor James to the

[3]

prostrated new father to whom he lent his own copy of Oscar
Wilde's recently published *De Profundis*—heady reading for a
young editor of the *Youth's Companion*.

I recall here the circumstances of my own birth because through
it, inevitably, Father was born, for me, as a father. My brother
Mark was born eighteen months after me, in 26 Brimmer Street, just
around the corner, where my parents moved almost immediately
after my birth. So that *home* in dream and memory for me is always
Brimmer Street, and it is inevitably there that I see Father framed.
Nearly fifty years after the trip to the Azores an article appeared
in the *Atlantic Monthly* (colloquially the *Atlantic*) entitled "Mark
Howe of Boston." Its author, Arthur Stanwood Pier, described his
subject thus: "A compact figure, in sober clothes, round faced, with
grizzled, close-clipped mustache and eyes twinkling benignly behind
[steel] rimmed spectacles." I prefer to recall him as not yet the
established old gentleman he was to become, nor as the overwrought
young father of a new baby, but as a sort of composite picture of
all the Brimmer Street years. We—his family—are sitting in the
bow window of the library which looks out on Brimmer Street. The
brick houses in our block—each attached to its neighbor—were built
in the last quarter of the nineteenth century. There is a little plot of
grass in front of each. The houses breathe, if they breathe at all, an
air of comfort and conformity. Henry James, once standing with
Father at the head of Marlboro Street, looked down its long expanse of similar brick houses and sighed, "Marlboro Street cannot
be said to be precisely"—time out for the Jamesian pause—"*passionate.*" Neither is Brimmer Street precisely passionate. Along it
we can see Father, walking with a rather heavy tread, his head held
high and back, his walking stick characteristically swinging forward
before it touches the bricks of the sidewalk. In the other hand he
carries a green baize bag, heavy with books. (He had the pleasure
once of hearing a girl sitting on a bench on the Boston Common
murmur to her companion as he passed, "They all carry them.")
If it is spring, he is wearing a "Boston leghorn" hat and across his
comfortable front can be seen swinging his father's heavy gold
watch chain. His tread up the high stone steps, the turning of the

lock, even the deliberation with which he takes out his latch key, everything is done at a comfortable pace. There is no sense that he is going to need fast, fast, FAST relief from anything he has been facing all day or anything he is about to face. "Fanny?" he calls out in a pleasant tone of voice, on a rising inflection. She was the lodestar, the starting point, and the object of return at the close of each day.

His voice is agreeably modulated, and his speech unidentifiable as characteristic of any one city. He enjoys teasing his Boston wife for her pronunciation of salt as *sollt*. It is not only her speech which is recognizably Bostonian; for all her wit and beauty and warmth of heart there is a certain Yankee crispness, shared with her three children. She and we, all so much less socially inclined than Father, come back to me as all but cowering behind the front door of 26 Brimmer Street. Its latchstring was so little out that the ring of the doorbell brought a shiver of something bordering on dismay. It was only Father who passed through it with ease and pleasure, no matter which way he was going. He was our ambassador to the world outside, as he was its ambassador to us.

A few excerpts from letters of Mother to me in the early 1920's indicate some of the ports of call visited by our family Ambassador-at-large. "Father [is] leaving for his Examiner Club Dinner at which O'Brien of the *Herald* is going to prophesy the outcome of the election tomorrow—everyone but Father concedes the victory to Coolidge. He does not forget his triumph when he was right and the *Herald* wrong about Hughes and Wilson." . . . "Father is meeting the Moscow Art Players at the South Station this afternoon just to make them feel at home!" . . . "Father is at a Headmasters and Trustees dinner tonight, hearing all the Educators breathing hot air on to the feast." . . . "Father is on the committee which is giving Amy Lowell a grand dinner next Saturday night, with speeches by Lowes, and Robert Frost, etc. All Boston (with one exception, who shall be nameless!) is going, and great will be the flattery and praise bestowed upon Copeland's only rival in the field of conceit!" And then, apropos "the Complimentary (not to say Flattery) Dinner which Amy Lowell's friends gave her last Saturday night. There were about 400 guests, —and sixteen speakers of whom your little

Lowes [John Livingston Lowes, with whom I had taken a course at Radcliffe] was the best, Father thought." . . . "Father found himself among the seats of the mighty, watching Amy smoke a big black cigar, while being presented with a silver bowl full of orchids." . . . "Father is in New York, being unable to resist the lure of the dinner given to Lord Robert Cecil, as the winner of the Wilson Foundation Prize."

In his comings and goings Father possessed the faculty of finding some bond of common interest with almost everyone he met. Mother called him the "bond salesman." If he heard one of the yeomen, outside of the Tower of London, singing for his own pleasure on a frosty morning, "Hail, smiling morn, smiling morn, smiling morn," Father was enraptured to be able to sing back antiphonally, "That tip'st the hills with gold, that tip'st the hills with gold." The bond—Boosey's book of "Glees," which had been a family staple during his Pennsylvania boyhood. Mother, when asked to exclaim over this or any other extraordinary coincidence which he came to lay at her feet, like a dog with a bone, often yielded to the temptation of asking him, with her quizzical smile, "Well, what of it?" But any dampener on his pleasure was like taking candy from a baby. It is only fair to add, however, that in all his encounters he was more genial than jovial, that there was more of sweetness than heartiness in his approach; he did not slap his man on the back, but smiled into his eyes. Mother said he was like a friendly dog who would go up to any stranger, wagging his tail, confident of liking and being liked.

Of course sometimes a "bond" misfired. I remember my discomfiture at an early birthday party of my own when Father insisted on trying to establish rapport with one of my guests. I introduced him to a little friend of mine named Rhodes, from Brookline, and he affably said, to put her at ease, "You must be some relation of my friend James Ford Rhodes, the historian." "I don't think so," the little girl quavered. Further exploration proved that she belonged to the Rhodes Brothers Grocery dynasty.

I don't know, but it might have been the same year that he gave me a small volume of his own poems. On the flyleaf is written, "To my very dear Mother—this first copy of the *magnum opus* of M. A. DeW. H. November 1897." Two pages later is written:

Dear Helen,

Eighteen years ago—eight years before you were born—I gave this little book to the sweetest old lady I ever knew. When she died, it became mine again, and now I give it to the sweetest young lady I ever knew—who is ten years old today.

M. A. DeW. H.

11 January 1915

He returns to his family as he left them—on foot. His office, his club, his church, and the Boston Athenaeum are all within walking distance. It's an easy walk to the subway to take him to Cambridge, and Harvard College. If it is a Monday, Mark Howe of Boston may have been either to a meeting of the Board of Harvard Overseers, the Directors of the Atlantic Monthly Company, the Trustees of the Boston Symphony Orchestra, the Library Committee of the Boston Athenaeum, or the Vestry of Trinity Church. It it is a Monday with no meetings, he will undoubtedly have lunched at his beloved Tavern Club in Boylston Place, and may be planning in the evening, if it is the first Monday of the month, to go to the meeting of the Examiner Club.

Nancy Byrd Turner, the Southern poet, was to recall to Father, years later, her first visit to Brimmer Street. "The three 'children' —well, that's what they were in 1916—remain as very vivid recollections in these latter days. Quincy . . . was fifteen and . . . just lately in long trousers, it seems to me. That was before long trousers were donned at 15 months. Helen, I can see now, the first night I ever met any of you, standing in front of the fire, long fair hair. . . . Mark distrusted me slightly, as some strange sort of outlander. He had on a white 'turndown' collar, set off by a Windsor tie." It is very much so, at the end of the day, that Father finds us three children in the library with Mother. No committee meetings for her, and no clubs either! How blandly we always gather there, ignoring the fact that it is the room in which Father does his writing. It is anything but a sumptuous room; in fact it is very nearly a shabby room. But it has atmosphere. A family has lived in it, been happy in it, sometimes got on each other's nerves in it, but always contained in the frame of reference that encircles it—books, books, and more books. Mother used to say that books multiply on shelves and tables; put down two at night, and there are four in the morning. The slip covers and curtains are of fading chintz, as are the covers drooping off the tables, but they are barely visible under the mounds of magazines and reading matter that bury them. Aside from the volumes in the shelves the room is benevolently dominated by the portrait hanging over the cannel-coal grate that Father always referred to as "Our Old Master"—Duveneck's "Lady with a Fan." Its rich dark tones are, indeed, Rembrandt-like, and the face of the Lady herself, in half shadow, an interesting and restful presence. She was given to my grandmother Quincy by a friend, for no better reason than that the Lady resembled her.

Enter Father. Bearing, inevitably, the Boston *Evening Transcript*. T. S. Eliot wrote of a Boston evening as "wakening the appetites of life in some, And to others the Boston *Evening Transcript*." To me, the conflict of growing up in Boston was that it brought both. Mrs. Bell, the Boston wit of a generation earlier than my parents, whom I dimly remember as a spry old lady in a bonnet and tippet who lived somewhere on the Hill, is supposed to have asked her husband every evening, "Anybody nice dead in the *Transcript*?" (This was the same Mrs. Bell who said, the first time she saw Isadora Duncan dance, "I have seen a naked Cabot.") One was sure that if anybody "nice" had died, someone equally nice had sent a letter to the *Transcript* extolling his or her virtues.

It is a wonder to me how Father did any writing at all at home, and yet, as there are chain smokers, he must have been a chain writer; as he sat at his heavy mahogany desk, once he had finished with the *Transcript*, there was always that green "Venus" pencil in his hand, with its black case and eraser at the tip, hurrying across the page, under the double kerosene "student" green-glass-shaded lamp.

Aside from the massive biographical work in progress (the mere number alone of such works from his pen helped to earn for Father the title used in the *Atlantic* article as the "Dean of Boston Letters.") Father was always writing an article, a chapter, a letter (for publication), a poem, an "occasional" verse, or words for a song to be sung by him at the Tavern Club, a resolution (concerning a fellow member of one of the innumerable boards on which he served, who was resigning, or had died), a "paper" to be read at one of the erudite clubs to which he belonged, or an editorial. Indeed it was precisely through so much of just this sort of writing that "Mark Howe of Boston" began to take shape as something of a local institution. His chore of writing an editorial was performed regularly every Sunday evening for more than twenty-five years, its destination the *Harvard Alumni Bulletin*. He wrote it in one draft, by hand, of exactly the specified length and then went out to mail it at the mailbox under the gas street light, in time for the evening collection. It must have been dreadful for the poor printer to confront his illegible handwriting on a Monday morning. (Mother said that Father's fingers were like éclairs.) From his pen, too, came the graceful note. Poor Father! He was so much politer to others than they were to him! He often had cause to observe ruefully that when a total stranger asked him a favor—an opinion on an unsolicited manuscript or a piece of literary or historical information—his correspondent was very apt not to express even perfunctory thanks for the time and thought given. As in so many aspects of life Father harked back to the ways of the generation that preceded his. Among his papers was a letter of Longfellow's, written in the poet's handwriting, to Miss Abby DeWolf, an elderly Bristol cousin of Father's who had written that she had "evidently sent a copy of her book of commonplace verse to Longfellow, and received in response this illustration of his kindness of heart."

Cambridge, Nov. 9
1873

DEAR MADAM,

I have had the pleasure of receiving your note, and the poems you were kind enough to send me, and beg you to accept my thanks for this mark of your consideration.

These poems I have read with interest and sympathy, and

feel how great a comfort it must be to you to be able to occupy the leisure which advancing years bring with them, with the exercise of your talent. If, as you say, you cannot hear the singing of the birds, you will enjoy all the more the sound of the voice that sings within.

Hoping that this consolation may never fail you, I am, Dear Madam

Yours truly
HENRY W. LONGFELLOW

If Father's notes of fifty years later, also handwritten, showed no less kindness of heart, they were hardly less flowery. In fact it has always been hard for me to understand what happened to his natural warm human juices when he "took pen in hand" to write a letter. We could actually hear him wheezing to himself as his lips framed the words he addressed, perhaps to a Harvard freshman. It seemed as though every fall there was a new one—more often than not connected, however tenuously, with the tribe of Howe. One such still possesses the note he received in November, 1923, surely in its stilted formal address no preparation for the genial welcoming "Uncle Mark" he was to meet for the first time. It might indeed have chilled him if he had been told that its author was one day to become his dearly loved father-in-law.

MY DEAR REGINALD,

(I suppose a great uncle may begin by dropping titles.) I am writing to ask whether you will not come to dinner with us next Sunday and make the acquaintance of some of your Boston relatives. If you are going to the Yale game on Saturday, I daresay you will be back in time to ring our bell at quarter past one. You will find that Brimmer Street runs out from Beacon opposite the Public Garden.

Hoping very much that you have no other engagement, I am

Very sincerely yours,
M. A. DEWOLFE HOWE

As Father was a stickler for the right word on paper, so he adhered to the proper use of a man's name. Books of reference—notably *Who's Who in America,* the *Harvard Quinquennial,* as well as the

Oxford Companion to English Literature—were what Mother called
a mania with him. He himself called them his only hobby. Do parents nowadays spangle their talk with quotations as much as Father
did? It didn't worry him—though it worried his children considerably—if they happened to be in Greek or Latin. He could write to
me in later life, *"Finis coronat opus,* dear novelist, and if you don't
know what that means (and I bet you do)—Reggie will tell you.''
Surprise and chagrin were mingled when we invariably had to ask
the meaning of some wise saw he would toss at us. *Solvitor ambulando* and *suaviter in modo, fortiter in re* were favorites, the latter
often given in an alternative version of ''Softly, softly catches the
monkey.'' His own first slim volume of verse he called *Rari Nantes,*
admitting that he himself might not have thought of Virgil's *Rari
nantes in gurgito vasto* had it not been for his father's use of it
every time he ladled oysters out of a large soup tureen! (Mother, to
whom the volume was delicately and indirectly dedicated long before she was engaged to its author, ungratefully translated the few
swimmers as ''Rare Nuggets.'') Any proffered gift or invitation
was apt to be accepted in W. S. Gilbert's words, ''The noble gal did
not decline, but simply said, 'With pleasure.' '' There was, as well, a
whole category of innocent merriment, emphasis on the innocent,
such as the dinner at which Professor Edward Kennard Rand of
Harvard proposed a toast to Father, *"Marcus Antonius De Lupus
Quam*—ET QUAM!''

As children we accepted the written word as a basic Fact of Life.
When people asked us the name of our little cocker spaniel, and we
answered, ''Brownie,'' we priggishly hastened to explain that it was
not because he was brown but because he looked like Mrs. Browning.
Her picture with her hair hanging in forlorn loops like Brownie's
ears, had been shown us in the frontispiece of the Cambridge Edition of her *Complete Works.* It was from the same bow window in
the library that my brother Mark, aged eight, had watched me come
howling down Brimmer Street, waving an empty leash, which he
immediately, and rightly, interpreted to mean as direful news as
Theseus' black sail. Brownie had just been run over by a car on the
Esplanade, and Mark, far more heroic than Aegeus who chose the

easy way, appeared downstairs at the front door to let me in and uttered, white-faced, what I consider the most selfless words I have heard that ever-selfless brother utter, "That's all right. It doesn't matter." This from the same little boy who himself was so tender-hearted that he had to be hurried past the display window of Lewandos' cleaning establishment on Boylston Street, where a full-size cat was standing upon her hind legs wiping off and hanging up to dry on a clothesline a row of chickens. One glimpse was enough to set him off into ululations to match those of mine which he attempted to calm by his stoic lie.

Father used to attempt to read poetry aloud to us on Sunday evenings for the simple reason that *his* parents used to read it aloud to him when *he* was young. I say that he attempted to read to us because the sad fact was that his hope that reading aloud would become a family pastime was never realized; we simply didn't want to listen. In one of Mother's anonymous essays, published in the *Atlantic*'s "Contributors' Club," "No Reading Allowed," she described a couple who, before marriage, thought that they shared in common the taste for reading aloud. Only after marriage did they discover that neither could tolerate being read *to*. Certainly when we all assembled, if anyone else did the reading, Father nodded off over his pipe, waking himself with a stentorian snore, and if he did the reading—the snores were ours. We were much happier if Father left the library, and went instead to the "back parlor" and seated himself at the piano, for family singing. On Sunday evenings there were hymns. They only served, however, to start the ball rolling. Father came uniquely alive—indeed it is where he sits most happily in memory for me—at the piano. His mother's instrument, which I still cherish, is a lovely rosewood Chickering of a shape and style long discarded, christened, he had been told, Cocked Hat. It still stands for me, as it stood for him, as the symbol of a happy childhood.

Father was not a musician in any accepted sense, but was endowed with that most enviable of gifts—an "ear." Under its guidance his fingers roamed easily over the keyboard; he was flattered one day at the Tavern Club when his friend the composer George Chadwick who was standing at his side commented, "You certainly know your way around the key of G." All the same, it disgusted Father that he had never mastered the skill of sight reading. He tried—too late!—to acquire it, struggling through a selection of Bach chorales, interrupted frequently by an explosive *"Pshaw!"* or *"Confound it!"* The closest that Father came to swearing was when he said the word *da—nation*. He was trying, exemplary son of a bishop, to make a nod in the direction of *darnation,* but the *a,* as he pronounced it, was unmistakably short.

Do you see the man I wish you to see? The words that flowed from Mark Howe of Boston in writing as in singing were used not to explore any subtleties of philosophical thought, not to exhort, or to plead: they were used as a bridge to connect him with his fellow man, as an expression of a friendly, outgoing nature. Father instinctively liked people. The perfectly adjusted man? The round peg in the round hole? Yes. Yes. I can answer stoutly to both queries.

And yet . . . The Sunday guest might already, in Father's greeting of him in the library, or particularly in his making the introductions to the rest of the family, have suffered a tremor of shock, and then of embarrassment. Father's family always waited, tense, in the presence of a new arrival, knowing that the moment must come. But it was at the dining-room table when, all charm and affability, he would embark on an anecdote, which I have been told by friends would be greeted by a stricken look repeating itself around the table on the faces of wife and children, that family tension mounted unbearably. It was simply because we all knew—who better?—that the anecdote would never be told smoothly to the end. *Some*where behind this apparently sunny nature lay—or had once lain—a shadow. *Some*where, conscious or unconscious, there must have been tension or strain. This hidden struggle was made manifest in a painful outer struggle. Father was cruelly handicapped by a bad stammer. It was in his anecdotes—so well known to us—that we could prophesy exactly the snag on which he was bound to be impaled. Many of his anecdotes began, "My father used to tell the story." There was, for one, the prayer of the nondenominational clergyman,

"Paradoxical as it may seem to Thee, O Lord, it is nevertheless true. . . ." That was a particularly hard one to embark upon because of the archenemy—the letter *p*. Father was adept at the devious game of synonyms that the confirmed stammerer plays. A p-p-policeman is hastily transformed into an officer of the law or the fellow that directs traffic. But the inexorable moment could not be avoided at the end of a supposedly funny story when a specific tag line or word had to be spoken. And we knew that it was that word that was going to be his undoing. When the moment we all so dreaded arrived, the poor man wrestled and tussled until either Mother or one of us who knew his stories, word for word, by heart, could bear it no longer, and freed him by supplying the missing word—thereby ruining the effect of his story. Father's amazing resilience of nature, pleasure in people ("seeing people always bucks me up," he would say), gushed up afresh after these rebuffs, and the next time, to the mingled admiration and horror of his introverted family, he would start all over again!

Words were the very coin of Father's realm, and he was prodigal in his use of them. Those that he left behind him tell much of the sources of his interests, his happiness, and of his strength. They all testify to a natural inclination toward sunshine and light. Yet somewhere, at some time, there must have been one Word that he could—or would?—not speak. What its name or to what deep dark soil of the unconscious its roots continued to cling remained a mystery. Among all that he did speak, that one Word, to the end, remained unspoken.

2

THE BRISTOL WAY

MOTHER WAS NOMINALLY A UNITARIAN. The designation, however, merely glossed over a deeply ingrained agnosticism. She showed more sense of irony than filial piety in calling one wall of our Brimmer Street dining room The Bishops' Corner. On it hung a veritable cloudburst of family witnesses to the Protestant Episcopal faith, exploding in lawn sleeves and a cascade of crucifixes. But the dominating figure—the largest photograph in the largest frame— was that of Father's father, the first Bishop of Central Pennsylvania. It showed a fine head and massive torso. But the truth was that, like an ambulatory iceberg in reverse, seven eighths of him appeared above the waist. Mother, who had met him only once, before she was engaged to Father, cut him down to size for us by saying, "The Bishop sat high." Indeed it was he whom she blamed for the lowly stature of her own children. He, dead so long before any of us were born, loomed for us not only portentously but a little ludicrously as the husband of three wives and the father of eighteen children—a number Father always found "rather mortifying." It was tacitly decided that our religious education was in Father's hands. Actually those hands never closed in a dogmatic stranglehold on any of us. Father's beliefs had nothing to do with dogma, reflecting rather a temperament whose natural expression lay in faith, hope, and charity. Quincy, as the oldest, was probably treated to the most specifically religious training, chiefly at St. George's, an avowed "church" school. I, like him, was started on Sunday school.

[15]

That phase didn't last long, when Mother discovered that my debutante Sunday-school teacher was telling her pupils that Buddha was only a carved idol and had never lived as a real man. I was removed forthwith from Sunday school. The fact that the debutante's name was Lowell, who, speaking only to God, had no need herself of any intermediary, did not help to mitigate in her favor. But I continued to go to church with Father, sitting squirming beside him in his pew in the gallery of Emmanuel Church—a church of which, incidentally, an errant Episcopal (!) cousin of Mother's— Bishop Frederic Dan Huntington—had been the first rector.

There was a ceremonial aspect to Sunday mornings with Father, from his polishing the surface of his top hat with the inside sleeve of his cutaway coat to the thrill of both words and music of the *Benedicite,* to which he, singing bass beside me, wagging his head from side to side, gave himself up with abandon. "O ye Dews and Frosts, bless ye the Lord, O ye Frost and Cold, bless ye the Lord, O ye Ice and Snow, bless ye the Lord: praise him and magnify him forever." During the sermon I sat close to him, and played with his amethyst watch fob or Phi Beta Kappa key and speculated on the meaning of the stained-glass window which faced us, showing four maidens in white, one of whom was pointing out to a young man a temple placed against distant purple hills and cypress trees. My wandering attention must have been sufficiently caught on one Sunday to cause me to ask in a stage whisper during the seemingly interminable list of *Thou Shalt Nots,* "What's adultery?" All I got from Father, to whom an evasion of the Facts of Life was instinctive, was a shake of the head to silence me. Even if Mother was a Unitarian, and didn't go to church, that hot potato was handed to her.

Father and I used to walk home down Commonwealth Avenue, then across the Public Garden. It embarrassed me when he tried— as he often did—to talk about what churchgoing meant to him. Not that he made any more orthodox statement than "I must say I enjoy at the end of a week of prose an hour of poetry." Perhaps this response to the poetic approach added to the relish with which he pointed out in the Garden the statue of William Ellery Channing, facing the Arlington Street Church, before which a devout Italian woman, newly arrived in Unitarian Boston had been observed kneeling in prayer. Father's remarks generally followed a wistful admission that he wished either Mother or the boys *liked* to go to church. Then he would add, "We always took churchgoing as a matter of course at Bristol." There it was again—Bristol! That Never-Never Land, so important to Father, and so remote from his children. Those friendly blue eyes that surveyed the Boston around him were bright with a recollected vision of quite other surroundings.

Father, in 1864, was born in Bristol, Rhode Island, because he was born in summer. Actually in that year his father was rector of St. Luke's Church in Philadelphia. But Bristol was writ large on the heart of both father and son. After all, had it not been the seat of Howes in good standing since the eighteenth century, as for the deWolfs since the seventeenth? For Father its very name spelled "the family." (And speaking of spelling, it was my grandfather who changed the small *d* to the capital letter, and added a final *e* to Wolf. His grandson George believes he made the changes to add "tone.") Members of that family to whom all his life Father was to feel so strongly bound came to Boston from Bristol only occasionally, and belonged, so far as we children were concerned, to an unknown world. It is a confession it shames me to make but, on looking back, I think there was something in the air of Boston—or, perhaps, in that breathed by Mother—that gave us the sense that to come from Bristol was a little less—a little less—(a little less *what?* I can't find the right word!) let's leave it simply at a little less than to come from Boston. There was no sense of social superiority on Mother's part, only a built-in distrust of a background redolent of ecclesiasticism—understandable in one sprung from the Unitarian tradition said to proclaim the Fatherhood of God, the Brotherhood of Man, and the Neighborhood of Boston. It seemed, furthermore, as though the Bristol Howes were not only Episcopalians but that their religion (so unlike the Boston brand!) seemed to put no damper on a natural inclination to enjoy life.

As we children grew older and were taken to Bristol from time to time we rather withdrew from the hordes of relatives—and how many of them there were!—who spent their winters in Philadelphia and were frighteningly different from ourselves. They greeted us and Mother, too, with resounding un-Bostonian kisses. There was a lot to drink for the adults, wonderful things to eat for everybody, and in one heavily laden family branch, affixed to the family tree through marriage, a pervasive sense of money that was vaguely shocking to our narrow Boston vision. The girls were all beautiful— indeed out-and-out beauties. I blush to think what manifestations of stiffness and suspicion our shyness must have taken. Mrs. Robert Homans of Boston—née Abigail Adams—has recounted her memory of once meeting my brother Mark in Boston at a gala evening of the Tavern Club to which ladies were invited, and making some passing remark about what a nice evening it was, to which Mark crisply answered, "I hate pleasure." It only went to show how far he had traveled from the traditions of Bristol!

Father never gave himself to any piece of writing with more enthusiasm than he did in late life to what he called a "Town Biography" of his birthplace. On its title page he quoted Kipling's lines,

> God gives all men all earth to love,
> But since man's heart is small,
> Ordains for each one spot shall prove
> Beloved over all.

Throughout his little book Father referred to the unique mingling of "worldliness and piety" which were characteristic of this flourishing seaport town of such architectural grace and grandeur. Like the southwest wind, known for relaxing the moral fiber of some of Bristol's citizens, even its piety belonged to a "temperate zone." That same temperate zone was destined to remain Father's theological as well as intellectual habitat.

A word that figured in Father's vocabulary, as it did in that of other Americans who were young on the Eastern seaboard in the eighties and nineties was "swell"—used not as an adjective but as a noun. In that limited sense of its time and place, it can be stated

categorically that Father was not a swell. The seventeenth child of
a clergyman's family was not likely to be that! But Bristol itself,
during the summers of the eighties was a place to which swells
came—from Philadelphia, New York, and Providence. (Father
wrote in 1950, "This, I find, is still an active little state with more
of a New York than a Boston exposure.") Photographs show Father
a gay young blade in a striped blazer, straw boater worn a bit
aslant, with a drooping mustache. The result was that all his life—
for all that the home of his mind and spirit was in the world of
letters—Father felt genially and happily at home with men and
women of "the world," neither troubled, on the one hand, by envy
of their yachts, mansions, idleness, or other possessions nor, on the
other, sneering or disdainful of pleasures and luxuries enjoyed by
men and women of cultivation and charm. If the Howe boys did not
own yachts, like some of the summer visitors and Newport neighbors, they were proud to count as friends the boatbuilding family
of Herreshoffs, so many of them blind. The Howes sailed the same
waters in carefree happiness in a succession of small catboats kept
moored off their stone dock. The largest of them was christened after
the beloved farm itself—*Weetamoe*. When years later one of the
world-famous Herreshoff racing sloops was christened with the
same name, Father admitted that the family felt "as if our privacy
had been invaded." Actually, both Herreshoffs and Howes were
only helping themselves to a name alive in the Bristol legend which
tells that the sister-in-law of Indian King Philip, trying to escape
from the pursuing British in a canoe, capsized and was drowned,
and her body washed up on the shore of what was to become the
Howe farm.

Weetamoe exerted its magnetic pull every spring. By the time
Father was eight years old, and his father was Bishop of Central
Pennsylvania, the family had moved to Reading. He recalled in
conversation and in print his memories of the move from there to
Bristol. The family would set forth in the early morning

A noble army; men and boys
The matron and the maid

for the long ride in a day coach, across Pennsylvania, all the way to Jersey City and the ferryboat.

If the ferryboat was exciting, the Fall River boat, a very galleon of juvenile romance, was still to be boarded. When the musical chime of the ferryboat mooring chains fell silent we stepped ashore on Manhattan Island. The North River Pier from which we were soon to sail was too near to justify the expense of cabs. Then we fell in for the march along West Street—crowded with drays—my father at the head of the procession, almost as "short and stout and roundabout" as the Bishop of Rumtifoo himself. . . . Whether consciously or not, he always gave the impression of having nothing to do with the stragglers in his train—my mother, bearing fardels like her leader, and like the several maids that followed her, and like ourselves, one of whom would carry a bird cage and another lead (or drag) a black setter who insisted on lying down at every such crisis as the passing of a railway engine or similar monster. . . .

Safe on the Fall River boat—most warmly blessed if it happened to be the *Bristol*—we had yet a great moment in store. Had the carriage-horses and the coachman, who had started for New York on a freight train on the day before our departure, arrived in time to sail with us? Then, planted on the forward deck above the freight gangway, we watched and waited, and swelled with pride and joy as we saluted our friend of the stable leading the pair on board. Band music and fluttering flags . . . float back in memory.

There was another memory of the Fall River boat, and none could be more grisly . . . passing from Hell Gate into the Sound there was the spectacle of a steamboat beached and in furious flames. The sun was setting directly behind it and against its blaze, beneath the canopy of smoke and fire, we could see small black figures, silhouetted against the sun, leaping from the decks into the water. The next morning all the world shuddered at the story of a hideous disaster—the burning of the excursion boat *Seawanhaka* with a shocking toll of lives.

On our early morning arrival at Fall River, there was al-

ways another boat to take. . . . At the Bristol wharf . . . a beach
wagon and carry-all were waiting for the drive of a mile or
more to the farm. . . . The gaunt Mrs. Gladding . . . had opened
the house and prepared the first—and oh, so late—breakfast.
Johnnycake, spread with butter from our own dairy, strawberries from our own beds—what famishing boy would not
welcome that indigenous repast, *apéritif* to a long banquet of
summer pleasures!

At the shore itself stood the stone wharf and bath house. . . .
Each of us claimed as "my stone" one of them, at a bed near
the base of the wharf, and on this stone each left his hastily
stripped clothing for the first swim, as for the many that followed. There was no nonsense of trunks in that privacy of
glorious, unfeminated light. And there was small need for
towels. The "pond lot," with its smooth surface that was never
tilled, ran down to the wharf, and racing naked as young Gre-
cians over its sward, we dried ourselves in the sun and wind.

I cannot attempt to record by name each of Father's family
circle. Of the eighteen children seven brothers lived to grow up:
four were half brothers, and two whole. Only one half sister survived. Of Father's two own brothers, the older was Arthur, the
youngest Wallis. All of the halves as well as the wholes, adding
throughout the years spouses and children, were integral parts of
the Bristol summers, most of them living under the hospitable roof
of Weetamoe. In the background stood, as so often in Victorian
families, the unmarried maiden relative or relatives, in Father's
case "Cousin Lizzie" and "Cousin Virginia" Smith—cousins of
his father.

The strongest bond between any of the children was that which
united Wallis, or "Wal" (pronounced Woll), with Father, nick-
named "Cal" (in honor, nobody seems to know why, of "my good
friend the Calendar," who figured in *The Diverting History of John
Gilpin*). His beloved younger brother personified for Father, all his
life, his own feeling for Bristol. When Uncle Wallis, as candidate
of all three political parties as president of the Town Council, led
the Fourth of July parade, mounted on a white horse, Father used to
say—as he did on many other occasions—"I consider Wal the head

of the family.'' It had not, however, been ever thus. The ''midget Wal,'' as his older brother referred to him, must have been a delight to his family from an early age. At five years old, taking his turn among the hierarchy of brothers at saying grace before meals, he said simply, ''O Lord, make us graceful.'' Graceful he was to remain, in mind, heart, and spirit for the ninety-four years of his life. Graceful, too, in very fact the midget of quicksilver must have been when, like Wee Willie Winkie in his nightgown, he ran not all over town but, fast asleep, along the ridgepole of the roof of Weetamoe to the horror of his transfixed family. The sensitive young Wallis must already have been showing in dramatic form the tension that caused him, too, to fall victim to the same curse that dogged his older brother. He also suffered a terrible stammer—actually, a great deal worse than Father's. Both brothers, talking over their common affliction, as they often did in later years (and, incidentally, never stammering when they talked about it!), were agreed that Uncle Wallis simply ''picked it up'' as an imitative admiring younger brother often takes on a mannerism of an older brother. This may be true. It was also true that Number Eighteen knew what it was to quail under the eye of his Bishop father.

Father, looking back in later years, characteristically attributed to the Bishop ''the best and kindest intentions in the world,'' excusing him on the grounds that ''the first principles of child psychology'' were unknown. ''My father was a firm believer in the power of the will. He could think of nothing better to say to me, even before strangers in whose presence I began to hesitate, than, 'Now, use your will—you can say it if you will only use your will.' '' Uncle Wallis, also as a very old man, could remember his suffering as a small child when the Bishop forced him, after he had rejected it for four days in a row, to down a spoonful of cold oatmeal, as unstrained as the quality of mercy which seemed so noticeably lacking.

All the same their father seemed to live on in genial and happy conscious memory for his sons as they continued to dip, all their lives, into the apparently bottomless reservoir of his anecdotes. My cousin George, that raciest spinner of tall tales, who has immortalized Bristol in his volume *Mt. Hope,* gleefully dips into the family

trough of several generations' testing. How familiar to our ears
were Father's words, "My father used to tell the story of the man
who . . ." It might concern the Bristol Gladding brothers who lived
together, and were so poor they were obliged to use corncobs for
fuel. When it got especially cold, one would say to the other,
"Stephen, put another cob on the fire, and let's have a rouser!" Or
the old man who would say, " 'Tis as 'tis. Can't be no tizzer." Inevitably the clergy figured: Bishop Griswold going one day to have
tea with his parishioner Aaron Usher, said on leaving, "I am glad
to see, Mr. Usher, in what a comfortable way you are living." The
answer was, "Oh, Bishop, if you want to know how we live you
must come when you're not here."

And so on, and so on, and so on . . .

The Bishop was far from being a killjoy in temperament. Who,
siring eighteen children, could have been that? Much of Father's
own instinctive liking for people must have come from this genial
propagator of his own seed and of the gospel, who was lovingly
known to many more fellow Bristolians as Uncle or Cousin Mark
than as Bishop Howe. Father recalled "his pleasure in good
horses, with a pair of which he was always provided for the daily
afternoon drive—reins in hand and so erect that he never would
have missed a back on the front seat." . . . "In many ways he was
less a Victorian than a belated Federalist of Georgian tradition. . . .
For one superficial sign of [his] rootage in the past, I take his long-
continued practice of heading his manuscript sermons with the text
in Greek . . ."

Father shared with his friend Van Wyck Brooks an "American
memory," replenished at its source by his father's memory of the
same kind. It gratified Father when, as an old man, in 1951, he
received an honorary degree from Brown University to discover that
his father, as a young man, had received the same degree from the
same university, exactly a hundred years before. Thomas Jefferson
was President when my grandfather was born; the War of 1812
began when he was four years old. He remembered "kneeling in a
chair at the front window and seeing the citizens march by in a
body with their spades and other implements, and the drum and fife,

to cast up earthworks in the south part of the town for its
defense . . .''

But this still does not tell us whether the Bishop could be held
answerable for the stammer which plagued his two youngest sons.
Perhaps the older sons should take their share of blame. One traumatic experience the two little boys went through—each at a different time—was being thrown off the end of the big stone dock into
deep water by an older brother who shouted at the terrified child,
"Swim!" That shock and fright could well have been enough to
cause lifelong aftereffects. It is certain that there was no physical
defect, as both brothers, all their lives, could—and did!—sit down
to the piano and sing, with no difficulty, the fastest tongue-twisting
W. S. Gilbert patter songs. For the benefit of any interested psychiatrist let me add one further footnote to this mysterious family
affliction. A son of Father's nonstammering older brother Arthur
was more cruelly afflicted than any other member of the family. Be
it added that this cousin of mine has carried his burden with such
dash, wit, and good humor that stories told by him and about him
as bon vivant and raconteur were legendary in the Philadelphia in
which he grew up, at a far remove from any possible exposure to
either of his stammering uncles. Another cousin, the daughter of
one of Father's half brothers, has a stammer so slight that whatever
small inconvenience it may have been to her it is, in the ears of
others, only one more of her many feminine and adorable attrac-
tions. There was nothing alluring or alleviating, however, for poor
Cal or Wal as they wrestled, from boyhood on, with their beasts
at Ephesus. Father, in his teens, was taken out of school for a time,
to make the first of many attempts made during his long life to find
a cure. The results were nil.

It is curious that the laws of inheritance have not exacted any
penalty from any of Father's or Uncle Wallis's children. Father
used to say as he watched Quincy and Mark and me in our various
callings, each of which demanded the capacity to use our tongues
before an audience, "I marvel at the fluency of my three children,"
and was quite aware that if he had not suffered under his handicap

nothing could have restrained him from speaking in public—and often!

There was little time, or temperament either, among the seven Howe brothers for introspection, morbid or otherwise. The Bristol summers were too full of activities to be enjoyed—six days of the week. On every day there were family prayers and "grace before meat," but on the seventh they were rolled away to St. Michael's in the family carriage. In the afternoon there was perhaps "an innocuous walk" up the gentle slope of Mt. Hope. Novels, on Sunday, were taboo. Evening entertainment was offered in the form of a game of biblical knowledge, called "I see," rounded off by singing of hymns on the piazza or around the piano. But for the other six days the Howe boys not only delighted in an all but amphibian life in and on the water; off the water they, along with the youth of their time, flung themselves into the interest of the brand-new game, imported from England—lawn tennis. Following the printed instructions which came with the game a court was improvised by means of a fish net and whitewashed lines on lumpy grass. A pair of homemade lopsided spoons served as racquets. Then there were the clambakes! Father always told us that a true son of Rhode Island was known by the skill with which he ate his clams, steaming from the mound of wet seaweed, dipping them in melted butter, and disposing of them over his shoulder with such dispatch that he could manage always to keep one clamshell in the air.

Tennis, singing, sailing, swimming, clambakes—these were only outward and visible signs of an inner happy family life. Indeed that family, in all its ramifications, past and present, seemed to include the whole town of Bristol. No matter what misapprehensions Father's priggish little Boston daughter labored under, in her credo that no community that was not within spitting distance of Boston's State House dome could be thought of as truly New England, Father's roots dug as deep and as far back into its soil as my mother's. Since one James Howe, along with his three brothers, came from the English Essex in 1635 or 1636 to the New England Ipswich the generations produced substantial New England sons—

college graduates, ministers, schoolteachers. It was when one Perley Howe, in the year 1770, arrived in Bristol, Rhode Island, and there married Abigail DeWolf, one of the fifteen children of the first Mark Antony DeWolf—as the name was then spelled—that a fresh, wild, and enlivening strain was introduced into the Howe blood stream. This Mark Antony DeWolf had appeared in Bristol from the West Indian island of Guadeloupe under the wing of the privateering, slave-trading, rum-running Simeon Potter. In spite of a name which very likely sprang from the common eighteenth-century Marc-Antoine, the young man was a Yankee by descent, his father Charles DeWolf having emigrated to Guadeloupe from Lyme, Connecticut, where he was born in 1695.

With the arrival of Father's piratical—excuse me, *privateering*—great-great-grandfather Mark Antony one Bristolian after another (which is tantamount to saying that one DeWolf after another) took to the sea. The past still flashed in lights and shadows in the waters that Father and his brothers sailed on and swam in. Those same waters, lapping distant corners of the globe, covered the bones of many of their forebears. There was even a Mark Antony DeWolf Howe who, as captain of his ship, built in Bristol, intended to take him around the world, went down along with his two brothers as first and second mate. The grandest seadog of them all was the navigator and explorer known as "Nor'west" John DeWolf, who at one time had himself been owner of and lived in the farmhouse which was to become Weetamoe. At the age of twenty-four he was in command of a ship in which he rounded the Horn with a cargo for barter in the fur trade on the northwest coast of America; thence with furs to China, where they were to be exchanged for Chinese goods to be brought back to Bristol. When he was a very old man he published a book concerning what proved to be a unique journey, with its crossing of 2,500 miles of the North Pacific, another winter on the coast of Kamchatka, further sailing in the spring to a Siberian coast town, and then a journey of 5,500 miles, on land and by river, across Siberia to St. Petersburg. At Tomsk he dined with the Governor and wrote: "I found a great many gentlemen there, but not one who spoke English, so that I was almost a dummy amongst them. I understood enough Russ, however, to learn that they were desirous of inquiring into the nature and organization of our government. I explained all the prominent points as well as I could, and they appeared to understand, for they praised our institutions highly. If I was able, under the circumstances, to form a correct opinion, there was a good deal of the spirit of reform among them.''

Father's comment on his story: "A young American discovering a 'spirit of reform' in the Siberia of 1807 is surely to be counted among our pioneers.''

Our last glimpse of Nor'west John is as an old gentleman, whom his grandchildren called "White Grandpa,'' living with his married daughter in Dorchester, overlooking Boston harbor. When they saw him gazing out to sea, with his old spyglass stretched to arm's length, they would ask, "What do you see, White Grandpa?''

Nor'west John, resisting the future, as he remembered the old square-riggers, always growled back, "I'm looking at those damned three-masted schooners.''

He enjoys his own niche of immortality in the pages of *Moby Dick*. His wife's nephew, Herman Melville, after describing a whale encountered in the Sea of Okhotsk, so large that the ship was lifted three feet out of the water and "the masts reeled and the sails fell all together, while we who were below sprang instantly upon the deck, concluding that we had struck upon some rock,'' added "Now the Captain DeWolf here alluded to as commanding the ship in question is a New Englander, who, after a long life of unusual adventures as a sea-captain, this day resides in the village of Dorchester, near Boston. I have the honor of being a nephew of his.''

DeWolf cousins abounded in Bristol, under a variety of names. All his life, if Father took the wings of the morning and dwelt in the uttermost parts of the sea, he was sure to find a "bond" with some member of the far-flung tribe. Professor Ralph Barton Perry at Harvard was one, as were Charles Dana Gibson, artist, and DeWolf Hopper, actor.

The mingling of past and present, swell and nonswell, as of drunk and sober, exploded every fourth of July in Bristol in a climax of festivity. Any man who had survived a Bristol Fourth—even to Father, wadded in his later years in the Boston Brahmin restraint of Cotuit on Cape Cod—knew that once in the land of Egypt he had sat by the fleshpots. Looking back, he admitted that "rum was a peril" on that day, but pellucidly added, "My mother's antipathy to strong drink must have been an agency for moderation."

Of all the beautiful old houses—rivaling one another in grace, elegance, and grandeur—in which these Fourth of July parties were held none was more flamboyant or imposing than "The Mount," built by Captain, later Senator, Jim DeWolf who, when he died in 1837, was the second richest man in the country. When the master of The Mount gave a dinner in honor of that naval hero, his daughter's brother-in-law, Commodore Perry, and his officers, after the Battle of Lake Erie, the black cook, Adjua (phonetically Adjuway), brought from Africa as a child with her future husband Pauledore, was already laying the foundations of a reputation which was the glory of The Mount for more than half a century. Even Father's Brimmer Street children were brought up on the jolly Bristol rhyme:

> Pauledore and Adjua
> Sitting in the cellar-way!
> Adjua and Pauledore
> Sitting on the cellar-door!

or its alternative

> Sitting in the cellar-way
> Down fell Adjua,
> Down went the cellar-door
> In fell Pauledore!

In the reverberating names of those black ghosts we are confronted with the grim fact that the gracious burgeoning of beautiful DeWolf houses and lavish DeWolf hospitality sprang from roots which were buried deep in the brutal filth of the slave trade. Bristol was the apex of an ugly triangle: molasses was transported from Cuba, in Bristol distilleries converted into rum, from Bristol the rum went to the west coast of Africa, to be converted into such cargo that even today it is shame to name it. Of all the Bristol slave-runners Captain Jim DeWolf's record is the most appalling—and, therefore, the most successful.

Father, in his own writing, has gravely, sorrowfully, and truthfully—if a trifle mutedly—recorded some of the appalling statistics of Bristol's slave trade. He had heard as a boy the story of the old trader "who sometimes had to put down his morning cup of coffee because he seemed to see blood on the surface of it, and when he saw it he remembered his throwing a slave with smallpox out of a boat, and chopping off his hands with an axe when he tried to pull himself back over the gunwhale."

Father tried to cheer himself by the thought that he was not a direct lineal descendant of the nefarious Captain Jim—the empty Howe coffers alongside the heavily laden DeWolf ones were proof enough of that—but he knew that final judgment must still be reserved on old "privateering" Mark Antony, whose blood they both shared. It is striking to observe Father's difference in attitude from *his* father's toward this blot on the DeWolf family scutcheon, as that of the town from which they came. The Bishop, in his reminiscences privately printed for his children, rather toploftily asserts concerning Bristol that "in one way or another some of our people having plantations in the West Indies there came to be a considerable colored population, and I recollect that for a while in my early days they occupied a certain part of town called Goree." He neglects to mention the fact that the nameplace, Goree, is situated on the west coast of Africa from which "this considerable colored population" was brought—in chains below decks. When the generation after Father's spoke up, however, in the person of George Howe, he did so loud and clear, with the names and numbers of the players. Father, then a very old man, was considerably saddened by having the record published. I tried to offer the bleak comfort of suggesting that many other New England families had been pretty bad too. "I'm afraid not as bad as ours" was his answer.

To go back to what might seem a totally unrelated subject—the Curse of the Stammer—that thorn in the flesh of two of the gentlest

of their generation. Would it be too farfetched to wonder whether
out of the family unconscious some once unspoken sense of guilt
was making itself felt? For words of protest or confession not
uttered in past generations, who knows, perhaps these two remote
and innocent descendants may have been called upon to pay the
price of struggle to speak any words at all. James Baldwin has said,
"It is the innocence that constitutes the crime." Our Gentle
Americans, nearly smothered under the mantle of Victorian
prudery, did not pray to be delivered from Evil; its existence was
unacknowledged.

A last look at that grandfather of mine. For me, he comes alive
through the reminiscences he left behind. The man who emerges is
one of vigor and courage—from the young undergraduate at Mid-
dlebury, Vermont, who at sixteen years of age was sent off "to
procure the paper necessary for the printing of a new magazine to
be called *The Christian Register,* memorable . . . from the fact
that [he] went alone in an open sleigh sixty miles with the
thermometer at twenty degrees below zero" to the incessantly
bereaved young husband and father. Those eighteen children!
Good, once, for a laugh, today they and their mothers shock and
distress as innocent victims of one man's private population explosion. With the loss of two wives and seven children behind him
he arrived as a young clergyman in Philadelphia with seven surviving children.

"After struggling on . . . for a year I began to consider how it
might please God to fill the void in my family circle. Of course, in
my very extensive acquaintance, and especially in my own congregation were very many unmarried ladies, whose position, intelligence and devotion to the church commended them to my
regard, but it was necessary for me, with such a retinue of children,
to seek one of singular maturity of character, whose endowments,
intellectual and moral, would give me promise of a happy influence
in molding the characters of these young immortals. Being thus
minded, I was, I believe, divinely led to seek the hand of Miss
Eliza Whitney, my present devoted wife."

Her immortality shone clear in the adoring, almost worshipful, tones in which her name was mentioned, not only as Wife and Mother, but as Grandmother, and "Aunt Eliza" to a far-flung empire. Father made no bones about his feeling that it was she, and not his father, who was the truly "spiritual" one of his parents. It was to his mother that he wrote faithfully, almost daily, when he was away from home. She lived long enough for me to remember her dimly as a story-book grandmother, in a white cap, an image in my mind that melts inseparably from pictures of Queen Victoria. I am not alone, as it was apparently the usual, even tiresome, thing to hear a stranger introduced to her for the first time ask tentatively, "Has anyone ever told you, Mrs. Howe, that you bear a strong resemblance to Queen Victoria?" That resemblance, inner and outer, was to place its unmistakable stamp on her son Mark. He inherited—ironically, from his Bishop father!—vigor, geniality, and a gusto for the good things of the World—but it was his mother who must be held accountable for both those qualities and defects covered by the all-embracing term "Victorian."

The Whitneys, like the Howes, of "sound Yankee stock," had come from England in 1635. My grandmother's father, Asa Whitney, was born on a Massachusetts farm and ended up in Philadelphia as an inventor and manufacturer of railway-car wheels and for a time as president of the Reading Railroad. The image of his mother was so hallowed for Father that I think he was not only amused but a little relieved when his family researches brought him back to his ancestor Levi Whitney, lieutenant in the Revolutionary Army at Bunker Hill, who was defended by John, later Judge, Lowell in a trial for the murder of his wife. She "seemingly in perfect health on the morning of April 11, 1779, died suddenly on the evening of that day. The suspicion and accusation against her husband were that he bought white arsenic, known to be a deadly poison, mixed it with egg and wine, and, in the legal terminology of the day, 'with force and arms, feloniously, willfully, and of malice aforethought caused his wife to drink and swallow it down.'" It is not recorded what arguments Lowell produced, but his eloquence caused the jury to vote Whitney not guilty and dismiss him "without delay." So, after all, Father's family skeletons did not all hang in the closet of the DeWolfs!

So now, returning to Boston, and the top-hatted cutaway-coated father I remember as a child, emerging from Emmanuel Church into the Sunday morning sunshine on Newbury Street, and making his way home across the Public Garden stopping to chat on the way with any friends he chanced to meet—and I could take a bet that he never made the crossing without meeting several—perhaps we can see a little more of what was within and what was behind him. "Proper Bostonian"? If one weren't an expert it might be possible to be fooled. But he was the first to repudiate the image. There was no company, nor any environment, in which he would not have been proud to be known as what he was—a Proper Bristolian.

3

I HAD NEVER SEEN A UNITARIAN

ONE OF THE INNUMERABLE ANECDOTES passed on by his father to *our* father concerned the visit to London in 1878 for the second Lambeth Conference, paid by the Bishop and his wife. At a banquet given by the Lord Mayor to members of the conference when my grandparents were ushered into the great reception room they were announced in ringing cockney as, "The Lord Bishop of Central Pennsylvan-*eye*-a and Mrs. 'Owe."

If Bristol, Rhode Island, was a little less than Boston, then Reading Pennsylvan-*eye*-a, lacked existence altogether for Father's Brimmer Street children. And yet, from the time he was eight years old, except for the blessed parentheses of Bristol summers, "Reading, P.A." was home for Father. It was, for instance, hard for us to believe, when he sat down at the piano in the back parlor to play and sing the familiar hymns, that he had ever been a small choir boy in Reading, and bopped on the head with a hymnal by the choirmaster. We enjoyed his rendering of the local dialect, with its "The cow has over the fence ge-jumped." "Johnny Schmoker," one of our favorite songs, must have had the same Pennsylvania-Dutch origin. Each verse began with an "Ich can spiele," then named the instrument Johnny could play, with appropriate sound effects: "Pilly willy wink, das ist mein Pfeife, Wach, wach, wach das ist mein Dudelsach," "Rub-a-dub-a-dub, das ist mein Drumbel," "Zum, zum, zum, das ist mein trombone"—then *accelerando!* all raced through, backwards. Wach, wach, wach! Rub-a-dub! Zum,

zum, zum! Pilly, willy, wink! and more too that I have forgotten,
until we ended up, puffing and laughing in a loud roar at home
base, with "DAS IST MEIN PFEIFE!"

There was, too, the carol "We Three Kings of Orient Are"
played, so Father told us, on this very piano by the author of both
words and music in his father's parlor in Reading. The same Rev.
Dr. John Henry Hopkins was responsible for another carol we
loved:

> Come, and I will sing you—
> What will you sing me?
> I will sing you One-O.

It proceeded from the One-O of "God Alone" to the "Twelve-O"
of the twelve apostles through many gradations—the "lily white
Babes clothed all in Green-O," "the cheerful waiters," and "the
ferryman in his boat." Its mystical mythical magic, as it had once
been sung by Cornish copper miners on Lake Superior, could charm
a child in any setting.

And then there were the songs that Uncle Arthur used to sing!
When the dashing Art in the early 1880's would return from
Brown, he dazzled his younger brothers with the latest song hits,
"The Man in the Sealskin Pants," and the Irish policeman on
the beat whom the servant girls greeted, "Are you there, Mor-i-ar-i-
tee?" There was to be, all their long lives long, something of the
hero worship which only an older brother can elicit in his juniors
in the feeling Wal and Cal entertained for Art. It is true that
Father and Uncle Wallis—professional men both—used to murmur
"poor Art" to each other, in talking of their Philadelphia stock-
broker brother—whom they saw as prisoner to the ticker tape of
"the market." All the same, Art was the gay blade of the three, and
as such he continued to be admired by his juniors. Even when he
was in his eighties, on an occasion when Father was preparing himself for a cocktail party in Bristol to be given in honor of this admired older brother, fumbling over a recalcitrant necktie before
the mirror (Mother used to accuse Father when he got into such a
state of being like the dandy hero of one of our childhood books,

Bunnikins Bunny) he was heard muttering to himself, "Art is a very snappy dresser."

Brown had been the family college until my grandfather became—ex officio—president of the Board of Trustees of Lehigh University. It was, therefore, natural that Lehigh became his choice for his two youngest sons, with the added attraction of the free tuition to all boys living in the Lehigh Valley.

Even in spite of this palliative there seems to have been a continual concern about lack of funds. The freshman Mark was "in a very bad way for shoes. I think for four dollars I can get a decent pair." On the point of buying for six dollars a fox terrier he had "long wanted to own," when a check from home brought five dollars less than expected, he "took it back to its owner with great sadness."

All the same, a happy nature was blossoming into self-expression. It was not difficult for Father's children to believe that in his college years he had excelled scholastically, edited and contributed to a wide variety of undergraduate publications, and even played Yum-Yum in the new smash hit of his day, *The Mikado*. It was much harder for them to believe, viewing his portly figure of later years, that he once was one half of Lehigh's tennis team, the other half "Charley" Davis whose more famous older brother "Dick"— known later to a wide reading public of his era as Richard Harding Davis—was to become Father's close college friend. The appearance of this friend at the beginning of Father's long journey through the years sounded a sort of leitmotif which was to recur again and again, stating that element in his nature which could attract other natures widely divergent from his own.

Richard Harding Davis must have been Father's complete opposite. Flamboyant in dress and manners to the point of exhibitionism (Father called it "a passion for exposure to the camera"), he was rebel, crusader, romantic. He could sign off a letter to his mother with a flourish, quoting a popular song of the day, "You're my sweetheart, I'm your beau," that could diminish the son of Eliza Whitney Howe—"Your loving son, Mark"—into a plodding pedestrianism. Davis obviously belonged to that company of

college students who become "legendary" even before the public
name is made. A dashing Don Quixote, he lifted his lance against
much of the established ritual of undergraduate social life of his
day—"cane rushes," hazing and secret societies among them. When
he himself, by way of reform, founded a new club, to meet at nine
o'clock on Saturday nights "so as not to interfere with our work,
and sing, read, eat, and box until midnight," the list of its first six
members, "the best of the College," rounded off with "and Howe."

The two friends, carrying out a literally sophomoric idea for the
class magazine *Epitome*, were called upon to write biographical
sketches of each other. In later years Father with limpid clear-
sightedness said of his own early attempt at biography, "and a
flat little performance it was." All the same, out of the corner of the
eye, we get a flash of Dick, who was "getting as little work as possible into ten hours a week" and "is taking what is known as the
'Davis Special Course.' . . . All students taking this course are on
all occasions obliged to wear knickerbockers, an ulster, and a Tam
o' Shanter, and to smoke a straight briarwood pipe."

"Dick," returning the compliment, referred to his friend as

a direct descendant of Mark Antony, the celebrated politician
and stump speaker . . . whose name, along with those of a
few other generals, he bears. . . . He was christened Mark
Antony DeWolfe Howe, Jr. Many another weaker nature
would have dropped under this burden; but though the effort
to support the . . . character of three such warlike cognomens
has embittered a naturally sunny nature, it has not destroyed
that reputation for morality which stands as pure and high
as his collars.

The dissipations he encountered while in that gay and
wicked Paris of America, Philadelphia, were counteracted by
the culture and refinement of Reading, Pa. . . . At the University he shines as an instructor of music as well as a student. . . .

He is noted more especially for the introduction of the
"Howe" walking-stick, the style of which would have been
more widely followed had his friends discovered the wood
pile from which it was selected.

In a letter to his friend, Dick Davis pinpoints the difference between them, admitting that "it is much more fun to reign in hell than to verse in heaven." He pays homage to one able to "shine in any firmament . . . which, being translated means . . . being head of the Burr, Glee Club, musical director of the Mustard and Cheese, 'Scribe' of the Arcadia and projector of banjo clubs, a necessary adjunct at all social gatherings and a crack tennis player." By contrast he sees himself as "a football player where football playing is considered an evidence of a weak intellect and a bad dancer though a good talker where good dancers are as numerous as the flowers in May (tra la) and where good talking is considered an evidence of bohemianism."

When, years later, Father became engaged to be married, his friend Dick wrote congratulations to his "Dear Old Man," regretting that he did not "have the honor" of my mother's acquaintance, but "I do know that she has one of the finest and best fellows I know to make happy. God bless you." Alas, that the gallant Dick should have been no longer living to witness yet one more example of his friend's ability to "shine in any firmament." Thirty years after his graduation Father returned to Lehigh to receive an honorary degree as Doctor of Letters. He was not half so pleased by the perfunctory handclapping that accompanied the ritual as he was by the roar of applause and cheers that hailed him at a totally unacademic moment. He was watching the baseball game with the archfoe Lafayette, and "a batsman struck a foul that flew high, very high, into the air. As it began to fall I saw it was coming in my direction. All eyes were upon it— and upon me, for it was dropping as if it held the very number of my seat. At the supreme moment, I rose, lifted my bare hands, and—thank heaven!—caught it. I would almost rather have had [my degree] withheld at the last moment than to have muffed that ball."

It was inevitable that the young Wal appear at his brother's side at Lehigh. And quite literally. Cal wrote home, "So far we have gotten along very comfortably in the one bed, which is a very wide one and this summer was supplied with a wire wove mattress. We time our dressing so as not to clash at the wash stand, and the drawers in the wardrobe supply Wal with a bureau."

Bright college years? Not entirely. For one thing, Father nearly died of typhoid fever, contracted because of the lack of proper sanitation in his boardinghouse. For another, David and Jonathan were still wrestling with their common enemy—stammering. Once more—this time of his own volition—Father dropped out of his classes, and repaired again to Philadelphia to seek another cure. Like the first one, the regime consisted of a long period of enforced silence. In spite of the fact that the stationery of Mr. Edwin S. Johnston proclaimed, STAMMERING CURED: RESULTS PERMANENT, Father continued to stammer.

As the time approached for the son to choose his life work the Federalist Bishop suddenly looms as the figure to whom he feels accountable. Writing now ostensibly to him, but surely also to his Victorian mother, Mark Jr. stands firm against what must have been at least an unspoken if not overt pressure to enter the Church. I often heard Father say, "I suppose if it had not been for my stammer I almost surely would have gone into the Church. Certainly my parents would have been pleased if I had." So easy is it for one's own memory to blur the outlines of actual fact. The young man, writing to his father, actually did not mention his stammer but dared to state, fair and square, the unpalatable truth:

> . . . I think a great deal about my future, and I am sorry to say (and I mean that) that I do not feel in the least called to the Ministry. . . . I hope you understand what I mean in feeling so strongly against [it]. I mean simply this—I do not feel in the least the spirit of Christian zeal which I think every clergyman should feel, nor do I feel at all that I should love the work *for the work's sake,* which, in my opinion, is no less important. I am sure that you will not feel at all like urging me to take the step, knowing that is my state of mind.

It is characteristic of the young man, as of the older man he grew up to be, that there never seemed to have been any of the inner struggle on the subject of religious belief that was racking the young intellectuals of his time. It is perhaps the more extraordinary as he particularly admired the poetry of Dowson, Henley, and Matthew Arnold, but he himself seemed to slip easily down the ways from the firm dock of Victorian tradition into the Sea of a less defined Faith. It was one, however, which was to keep him afloat always. Its melancholy, long, withdrawing roar never sounded in Father's ears. Francis W. Newman, quoted by William James, could have been writing of Father when he defined the category of the "once-born soul." Those like him "generally have no metaphysical tendencies: they do not look back into themselves. Hence they are not distressed by their own imperfections: yet it would be absurd to call them self-righteous, for they hardly think of themselves at all."

If Father failed to hear a call to the Church the call that he did hear, unmistakably, as his years at Lehigh drew to an end, was the one that beckoned him to the world of letters. The fact that he did not automatically choose Brown as his college showed that he was beginning to make decisions for himself. He sent for catalogues, describing courses in English given at Yale, Columbia, Johns Hopkins, and Harvard. Much impressed by a young gymnasium instructor who had come to Lehigh from Harvard, it was there he decided to try his luck. This "unconscious ambassador" was a young man named Herrick, who was to die soon after, younger brother of the novelist Robert Herrick, yet to become Father's friend. The choice of Boston and Harvard was a natural one. A young man of the 1880's whose deepest yearning was to become a poet, knowing at the same time that he would have to earn his living—and more and more drawn to the hope of doing so in the world of letters—must have felt a pull toward Boston. The firmament of that city was still lit—if ever so faintly—by the afterglow of the great literary figures who had just dipped over its horizon. He quoted to himself a song about Columbus—as I heard him often quote in later years—"Somewhere there's something that ain't been seen yet."

Father once heard a group of Inner Bostonians discussing the possible election to membership in the sacrosanct little "Wednesday Evening Club of 1777" of a certain distinguished man who had come to live in Boston from another city. The inevitable question was asked: "What was his class?" The answer rang with a cold finality: "He had no class. He went to Yale."

The first impact of Cambridge and Boston could not have struck the new arrival from Pennsylvania with a more icy chill than if he had, in fact, come from New Haven. Attending his first "Harvard Assembly" at a hall on Berkeley Street in Boston, Father, like other students who could not afford the "hack hire" for his return to Cambridge, walked to the corner of Charles and Cambridge streets to wait for the horsecar that would trundle out to Harvard Square. In later life he recalled:

> It was a bitterly cold night, and after the long walk from Berkeley Hall I found myself shivering on the street corner with two other young men whom I did not know, but recognized at once as having been at the very party from which I was returning. They were engaged in animated conversation. . . . My instinct was to amalgamate the three strayed revellers with a remark upon the coldness of the night and the suffering which we shared. But no, I said to myself, let me learn the customs of the country. It was two to one, I thought, and they should take the first step. Did they take it? Not at all. They were happy in their own companionship and left me congealed in solitude. If I had tried to break the ice, I might have fallen into cold water . . . A little later I learned that my silent encounter had been with two brothers named Cabot, one of whom was yet to become an eminent authority on social ethics. . . . That night he helped me to feel that my Pennsylvania Bethlehem was for the moment as far away from Boston as Bethlehem of Judea.

The newcomer's first taste of Cambridge hospitality was not much more enlivening:

> I have just come now from the Haskins', who gave a nondescript kind of a party. Among the women there were a few— very few—who could stand being looked at twice. The rest were—Cambridge, and all is said. We first had charades, rather cleverly done; then the lightest of suppers, cake, fruit

and coffee of which a graceful individual spilt a cup all over my shirt-front. Then we played Clumps, a variety of 20 Questions. They chose such ridiculous subjects as the eighth word of the second book of Homer's Odyssey and "the second puff of the ill wind that blows nobody good," both of which were within the grappling power of the Cambridge mind.

Father admitted in later years that "I believe I had never seen a Unitarian before coming to Cambridge." Now, striking out in a spirit of exploration, he ventured into King's Chapel. He wrote home of an unexpected distraction in the shape of Dr. Holmes:

I am afraid I worshipped man most of the time, for I could not help staring at and admiring the genial old gentleman so near me. The congregation was very small and made up principally of people who looked as old as the church. Most of the men wore choker collars and voluminous black cravats, the women—purple bonnets. Old Professor Peabody of Harvard preached just such a sermon as you would expect from a Harvard Professor of Philosophy and a Unitarian minister combined,—all very scholarly and polished, but containing a great deal more about the philosophy of the sense and reason than about Christianity. Passages of it, however, elicited emphatic nods of approval from the Autocrat.

The hungry sheep may have looked up to Dr. Peabody, to find himself not fed; it was another story, however, when he found himself returning again and again for the nourishment he welcomed in the preaching of Edward Everett Hale at Harvard. But, he wrote, "It was Phillips Brooks, condemned by his own brethren thereafter for tolerating just such preachers, who opened my eyes widest of all." The Pennsylvania *émigré* was dazzled by his first sight of Trinity Church, which he found "beautifully rich and warm, and the size . . . adapted to the rector." A few years later, on an Easter Sunday, his "wish through the whole day was not so much that I could be in Reading, as that all of you could be here." Writing home, in January, 1887, after a Christmas visit, the homesick Mark did "not even feel—as I did when leaving Reading—that I am a friendless youth in a strange land, for on the horse-car which brought me to Cambridge yesterday morning I met Mr. Barrett Wendell who said that his wife would be at home that afternoon and would be glad to see me. I went in and had a very pleasant time at the small 'tea' I found in progress."

Aside from the general sense of social thaw there were courses to be enjoyed. Father, in later life, found himself to have been "incredibly stupid" in his ignorance of the existence of Norton, Shaler, Palmer, or James. He did, however, "sit under" Hill, Briggs, the young Wendell, and Child. Among them it was to the last-named that he felt the most lasting sense of gratitude, not only for his introduction to Milton, Bacon, and Shakespeare but for his understanding of the distinction between *will* and *shall, should* and *would*—a distinction which, alas, never was to rub off on his children. Further, he recalled, "I learned to distinguish between the best and the less than that in writing, and, by a parallel scale of measurement, in men. . . . I formed under Child some of the standards of taste which I have long accepted as valid." Francis J. Child (appearing to Henry James as "all finely circular") was known as "Stubby." To Father he seemed "never to justify more the sobriquet than when seen, short, rotund, curly-haired, plodding across the Yard, his large loose bag of books almost trailing on the ground."

To welcome the newcomer's literary efforts there were the *Advocate,* the *Lampoon,* and the *Harvard Monthly*. When, at the end of his first year, Father was offered the position of managing editor of the latter, although longing to accept, conscientious son that he was, he wrote to his father that he realized that another year of causing expense at home was more than his due. Virtue was rewarded. He received a Shattuck Scholarship of two hundred dollars, which would pay his room rent and two thirds of his tuition fee. Even though only a graduate student he was—contrary to present-day practice—absorbed into the graduating class as a proper son of Harvard, receiving his A.B. degree in 1887 and his A.M. in 1888. He gratefully accepted the position on the *Monthly,* not realizing at the time that his predecessor and his successor—one young man named Santayana and another Berenson—were to cast, retroactively, a special luster on the niche. As the end of his second year at Harvard approached, the time for deciding his lifework had to be faced. He was much tempted to become a teacher, but had to accept the fact that his stammering would make an insuperable handicap. When, through the good offices of Professor Child, Mr. Horace Scudder, editor of the *Atlantic Monthly*, recommended him as an assistant in the editorial department of the *Youth's Companion*, he accepted. He himself wrote that "in the little world of Boston letters late in the eighties there was hardly a humbler post." All the same it was that little world which was to become his oyster.

Presently Cal and Wal were tucked into Boston lodgings together. Uncle Wallis, arriving to study architecture at M.I.T., joined Father in rooms, first on Charles Street, behind Clough and Shackley's drugstore, later on Mt. Vernon Street. Ultimately the brothers were to eat their dinners at the boardinghouse of Mrs. Knowlton on Chestnut Street. It was undoubtedly at the table of this vivacious housekeeper that the two polite young stammerers, on being introduced to a newcomer at the table, opened their mouths in unison to get out the best they could in the way of a greeting when the new arrival put them promptly out of their misery by proclaiming his own. He held up three fingers, managing himself to splutter out only "Th-th-three."

What a satisfaction must Cal and Wal have been to the pious heart of their Victorian mother, as they saw in the New Year of 1894 over their fire, "talking and thinking much," and regretting that they could not be reading the ninetieth psalm with her! Even the Bacchanalian rites of Beacon Hill's *vie de Bohême* could not have caused too deep a concern:

"Our Welsh Rarebit—of which Wal foretold you—was quite a success, we thought, last night. Four of the prettiest girls in Boston . . . graced our humble quarters, and seemed on the whole to enjoy being here. The study of family pictures—especially in the groups of monumental extent—occupied no small share of their attention." Perhaps it was the echo of the laughter of those pretty girls (could they have been laughing outright at the sight of so many descendants of one bishop?) that brought him up with a sharp twinge of conscience as he hastily added, ''Don't be afraid of our doing anything so un-Lenten next week. We have not lost our memories yet.''

The hallowed presence of that white-capped mother back in Bristol was constant to her sons. The one who concerns us wrote her, ''It disturbs me to find that much as I hear [Phillips Brooks] I don't grow any better, and I know the trouble is not with the preacher. It is the same with books. I have finished *God in His World,* and though from what everybody says and my own critical judgment tells me, it must be a very fine book, my impression of it all is most hazy and, I fear, its effect upon me nil.'' He had already written from Harvard, ''I wish with you that my writing could be directed to some purpose more distinctly useful, but how many ordinary mortals have the opportunity of doing good all the time.'' If one couldn't ''do good,'' at least the two brothers could go to hear Phillips Brooks preach during Lent. At the noonday service at St. Paul's ''the church—aisles and chancel—were packed with men, and the volume of sound that rose in the simple hymns was most stirring. It might have come from medieval crusaders or Knights of the Holy Grail if the rumble of carts and gongs of electric cars without had let us quite forget our *fin de siècle.''* In due course Father became part of the mufti chorus of men and women which supplemented the four soloists of the choir at Trinity Church, in a balcony over its west door.

On the occasion of Phillips Brooks's consecration as Bishop, Father, from his chorister's point of vantage, thrilled to see his own father serve as one of the seven consecrators participating in the ceremony. When Phillips Brooks died in 1893 this one parishioner and chorister was carried away by the sense of the ''irreparable loss. . . . It is all too soon to realize the fullness of it; but the diocese, the city, the country, and the world have surely lost the one man the most needed in this day. You have no idea of the way the Bishop's death has affected the whole community here. It is the one subject of talk in all classes. Today flags are at half mast. . . . As I write I hear the bells tolling and almost see the throng inside and outside of the church. . . . Oh it is all too sad and dreadful.''

It is not only concerning Bishop Brooks's death that he writes to his mother; he also writes her when his own bishop father has a birthday,

"Please extend to Father my most hearty and filial greetings upon his approaching birthday . . . I was never prouder to bear the name which reaches threescore years and ten with glowing honor."

His mother's own birthday finds him "just as ready to say 'I thank God for my Mother.' . . . May every year make your days lighter and happier—as all your years that have gone have made the days for other people. If one of your own boys cannot know how this has been—who can? God bless you, Mother, and make us all better deserving of you."

Aside from increasingly demanding work the young man was making new friends on all sides. His half brother Reginald was rector of the Church of Our Saviour in Longwood, and he and his wife were welcome surrogates for the Bristol tribe. On December 23, 1890, Father wrote home, "As I have been asked to Longwood only for dinner on Christmas Day I have just written to Clyde Fitch asking him to dine with me tomorrow night. Wallis will tell you something about him."

The name of Father's new friend echoes today with the hollowest of all empty sounds—that of the writer of a string of smash hit plays, none of which are known to a succeeding generation. When Clyde Fitch died at forty-four, burnt out from overwork, at the height of his popularity there was no more famous or successful playwright in America. Ethel Barrymore had made her debut in his *Captain Jinks of the Horse Marines,* Richard Mansfield made his *Beau Brummel* famous, or, perhaps, vice versa. At one time four Clyde Fitch plays were running simultaneously in New York. He had been brought as a guest one evening to read his new play, *Frederick Lemaitre,* to the members of the short-lived Mermaid Club of which Father was a member, along with George Santayana, Norman Hapgood, Robert Herrick, and H. T. Parker. Founded by George P. Baker, its purpose was "to cultivate a serious interest in the stage."

Robert Herrick recalled the evening: "We were gathered in a low-ceilinged room of the old house next to Christ Church, whose cracked chimes broke across the dramatist's emotional periods. I can see him as he was then, slight, dark, with black hair brushed back in a wave from his forehead, over which in the tenser moments of delivery he would pass his hand. I can recall my thrill at the daring freedom and zest of his delivery. We did not read our papers at The Mermaid in that way." It was following this occasion that Fitch returned to Father's lodgings with him, and the two young men sat up talking late into the night.

Once more, some quality in Father was attracting a man as different from himself as Richard Harding Davis had been. Fitch at Amherst had made as much of a mark for conspicuousness in his dress as Davis had at Lehigh. In snatches from his letters to Father during the nineties we can sniff over the years the smell of grease paint, suffer vicariously in the sense of nervous exhaustion from hard work under pressure ("I am working like a *Dorg.*" "Golly! but I've been working." "Racing through one act against a deadline so as not to disappoint a man. . . . I sat up most of the night, and then he disappointed me! Toujours! Toujours!"), and tingle with the excitement of his innumerable first nights. Father attended *Betty's Finish* at the Boston Museum, as guest of the playwright, and received from New York, in a letter, "a violet from last night's boutonniere." In February, '91, from the Albany, Piccadilly, where he was staying during rehearsals of a new play, Fitch wrote, "The truth is I am completely fagged out and don't feel up to writing anybody or anything, but I want you to know I think of you as staunchly and affectionately altho' I may not put my hand and seal to it. . . . I had supper with Irving Saturday night—very jolly. He does Henry VIII next year . . . 'God save the Mark' Howe! Au revoir Staunchly yrs." Three years later, back in England again, "London is very dull this year—theatrically. . . . Of course we had *Duse,* great, supreme artist! and now Bernhardt one whole grade beneath Duse. . . . How are you? Let me have some word. It isn't good for friends to let go hands for too long."

Father visited Fitch several times in New York in his apartment in the Carnegie Building. Of one such trip he reported to Reading, "I lunched with Fitch at the Players Club—a most fascinating place—and spent a good part of the afternoon in his picturesque rooms—full of tapestries, old prints, palms and everything queer." And yet Clyde Fitch, the sophisticated, effete darling of Broadway, could find room in his heart for what his friend Mark's little corner of Boston had to offer. "I feel miles away from it all, back in this commercial city. Boston's is certainly the atmosphere to live in intellectually. The only danger is from *ruts,* and getting hum drum. Here we have a bigger sweep, more *world,* but more *worldliness* too, and no sympathy, and that is the heart of Boston,—its sympathy." It must have been chiefly sympathy—including the sense of *simpatico*—that he found in his "dear old Mark." His letters are punctuated with uninhibited "my dear fellows." "This has been a dreary winter for me. I wish you'd run on to New York and make it a bit brighter. Have you read Peter Ibbetson and don't you love the first 1/2 or 2/3?" When his friend Mark sent him a slim volume of his own poems, "The set up of the work is good and true, as the inside. Just as you are—*out* and *in!*" Then, "I've been desperately ill,—nip and tuck life or death—but here I am again like the Jack-in-the-box. I liked your letter about 'a wave of Life' better than any that I have received." He meets "a Dr. something-or-other" from Bristol. " 'How many good things come out of Bristol,' I said to him, mentioning Mark Howe among them. When I had mentioned you he was rather staggered. He said you *were* a nice fellow and could drink more whisky than the 'next fellow,' or words to that effect. I confessed that our friendship had been formed from a slightly different point of view!"

Fitch might well have been thinking of a return of hospitality which the Country Mouse offered the City Mouse on the occasion of Father's taking him to a New Year's Eve midnight service at Trinity Church where Fitch was carried away by Phillips Brooks's preaching and returned afterward to Father's rooms for a long talk into the early morning hours. Perhaps it was the artist's response to human qualities that enabled the playwright to put his finger on that in Father which drew friends to him. "I don't mind telling you that you *lift me up,* a little, strengthen me in my purpose, and I am glad of that." Yet Fitch did not use Father solely as a reflecting mirror of himself. "What do you do without Phillips Brooks? Have you read any of Davis's articles on Mexico? And how does life go with you? Are you in love?—Or do you wish you were?—or weren't? And has the poetic muse been tickling your brain any lately? And what's been your chief pleasure this winter? Does the Mermaid still swim?"

The nostalgic whiff of this particular friendship, as from the violet of the first-night boutonniere, must have grown fainter over the years for Father. The innocent pleasures of Boston in the nineties were beginning to encircle him. Aside from the Longwood Cricket Club for tennis, there was the Papyrus Club "which took its Bohemianism a little too seriously, and the Puritan Club, which did the same with its youthful respectability." In 1893 he was elected to the Tavern Club. I think it is fair to say that no single association of men gave Father more pleasure over his many years than his membership in "the Tavern."

Doors were beginning to open. The brothers called upon "the Williamses of Buffalo. Wallis will explain what I mean by saying that though they talked more glibly than ever of their friendship with Mr. Howells etc. etc. wisdom should prompt them, unless they crave a Lapham immortality, in keeping out of the novelist-photographer's way. He will have them in a book before they know what struck them." And "W. and I are both asked to join a Dancing Class—i.e. to subscribe not very heavily for a series of five dances—under the auspices of some very Bostonian matrons." "I have been to dinner parties with still another to come tomorrow. . . . Last night a musicale at Mrs. Cabot's followed the Wells's dinner." "Since Easter my social enjoyments have been more than commonly frequent. The 'Orchestral Clubs' musicale, the Horse Show to which I went with the Parkers, tea and hymn singing at their house on Sunday evening, a call and walk with Miss Ferriday . . . all these things and several more of like nature have made the last ten days rather unusually gay for me."

Miss Ferriday must have been produced as a red herring. At last there was one emotion the son was not confiding to his mother. Early in 1889 he had learned that the Parkers' was not the only Boston household "gay" enough to sing hymns on Sunday evenings. There was another, at 82 Charles Street.

"For about six weeks Mrs. Josiah Quincy, whose daughter I had met at the Parkers', has been asking me to come to their house on successive Sunday evenings and try some of Bach's chorales and other sacred music. I have not been very anxious to go, and have always had something else to do, but last night went for the purpose of trying a Miserere by F. Boott . . . And who do you suppose was there? The venerable Boott himself!—the man whose music filled the Bristol house with melody and the hearts of the auditors with weariness so often last summer. He was a very genial old gentleman, and bore our murdering of his music like a martyr. He and a dreadful tenor were the only people there beside the family, so that the gathering was extremely quiet—not at all in the nature of a salon. Still—I am not sure that I shall go again—though I have promised to."

"The only people there beside the family"? Not quite. Father did not record for his mother's benefit as of any importance, as it certainly carried none to him on that occasion, the fact that one member of the family held herself aloof from the party. Not exactly like Cinderella, she was, all the same, the youngest daughter—then only eighteen years old—and did not join the party. All Father saw on that evening was a very pretty girl, with a pile of golden curly hair and large, light, green-blue eyes which, as he recalled later "glowered" at him from the other end of the hall. Boy did not even meet Girl. But he was looking not only at one more Unitarian; the Proper Bristolian had seen his first Introvert.

4

TRAGICOMIC AND TRIANGULAR

WHEN THAT SHIVER AT THE SOUND of the doorbell ran through 26 Brimmer Street the word that leaped, in a stage whisper, to our lips, was "Caller!" Placid North-of-Ireland Lizzie (she pronounced her own name Luzzie) who blessed our household for more than twenty-five years—hair sleek, black uniform, apron as unruffled as her calm countenance—would appear in the library and extend to Mother a silver salver, bearing a calling card. Mother's first and most usual exclamation was, "Oh, Lor'!" before pulling herself together with an "Ask him to come up, Lizzie." By the time that *he* ascended the stairs Mother was ready for him, in the "back parlor." Of that thin red line of callers there was one who sent up no card. Not because his dropping in on Brimmer Street was casual. On the contrary, it was so much the reverse that preparations had been carefully made beforehand. There was no appearance, public or private, made by Professor Copeland that did not smack of the showmanship of a theatrical star.

Perhaps the fate that overtakes a man of the theater applies equally to a great teacher whose name, for succeeding generations, dwindles to a legend. Walter Lippmann, speaking of Copeland's magic as a teacher, bore witness to the conviction held by his students "that but for their luck in having known him, they would be more deaf and more dumb than they are, that in truth he has helped them to live, is the reason why he is the object of a cult in which there is such fervor, such affection, and such gratitude."

Though "Copey"—as he was known at Harvard, although to
my parents he was either Copeland or "Cope"—did not come often
to Brimmer Street, his visits were always something of an occasion. He certainly was not one to whom children "took" easily,
or he to them. I remember still the awkwardness I felt as a child
on an evening when Mr. Copeland was there and, as I kissed my
parents good night, one of them murmured that it would be nice
to kiss him too. He drew back in an embarrassment which immediately communicated itself to me; and the gesture was never
repeated. Small of stature, with a top-heavy head, his features were
wrinkled, wise, and clever, like those of an old Chinese. On a wall
of his room in Hollis Hall hung a portrait of a Spanish peasant,
painted by his friend Waldo Peirce. "I like to have him here," was
Copeland's own comment, "because no matter how old and ugly
I may get, he'll always be older and uglier." I can still hear the
deep, resonant "stage" voice that made him the beloved Copey of
his public readings, when, as a child, I answered our telephone—
sometime after 1916—just after its exchange had been metamorphosed from Haymarket to Lafayette. Instead of asking to speak
to anyone, or giving his name, he simply vibrantly proclaimed,
"Lafayette, we are here!"

This rich voice of the actor, adapted to both tragedy and comedy,
coupled with a marked—who knows if it might not have been
great?—talent, chafed in the prison house of an insignificant exterior. It would have been hard enough for any son of Calais, Maine,
in the 1890's to flaunt the standards and conventions of his upbringing by choosing to become an actor, but if he had not been
crippled with the Achilles heel of vanity and had been willing to
accept the roles for which nature had made him, he might have
approximated the style of a Barry Fitzgerald. As it was, Edwin
Booth was one hero and John Barrymore another. The result was
an unhappy man. His biographer, J. Donald Adams, summed up
his "strange and baffling ambivalence . . . he was caustic and
tender, demanding and generous, rude and punctilious, timid and
courageous, indolent and indefatigable, self-centered and even,
sometimes self-forgetting."

I cannot speak for his relations with women, aside from Mother. From what Father himself told me, as well as what can be read between as well as in the lines of his letters, it is clear that at least one side of him longed to play a man's—indeed, perhaps, a lover's—role. What fears, uncertainties, self-consciousness, or other hidden forces held him in check we can only guess. As he grew older, inevitably his crotchetiness and personal vanity increased and, in direct ratio, Mother's warmth of feeling for him cooled. Perhaps because she had known him more intimately than those who could laugh at him as a "card," she was saddened, and all but disgusted. "He's simply not the Copeland I once knew," I have heard her say often. She wrote to me in the 1930's, "Poor Cope! He is in the Stillman Infirmary suffering from acute Egotism, which the doctors think is arthritis! I went out to call on him, and, as he said, his room looked like that of a dying prima-donna, being filled with flowers sent by satellites. Two terrible specimens of undergraduate humanity came and sat by his bedside like mutes during my call, and did not add to the gayety of the occasion." All the same, once a year flowers arrived for Mother from him. The occasion was the anniversary of his mother's death. When it occurred Mother had written an appreciation of her which the son had never forgotten, published anonymously in the *Transcript*. Her letter to me continues, "Talk of elderly romances! At this moment enters Copeland's annual floral tribute which surpasses all records! A superb pink cyclamen plant the size of a large shrub and covered with huge blossoms which even I cannot kill at once."

When Father was over ninety years old, lying in his father's old four-poster bed during a weakening attack of bronchitis, he chose the moment to hand me a packet of letters. They were letters from Mother, covering the seven years of his siege for her consent to marry him. Mother had written me many years earlier, "Father is sitting happily gloating over a pile of his letters to me, written twenty-six years ago, and now being consigned to the flames after their final perusal." She admitted that Father murmured occasionally that he would have liked me to have been allowed to see in his own words how he had always felt about her, "after we are dead and gone. I have no such post-mortem wishes, and I am making dangerously large fires these days with old letters of old days.'' The packet that Father handed to me—of Mother's letters to him—he asked me to burn, unopened, in the grate of his library. This I did, watching them curl away into black wisps, and then into nothingness. But there still remained one packet which reveals much of my parents, as well as of the friend who wrote them.

When J. Donald Adams published his book *Copey of Harvard* he asked Father for any letters he might have from his old friend. Father gave him all he had, with the exception of this one packet. ''I can*not* hand over Copeland's letters to your mother,'' he said to me at that time. In fact, whenever Father spoke of Mother and Mr. Copeland he lowered his voice to a near whisper as though he were retailing the raciest find of a contemporary gossip columnist. ''There's no question,'' he would say, ''Copeland was devoted to her. What he wanted was not marriage, but to get her to admit that she preferred him to anyone else.'' The role of a sort of poor man's Shaw, enjoying a ''literary'' flirtation with a young lady quite capable of giving as good as she got, perfectly suited him. Had it turned into anything more dangerous the chances are that he would have fled.

Copeland's letters to Father, covering a span of some fifty years, were most of them signed ''Your oldest friend.'' I doubt that for either of these two arrivals in Boston from the New England hinterland in the late eighties there was any friendship of longer or more solid duration. Actually it was a friendship passed on by Uncle Wallis, who had first run into the young journalist from Calais, Maine, working at the time as literary and dramatic editor on the Boston *Post*. Their meeting place was the small room on Mt. Vernon Street where he and Father ate many of their dinners, named the Hole-in-the-Ground. In short order Copeland was Father's friend too. And presently, through his new friend Mark Howe, he came to know Miss Fanny Quincy.

The letters written home to Reading and Bristol by the confiding son unveil the features of this young lady only in glimpses. She was one of the ''four of the very prettiest girls in Boston'' who

had been offered Welsh rarebit and a sight of the massive Howe
family group photographs. It was undoubtedly her compassionate-
hearted sister Helen who was responsible for "a musicale at the
Quincys . . . where a blind girl sang most pathetically." I cannot help wondering whether the far more critical Fanny did not
find almost as pathetic Mark Howe's attempt to please when, in
his own words, "by way of contrast," he "favored the company
with the *Jumblies* and *Bachelors Buttons.*" His pleasure in singing
found one happy outlet in the "Boosey Club." To repair to a
tintypist or photographer seemed the first move on any occasion
when one or two young couples of the nineties were gathered
together. "The Booseys were photographed yesterday—a most
handsome group," wrote the wan young man with a droopy
mustache shown in the group picture I cherish today. At its center
perches a pretty girl, with a flowered hat high on her wavy hair,
and velvet ribbons on her bodice. In the words "Miss Quincy en-
quires solicitously about you. She has just been through the Grip
herself" I deduce that Mother must have paid that one visit to
Bristol during which she saw, for the only time in her life, the
Bishop plain. When he tells his mother that he went to the theater
"with the Quincys" we have the full extent of the reference Boy
was to make to Girl.

I was brought up, however, on the racy bit of family lore which
recounted that Fanny Quincy used to go to first nights with the
young critic of the Boston *Post*—ALONE. In the Boston of the early
nineties such an act of social emancipation was perilously close to
being risqué. Not only intellectually but certainly temperamentally
Copeland would have proved more congenial as one of two on the
aisle than the "roué of Reading, P.A." who found the acting of
Booth and Barrett in *Othello* "wonderfully powerful but not the
most pleasant way of passing an evening. It was too harrowing."
Copeland's love and knowledge of the theater must have been shared
by his companion. In any case it was she who arranged in her parents' house at 82 Charles Street one of the first—more than likely
the very first—of the Charles Townsend Copeland readings, later to
become the rage for enthusiastic audiences addicted to platform

performances. This must have been an opening gambit in the game which took off from there, carried on, on both sides, with obvious relish.

Letter Number One refers to that first reading:

April 4, 1891

MY DEAR MISS QUINCY,

Whatever you do—whether you ask me to come to see you or dismiss me when I am come—it is the good, the true, and the beautiful.—Heaven knows I do not want to have anyone coerced into going to my reading, but I feel that Professor Thayer and Brandeis might think it odd if they were not informed of it. . . . —Are you are not repenting by this time of having undertaken such an affair? It must be an awful amount of trouble.

I hope you read me this morning . . . and I hope you will believe me always

Your obedient servant,
C. T. COPELAND.

Hard on the heels of the reading itself:

MY DEAR MISS FANNY QUINCY,

Let me acknowledge and thank you for what you describe as the result of your labors—for what I more grossly term the sum of fifty-seven dollars. But it is not easy or even possible to thank you for the tact and grace and kind cleverness with which you managed the whole thing, and gave it whatever success it had.

Presently he is reminding her not to forget "our little expedition for tomorrow afternoon. It has been the hope and guiding star of my week." In answer to some invitation from her he writes his "Honored Patroness, Yes, with enthusiasm if I may sit beside you: no, with scorn, if I may not."

And in answer to another:

MY DEAR MISS FANNY QUINCY,—

Did I say I was old? I thought I said only that you are young—which nobody can deny, though you do write notes so alarmingly clever that my pen is divided between shyness and complaisance in attempting an answer. I will confess to you that I am as old as they say Hamlet was when he got up that tactful little theatre party at Elsinore, and yet I have never been to one in my life. It is high time, and I will present myself on Friday at as "sharp" a 7:30 as can be whittled off the end of a laboring day. . . .

Accept my venerable thanks, and believe me

Yours to flatter,
C. T. COPELAND

Eighty-two Charles Street is only a stone's throw from Mt. Vernon Street. Now, however, the friendship is ripening sufficiently to warrant an invitation to the family house at Quincy.

Duty points in several other directions all at once, but Quincy will be the lode-star of my inclination next Saturday. I shall come by the half-past four train—the earliest, pray note, named by your Serene Excellency—cherishing the hope that you will take me for a walk. . . .

In reply to the next move her "Excellency" is asked to "Accept my humble and hearty thanks—that is a phrase from the Prayer Book—for the beautiful, true portrait of Yourself."

Mark Howe has not appeared in Copeland's letters. Suddenly he does so—in an abrupt note—as an off-stage Miles Standish:

Mark is a bully fellow: I hope you will always remember that and that I said so.

The one letter to himself which Father did not give to Copeland's biographer was written on the same day, clearly on the heels of some moment of truth arrived at in a night session between the two friends concerning their relations with the same girl.

DEAR MARK

(Whether you like it or not), I ought to have said tonight that the "one or two other things" by which I set such store were interspersed with varied statements of the fact that she "cared for men and for her girl-friends in *exactly* the same way." This, I think, removes the offense of my communication, and a lawyer would see that it also lessens its value as evidence,—especially since the whole was clinched with the celebrated formula of the five reasons. It was all too tragicomic and triangular and without known precedent, for me to understand. But one thing I perceive with the help of solitude, and that is that [Here, a word—or words—have been cut out of the paper.] you are at last deeply—and, I hope, for her sake and yours, irretrievably—interested.

These declarations are queerly written, but I think I have said what I meant to say,—I don't know whether you went straightway to sleep or not: I had a curious feeling for half an hour, more or less, of being with you as much as if I had not come away. At all events, I promise, here upon my bended paper, never to stay under your roof again beyond eleven o'clock. Hold me to the oath! I have been outrageously selfish about it already. . . .

This drunken rag of a letter has not been written merely out of "nervousness," but for the point of honor from which it started and also to say things with my pen as I never can say them with my tongue. I shall be exceedingly glad to know that you have received it. . . .

If you never come to see me or take me to walk of your own motion—as they say in the law—I shall feel that your wonderful and patient charity is only that and nothing more.

Love me a little and do not despise me too much, and—*ora pro me. Dominus vobiscum* is the prayer of your servant and friend

                                        C. T. COPELAND

This letter was written on April 25. Only a little more than a month later it was Father's turn to make his way in the direction of the "lode-star" of Quincy, Massachusetts. Even as a very old man he was to go back, again and again, to a certain "fatal" Memorial Day when, in Quincy, he tried his luck—in vain. There was a walk, during which the wooer and the wooed sat, on bench or wall I know not which, while the self-torturing young woman poked her parasol into the sand at her feet. As her suitor pressed her for the answer she was so loath to give, with her eyes turned from his he watched the tip of her parasol trace out the two letters—N-O.

John Alden was undoubtedly turned to for comfort. Copeland wrote, a few days later:

My dear, charming, unhappy Friend,—I had every intention of writing you an apology before your reproachful letter came. The apology was to relate to the way I spoke, because, although I had not the luck to be born in Boston, I yet have some notion of how a man should speak to a lady, and how he should not. The second method I exemplified on Tuesday. But as to the substance of our talk, I never thought and surely never could have said I thought that you intended from the beginning to work the woe. My bitter complaint against you is that, after you discovered it to be working, you should have done as you did. But we will talk of that if you want to; it is impossible to write about it.

Mark is absolutely what a man should be under the conditions. He is not bowled over, and I think he will do better work and more of it as a direct result of this experience. All the same he will not forget you—how could that be possible!— he blames you for nothing, and my only fear is that, if he married some other girl, he would still remember you. He should make you happy and you would make him happy, but the gods who sit above have willed it otherwise; and there is nothing to do but remind you of Rosalind's advice to Phoebe that she should thank God, fasting, for a good man's love. . . .

But it is truly absurd for a man who is not yet old enough to be a Dutch uncle, to be writing in this strain to a pretty girl. It is because you are so much more than beauty and wit could make you that I do write in this way, and that your conquests are likely to bring you as much grief as triumph.

Don't cry any more of your eyes out. What is done is done. But if you do indeed value my good opinion, remember what you have promised me.

When I think of you and when I think of Mark, the tears come into my eyes and I am no longer the quoting, literary, naught-availing person you believe me to be. I still avail naught, but I pray into the dark that the powers which have let you and me know a man who is so much better than either of us—gallantry to the winds!—may make you feel as well as

see that you have let happiness drift by for the lack of putting
out your hand. If that day comes, you will remember what I
said, and think better of me. You will lay up nothing against
me—not even this foolish, half incoherent letter.

　　Accept my homage, Mademoiselle. *Je vous présente mes
respects et mes voeux les plus sincères.*

C. T. C.

After this one straightforward declaration of his inner feeling—
ironically more for Father than for Mother herself—the play
actor must have been grateful to the young woman who would toss
him just the cues that would evoke just the sort of lines he most
enjoyed speaking. On her side there must have been cause for
gratitude too. What strains and stresses were tearing at the heart
of Fanny Quincy at this time her daughter today can only guess.
In one letter Copeland can speak of himself as "servant and adorer
of one New England woman" and in another breath an unmistakable sense of relief that he knows nothing will be demanded of him:
"I have every confidence in my ability to conduct my side safely,
and I cannot flatter myself that there would be any danger for
you." Undoubtedly Mother had no desire to work any more "woe,"
so decided to recede a little. Her swain's response was "But I applaud your resolve to give up theatre-parties à deux." Their game
went on nonetheless. One move included Mother's giving him a ring
which "surprised and delighted" him. "I thought it only a joke
until you wrote of your interview with the jeweller. A bleeding
heart would have pleased me most, but the true-lovers' knot has
already excited favorable comment." In spite of the "trouble that
is likely to come from it," he swears that it "shall never leave my
finger until Charon takes my hand to help me into his boat."

　　Returning during the summer to his native Maine he writes to
"Mademoiselle":

　　The story is off: I promised to write it when you liked me
　　better than any other man. I can't write it merely with the
　　inspiration of your not liking any other man better than you
　　like me. See your responsibility! . . . I went to a hop last
　　night, and am going to a tea this afternoon, and a reception

this evening. They say I look bored: I should be surprised if I did not.—Who are the special victims of your wiles just now or has the Viking come already?

Whatever opalescent lights and shades shimmered across the surface of Fanny Quincy's involvements with the opposite sex there is no question that through her complex nature ran an undercurrent of deep feeling—feeling doomed to be forever shot with dread and self-doubts. Five months after she had been assured that "Mark was absolutely what a man should be," she wrote to her confidant, addressing him—a daughter of her time—as "Mr."

My dear Mr. Copeland

I was sorry not to see you last night, but if you will choose the middle of my night for your visits what can you expect? On your arrival I was engaged in my usual evening pastime of crying! This time for no better reason than that I had to begin another week in this vale of tears. However, I had something to cry for when I heard that you were downstairs, & that I was unable to see you. I really was sorry not to use the ticket to Mrs. Winslow's reading, but I truly had an engagement which I ought not to break. I have been so depressed lately, that the other day I was on the point of writing to you that I would go to the theatre with you so often as you would take me & let "what people say" be d——d. But I have now come to a final decision which I regret to say is *No,*—though you know how much I have enjoyed the little sprees—All my lady friends are married, & almost all my gentlemen friends are engaged, so I am utterly deserted. I am in a Boy's Club & play games with the horrid little brats every Tuesday evening— That's what it is to be really charitable. If you had a grain of charity in your composition you would tell me what afternoon you would go to walk with me, or at least you would come to see me some time before 10 P.M. If my depression continues, you will see "A Tragedy in High Life" in the Morning Post soon, & you can go identify me at the Morgue— It will be my last wile.

Yours de profundis
Fanny H.Q.

How grateful the youngest Quincy daughter must have been when she learned she was to be removed to Europe along with her mother and father and two sisters, to be gone, like a proper Henry James heroine, for two years. Part of the time was spent at the Villa Mercede at Bellosguardo in Florence where her half uncle Henry Huntington was American consul, and much of it in England. When, for the removal of an appendix, I was in a nursing home in Dorset Square more than thirty years later, Mother wrote me: "It is the *one* place in London that is vivid to me, for it was our headquarters for many weeks, and I used to sit of an evening in the little green enclosure with a fellow boarder at what I *think* was No. 32—while he apologized for not being able to ask me to marry him as he was already engaged!"

Of the young men she had left behind her in America Mark Howe at least was taking his medicine—straight. In fact his disappointment seemed positively to have whetted his palate for a taste of the seamy side of life, a taste, to date, so alien to him. Even before he had had to bite the dust that spelled out Fanny Quincy's fateful no he was writing his mother that he was "heartily sick of so many distractions. I don't do what I should like and ought to be doing, and altogether indulge myself in as thorough dissatisfaction with my course of life as I have ever felt."

Confronted with the loss of the girl he wanted to marry he decided to turn his back entirely on the segment of Boston which she and his "distractions" represented. He would continue with his job on the *Youth's Companion,* but he would move to Andover House in the South End, and give his evenings toward participating in the work of the newly founded settlement.

Doing good or do-gooding, the young man was now to respond to the strong appeal made to him by a new friend, certainly as different from Clyde Fitch or Richard Harding Davis as Mark Howe was from all three of them. Robert A. Woods, freshly returned from London and an apprenticeship at Toynbee Hall, must have been the first voice to speak to this son of the eighteen-nineties in the explicit accents of social conscience, as such. Andover House—later to grow into the South End House—was only the first step in the career of this pioneer in the Settlement House movement. As it was, Mark Howe, Jr., had considerable difficulty in trying to describe to his bishop father how there could exist any acts of organized community charity performed under any other auspices than those of the Church. All the Bishop could do was repeat, "I don't understand. I don't understand." But it was not only members of the Christian Church who in those early days of "social work" did not understand. Father used to quote a story Robert Woods brought back from Toynbee Hall of the young Oxford graduate who was cutting his eyeteeth in this new field, and asked of his preceptors what he should say in his first encounter with some of his underprivileged East End charges. He was told, "Talk to them as you would to any of your other friends." On a midsummer's day, launching, with this instruction in mind, a trial conversation with his first have-not, he began, "I say—are there many people in town just now?" The answer came back promptly, "I think, sir, there are something like seven millions."

A Dickens might have had fun with the efforts of the well-meaning young littérateur among the submerged thousands of the Boston of the 1890's. When he attempted to entertain a "group of poor people in the West End" with stereopticon and song he was forced to admit that "my several solos—sung at the people's backs—did not stir them to cheers or shouts or applause."

Then there was a "waifs' dinner" and a boys' club before which he sang, to be impressed by "about half a dozen girls, who *can* do whatever they want in Boston society [and who] give up one evening a week to meeting the young 'toughs' they have gradually attracted from the street. The boys are of the lowest sort, but the older ones, who have been in the club for some time, show the influence that has at least touched their lives. What excited my greatest admiration was the pluck, the real bravery of the girls who face these boys as they do and try to make them better."

There was a visit to the Church of the Carpenter where "three ministers without salary live with their flock and try to put 'Christian Socialism' into practice. We found the church by going up one flight of stairs, then over a shaky roof and down a few more steps, which landed us in the upper chamber which serves as sanctuary, and on Sunday night—with the chancel curtained off— a big supper room. The whole affair was very curious—like something one might read about as taking place in East London or Paris. I could not realize that I was in good old Puritan Boston.''

No matter how high his motives or determined his resolve to make others or himself ''better,'' the young man had obviously been cast by temperament as well as fate to play another role. Skipping temporarily over the various moves that were to open a new chapter for him, suffice it to say that within a few months he had resigned from the *Youth's Companion*, was established as assistant editor of the *Atlantic*, and had returned to Charles Street.

It was not to be long before Wal returned to Bristol, to marry the town's prettiest and most popular girl—the only child of Dr. George Locke, the rector of St. Michael's. So vague and dreamy was the rector that Father, meeting him on the first day of his summer holiday, walking to Bristol's railroad station, asked him, ''Where are you going to spend your holiday this summer, Dr. Locke?'' The gentle soul answered with his usual sweetness, ''I haven't quite decided whether to go to North Carolina—or Portugal.''

Otherworldly as he may have been, his beautiful daughter Mary (to us she was always Aunt Molly) was of the earth earthy. It was difficult for us children to reconcile the expansive and expanded Aunt Molly we knew in Brimmer Street with the photograph of the wasp-waisted bride which hung on the wall of my parents' bedroom. But the cyclone of vitality which had often lifted us in its path was obviously nothing new. Left motherless in infancy, Aunt Molly was brought up not so much by her dreamy father as by the whole town of Bristol. It was therefore the most natural thing in the world for the high-spirited bride to invite the entire town to her wedding. In her exuberant extraversion she did so, however, without fully realizing the anguish of stage-fright her stammering bridegroom would be called upon to meet. In fact, rather than meet it at all, he simply lost consciousness, slumping into a quiet faint at the altar into the sustaining arms of Cal. Surely it was Cal's finest hour! He rose to the emergency with such presence of mind that he forgot to remember his own stammer, and not only spoke up "I will" with resounding clearness but "I Wallis take Thee Mary" as well.

I have heard Father describe seeing his mother break down and cry—an unheard-of indulgence for her—on the heels of the ceremony which had put her youngest son through such a strain. She must also have had increasing cause to wonder if it was not getting to be high time for the older brother to get to the altar under his own steam, and speak up his own "I will" and "I Mark . . ." On his move to Andover House she had apparently applied gentle pressure on the vulnerable spot in the wall of his reserve. He wrote back, "You ask about the Quincys going to Washington: I think there is no likelihood of such a move, especially as they are all planning to go to Europe for a year or two. Much love to all, As ever, Mark." He was as ever Mark when a month later he wrote "Miss Abby Quincy died last Saturday, and the papers report the safe arrival in Gibraltar of the ship bearing her two great-nieces." Whether her aunt's death offered Fanny's suitor an excuse for writing I do not know, but Copeland clutched, some time later, at the straw of the death of an uncle.

Adams House
No. 553 Washington Street
Boston 20th Jan.

DEAR FANNY,
I have just heard of the death of your uncle, and that gives me courage to send you a word of amity and compassion, although you said you didn't want to hear from me again. I don't know whether you cared about him, but I do know by experience that the chill touch makes us think how easy it is for death to take the very nearest and the very dearest.—I shall try to write to you soon again. In the meantime it would make it more possible for me to write freely and naturally if you could bring yourself to send me a word. The writing of letters is agreeable to you but—as you well knew and know—almost constitutionally out of the question for me. Yet if you had taken my poor paper in the *Atlantic* as an answer to your welcome and attractive epistle from Italy,—I sent the

Atlantic to only two other people in the world—and written to me again in some other vein than a shower of curses, I should have plucked up courage and addressed you with my own hand instead of through the pages of a magazine. As it is, I have no more courage than to send you my best love and best wishes and an eager hope that I may see you again soon. *Do* write to me,

                                             C. T. C.

In spite of the protracted separation Father held on. The fact that he had made his first trip to Europe on the S.S. *Paris* in May, 1893—with Mr. Ignace Paderewski, Mr. Augustin Daly, and Mr. Charles E. Dana listed among its passengers—did not prevent his setting sail again in November, 1894, on the steamship *Mohawk*, whose steerage passengers numbered five hundred cattle and over a hundred horses. As to the human cargo he wrote: "The people— there are only fifteen of us— are as odd a jumble as you could find. The 'prima donna'—so to speak is a Mrs. Butler, known to the public as Annie Oakley—a famous rider and shot in Buffalo Bill's Wild West Show,—and as nice (if ungrammatical) a little woman as one often meets. You would smile if you could see me playing accompaniments for her extraordinary singing. Her husband is with her—a very decent sort of a horseman." It certainly would make Father's children smile if only a program of that ship's concert had been preserved for a future collector's item: "*Songs*, Annie Oakley. *At the piano*, M. A. DeWolfe Howe." All that does remain is the photograph of a girl in a huge sombrero, her hair hanging below her shoulders, and her bosom plastered with medals. On the back of the picture Father has written, "Autographed and given to me by 'Little Sure Shot' when we were fellow-passengers. . . . I remember well her standing on the after-deck with her rifle and hitting every coin we tossed high into the air."

This trip was taken for the simple purpose of spending one day with Fanny Quincy. The persistent suitor reported it coolly for the benefit of his mother: "On Saturday I was very hospitably received by the Quincys in Brighton, though their house was not large enough to provide me more than some pleasant breakings of bread with the family. On Monday I returned to London, glad of my glimpse of old friends and an interesting place." Much less glad he must have been to have had that repeated NO ringing—yet again!— in his ears. This time it was delivered on the beach at Brighton. All the same, he returned home carrying with him a stickpin, bearing the emblem of the lion of St. Mark's, bought, he was told, expressly for him in Venice, and a lock of that gold hair. Was it any wonder that he could not entirely despair?

Certainly there was no room for despair in the mood of the young man, nearing the end of his twenties, who had every reason for entertaining the highest hopes for the career opening out before him. Mr. Horace Scudder, the *deus ex machina,* who had placed Father on the *Youth's Companion* in the first place, appeared to consider that, after five years' apprenticeship, the time was ripe for offering him the position as his own assistant on the *Atlantic,* published at that time by Houghton Mifflin. At the same moment another fork in the road—that road not taken—presented itself in the form of an offer from *Harper's* in New York. After an on-the-spot inspection, made at the instigation of his friend Dick Davis, "There will be great chances, I think, for their group of young men of whom I should be one," Father wrote home. He saw the opportunity as an offer of a "bustling expansive career" but "the other sort of life—such as the distinctly literary nature of the *Atlantic"* was a stronger magnet. He did not spell out for home consumption his strongest motive for wishing to remain in Boston: the simple fact that it was the city which contained Miss Fanny Quincy.

He even managed to live through an interview with Mr. Henry O. Houghton, which must be unique in publishing history. The nervous candidate for the job got himself tied up in the most excruciating manifestation the stammerer knows—total silence. The result was that when he extricated himself at last with a spoken word—undoubtedly not the one he had been trying for at the first shot—he looked up, to find that Mr. Houghton had fallen asleep! No Emily Post, no *How to Succeed in Business* advice was handy. He asked himself, "Should the first motion of an Industrious Apprentice take the form of waking up a nodding Master? Should one cough, or drop a book, or utter any cry for help? Luckily I held my peace, could soon say to myself, 'Listen, the mighty Being is awake,' and depart in assurance of a salary I was glad to accept.''

Two years on the *Atlantic* (in those innocent days the magazine miraculously appeared every month with no other editors than Mr. Scudder, Father, and—as he recalled her—''the amazingly erudite and conservative Miss Susan M. Francis'') offered the opportunity to plant his feet more firmly on the ladder which, surely, could lead nowhere else but up. Had he not received, as token of the position awaiting him at the end of the climb, a small publication, inscribed by its author, ''H. E. Scudder to his Understudy''? There were writings of his own as well, beginning to appear over a wider and wider field. ''It seems to me now that I do nothing but read— read—and write—write to the almost entire exclusion of living— as I understand the word,'' he wrote home.

It is hard to know, so long after, whether it was overwork that brought on the trouble that was building up for him in the wings. Here and there through his letters, written in the characteristic major key, allegro giocoso, we hear beneath a minor tremolando in the strings—like that which prophesies her fate to Carmen. ''Blue is good for the eyes—hence my first choice of writing paper'' starts off one letter. In another he confesses that ''some late reading so troubled my eyes that for a week I have had to be very frugal of their use at night.'' He has been to the oculist, who ''has rejoiced my soul by saying that the new manifestation of evil in my eyes seems to be something temporary and unimportant,'' although he is forced to add, ''Of this he cannot yet be *perfectly* sure . . . if only he is a true prophet I shall grudge him nothing of his big fee or my lost month.'' The tone grows unmistakably more serious: ''My writing at all will show you that my eyes are still usable. On Monday and Tuesday I was greatly alarmed by finding on the outer side of my bad eye quite such a spot as made all the trouble on the inner and the doctor was inclined, too, to regard it rather ruefully. He decided, however, not to remove it by force of arms. . . . I cannot feel quite out of the woods; but if I can hold my own or gain in general physical condition I really think the trouble will disappear. . . . After I wrote last week the cloud which I saw forming on the horizon developed itself into the largest excrescence that had yet adorned my eye—and still another scraping was the result.''

It was becoming painfully apparent that, in addition to the fear of losing the girl he hoped for, there was every likelihood of his losing his professional career as well—along with his eyesight. No less than total blindness was the threat.

There were the heartbreaking rising and falling of hopes as he returned again and again to the doctor, and the symptoms of pain increased. Finally, in the spring of 1895, he wrote his mother, ''It seems to me therefore that the best thing to do is to quit Boston and the pressure which I cannot escape so long as I stay here,—and for six months or a year to try something quite different. Would it break your heart to have another son come home disabled? Living in Reading for two months and in Bristol thereafter I could certainly do enough work with safety to keep me in carfares and pin money—perhaps a little, or considerably, more.''

Presenting his resignation to Mr. Scudder must have been one of the most painful acts of father's life. He wrote staunchly, nonetheless, ''the sense of being beaten—temporarily—is galling, but worse defeats than mine have turned into other things, and—we shall see.'' If only he could have been sure even of that! There was no self-pity as he actually welcomed the opportunity for physical labor, at the same time getting his mind off his own troubles, when he went forthwith to Reading on the heels of his father's retirement from the ministry, to help to move his parents with all their household belongings to make their permanent home in Bristol. The Bishop, who had so looked forward to a succession of twilight years at his beloved Weetamoe, enjoyed only a few months. He died suddenly in that August, confronting Father with yet one more breaking of a tie—and his first taste of loss in the ranks of the family on whose solidarity he had so long depended.

Copeland wrote him from Campobello: ''I want you very much to leave the *place* of sorrow—there is distraction in that, if not comfort—and come to visit me a week. . . . These waters are of the

water of Lethe, and no man lifts his eyes to these hills without help.
I will be as good to you as I know how, and we will walk—or like
Landor you shall 'walk alone—upon the Eastern uplands.' All this
sounds like print, or rather (and worse) like something not quite
good enough to print. . . . Yet even *in literis* I can tell you that I
think of you daily and often.'' Not only would the devoted son not
leave his sorrowing mother, but the neophyte farmer—because
farmer was what he had decided to become—could not leave his
duties. Going through the motions of an efficiency expert he sub-
scribed to a farm journal, sent for government pamphlets on farm-
ing, and set up a system of accounts, ''which in the end proved
nothing but that we seemed to be getting our vegetables, butter,
and milk on moderate terms.'' He gave himself up to the pleasures
of the haying season, seated on a horse-drawn rake, delivered milk
before breakfast to a few summer customers, and left the real
running of the farm to the head farmer, Michael Callan. Father was
to quote all his life one aphorism of Michael's: ''When I laid before
him some such plan as breaking up a field that had been too long in
grass, he would come to me the next day and say in his three-
dimensional brogue, 'The more I think of it, Misther Mark, the
less I think of it.' ''

I cannot put a definite medical name to the ''trouble'' that had
afflicted his eyes. Father himself, totally unmedically minded and
strangely uninterested in any symptoms of his own, never specified
it definitely. It was probably iritis, with ulceration of the iris in
aggravated form. Its symptoms came and went in cycles. ''There
were weeks of black patches and dark rooms, when light was a
blinding pain.'' There were also ''lucid intervals,'' in which he
could write—and even read. As for his reading—it was done according to the custom of the family—aloud. During their long evenings together he read *War and Peace* aloud to his mother. There
was, as well, the perennial, inevitable antidote to which all Gentle
Americans have ever had recourse under stress of mind or body—
Jane Austen.

One wonders if the mind of the reader wandered from the words
he was pronouncing, perhaps to consider how his light was spent—

cooped up with an old mother, on a back road in Bristol, Rhode Island, the only other company being his knowledge that he had lost both the job and the girl of his choice.

If pity is akin to love, perhaps it was pity that turned the tide. In any case, the resistance of Fanny Quincy, after four more years, broke down. It broke so far down, in fact, that she consented to share the distinctly doubtful future of her husband—under the same roof with his mother. By April, 1899, she could write her mother-in-law-elect, ''This has been a very new and a very happy winter for me in many ways,—much happier for feeling (as you have made me feel) that my contentment is *not* at the expense of your renunciation. I think I have learned to know and value Mark in a way that is not quite possible unless there is a bond of hope and confidence that binds two people together, and though there are still—and always will be—moments of self-distrust and sadness and dread, yet I think I can heartily echo Rosalind's sentiment that a woman should 'thank Heaven fasting for a good man's love.' I hope he will be no worse for the love of a *very* mediocre woman!'' Mother only once let me get an oblique glimpse into what that time must have been for her when, speaking of a friend of mine, she wrote of ''those terrible days before the marriage of anyone who does not rush into the thing with the heedlessness of extreme youth are simply days to be lived through somehow—and then forgotten, if possible!''

It was characteristic of her to wince over the feelings of others with an intensity that made them her own. In his search of a cure for his eyes Father had recourse to a Providence oculist, and later to one in Boston, who continued the same grueling treatment of cutting and burning away a ''superfluity of bone in the upper recesses'' of his nostrils. She could agonize not only over his pain but over what his mother's feelings might well be in facing the arrival of an all but unknown daughter-in-law.

> . . . the room being torn down preparatory to its reformation, the plumbing in Mark's poor nose being overhauled, you must feel that life is buzzing around your ears at a pretty high pressure. I am only regretful that my part in the programme must be rather an annoyance to you, for all the carpentering, and

papering that is happening so close to your own room must be
rather a trying reminder of my approaching advent. . . . I
hope that Thursday the 21st will not seem too early a date
for you to accept me in the role I am most truly anxious to
fulfill with credit, that of being a further bond—or rather a
nearer bond—instead of a barrier between you and Mark.

After Uncle Wallis's public debacle it could not have been difficult for my grandmother Howe to accept a wedding ceremony
done less in the Bristol than the Quincy way. A small house wedding
involved the groom's being stuffed into a broom closet, to await
his cue.

Another lively imagination—remaining at a safe distance—also
was conjuring up pictures of how it all might be. The mingling of
pique, pain, bravado, and true depth of feeling writes the perfect
Finis to the story of our particular merryman moping mum.

Calais Maine

DEAR FANNY,

   The news that next Thursday is to be the Day, came with
startling suddenness. I was sure you told me that it was to be
in October and that I was to be asked to something after what
the newspapers call "the ceremony."— Here is a very little
cheque, but I should have to press the whole decimal system
into the service to express the book and volume of my love and
happy wishes to you and Mark. You must forgive my crude
way of making a gift, for there is nothing here but hills and
the river. Don't buy a cologne-bottle this time: buy something
that will last until the donor's face is wrinkling into dust.

   If you and Mark want a telegram on the fatal day, you must
tell me when and whither to send it. . . .

   Is "the tie that binds" to be secured with the Anglican
knot? Will the Voice breathe o'er Eden, or will *Lohengrin*
be honored?—Live long, dearest Friend, and keep always a
little whimsical tolerance for

                                     Your faithful
                                         COPE

Saturday night
16th September, 1899

I must record a poignant and ironic postscript. I well remember the look of sadness on her face when Mother once said to me in substance, "Almost every woman has cared very much for some other man than the one she finally marries." If she seemed to be playing the heartless flirt with both Copeland and Father it is because there was another serious contender. Father used to refer to his existence, saying, "I don't know what made her decide on me. Up to the last minute it looked as though she wouldn't." I never knew any details as to his profession, who it was that he finally married, whether Mother ever saw him again after her own marriage, or when he died. The only thing I do know is his name. And it does not figure in these pages.

5

THE LITTLE WORLD OF BOSTON LETTERS

THE MOST DISMAL ROOM in 26 Brimmer Street was grandly called the "reception room." It opened off the hall, at the front door, and was continually chilled by drafts. The hall itself was pretty dreary too. Its main feature was what I can only call a *thing*, inset into the banisters at the foot of the hall stairs—a lyre-shaped object a couple of feet high. Perhaps it had once been intended for some sort of lamp. My parents said they vowed the first time they saw it they would not allow it to remain in the house twenty-four hours after they moved in. It was still there when the door was finally closed on Brimmer Street, twenty-eight years later. There was no "powder" room on the ground floor—only a lowly washroom, stuffed with sleds, galoshes, and roller skates. My doll carriage was kept in the airless broom closet under the stairs where there was also what my parents always referred to as the "W.C." The reception room was furnished with what were clearly leftovers—wedding presents and mementos for which no other place could be found: a bronze plaque of my uncle "Joe" Quincy as Mayor of Boston, a Braun photograph of "The Man With the Glove," a framed illuminated parchment rendering of the Tavern Club's anthem, *"Meum est propositum in Taberna mori."*

It is odd that in a room which was so little associated with important family happenings one of my sharpest childhood memories of Father comes into focus. I am ten years old. Father is looking out the window at Brimmer Street, with his back to the room. He must be talking to Mother. He is saying, in a voice of sadness, unprecedented to my ears, "I have lost one of my best friends." That friend, I know now, was Mrs. Annie Fields.

James T. Fields, publisher of Dickens and many of the great of his day, as a widower in middle life, had married the nineteen-year-old Annie Adams. As she inevitably survived him by many years the house at 148 Charles Street was a center of hospitality—first with both host and hostess, later with hostess alone—for a span of some sixty years. There had been men of letters from abroad—Matthew Arnold, Thackeray, and Dickens pre-eminent among them. "Few were our native authors," one can hear Henry James's accompanying sigh, "and the friendly Boston household had gathered them in almost all." Aside from Longfellow, Emerson, Whittier, Hawthorne, there were Winslow Homer, Sargent, Modjeska, and Edwin Booth representing the other arts. The ambiance of a house which was "not a place where one could hear about the past, but . . . a place where the past lived on" was of course totally lost on the children of Brimmer Street. For us Mrs. Fields lived on only when an errant blob of applesauce found its way to cheek or chin, and Father would say, "Jamie, there's a gazelle in the garden." Thus Mrs. Fields was purported to have indicated that there had been a slip, 'twixt the cup and lip of her full-bearded mate. The *utterly utter* was not confined to Mrs. Fields's vocabulary alone; the subject matter touched on in Charles Street was only of the highest. Willa Cather recalled her saying yearningly, "You know, my dear, I think we sometimes forget how much we owe to Dryden's prefaces."

For Father, as for the young Willa Cather, Mrs. Fields served as a link in the chain that led back to "the great shades" who, Miss Cather felt, were most likely to appear at teatime, coming up the deeply carpeted stairs into the long, narrow, heavily curtained drawing room, looking out across a garden to the Charles River. And yet that chain, at its nethermost tip, could be stretched to touch even Quincy and me, at approximately nine and four years old. All that remains for me of one visit to that drawing room is a misty

impression of two old ladies, letting loose for our benefit some balloons which floated airily beneath the high ceiling. One of the ladies
wrote to Father afterward, saying, "We had such a *dear* time with
Helen and Quincy on Monday. I call them very dear young persons
with manners of the very best." Her letter is signed, "Yours affectionately, S. O. Jewett." I doubt that at the time I identified her
as the donor of two books of her own authorship, inscribed to me in
the month of my birth "from one of her oldest friends." Quincy
figured more prominently in the life of the salon than I. In the same
drawing room in which, after one of his public readings, Dickens
had made burnt brandy punch and sung comic songs, the same
drawing room to which Emerson so often came, bringing one day
his wife and daughter, murmuring that there was not such another
in all Boston, while he "looked about and told them the wrong
names of the painters," Quincy, whom the ladies most often called
by his pet name of "Kinky," recited "The Sands of Dee." The
miniature future broadcaster held his audience spellbound, from
his opening, "O Mary, go and call the cattle home," building up
toward the climax which he gave forth with full tremolo,

> They rowed her in across the rolling foam
> The cruel crawling foam
> The cruel hungry foam,
> To her grave beside the sea.

leaving the tenderhearted ladies dissolved in tears.

It was Copeland who first brought the young editor of the *Youth's
Companion* to call on Mrs. Fields. Behind her back, Copeland bap-
tized her with the name of the mythological Greek nymph Clytie.
To be "taken up," and into such a rarefied atmosphere, must have
made the air the Proper Bristolian was breathing at the *Youth's
Companion* seem even cruder by comparison.

The *Companion* of those days enjoyed—as Father was fond of
quoting from another context—"merely a national reputation"; a
circulation of some half million was a phenomenon at the turn of
the century. Father recalled its "Premium Number," a glorified
illustrated mail-order catalogue. It offered:

toy steam-engines, skates, books, sewing-machines, real and toy, caps and gloves—even, for at least one year, live goats . . . Men who were once boys in country towns, East and West, have told me of the excitement that attended the delivery of the mail on one October Thursday in their communities. Boys and girls, snatching their papers from the postmistress, began rushing from house to house in search of fellow townsmen, of any age, who had not already been drawn into the *Companion* fold. . . . The names with which it burgeoned forth every year were not merely those of C. A. Stephens and fellow specialists in *Companion* fiction, but also the most conspicuous in the world at large: Tennyson, Gladstone, Henry M. Stanley, Mark Twain, Theodore Roosevelt, Whittier, Phillips Brooks, Sara Orne Jewett . . . A single group of writers promised for one year consisted of Barrie, Stevenson, Howells, Kipling, and Mark Twain. . . .

Early in the century, I remember, there was a succession of short poems, in a small, clear, black handwriting from an unknown poet in New Hampshire, whose writings seemed to me to strike a fresh and enchanting note. He has told me in recent years—and I take no shame in cherishing what he said—that my anonymous letters from the *Companion* were among the very first to give him any encouragement to proceed as a poet. At Christmas of 1931 that poet, whom I came to know when the *Companion* was far behind us both, gave me a copy of his "Collected Poems," with these words written on the fly-leaf:
"To MARK A. DEW. HOWE
who many a year ago (a score and a half or so) wrote three words into one of the poems in it, but who won't remember which they were (and I won't tell him, because I don't believe in giving the critics any more help than I have to give them).

ROBERT FROST"

I think Father believed those three words to have been tucked away somewhere in "A Boy's Will," but Robert Frost never told him so!

So, in spite of that Premium Number, to work for the *Youth's Companion* was not slumming. Ellery Sedgwick, later of the *Atlan-*

tic, was one of its editors, as were Paul Revere Reynolds, to become dean of New York literary agents, Charles Flandrau, before he became known for his books on Mexico, and John Macy, that unsung optimist who, married at the time to the great Ann Sullivan Macy, was hoping to preserve a marriage contained within the most extraordinary prefabricated triangle in history. In the Art Department a young Gluyas Williams was already beginning to feel his oats.

Photographs attest to Mrs. Fields's beauty in age as in youth. Henry James was to respond to her charms, even stoutly emphasizing—as Father himself attempted to do—her sense of humor. No need to say which of the gallants is speaking: "All her implications were gay since no one so finely sentimental could be noted as so humorous; just as no feminine humor was perhaps ever so unmistakingly directed, and no state of amusement, amid quantities of reminiscence, perhaps ever so merciful."

What the neophyte, as his elders and betters before him, found in Mrs. Fields was that rarest and most precious gift a writer can come upon—the spark of genuine interest and belief in his work for its own sake. Willa Cather could testify that "she rose to meet a fine performance always—to the end."

At the time that the underling editor on the *Youth's Companion* had made his decision to throw up his job in favor of an opening on the *Atlantic,* he had written back to Bristol: "I saw Mr. Ford and resigned. The old gentleman took it really quite sadly. . . . That evening—where do you suppose I went for advice? To Mrs. James T. Fields who knows the magazine world of Boston and New York quite as well as any living being. What she said happily confirmed my own views."

When the threat of losing his eyesight and the actuality of losing his position on the *Atlantic* drove her protégé from Boston the tender patroness followed him—with letters.

"Dear Mr. Howe, I hope you will be able to pass next week here! On the 29th I am going to have a little dinner in memory of Keats (it is his birthday you will remember) and so if you will come that day and stay as many days after as you like, you may be able to slay

several birds with such a pebble of a visit.'' Surely on that occasion
the conversation piece must have been two treasured objects, kept
reverently under glass—a lock of the poet's hair and a drawing of
his features by his close friend Severn, who had given both to Mrs.
Fields. Yea, though he walked through the valley of the shadow
of death Mrs. Fields, with her Victorian maxims, was with him.
''I am not forgetful of you in these days of experience where neither
youth nor age means much to us! The strong light of death shines
upon our lives and we find there is but one day after all in which
we may do our best, one day for progression towards the beginning
we call life indeed.''

What, in youth, he would have liked to become throws, perhaps,
more light on the true essence of a man than works actually performed. The apprentice farmer in Bristol, like the apprentice editor
in Boston, wanted nothing so much in life as to become a poet. He
had already, to his credit, one privately printed volume of verses.
Now, in 1897, came his first commercially published book of verse,
published by Copeland and Day, a firm long since extinct. Behind
his dark glasses he must have been pleased to read Thomas Bailey
Aldrich's words:

> when the day comes for you to gather all your books of verse
> into two or more volumes you will find next to nothing in this
> to leave out. . . . [The poems] are wonderfully even and firm
> in texture, and have no uncertainties in the pattern. . . . Read-
> ers with insight and sympathy are always in the minority, so
> far as poetry is concerned. . . . If you had wished for present
> popularity, you should have written in some loathesome dialect
> not spoken anywhere on the face of the earth. I wonder
> how *Lycidas* or Keats's *Ode on a Grecian Urn* would go in
> Kiplingese!

It must have been concerning one of his volumes of verses that
Mrs. Fields gushed:

> DEAR MARK!!!
> Nothing could be more exactly right; but I believe you have
> taken pure joy in surprising us after so long a time.
> I am hoping to see you to say the inexpressible!

Yours, with an unaccountable sense of personal satisfaction . . .

The poet-farmer continued, however, to plow the furrow of prose. There was his column "Boston Letters," contributed to Scribner's little monthly, the *Book Buyer*. His successor on the *Atlantic*—and not long after to Mr. Scudder's position as editor—Walter Hines Page, made opportunities for him to do anonymous book reviewing. He was already beginning to feel his wings grow stronger in a series of biographical papers for the *Bookman*. This latter was to serve as springboard from which he jumped into the waters of true authorship with *American Bookmen*, published in 1898. He was to remember one of those special moments of a lifetime "that stand out in red or gold" when he carried away from the Bristol post office a package of a dozen "author's copies" from Dodd, Mead, and Company to the beach-wagon, and drove his precious burden back to Weetamoe.

Next came the launching of a series of "Brief Biographies of Eminent Americans," published by the young firm of Small, Maynard and Company, under the covering title of the "Beacon Biographies Series—edited by Mark A. DeWolfe Howe." The little volumes, of about twenty thousand words each, were charmingly designed by Bertram Goodhue. The series began with five titles of which Norman Hapgood's *Daniel Webster* was one and Father's own small biography of *Phillips Brooks* another. Copeland was to do an *Edwin Booth;* the "glory of the series," in Father's opinion, was Owen Wister's *Grant*. Father was never to belong to the "debunking" school of biography, and with this first venture he had found at least one member of his potential audience. The New England author Margaret Deland found *Phillips Brooks* "a model of what a biography ought to be: true, first; reverent—fair; marked by a fine reserve, but by an even finer sense of proportion . . . I hope you will not think that I am speaking without reflection when I say that I have never read any biography which gave me such delight in this way, as yours of Mr. Brooks."

As the threat was lifted from Father's eyes, thanks to the painful treatments on his nose, he and Mother returned to Boston in 1900, settling first in Mt. Vernon Street. His position on the *Atlantic* had been filled, and he was grateful indeed to be received back into a half-time position, not too demanding for his eyes, with the *Youth's Companion.*

His professional career was obviously no longer Father's chief concern after he and Mother were married in September 1899. The couple had withdrawn on their "wedding journey." (Gentle Americans never embarked on as crude an interlude as a honeymoon.) The bride refused to play the conventional romantic role: my tattered volume of Olive Schreiner's *The Story of an African Farm* is inscribed "To Mark Howe for his wedding trip, from his sincere old friend, F. H. Quincy." That sincere old friend was to become the mother of a son, Quincy, born in midsummer, 1900, in Boston. I have heard her say—and small wonder that it was so after a labor lasting two days—that the happiest moment of her life came in hearing his first cry. When she returned to Weetamoe she could even make her churchly mother-in-law laugh when the presence of the new infant brought inevitable nighttime disturbance and she quoted Scripture: "We shall not all sleep, but we shall all be changed." The voice of Copeland was heard upon the child's birth, writing to Father: "God bless you and Fanny and the Boy! As he won't be named for me, I don't much care what he's called; but should like to know his weight and the color of his eyes. . . . Where was little Mark Josiah born? . . . I hope you and F. are both better than can be expected. Hurry the child to church; she may object when she gets stronger." How little "she" objected was revealed when four years later the grandmother in Bristol heard that "Quincy is well, and the joy of my life. He inherits a love of church-going from you, and sits like a mouse through a musical service at the Advent. He is very high church I regret to say! Lovingly, Fanny."

The process of fusion between the Bristol and Boston Ways was gradually advancing as the ramparts of the older generation began to totter and fall. The blow of the sudden death of her mother by pneumonia "is a killing one for all of us," Mother wrote to Mrs. Fields. After Mark's birth, a year and a half following mine, there were a few summers in Bristol, only dimly remembered by us both. There Grandpa Quincy accompanied us, and struck up a lively and congenial friendship with Grandma Howe, across the gulf of their opposing views on religion, to the mingled surprise and amusement of their children. I have heard Mother say that her own happiness at the instant of the realization of my existence could not rival what she felt at the sound of Quincy's first cry because between the two births her mother had died and "nothing could ever be the same again." For the Gentle Americans a Mother was deeply loved, and as deeply mourned when lost, not yet metamorphosed by Freudian innuendo into the monster Mom who dominates our latter-day psychoses. The death of Father's mother was for him, too, a searching grief. He wrote:

> Once when you left me in a room alone,
> Sudden the world seemed void and black.
> So that my heart cried, "Were she gone,
> Gone, never to come back!
> Some day, how will it be?
> What will remain for me?"

His unabashedly reverential love for an almost divine being expressed itself in florid Victorian idiom:

> ... reared within my heart
> A secret, inner chamber stands apart,
> All furnished forth with her ...

Those furnishings were to be with him all his days.

Mark and I were too little to be worthy of much of Mrs. Fields's attention but by the time Quincy was twelve and thirteen years old he was in a fair way of being wooed as assiduously as the literary lions of old. On Washington's Birthday, 1912, Mrs. Fields gave him a volume of valuable autographs. In his thank-you letter the recipient clear-sightedly states, "My father and mother are very much pleased with it and they are very glad I have it." At Christmas his thanks for a "nice box of butterflies," led to the inevitable enumeration of other Christmas presents received, ending up with a flourish:

[Mark and Helen and I] "now have a dog, two paraquets, and a canary. I hope we will have enough live stock to last through the winter."

The yearning sibyl of Charles Street obviously confounded his parents by an invitation to the thirteen-year-old schoolboy to come and pay her a visit. With Mother away, the man of the family was thrown into a social panic, floundering about between thanks for such kindness "and temerity!" and a variety of excuses. "For the good of his soul, such a visit as you propose would be one of the best things in the world. But my imagination baulks at its being equally good for you! . . . there are music-lessons, and a small menagerie of pets for whose care he is responsible, —and sometimes—studying at night. . . . Perhaps Fanny's more flexible mind will compass the possibilities."

That mind produced the solution:

If you felt like asking him to supper with you and pay a little call after the evening meal either Friday or Saturday he would feel immensely flattered, and I think you would get at his little ego better than if either parent accompanied him!

That little ego didn't do too badly with its own set of excuses:

Thank you very much for asking me to visit you. My mother thinks that I can spend Saturday night and stay for dinner Sunday. I am going to a football game on Saturday afternoon and I am wanted at home to help to take care of Helen and Mark. I am sure that we can have several nice talks while I am staying with you.

Yours affectionately,
QUINCY HOWE

In actuality Quincy was so far from "taking care" of Mark and me that the only hour of the year in which he stooped to the concerns of such small fry occurred on Christmas Eve when he read aloud to us "A Visit from St. Nicholas."

Although Quincy himself does not remember whether this much-discussed visit was ever paid or not, he does remember being "parked" in Charles Street one autumn, while the rest of the family remained on Cape Cod and he returned to the Country Day School. His general recollection seems to be that he himself did a great deal of talking. What a different companion Mrs. Fields must have found this twentieth-century schoolboy, normally free of any aesthetic or literary interests, from Leigh Hunt with whom she had rhapsodized over the "starlike beauty of Shelley's face." I have tried to squeeze further recollections from my brother in vain: "Do you remember what James spoke of as 'the quite lawful art of causing a black lace mantilla to descend from her head and happily consort with a droop of abundant hair'? Or Miss Cather's impression that she was 'very slight and fragile in figure, with a great play of animation in her face and a delicate flush of pink on her cheeks'?" "No. 1 only remember an old lady."

Mrs. Fields was by no means the only magnet to draw Father to the long drawing room in Charles Street. There were, in my parents' circle of friends in Boston, several households consisting of two ladies, living sweetly and devotedly together. Such an alliance I was brought up to hear called a "Boston marriage." Such a "marriage" existed between Mrs. Fields and Sarah Orne Jewett. Father wrote of it as a "union—there is no truer word for it." What Henry James, whose *The Bostonians* was published in 1888, found to "catch at" in the friendship between the Charles Street ladies we can only guess. All we get is that "their reach together was of the firmest and easiest and I verily remember being struck with the stretch of wings that the spirit of Charles Street could bring off." He writes of them both with such affection, nostalgia, and downright chivalry that we are left confronting merely shadows.

When Sarah Jewett's wings stretched in verse, they gave us *Together*.

A few lines suffice:

> When everyone has said good night
>   In fading firelight, then in peace
> I idly rest: you come to me—
>   Your dear love holds me close to you.
> If I could see you face to face
>   It would not be more sweet and true.

When, after her friend's death, Mrs. Fields brought out a volume
of her letters Father laid a restraining editorial hand across her
enthusiasm, particularly "regarding the nicknames—especially
where an assumed childish diction is coupled with them. An occas-
sional 'Pinny' [the tall, slender Sarah was so called because of
her head which was no bigger than a pin's] I should think might be
left, but four-fifths of them—I think—should go for the mere sake
of the impression we want the book to make on readers who have no
personal association with Miss Jewett. . . . I doubt . . . whether you
will like to have all sorts of people reading them wrong." In the
copy of these letters inscribed to "Dear Mark and Fanny with
ever true affection from Annie Fields" I have found tucked three
letters, all addressed to Mrs. Fields, two in Miss Jewett's own handwriting and one typewritten copy. It is in this copy that one sees
the gentle pencil has been obediently at work. Miss Jewett's nickname for Mrs. Fields has been obliterated throughout. Is it any
wonder, when we learn that it was "Fuff"? Concerning a paper
Mrs. Fields must have written about Leigh Hunt Miss Jewett says,
"You must write all your stronomizing proclivities will let you(!)
about the bookatees and their being your dear bookatees. . . ."

> Good night dear dear Fuff—if you could only dream how I
> want to see you! What is in bloom in the garden? I wish I
> could send you a sniff of our big flowering currant bushes.
>
>   Your own P.L.

She had written earlier:

> I think your book is the dearest book I ever saw! I don't
> know that it is polite to speak of the cover first, but it is *so*
> pretty! . . . I do think you were very good to send me Under
> the Olive—I know how many friends you have, —but I take
> it, as I know you will let me, as a sign of something that is
> between us, and since we have hold of each other's hands we
> will not let them go—
>   . . . I shall be very fond of the little book for its own sake,
> and also for yours, and many a line will seem as if it were
> spoken and not written to me, and bring back other things—

that you have said and I like to remember. . . . I do hope to
be in Boston again and I should like dearly to make you a
little visit. And we will play with each other whenever we have
a chance, and talk about the rose teaset—and find time every
day for one handkerchief doll at least.

Father was obviously distressed to have to recognize the sentimentality in "Miss Jewett"—as I was brought up to hear her
called. To recognize the existence of a personal sentimentality, however, is only to emphasize the mystery concealed in the tangled skein
of gifts from which the artist weaves his finished tapestry. In her
stories of New England the clear *unsentimental* tone of Sarah Orne
Jewett still reverberates, authoritative, unobtrusive, true, with—in
Willa Cather's words—"a quality which any ear trained in literature must recognize."

It was during these years of editorial apprenticeship dealing with
most of his writers by correspondence—and not face-to-face as with
Miss Jewett—that Father was laying a firm foundation of the craft
that was to stand him in such good stead in his own biographical
writings: a sense of form, style, and proportion. What was relevant
and what was irrelevant to the subject became part of his own
equipment as a writer.

It was as the so much younger editor (first, on the *Youth's Companion*, then on the *Atlantic*, and again on the *Youth's Companion*)
that Father offered Sarah Jewett editorial judgment she appeared
to value.

I did not mean in the least to be impatient about the little
story which I had sent you. An old writer like me learns to
ignore the "fortunes of war." . . . I do not send my work "on
approval" any more except to a friend like you since we are
on quite different terms from the plain Editor & Contributor
relations, but I hope that you will always say just what you
think as you have done now. You know what a warm interest I
take in both the Companion itself and your connection with it.

And now about the cheque! It doesn't seem very easy to take
it, at first thoughts, but neither does it seem easy to send it
back since that might seem to have a pettishness that does not

exist! Will you therefore mark the sketch *Left Out* (instead of
Counted Out), which I believe comes closer to its meaning, and
then put it in a pigeon hole? You can use it in your announcement (out of which I refuse to be left!) as before the time
comes for printing, either you shall have something that you
like better, or this story shall be made better, itself.

Lest we idealize such a relationship across mists of time, it is
almost heartening to hear the human ring of her voice in a P.S. "I
am not usually so mercenary but I should be glad if you could have
the cheque sent me as soon as may be. It is one I wish to spend
now!!"

Thomas Bailey Aldrich, as editor of the *Atlantic*, had said that
whenever Miss Jewett sent him "one of her perfect stories the whole
number seemed to bloom." No wonder that she wrote to her editor
on the *Youth's Companion* that she hoped the "Green Bonnet"
would remain in fashion until another spring.

No more Green Bonnets for me, or short sketches which are
soon written—I am still hard at work on the story which
begins in the November *Atlantic* and there is a long stretch of
hard work ahead before I can put it out of mind. I feel just
now as if I had all the cloth without having my coat made!—
I have written most of the chapters, but every one must be
written at least once again and put into shape.

And yet her relations with the *Companion* continued, happily.

The Companion gave me a great surprise and pleasure, I
was monstrous pleased to be put on the first page "fea-
tured"!! and with such a really nice and really illustrative
picture! They are so few in my long history as a writer! The
little boy is charming—and our story which began in a bit of
frolic turned out better than might have been expected,
didn't it?

When an accident to her carriage in South Berwick threw Sarah
Jewett out, causing a slight concussion, her concern was not that
she was incapacitated for writing, but that she could not be with
Mrs. Fields, who had been ill. "I know so well what a difference it

would make if I were there. . . . I try to be reasonable, for if I were no stronger than now I should only make things worse by being there! I do hope that you and Fanny can be let in to see her *very* soon.'' Recovery was painfully slow, and she admitted to being ''rather dull and confused after the accident'' though she could close ''with much love to Fanny and Kinky and yourself, believe me Your affectionate friend.'' She herself did not know that she was never to write again. A letter to ''My dear Friend'' confessed:

I ought to have written you at once but I could not help clinging to the hope that it might be right to say *Yes*, in loud and cheerful fashion. But alas, I am not yet fit to think about the smallest bit of work. I should think about it all night as well as all day! As I am getting on so slowly that I still have to be very careful of even reading and writing notes —I get downstairs for part of the day, and lead a really hulking life in my room for the rest of the time!!

But Mrs. Fields is better and things are going well with her, which is a great happiness to me.

I venture to suggest that you should ask dear Mrs. Julia Ward Howe to make the ''Easter wishes''! . . . I think it is just what she could do beautifully, and a word from her would come to so many, many people as a word from a friend.

Perhaps some day too, she could write some charming little short papers about her Greek experiences—there is one about a Brigand's Head in a Bag!!! She gets a little lonely in these days with so many friends gone and her old activities hindered by 84 years— but her brain is the brain of a young student in the best of trim!

Yours most affectionately
S. O. JEWETT

It was an ironic stroke of fate that Mrs. Fields, so much the older of the two friends, should have been called upon to survive the younger Sarah, at whose funeral a poem by Father was read.

For all that he was holding down a full-time office job, his habit of unremitting industry, which is so much part of my own memory of him, must have been established early. There were not only several volumes of verse, and the editing of the ''Beacon Biographies Series''; there was, in 1903, a sizable tome, *Boston, the Place and the People*. Father's erstwhile teacher, Barrett Wendell, had nothing but kind words for his pupil's writing. Speaking of a chapter of the book, ''The Boston Religion'' (inevitably, Unitarianism), he wrote:

It is the best statement of the matter it deals with which I have come across; and whets my eagerness for your book. And it is admirably written. You have just the unobtrusive command of style which marks a real man of letters, as distinguished from an amateur. But I wonder if your latent orthodoxy is, after all, so deep or as heretical as mine. . . . We can say, of course, that the historic church is a dream or a dreamer. But I cannot see how we can claim any spiritual fellowship with it, and not find the Boston Religion a trap for souls—more alluring in its transient earthly purity, than all the snares of the flesh together.

In his spare time out of the office ''in four years of hard single-handed work'' Father also plowed through three ''Saratoga trunks'' full of papers, to come out in 1908 with a two-volume life of the historian George Bancroft. This was the first of many such works which he undertook at the request and in the pay of the family of his subject. The book came out seventeen years after Bancroft's death at ninety-one, so that its subject was already more of a tradition ''lapped in lead'' than a man whom the living remembered. Years later, looking back, it caused Father to warn others (I take it today to myself) ''if any man's life is to be written, no matter what a figure he has cut in the world, let it be with reasonable promptness.'' At the time, however, the biography was well received, even calling forth a nod of approval from no less august a critic than Charles Eliot Norton.

You have done your work not only with literary skill and taste, but with admirable tact, discretion and good judgment. Your general treatment of the subject is in the right tone, while your treatment of special incidents is often masterly in its reserve as well as in its expression.

I have not been an indulgent reader, but I have found noth-

ing that was not to be praised in your work, with the exception
of a few words at which I stumble. Bancroft is happy in having such a biographer. . . . But how completely his History is
relegated to the shelves from which the books are not taken
often enough to keep them from getting dusty.

There were other older men than Norton on the fringes of
Father's life. When he wrote for the Tavern Club a memoir of
William James's friend and colleague Richard Hodgson, James
wrote him:

MY DEAR HOWE—for your words about our common friend
melt out the "Mister"—I have just read your Memoir of
R.H., and the tears have been in my eyes. A truer, better,
heartier thing could not possibly be written. *La voix du coeur
qui seule au coeur arrive*—just the points, the words, the tone.
And the resultant picture quickens all one's memories of the
incomparable and unconquerable Richard, to the aching point.
Such independence of life with such absence of *defiance* was
most rare.

I have been comparing the various utterances of the pro-
fessed R.H. through Mrs. Piper since he appeared there. Dra-
matically most like, but in content most imperfect—& on the
whole to me very puzzling.

I bless you for the Memoir, and for doing it so well.

Faithfully yours,
WILLIAM JAMES.

And a few days later, giving the addresses of various friends of
Hodgson's who would want the memoir, James asked for "six more
to me, who will address them to certain female loveresses of Hodgson at a distance who will prize them greatly. You don't probably
know how much friends of R.H. *will* prize those life like words of
yours."

There was one other old lady, aside from Mrs. Fields, who would
be soon leaving the stage, over whose shoulder Father could dis-
cern still other ghosts and shadows. Although Mrs. Julia Ward
Howe was old and famous she still could have enough humility
about her professional standing to sign a letter to Father as a junior

editor of the *Youth's Companion* "Yours with much respect," telling him that she has made "long journeys, with lectures in distant
cities, etc. etc. If it is not yet too late for me to speak of the poem
mentioned by you as desirable for the Youth's Companion, I shall
be pleased to confer with you about it. I suppose that you are very
busy, but could you not call upon me some time soon?" When his
Bancroft biography appeared she told him, "I have read it with
great pleasure and am sure that it will have and keep an honorable
place among modern biographies. The scattering season is now at
hand, but if my life is prolonged to another season, I shall hope to
see you and Mrs. Howe at my house." Whether before or later I do
not know, but I seem to retain a hazy impression that Julia Ward
Howe was the old lady in question when Quincy, as a very small
boy, was taken to see her by his parents, and before being ushered
into her presence asked a question which became part of the family's
little language, and served on many future occasions. *"Does she
know about me?"*

A dinner party at Mrs. Fields's table rings the curtain down on
this little world—and on my own attempts to reconstruct Father's
memories of it. If his own penciling on the back of an old envelope
was correct, the assembled guests, aside from himself, and Mrs.
Fields as hostess, were Julia Ward Howe and Henry James, as well
as two minor Boston novelists, both friends of Father's, and their
wives—Robert (later Judge) Grant and T. R. Sullivan. Mother's
absence was explained by my very recent birth. Henry James was
to describe the party ten years later in the *Cornhill Magazine*
(reprinted in the *Atlantic*), as "a haunted little feast as of ghosts
if not of skeletons."

The ghosts at the banquet were personified in "the image of that
immemorial and inextinguishable lady Mrs. Julia Ward Howe, the
most evidential and most eminent presence of them all, as she rises
in her place, under the extremity of appeal, to declaim a little
quaveringly but ever so gallantly, that 'Battle Hymn of the Republic' which she caused to be chanted half a century before and still
could accompany with a real breadth of gesture, her great clap of
hands an indication of the complementary step on the triumphant
line, 'Be swift my hands to welcome him, be jubilant my feet.' "

(It is amusing, parenthetically, to recall a letter of Richard Harding Davis's, written in 1891, telling of his going with friends to the house of Mrs. Howe: "There were only a few people present and Mrs. Howe recited the Battle Hymn of the Republic, which I thought very characteristic of the city.")

Father was to recall his own minor role among his elders and betters:

> This was the assignment for the youngest member of the party to convoy Mrs. Howe, on what happened to be a night of snowstorm and icy sidewalks, from her house in Beacon Street to Mrs. Fields's in Charles Street. The journey thither and back was achieved in one of those two-horse Kenny & Clark cabs then much in use. I remember with a special enjoyment the utterance of Mrs. Howe as she slumped into her seat for the homeward drive. Diminished as she was in stature by her nearly ninety years, she declared with an air of finality "Annie Fields has shrunk."

I jump ahead for a moment to 1915, when Henry James wrote to Father, obviously in response:

21, Carlyle Mansions
Cheyne Walk, S.W.
July 20th, 1915

MY DEAR MARK HOWE,

Forgive my having to use this form of thanks for your good letter, of so friendly a tone, about my Cornhill paper. (It was only derivatively in the *Atlantic*—Reginal Smith, editor and publisher of the Cornhill, who had considerably known Mrs. Fields, pressingly proposed it to me and without him it wouldn't have been produced. The *Atlantic*, alas, has but spoiled my title: I found "Mr. and Mrs. Fields" a title, but "Mr. and Mrs. J.T.F." none at all. By such a hair do these things hang, and so all but non-existent, on your quarter of the earth perhaps especially, is any sense for them.) Your appreciation, however, reaches me, alas, but through the most muffling and deadening thicknesses of our unspeakable actuality here. It was to try and get out of that a little that I wrote my paper—in the most difficult and defeating conditions, which seemed to me to make it, with my heart so utterly else-

where, a deplorably make-believe attempt. Therefore if it *had*
any virtue, there must still be some in my poor old stump of a
pen. Yes, the pipe of peace is a thing one has, amid our storm
and stress, to listen very hard for when it twitters, from afar,
outside; but when you shall pipe it over your exhibition of
dear Mrs. Fields's relics and documents I shall respond to your
doing so with whatever attention may then be possible to me.
We are not detached here, in your enviable way—but just
exactly so must we therefore make some small effort of escape,
even into whatever fatuity of illusion, to keep our heads above
water at all. That in short is the history of my Cornhill scrap.
I have liked hearing from you; you recall to me occasions
which your participation in them made so pleasant to me—
well do I remember the Charles Street dinner, and also my
happily dining with yourselves. I commend myself kindly to
Mrs. Mark, and am yours all faithfully

HENRY JAMES

The year 1903—two years before the dinner in Charles Street—
had seen the publication of Father's *Boston, the Place and the
People.* Sarah Orne Jewett had written him in that year, on
Christmas evening:

MY DEAR FRIEND,
    You are very kind to send me your Book—I am delighted
to have it with your name and mine in the beginning, and I
am not writing before I read it, because I have read it already
with the greatest delight and admiration.
    —I have been waiting for many days to tell you so . . . that
I have found it strangely difficult in this last month. . . . On
some days when I could read I caught eagerly at the Boston,
and I wish that I could say now how fine I think it is as a piece
of work: charm—perspective, proportion, dignity—*readable-
ness* are all there. Yes, and *seriousness* which is so often left
out of books in these days—we are sometimes afraid of not
being amusing enough— You often take the humorous point
of view, but never descend to the showman's banter—I have
just looked into a book that is spoiled by it. . . .

Yours, very affectionately . . .

It is in connection with this same Boston book that several years later (the letter is undated) she writes:

My dear friend, I have been meaning to copy this piece of a late letter from Mr. James—and now that it is written off I wonder that I don't just send you the letter itself! He adds further words to tell me that if I demand the book he means to wait for a private conveyance—books going to America meet with such dangers by the way!—I can but smile sadly, and with your "participation" let our dear friend keep it! I didn't know where it had gone, my only Boston! For I wasn't at that dinner nor did I see him until some weeks later and when he came, later than that, to Berwick he never dared to confess. But isn't it nice that he likes it? I think you ought to have more pleasure than I over the message but I had a great deal. I hope that you won't stop to write about it but come very soon so that we can talk about my borrowing so valued a work, being now in real need!!

Yours affectionately,
S.O.J.

On another sheet of paper she had written:

Mr. James writes me (after speaking of Mrs. J. W. Howe as) "the greater, the greatest Mrs. Howe (not less than the lesser) and to convey a renewed benediction to that very pleasant young author-man who was with her at Mrs. Fields's that day at dinner, the DeWolfe of that ilk, whose big Boston-y book I so handsomely stole—"

This may seem an incoherent little affectionate message at first sight, but I think you will both make it out as H.J.'s narrative vein!

And on yet another piece of paper, in her fine handwriting, Miss Jewett had taken the trouble to copy out the following, from Henry James:

. . . and apropos of books I find I have in my possession a volume of *yours*, a very valuable one, the presentation copy of DeWolfe Howe's very handsome and charmingly done "Boston" which you must have lent me the night you and he and

I—and Mrs. Howe under his charge—dined together at Mrs. Fields's in so interesting a fashion. It appears to have tumbled recklessly into my luggage on my departing later on—and the perusal of it here this autumn (for I had never time before) has made up to me a little for having failed to see again that most engaging youth the Author in spite of my having (at the dinner in question) counted on putting my hand on him afresh, —at a date that never became possible. And all this under the empire of his and yours and every one's irresistible charm. Will you kindly, if you have the little Boston chance of it, say something of this to the said gallant and genial DeWolfe for me, and mention to him by way of a message from me, that the reading of his encyclopaedic little work greatly helped to put me in the mood for writing—3 months ago—a small impression of the admirable city (which has yet to be published). This is a very long story to trouble you with, but the moral is that I hold the volume at your disposal (unless you tell me with his participation to cherish it forever in memory of that rare evening).

And so, if Mrs. Fields "went back" for Father, Father himself, mourning her death in the Brimmer Street reception room, "goes back" for me. I have up to now been able only through imagination to attempt to recapture the flavor of the headwaters whence he came. I leave here my approximation of Father's memories—those shadows of a shade—and, in returning to Brimmer Street, shall pursue instead the flesh and blood of my own.

II

Boston—the Place and the People

6

WE WERE NEITHER LONG-TAILED NOR SHORT

WHEN FATHER, WITH HIS BACK TO ME, looked through the win-
dowpane, Brimmer Street undoubtedly appeared to him in some
sort of social and historical perspective and not, as to me, like the
inevitable backdrop to the very Cosmos itself. Only now that I am
more than ten years older than he was then, do I see it, and my
parents whose habitat it was, in relation to the Boston frame that
contained them.

Caesar divided Gaul into three parts, Proust his Paris into two.
There are many ways in which my parents' Boston may be sliced
or peeled; one's bound to lose some of the juice in any of them.
They and their contemporaries used to refer to a subdivision of one
Boston clan as the "long-tailed Forbeses" and the "short-tailed
Forbeses." The tails referred to the horses owned by the two
branches of the family—one left to flop and switch in a state of
nature, the other fashionably docked. (This branch of the family,
some members of which had lived in Paris, was also known as the
"French Forbeses.") The Mark Howes of Brimmer Street certainly were not short-tailed, but somehow I can't quite admit to
their being long-tailed either.

Sticking to a simple geographical division, and yet at the same
time skirting a social implication inherent in it, one might say that
the two "ways" in Boston were the Hill and the Back Bay. Father
and Mother, living on Brimmer Street, belonged to neither, although they touched both.

The "back parlor" faced the Hill. As the library, like the reception room, facing toward the Back Bay, was dominated by Father, so the parlor was Mother's room. Actually, it looked out across a dreary waste of back yards, before any Beacon Hill Garden Club had been created to redeem them, toward Charles Street. The Number Ten fire engine on Mt. Vernon Street was so close that we could hear the alarm go off, day or night, preceding the clanging of bells and the clatter of the hooves of the great Rosa Bonheur horses. There was also at our back what we called simply "the Negro church," a fine Federalist brick building. How its exclusively colored congregation found itself in such an unlikely neighborhood I don't know. "Discrimination" was a word as foreign to the vocabulary of Brimmer Street as "integration." We saw no farther than the ends of our own White Anglo-Saxon Protestant noses. Father himself used to deplore the fact that he did not rub shoulders with any such diversity of people and races as that to which Uncle Wallis, living in Bristol, was exposed. The small town itself, since the Howe boys were young, had burgeoned with Italian and Portuguese citizens, employed in the rubber works, and in Providence, where Uncle Wallis practiced architecture, his daily associations brought him into touch with a wide variety of clients, contractors, builders, electricians, as well as workingmen of many skills. I can assert categorically that Father was not arrogant; but bland he could be. On the whole, he simply serenely accepted the fact that his lines seemed, to him, to have fallen in pleasant places. Although he lived to vote for John Fitzgerald Kennedy as President, as he had voted for him as Senator, it is not easy for me to record the truth that Mother and Father would not have been likely to know their fellow Bostonians, Mr. and Mrs. Joseph Kennedy. The Kennedys and Fitzgeralds were Irish; they were Roman Catholic. Higher than either of these two hurdles to Proper Boston, however, remained the simple fact that the Kennedys were *new.* Old Boston and New Boston went their separate ways. The fact, however, that Mother's brother had been a Democratic Mayor of Boston, and that Father himself, since 1888, as he emerged from the ready-made Pennsylvania Republicanism he had accepted in his youth, had always voted for the Democratic candidate in national, although rarely in city elections, helped to make him something of a *persona grata* outside his circumscribed circle. Indeed he lived long enough to receive on his ninetieth birthday a warm and flowery telegram from one of Newer Boston's most flamboyant figures—James Michael Curley.

By the next generation the dry ice in which the Gentle Americans were preserved had begun to thaw; and in the generation following mine two of Father's three granddaughters of marriageable age have filled the vacuum which Nature abhors by freshening the family blood stream with Jewish husbands, and his grandson brought home his bride from Germany.

Number 26 Brimmer Street presented the outward and visible sign of the halfway meeting point between a Long-Tailed and a Short-Tailed way of life. There was nothing "high style" about a family summoned to the dinner table by the tinkling of a dinner bell from the downstairs dining room; and napkin rings were in order. According to the standards of the time and place we lived modestly, but comfortably. Money was a subject that was taboo as being vulgar, so I have no idea what my parents' income was at any time during their lives, although each had "a little something" with which to supplement Father's modest professional salary and income from writing. The fact that Mark and I appeared, for instance, to be under the wing of a French governess was deceiving. Actually my adored "Mademoiselle" was the sister-in-law of a Williams professor, known to friends of my parents. When she arrived in Brimmer Street in 1915 she had just lost her fiancé in the war. If she was paid anything by my parents, which I rather doubt, it must have been negligible. While Mark and I were at school she gave French lessons to the ladies of Boston who, finding her charming and appealing, "took her up." Some of the Francophile husbands were all too happy to join the hands-across-the-sea welcome. Mademoiselle had a way with men, wrapping Father, among them, around her little finger, as she beguilingly perjured herself, "Monsieur Howe a un accent délicieux!" She did, however, *taquiner* a little, and called him, with no perjury whatsoever,

"Monsieur Howe qui ronfle à l'église!" I was a little confused that her dead fiancé, with his waxed mustache, as shown in a frame decorated with the tricolor, looked alarmingly like the Kaiser. As the one living token from her lost love, she brought with her a little Griffon Bruxellois, with squashed nose, and tongue sticking out between his teeth, who, kicking his tiny front paws up in the air, trotted at her heels wherever she went. His real name was Kiss— but Mother preferred to have him called "Quisse," in Mademoiselle's own pronunciation, without feeling it necessary to explain the provenance of the name. Both my parents heartily disliked Kiss, who had a yapping bark, and on many occasions merited the reprimand, "Méchant chien, qui a fait pipi sur le tapis!" I, on the contrary, loved him.

Although in comparison with most of Proper Boston our means were modest, all the same, on looking back, I recapture the sense of solid comfort, if not downright luxury. The house was six stories high. Our mutely long-suffering laundress, Nora Hyde, worked for two days a week (the figure three dollars sticks in my mind, as covering her day's work) at the deep inset soapstone tubs in the dank, drafty basement laundry under the front doorsteps, and next to the furnace. The kitchen, opening onto the back yard, was also in the basement. All food for the table was placed on the dumbwaiter, and the heavy rope on which it was suspended hoisted by hand. The top story of the house was docilely occupied by three devoted Irish maids who never complained about its absence of heat any more than they did of the five flights of stairs they climbed for their cheerless "rests" in the afternoon. The maids' "day off" fell every Thursday and every other Sunday, the day starting after the lunch dishes were washed—never before two o'clock in the afternoon. After the routine midday dinner on Sunday, with the inevitable roast beef, Yorkshire pudding, vanilla ice cream and chocolate sauce, it must often have been nearer to four than two that their work was done. (A tiny footnote to social history perhaps worthy of record is the fact that in Father's youth the family always ate cold roast and cold rice pudding after church on Sunday, so as not to cause the servants to commit the sin of working on the

Sabbath. Today, even those descendants of the Gentle Americans fortunate enough to have any "help" at all, must kiss her—how rarely them!—good-bye on Friday evening, till Monday morning after breakfast. And, taking a leaf out of the Gentle American way of life of a hundred years ago, they subsist on Sunday on cold leftovers.) Yet our Irish maids stayed with us on an average of twenty-five years!

There were two dynasties, supplying, in addition to those who lived with us under the same roof, "accommodators" on days out, and otherwise assuring Mother of shock troops of replacement in time of need: the South of Ireland Sheas and the North of Ireland McClays. Our nurses were from the Nova Scotia clan of McLeod. Father was devoted to them all, but took particular pride in the fidelity with which Protestant Lizzie maintained her own habit of pious Sunday churchgoing in the face of the two Roman Catholics who attended Mass. Every evening, at the time the lamplighter was lighting the street lamps below in Brimmer Street, Lizzie came upstairs to draw the curtains and to light the gas chandelier that hung from the ceiling. For this rite she used a lighter, consisting of a long, wooden-handled brass rod with a slotted device on the end for turning on the gas key, and with a curved fork just below it, sprouting a flaming wax wick which ignited each gas jet as its key was turned. Later we went through a phase of C-E Z gas mantles, which gave a terrifying pop, and shed a lurid white light. I am sure that gas was burned in 26 Brimmer Street long after electricity had been installed in the houses of all my parents' friends.

When I brought home from boarding school my friend Elizabeth Morrow, daughter of the then Morgan partner Dwight Morrow, I remember her fascination with our kerosene lamps. Soon after, Mother took me for my first visit to New York when I was about fifteen years old. (I wore a hat for the occasion bought at R. H. Weathern, trimmed by us both with a sheaf of wheat and a bunch of iridescent grapes in the front.) On that visit the Country Mouse went to the Town Mouse, and I to the Morrows' huge Fifth Avenue apartment overlooking the Park. When we went to a matinee I was enthralled by Elizabeth's beautiful coat, whose loose sleeves were trimmed with fur. I thought simply, how *pretty* to have great fur bands on the cuffs of a coat, and how *beautiful* Central Park looked compared to Brimmer Street. Any remote connection between these fascinating manifestations of life in New York and a necessary bank balance to supply them never occurred to me. I vaguely felt that Elizabeth and her world were different but never could have pinpointed what that difference was. Never in explorations into the outer world or its incursions into our world was the word "money" used.

We were no more high style upstairs than down. On those evenings when our parents were going out to a dinner party we children, after our own supper, congregated in their bedroom, with its straw matting on the floor and coal grate, to watch them get ready. There was, at the foot of the Bishop's four-posted double bed in which all eighteen of his children must have been born, a chaise-longue. Tom Brown at Rugby could have shown no more courage than Father, kneeling down on one side of this bed to say his prayers every night under the blue agnostic gaze of Mother. If one of us lolled on the chaise longue another might rock in the comfortable rocker from Grandma Howe's Bristol bedroom. Preparing for the party, Mother stood before the mahogany "cheval glass" or before the mirror that hung over the handsome high chest of drawers (there was no dressing table in Brimmer Street) adjusting her hair with an invisible hairpin through the mesh of her hairnet, and dabbing her nose with a little powder from a Dorine compact, in its Rachel tint. Father, meanwhile, was going through the business of "stropping" his razor, and shaving—I am sure I remember it so in the earliest days—in the bowl of a washstand set that stood in the corner of the room. Then came a wiggling into his suspenders over his stiff shirt as he tried to fasten a recalcitrant collar button with his rather clumsy fingers. I do not recall ever having seen Father lose his temper at a human being, or speak unkindly to any creature, but I do distinctly remember his working himself into a fury over that collar button, with a fuming "Confound it!" or "Da—nation!"

As to the actual physical cartography of Boston, 26 Brimmer

Street was "next but one to the Church of the Advent," as we learned to say by rote to taxi drivers. Today, living in New York, I am still nostalgic for the ease with which in Boston we could call a taxi to the door, and leave it by simply giving the driver a charge account number. Father's segment of Boston was still so much of a small town that in his old age the drivers of the Town Taxi and the Boston Cab treated him with the personal solicitude other men pay vast sums to elicit from family retainers. At the end of the street that opened onto Beacon Street were the fine brick mansions of the Richard Searses (he, known to Mother and her sisters as "Rickety Dick") and the Bayard Thayers. (One of these houses is now the Charlotte Cushman Club, the other the Hampshire House.) We were actually as well as symbolically at the other end of the street which finished off in a plot of ground belonging to the Old Ladies Home—now gone. The Brimmer Chambers, catty-corner to it, was filled with bachelor friends of my parents, several of them "callers" who came to see Mother.

Our most distinguished neighbors were Admiral Byrd on the other (water) side of our block, whom, alas, we did not know, and in the next block in a fine old family house Professor Samuel Eliot Morison, whom Father knew well. How handsome and haughty was this professor-horseman, admiral-and-historian-plenipotentiary-yet-to-be as he strode along Brimmer Street in his riding clothes, reminding me always in manner and appearance of Darcy of *Pride and Prejudice!* Opposite us were the Arthur Hills, with their noble dynasty of dachshunds, who walked abroad in a flock, headed by their founding father, "Mr. Gray." Next to them were the Frank (Francis) Welches in their huge house, filled with French furniture brought from their apartment in the Avenue Marceau in Paris. In Boston Mr. Welch was known as "Bad Frank Welch," as opposed to "Good Frank Welch." Different Boston families, bearing the same name, presented a certain problem. One heard on some lips of the "right" as opposed to the "wrong" Ameses, although a gentler line of demarcation could always be made by referring to the "other" Ameses. Father himself was not immune from this Boston habit of hairsplitting. He was a great stickler for the use of the proper middle initial: when he went to pay a call on Sunday afternoon he made it clear that it was on Mrs. William *C.* Endicott. When I once asked him who was another Mr. Such-and-such Endicott, he blandly answered, "Oh, he is one of the *shoe* Endicotts."

This is perhaps as good a place as any in which to admit to the particular subspecies of snobbery which had marked us. If it was implicitly accepted that the circle of my parents' friends belonged to a homogeneous background, that background had long been accurately pinpointed by Dr. Holmes. It took for granted "family traditions and the cumulative humanities of at least four or five generations." The man who sprang from it must have "tumbled about a library and feel at home wherever he smells the invigorating fragrance of Russia leather." Yesterday's Boston may have had its brand names, but they were not those of today's name brands. If a name had been made in previous generations through achievements in government, law, learning, science, letters, or the church, it was a little more congenial to our preconditioned Brimmer Street palates than if it had been made in trade or if much money had stuck to it. Much of this slant I am now sure sprang from both Mother's temperament and the story of the family behind her—of which more later. The distinction which had gone with the name of Quincy in New England from pre-Revolutionary days had dwindled down to a trickle along with the fortune that had once gone with it.

In the middle of the nineteenth century there had been one move made by the family from their "seat" at Quincy to their house in Park Street when, due to faulty packing, an enormous amount of china was broken. To my eyes the mark of a proper Lowestoft vase or plate was a crack across the front, and a rivet on the wrong side. It was Father's shrewd perspective on New England history that prompted him lucidly to declare that those families who had held onto their prestige and power were those who had held onto their money. Somehow we vaguely felt that money long ago was all very fine, but that money today was a little—"common." I will not admit to the charge of "shabby genteel," because—to my ears at least— "genteel" implies a phony veneer, with emphasis on nonessential appearances. If Brimmer Street lacked a certain worldly gloss, it stood four square in its commitment to "amount to" something (there was no dwelling on achievements of dead ancestors) and that amounting was never to be tallied in dollars and cents.

A long detour from "bad" Mr. Welch. To me his badness consisted in holding in thrall, as a virtual prisoner, his warm, vital, much younger wife whom he had met on shipboard many years before on her way to Europe to study for opera. It was not only because she came originally from New York, and had therefore no New England shackles to burst, but because there was something in her very looks, as well as in her beautiful singing voice, that made one feel she might have made another Frieda Hempel. If "Aunt Agnes"—as she came to be for me—lived to regret her marriage, she carried off her disappointment with a high and gallant hand. During my growing-up years, when I was nursing ambitions for the stage and smoldering in adolescent protest against all that seemed stultifying about Boston, her French salon with its red damask and gilt Louis XV furniture glowed like one live coal in the dusty grate of Brimmer Street. She gave me singing lessons, always in French, and then, through me, reached across the street to my parents.

There were other Brimmer Street figures, whose names we did not know, who were almost as familiar to us as those whose names we did know. There was the tawny-haired lady whose brown cotton stockings always seemed to be falling in folds at her ankles who illustrated, through her resemblance to her own Irish terrier, Mother's belief in the law that dogs and their owners generally come to look like each other. There was the "ship under full sail"— a large, placid lady who lived in the rooming house at the end of the block, whose huge picture hat, with the wind behind it, appeared to supply the momentum to send her floating slowly down the block. There was our postman whom Mother called behind his back "Little Cunnit," derived from cunning. ("Cunning" was used by my Gentle Americans as a term of endearment, never "cute.") On Wednesdays we were visited by the Italian organ grinder who, whenever a new baby was born to his wife, would hand in via one of us children who had run out with our fifteen (!) cents an envelope addressed on the outside to "Dear Madam." One of the denizens of the Brimmer Chambers, who seemed to be passing whenever we looked out the window, was christened simply "Pippa." There was the old "begga rooman who goes to door to door"—as I am told I described her—as well as the cab and horse, whose name was Diamond, under whose quivering velvet nose we were allowed to extend, on a correspondingly trembling palm, a lump of sugar, who stood at the corner of Otis Place and Brimmer Street. Other Brimmer Street memories include the covering of tanbark that was laid down in the street to deaden the noise of wheels because Mr. Warner, across the way, was dangerously ill. Then there was the frightening Mr. Smith, the neighborhood drunk and bum whose trousers were perpetually falling down, revealing a foundation garment of newspapers.

Certainly nobody could be frightened of Miss "Mamie" Blake who lived also in our block, on the water side of the street, in a big corner house, with her old mother. Miss Blake used to drive my parents, and me too, sometimes, in her shining little black carriage, with the coachman on the box, to the Saturday evening Symphony Concerts. Our seats were in the balcony and it fascinated me to look at her head from above, with its little cap of white hair—white only on top. She was one of the many single ladies of Mother's generation in Boston who laid down her life on the altar of filial devotion. After the death of the last parent such a daughter lived on alone in the large house that had once held a family, with the servants growing older and feebler until they became charges rather than a prop for her old age. Mamie Blake was not only a Gentle American; she was the living embodiment of the genus Maiden Lady. She blushed easily, and had an engaging little stammer. Mother's darts of sharp comment amused her almost in spite of herself, so that the blood would mount higher than ever above her stiff-boned lace collar, as she exclaimed, "Oh, Fanny!" There was always much talk of "Uncle Henry" between Miss Blake and Father on the way to the Symphony Concerts. "Uncle Henry" was Major Henry Lee Higginson. The "Major" was won in the Civil War, and the fortune that enabled him to found the Boston Symphony Orchestra was won in his family's banking business. Father was much involved with Major Higginson in those early days of the Orchestra of whose original Board of Trustees he became a member in 1918.

Aside from Pippa, whom my parents did not know, there were other denizens of the Brimmer Chambers who passed our door as often whom they did know. Mr. Stephen Cabot, the retired headmaster of St. George's School in Newport, was a familiar figure, going to or coming from the New England Kitchen on Charles Street. The New England Kitchen was the distilled essence of the atmosphere covered by the word the "Hill." The clientele of this depressingly respectable restaurant was made up of a mingling of lower-income white-collar workers and stragglers from Long Tailed Boston, the latter with their millions stashed away in State Street vaults. Each group was indistinguishable from the other: both dowdy, wholesome, and their minds fixed more on the books or papers propped up on the table before them than on the plain fare it set forth. Probably as Mr. Cabot walked by our house, his head thrust forward, swinging his walking stick, eyes downcast, he was not wondering—as so many visitors to Boston have wondered—why the city is so lamentably short in attractive restaurants. The chances are that his eyes were lowered so as to avoid the embarrassment of having to speak to someone he knew.

Suffering myself from this mysterious Boston complaint, I cannot diagnose its cause, only describe its symptoms. Any outsider would, I am sure, lightly dismiss the victim of the disease as "snooty," but that no more explains it than to explain the sufferer from a common cold by saying that he's contagious. I go so far in identifying myself with those who walk under its curse that I could well have duplicated the behavior of the unidentified Cabot brothers to Father on his arrival in Boston on the frosty street corner. My general feeling would have been, "He doesn't want to talk to *me*." I can only testify that it *feels* more like inadequacy than arrogance, but I do not dare go further. I am sure that one of the prime reasons for Father's success with the prisoners of Boston shyness was his own friendliness, free of self-consciousness, even in spite of his stammering. "Hello, Steve," Father would say if he saw Mr. Cabot coming, and the clear blue eyes would lift in greeting—and relief.

Mr. Stephen Cabot had a brother almost as shy and modest as himself who, instead of walking past our front door, mounted its steps and came in. The arrival of "Fred" Cabot occurred once a week, right after breakfast. His reason for choosing that hour for a call was that, before his day's work as Judge in the Children's Court, he delivered, by hand and on foot, the eggs which came from his nearby farm, and which he sold to a select clientele up and down Beacon Hill. Irrelevant and immaterial was the possession of a large family fortune. Judge Frederick Pickering Cabot was not only a pioneer in the attempt to understand and ameliorate the causes of what was not yet called juvenile delinquency but was President of the Boston Symphony Orchestra's Board of Trustees. His classically noble features are perpetuated in a marble bust which stands today in the lobby of Symphony Hall. It is told that when he came out on its stage one Friday afternoon to make some official utterance a little girl in the audience was heard to exclaim, "That's our egg man!"

When he came to deliver his eggs in Brimmer Street he and Father were apt to withdraw into the drafty little reception room for a colloquy on Symphony matters. This same depressing little room was also used for another post-breakfast call, this one by Dr. Henry A. Murray, many years Father's junior, not yet renowned as Professor of Clinical Psychology at Harvard. Father drew the brown velvet portieres closed after himself and this fellow stammerer to foster the illusion that they were unheard as well as unseen as their two voices lifted in doleful moaning and intoning, *may, may, may, mee, mee, mee,* etc. Over a period of several years the two men put themselves under the treatment of a Dr. Green, whom they went regularly to see in New York, returning to give each other moral support by doing his prescribed exercises together. Part of their homework consisted in giving each other a miniature lecture—the subject chosen to taste. One half of this captive audience was eventually completely cured; the other—Father—always believed that he too might have been healed had he started the treatment when he was much younger.

There were not only "loners" who came to see Father in Brimmer Street. Inevitably, some of the dinner parties for which we watched him and Mother dressing were given under their own roof. Father's serving of cocktails—before Prohibition—was part of his perennially effervescent and yet guilelessly innocent cordiality. I am afraid that orange juice had found its way into the gin and that the mixture was served, already poured, into the very small, delicate stemware glasses, decorated with clusters of green grapes, and passed about by the extra waitress. Father, with a genial clatter of ice and very little else, in the bottom of the shaker, would press a drop of "dividend" on the men; any thirsty ladies had to be content with the one eyedropper dose dispensed to them the first time around. In my adult years Father used to inveigh against the habit of a host offering his guests a *choice* of cocktails. "It's part of good manners to accept what is offered you" was the gist of his protest.

"Entertaining" always loomed for Mother as a prodigious effort. It was certainly not because she was an inadequate hostess. Bertha's dinners were delectable. There were apt to be oysters from Welch's Fish Market nearby, followed by a marvelous lighter-than-air fish mousse. Filet mignon, with mushroom sauce, and hot homemade rolls figured, and Bar-le-Duc and cream cheese, served along with the salad. Bertha's meringues, with crushed strawberries, were an achievement, if a mold of ice cream with a sherbet center had not been ordered from the Women's Educational and Industrial Union.

The table looked lovely. The blue Canton willow pattern china from Bristol, used every day, was superseded by a beautiful green and white service (still nameless to me) from Quincy, and the Lowestoft plates for dessert, with Great-great-great-Grandmother Abigail Quincy's monogram. I am happy to record, in view of the skimpy cocktails, that there were glasses for two wines and champagne. The candles wore their best pink silk and silver shades with beaded tassels, and for centerpiece there were flowers in the middle of the three-pronged silver epergne.

No guest worth his salt could have found Mother a dull table companion—and *everybody* liked Father! That is, until Prohibition. That miserable amendment forced him into the position of changing his natural spots. Sometimes I think taking the stand he did during those years—which was, quite simply, that of obeying the law of the land—was the single bravest action of a man to whose convivial and noncombative nature it would have been so much easier to go with the tide on which his friends were happily carried—friends who did not hesitate to laugh at him as both priggish and stuffy. And all for the sake of a law in which he did not believe! He went through—to the avowed derision of his bathtub-gin-drinking undergraduate son—a lot of what today would be called "jazz" about putting down cellar some uncorrupted California grapejuice. Then, with the addition of yeast, the passage of time, and, I daresay, some muttered abracadabra—lo, it had become—well, if not wine at least a Brimmer Street version of wine. And—because he had neither bought nor sold an alcoholic beverage—the letter of the law had been obeyed.

When I airily speak of "everybody" as liking Father I must hasten to pinpoint him in his neither Long- nor Short-Tailed World by stating that of course there were Boston doors which were not opened to him, or which he did not open. One such was the door that led to such Upper Bohemianism as the city afforded. Father, for instance, could never have become a member of a certain intimate Société Gastronomique whose reverence for the best food and drink expressed itself in an entire mystique—club banner in the corner of the dining room of the host of the evening, and cook brought blushing from the kitchen to be toasted at the end of the meal. Writing to me, in his late years, of a dinner with a host whom he identified as "whose-God-is-his-belly" he described the dinner as "pluperfect, with a French menu handed round before the Oysters Rockefeller, and eels (as I discovered *anguilles* to mean) cooked in red wine. But the host's barbaric gloating over it all—smelling his wines and using them for a tooth wash—nearly turned my firm old stomach."

Another milieu in Boston where Father did not shine was that of the salon. If, as a young man, he had been grateful for the welcome he found in Mrs. Fields's drawing room, in middle age there was no hostess before whom he was disposed to burn incense. He was not among the faithful who orbited about Mrs. Fiske Warren, whose porcelain beauty Sargent had immortalized and whose aesthetic yearnings, it was said, had been put on a pin by T. S. Eliot in his "Portrait of a Lady." Nor did he attend any of Miss Rose Nichols's rather intense political forums, farther down the slope of Beacon Hill. Father's stammering undoubtedly presented a hurdle to any potential hostess as well as to himself but, even more, his disarmingly healthy lungs demanded a simpler, clearer air than one even faintly redolent of the hothouse. Showing unfeigned enthusiasm for the many aspects of life that interested him, and an equally unfeigned boredom in the face of those that didn't, he was neither precious, exhibitionist nor sycophant, sublimely innocent of the art of "playing up." "Outré" is a word I never hear today: my parents often used it. Surely it would have applied, when feelings were running high during a World Series, and Father met Mrs. Jack Gardner at a concert in Symphony Hall with a pennant tied across her brow proclaiming, Oh You Red Sox! He might have used the same word when Amy Lowell smoked one of her own after-dinner cigars on occasions when my parents dined with her. Though Father knew both of these flashing "personalities" he was intimate with neither.

Another Boston door that Father never opened was one that led either to the riding stable or the gaming room. He didn't know one card from another and had as little interest as aptitude in games of either skill or chance. Though in his youth he had ridden such horses as Bristol afforded, one could never have imagined him as a member of the North Shore's fashionable Myopia Hunt Club. Perhaps, actually, his membership or nonmembership in certain clubs tells as much as anything about him. No power on earth, for instance, could have made Mother want to join the Chilton Club, made up of the elite of conventional Boston ladies. Nor was the Tuesday Club or the Parliamentary Law Club (known lovingly to its members as "the P. Law") her dish. Many of the ladies of Boston's first families, with high-brow proclivities, belonged to one

or the other, and sometimes both. At one a "paper" was read pre-
paratory to launching a general discussion; at the other debates
were held under the rules of proper parliamentary procedure. The
sort of subjects touched upon (I do not transcribe literally) were
limitless in sweep: "Does all true Art express some moral purpose?" or "What is the happiest decade of a woman's life?" She
was, however, one of the small group of women which called itself
"The Nucleus," hoping someday to burgeon into an approximation
of New York's Cosmopolitan Club, with an avowed emphasis on
"interesting" if not downright talented or professional members.
But as the token members from the Radcliffe community or from
the working Boston press were few and far between, and as the club
grew more and more "social," and its luncheon meetings more and
more noisy, Mother, at the time of her death, was on the point of
resigning. Father, on the other hand, who had many Short-Tailed
men friends in Boston's "exclusive" Somerset Club who periodically asked him if he wouldn't like to have his name put up for
membership, always replied with perfect affability as well as honesty, "I should enjoy it very much, but I simply don't feel I can
afford it." Of his lifelong love affair with the Tavern Club I shall
speak elsewhere. When, as an old gentleman, he used to dine or
lunch at the Somerset Club he commented with pleasure that all the
waiters and stewards greeted him as "Mr. Howe" with as much
respectful attention as though he *were* a member. This fact was only
part of the guileless pleasure he took in certain amenities—which
he could either take or leave alone.

It would take a provincial Proust to explore the intricate weaving
in and out of Boston's different "ways" and to show how those of
its Short-Tailed world of Fashion, supported by money made in
Business, could still make use of a little cross-pollination from the
Long-Tailed world of the Arts and Professions, who, in turn,
needed patrons for their very existence.

There was in the Boston of the twenties (I do not know if it still
exists) a club which was archetypical of the upper crust of other
American cities who, not satisfied with their social assurance, feel
impelled to add intellectual pretensions to it. I, as professional enter-

tainer, have had firsthand experience of such a club in many more cities than Boston. I have been greeted by my hostess in at least a half a dozen of them with the same, ''It may interest you to know that Ruth Draper gave her *very first* performance in this room.'' The club generally boasts some fifty to a hundred members of both sexes who commit themselves to meeting three or four times a season, late in the evening, to listen to an ''interesting'' speaker. The members sit on gold caterer's chairs in the largest room (preferably one of the few ballrooms still extant in the city) in the largest house of one of the members. Certain of the members indeed are chosen for no more complicated reason than that they live in a large house. The ladies put on their very finest buttons and bows, and the gentlemen are dressed to match—often to white tie and tails. Before the meeting small dinners are held in the houses of other members before they ''go on'' to the event of the evening. By the time they settle down onto their uncomfortable gilt chairs, cocktails, wines, champagne, and liqueurs have done their work so well that the double chins of the ladies fold over one by one into their pearl chokers, until released, like a Jack-in-the-box, on the cue of a stentorian snore from the sleeping mates at their sides. Boston's such club was called the Contemporary Club. Once John Mason Brown has delighted such an audience—as only he can, with food for the mind presented with consummate skill and grace—then, they ask themselves, who else is there? If it's a visiting Britisher the chances are that if he is an erudite scholar his mumbled er's and ah's will render his speech unintelligible, and if he is a titled lion he will, along with his audience, be couchant on the field of after-dinner lethargy. Boston's Contemporary Club, in the days of my own recalling, was palpably happier when being entertained by a conjurer, producing rabbits from his hat and colored handkerchiefs from his sleeve, than they were in listening to an analysis of the Dawes Plan or *The Waste Land*. Be it recorded that on one occasion the gilt chairs creaked and rocked under the pressure of their hysterically delighted occupants as they witnessed the gyrations of a still-to-become Editor of the *Atlantic*, dancing with—a broomstick.

Father's presence on the Governing Board was witness not to the hope that he might supply a ballroom for the meetings but that he might serve as link with that other world in which the elusive commodity ''talent'' was to be found. The Contemporary Club was not alone among such social organizations, whose members for the most part were in a position to live on the income of their income, in attempting to wring from a speaker the lowest possible fee in the bland self-assurance that any artist fortunate enough to have his existence recognized by such a body should find his reward in the upping of his status, if not his bank balance. One artist so engaged in 1924, with Father as go-between, wrote from Vermont:

> . . . One hundred and fifty is my usual fee; but I do not always ask it of friends. Speaking as poet to poet, how much do you think the club would think fair? Set it at that.
> We'll be delighted to stay with you and Mrs. Howe. You are too kind in all this.
>
> Ever yours,
ROBERT FROST

''Poet to Poet!'' The seeing eye of the true poet could recognize in kinship a fellow creature who maintained at his core a citadel of inner freedom. It was to this impregnable citadel that Father could happily withdraw from—just as he could happily go forth to—either his Short-Tailed or his Long-Tailed friends.

7

CALLERS

I never knew a man with less of the flirt in him than Father. Perhaps he illustrated the paradox that the man most successful with women must have something of Woman in him. Father had none; he just plain wasn't interested in feminine psychological or emotional vibrations. He was a monogamous and devoted husband, and that was that. Mother's own stern sense of what was appropriate in a wife, and what not, was enough to still any provocation for jealousy. Not that Brimmer Street abounded in such provocations. Aside from those neighbors who passed our front door, or those who closeted themselves with Father on the ground floor, there was that trickle, already referred to, of "callers." They did not fit into the classification of either Long-Tailed or Short. Each was an individual in his own right and, for each, Mother was the object of his call. Had either of my parents been different, potential dynamite could have smoldered in the occasional appearance in Brimmer Street of two real "lady-killers." Both came first as inconsolable widowers, and continued to come in subsequent incarnations as disillusioned divorcés. Mr. Guy Murchie, the romantically handsome protégé of the early Copeland and ex-Rough Rider of Theodore Roosevelt's, was one. The other was the strikingly handsome, tall, and distinguished future Canadian Senator John McClennan, from Montreal. The death of his young wife had been a great grief to Mother during the early years of her own marriage. The *sotto voce* conversations that hummed in the back parlor testified to the efficacy of the consolation Mother was able to give.

These two star performers appeared only very occasionally in Brimmer Street. There was, however, what one might call a resident stock company, not one of whom carried with him even the faintest whiff of danger. (I do not quite classify Professor Copeland as a caller. The groundwork for his appearances in Brimmer Street was too well laid in advance.) Mr. Berkeley Updike, like Mr. Stephen Cabot, lived in the Brimmer Chambers and passed our front door, with his characteristic walk, head thrown back, and quick, short steps, as often as Pippa. The fact that the name of Daniel Berkeley Updike, as founder and head of the Merrymount Press, is still revered wherever good printing is recognized as a high art meant nothing to the Brimmer Street children, who instinctively scattered when that most precise and cultivated of bachelors appeared. It was somehow in the air not only that he didn't think we were much of a credit to Mother but that he didn't think Father "up" to her. Certainly Father himself was aware of a vague malaise which made him wonder if he was "up" to Mr. Updike. Had he not, after all, written to his mother as long ago as 1887, after spending an evening with his fellow Rhode Islander at Young's Hotel, "Berkeley Updike strikes me as a remarkably nice fellow. He is one of the best talkers I have ever met, and has excellent ideas. I mean to see more of him unless I find that I bore him?" He and Father had first known each other as boys, with relatives in common; Mr. Updike was already established in the office of Houghton Mifflin when Father himself came to work there. An added bond was Father's first splash into the pond of verse, *Rari Nantes,* privately printed in 1893. Its eighty copies carried the colophon description "from designs of D. B. Updike"—the second of all forerunners to the long list of distinguished Merrymount Press publications.

As the years went by Father felt that he *did* bore Mr. Updike. He understated that temperament so alien to his own when he wrote that "Updike would hardly have qualified for Dr. Johnson's term of 'clubable.'" It is not surprising that the finicky exterior threw poor Father into paroxysms of stammering—a distressing vicious circle, because the painful manifestations of the stammer, in turn, only further exacerbated the thin-skinned, aesthetically fastidious Mr. Updike. We children felt chilled by the disdainful toss of his head and the short, mirthless laugh, never suspecting that we, on our side, had the power, which we used unconsciously, of hurting him. There was a windy summer day at Cotuit, when he was dressing in one of the little cubicles of our tiny bathhouse, and I, not knowing he was there, chose the moment to ask Mother in the cruel and loud tones of childhood, "Mother, why didn't Mr. Updike ever get married?" I felt a shiver of dismay as I heard the clearly enunciated question of some vague matter of wind or tide which promptly floated out from the bathhouse, telling me that my barb had struck home. My aunt Mabel, meeting him in Mother's parlor, not having seen him for half a lifetime, unwittingly let fly another dart. Her greeting was "What have you done with your years, Berkeley?" He gave his nervous little yip and asked, "What have I done with my *ears?*" The fact that he very obviously *had* done something, or rather something had been done to them, by means of clever surgery which had reduced their size, compounded the general distress.

There could not have existed that genuine friendship between Mother and Mr. Updike if his surface manner had been the whole man. He was obviously one of those who, ill at ease in the company of "clubable" men, was at his best with one sensitive, cultivated woman. It was said by one of his peers that, like his *Printing Types,* Berkeley Updike was "not made in a hurry." Neither his social nor even his distinguished professional life contained all of him. Just as he had an eye for genuine quality in printing and was impatient of work that was "pretentious, showy, or egoistic," his comments, however acid in form, were never spiteful in substance. At the center of his being was a deeply spiritual sense. He was "too much a 'recollected' man to allow conversation to degenerate into mere gossip." If Mr. Updike's life was shaped into a certain rigidity of pattern, "he was himself the centre of the pattern and he might have lost in humanity but for his religion, his humour and his reading." I remember at least one instance when Mr. Updike's

humor mingled with his religion to make an anecdote which amused
Mother and Father. On an Easter morning he attended the early
communion service at the small private chapel in Sudbury belonging to the Gothically oriented architect Ralph Adams Cram. Mr.
Cram himself belonged, if a little self-consciously, more to the age
of stained glass than the picture window. Greeting Mr. Updike after
the service he brought out, in one monotone phrase, "Christ is risen
give the proper answer." Mr. Updike, conversant enough with the
medievalism expected of him, was able to snap back, on cue, "Christ
is risen indeed."

Mr. Updike's reading ranged widely, focusing perhaps particularly on the eighteenth and nineteenth centuries—both French
and English—in literature, history, and above all, memoirs. I have
the feeling that he must have been the source of an extract copied
out by Mother as "Ten Commandments of Madame Campan,"
lady in waiting to Marie Antoinette, who afterward kept a little
school for daughters of the nobility. (The Gentle Americans were
given, like hoarding squirrels, to tucking away little nuggets of
wisdom or interest.)

> De la dignité sans hauteur,
> De la politesse sans fadeur,
> De la confiance sans hardiesse,
> Du maintien sans raideur,
> Des grâces, sans affectation,
> De la réserve sans pruderie,
> De la gaieté sans bruyants éclats,
> De l'instruction sans pédanterie,
> Des talents sans prétention,
> De l'envie de plaire, sans coquetteries.

I suspect that it was thus that Mother appeared to him. But—as
was so often to prove the case where Mother and Father were concerned—it was Father who triumphed in the end. Some mental
block prevents my remembering which parent it was who told me
that Mr. Updike one day said to Mother, "I used to think that
Mark wasn't good enough for you. Now, I know that he is." If

Mr. Updike, through the years, came increasingly to respect and value Father's qualities, it is also possible that those qualities had developed with time. Perhaps Father's capacity for crystalline obliviousness of any snub directed toward himself was one of them; the verb "to rankle" was not in his lexicon. Turning the other cheek was a natural and simple reflex for Father.

There could hardly have been a greater contrast to Mr. Updike than that presented by another friend in Brimmer Street, though he never did anything so conventional as pay a "call." Robert Savage Chase—"Rob" or "Robbie," as he was to my parents—was small only in inches; he towered as a man. Robbie Chase's name was unknown in his lifetime. He knew the insistent nip of poverty. Rebel, reformer, true Bohemian, and an artist in living and loving, let his name stand here, remembered in love and honor.

He was a tireless foot soldier in the army of those who march in the unending slogging campaign against human injustice. As part of that campaign he hoped to see the crumbling of the barricades behind which he believed the Gentle Americans lived their lives. And yet, from across the barrier of totally differing ideologies, Father, with the quality that had already attracted men of an opposing stamp from his own, made a lifelong and devoted friend. Robbie had known him and Uncle Wallis from their very earliest days in Boston. I rather think he must have met Uncle Wallis at M.I.T., where he had come from St. Louis, I assume to study architecture. He made such living as he made at all from mural painting, chiefly in the mansions of the very rich, and from his accurate copying of old paintings. He and his wife, Jessie Anderson, provided not only spice but a very special sweetness to our otherwise bland Boston diet. Originally they lived in Newburyport. There were twins who died; then the family came to Boston to live in a tiny house on the "backside" of Beacon Hill, in Bellingham Place, one of the mews-like oases that are to be found among the surrounding slums. Mrs. Chase, who wrote several children's books, brought in through private tutoring the only sure income on which the family lived. Their remaining daughter was Betty, approximately my age and the roly-poly, rosy apple of her parents' adoring eyes. Precocious as a child of such parents was bound to be, Betty showed an early talent for the violin. Her parents' meager earnings were poured into her private lessons with the violinist and composer Charles M. Loeffler, who predicted great things for her future. Robbie played the cello, Mrs. Chase the piano; chamber music was the backdrop against which were highlighted painting, politics, and poetry. Robbie's gods were Keats, Bach, and Karl Marx. On a day that the Back Bay visited the Hill, in the form of Mrs. Bentley Warren from Beacon Street calling in Bellingham Place to consider giving the artist a possible commission, she spied Keats's death mask and remarked that she had happened to read his "Ode to a Nightingale" that morning. Robbie, sealing the friendship which flowered on the spot, promptly kissed her.

Robbie's mind would have been that of a one-track fanatic if it had not been irrigated and irradiated with the bubbling springs of a fresh and impish humor. It was Mother—withdrawn and inherently melancholy as she was—whom Robbie elected as his soulmate in the higher realms of laughter. Clean-shaven and ruddy, roly-poly as his daughter Betty, Robbie's resemblance to St. Nicholas lay in the fact that when he laughed he shook like a bowlful of jelly. Perhaps he was even more like one of the Cheeryble Brothers. When he laughed his little crinkly eyes brimmed with tears which overflowed down his suffused cheeks; his voice became so choked, his shoulders so convulsed, that it would have been easy to mistake one of his paroxysms of amusement for one of grief. Newspaper clippings and photographs concerning grotesque happenings and people were continually flying back and forth between him and Mother. But what Robbie flung himself into with the abandon of the true artist was the practical joke. He worked on one each year, to come to fruition on Mother's birthday, which was the same as Betty's. One year flowers arrived throughout the day, on the hour, from florists all over the city and suburbs, with a different card—each with a name more unlikely than the last—in each. There was no question who was behind them all. Mother really suffered under that demonstration, knowing how ill Robbie could afford it. Another celebration was relished more in imagination than it would have been in actuality. Mother wrote me:

Rob Chase paid Quincy and me a Bolshevistic call last night, clad in a low-necked blue flannel shirt. He had planned an extraordinary celebration of my birthday, the actual engaging of a small orchestra of Italians from the North End, who were to bring camp stools and sit on our little grass-plot, playing steadily from 8 A.M. till 5 P.M.! He had trained them to refuse all money, to decline to leave the premises, and to say, "I don't understand" when they were ordered to go away! He took it *most* seriously, and had come to make sure that I should not be away on the 14th,—then suddenly he thought how Father would look when he came home at lunch and found the orchestra still playing,—and then at night,—and would find them still at it,—so he confessed the scheme to me, and thank Heaven, he is not going to carry it out! I can imagine Van Allen's [the rector of the Church of the Advent] disgust,— although Rob had specially ordered one religious number to be introduced, out of regard to our ecclesiastical neighbor!

To Rob himself she wrote:

DEAR ROB,
    I liked the tulips as much as Mark liked the unheard melodies! He was grateful to you for *not* sending the orchestra, and I was grateful to you for thinking of sending it. It was a beautiful thought and I am proud to have inspired it,—but oh what terrible results you have spared us, of infuriated rectors, bewildered lawyers, perplexed neighbors, and powerless policemen!
    . . . But the tulips are so beautiful and bright that they really make a sound,—a pleasing and triumphant scarlet song, of the victory of old age, which can still receive tulips, and not in a funeral wreath!

(Actually Robbie had sent a funeral "piece" the year before, in ghastly colored wax, a product of the mortician's art—also from the North End.)

Mother achieved her greatest triumph on an occasion which had nothing to do with a birthday. Robbie, announced first by Lizzie, arrived one evening after dinner to find Mother in the parlor, ready, though not exactly eager, to receive him at such an unusual hour. He appeared, and stood silent on the threshold of the room— holding in his hand a long riding whip. Mother looked a moment at the strange apparition, and then came up with, "Didn't Nietzsche say 'When thou goest to women forget not thy whip'?" "I *knew* it, I *knew* it!" he crowed, as the tears of delight gushed, and he abandoned himself to the throes of his own amusement. Mother always said that the Lord simply opened her mouth. It was an incredible fluke that she happened to know the very passage that prompted the trouble he had taken for that one instant in which she might irretrievably forever stand—or fall—in his esteem. There really seemed to be some force of telepathic sympathy between them. It happened more than once that he telephoned the house in Brimmer Street on the very evening that we had just moved back from Cape Cod after the summer. "I just wanted to say 'Hello,'" was all he had to say. "How did you know I'd be here today?" "I knew, I knew." But we never learned *how*.

Father called himself a "liberal"; Robbie Chase, with reason, might have been called a "radical." And yet his radicalism was as idiosyncratic as the rest of him. He was never a member of the Communist party. The light he chose to follow came from the rather flickering Socialist-Labor party whose leader, Daniel De Leon, he thought "the only profound Marxian in our country." The wonder was that Robbie never dropped Father as a friend; rather he clung to him. "You will always be *Mark* to me even tho never *Marx*," he wrote. Nevertheless, he could not resist the temptation of trying to convert Father. Mother wrote me, "He [Robbie] now preaches the Socialist doctrine on the Common of a Sunday afternoon, and got going on the subject last night here from 8 to 11:15 until I thought I should go crazy! Father insisted on trying to argue with him, between coughing and stammering, and of course they had no meeting ground." In later years Robbie envisaged Father as "sit-

ting next to my fireplace over a pipe and a stoup of Snow Hill
Street chianti." In such a setting he would urge no repinings over
the "old song of the spheres"—but "a realization that the past
and such of the present as is overhang of that past is only the
savagery of man."

In a stream of letters to the *Transcript* over the years, signed
"Meliora Spero," Robbie was ever on the side of protest. Harvard
College got the back of his hand when it gave an honorary degree
"to an official representative of the Roman Catholic Church. If
Harvard and this country stand for anything, it is the opposite of
that for which the Roman Catholic Church stood 300 years ago and
still is bound to stand today."

One happy meeting ground for Robbie and Father was the
interest they shared in the New England—and particularly the
Boston—past. Saving the Mall in the North End was one of Robbie's
crusades; trying to rally his fellow citizens to stand "round the
grave of Jas. Otis Jr. on the anniversary of his death May 23rd
in remembrance of what he means and should mean to Boston and
the country at large in respect to the winning of American Independence" was another:

> But nobody seems to care and everybody is too busy to con-
> tribute by their presence in standing by while the wreaths of
> the State and the City are placed on his grave. . . . My only
> place in the matter is that of one who sees in him a figure that
> should not be forgotten and one who marvels at the vision and
> devotion of those men—Jas. Otis, Oxenbridge Thacher (who
> does not even appear in the American Biography), Josiah
> Quincy Jr., Joseph Hawley, John Adams, Sam'l Adams,
> Joseph Warren and the others who risked life itself and as
> with Quincy and Warren gave their lives and in the case of
> Otis life and more than life to their country. How in thunder
> did they put it over!

Though the past was alive for Robbie, it was toward the future
that he looked. His juniors gravitated toward him as effortlessly as
to Santa Claus. Quincy and a handful of Harvard contemporaries
used to spend an occasional evening at Robbie's little house in Bel-

lingham Place, and attend what he enjoyed calling his "college."
Although Eugene Debs's imprisonment as a conscientious objector
and Sacco and Vanzetti's long imprisonment and ultimate execution
were discussed as burning issues of the day, the conversations, on
the whole, were theoretical and analytical and given to exploring
the weakness of the capitalist system, as they cut their teeth on
Spengler's *Decline of the West*.

As a parent Robbie showed more idealistic theory than common
sense, and it was as a parent that Fate brought him his severest
sorrow. He only occasionally looked a little pained as Betty put
him through various ordeals on her road to what they both believed
in as the total emancipation of women. Somehow she gave up the
violin—after years of work and hard-earned money spent on her
studies. She flung herself, instead, into a Bohemian life, 1920
vintage. Robbie reported to Mother that some friends of Betty's had
waked the household by calling her on the telephone at 4 A.M. and
asking her to "come out and drink gin." "It's all right, Fanny,
it's all right" was the father's comment, made with only a shade
too much bravado. Mother wrote me, "Betty Chase returned to
N.Y. last winter, after picking strawberries in New Orleans, and is
now taking a secretarial course. Her father was in N.Y. last week,
but did not go to see her—he went and stood under her window,
but did not wish to break into her life! 'But it's all right, Fanny,
it's all right.' "

I don't remember all the phases through which Betty passed. In
one of them, it was rumored she was living in the sands near
Provincetown, in a house built of cigar boxes and packing cases,
with an old saint or sage. Then she wandered through the streets
of New York, with or without the sage, I don't recall—with a
hurdy-gurdy. And then the word came: she had committed suicide,
by putting her head in the oven, leaving a note for her mother.

From the ordered bourgeois bastion of Brimmer Street there were,
needless to say, no "I told you so's" to the parents who had been
almost doctrinaire in the hands-off attitude toward their one ewe
lamb. Chiefly, perhaps, because there was the sense that the Chases
lived nearer the kernel of life-as-it-should-be than any of us. Those

two stalwart parents bore their tragedy with bravery I have never seen surpassed. As he grew older, Robbie's face, topped with the closely cropped white hair, took on a strength and nobility that had been lacking in the rubicund little Cheeryble Brother. Mrs. Chase's appearance was as remarkable as and not unlike that of a smaller Gertrude Stein. Her hair was cut close. In the winter she wore a hood so that she looked, at first glance, like a gnome, until one saw the luminous beauty of her face, high cheekbones, big warm smile, and pale-blue eyes, which in repose were filled with the sorrow that crept into them, until, self-effacingly, it moved off to make room for the abounding delight she took in anything done or said by Rob. Like him, she, too, shook in amusement over the jokes life seemed to turn up for her on every side. After Betty's death, I remember her saying to me, ruminatively, as though she were diagnosing someone else, "It's a queer feeling not to be a *mother* any more." When she had to have an operation for cataract, Robbie nursed her at home, and every morning she reported that he put something different on her breakfast tray to make her laugh.

By this time they had moved to an old house, away from Beacon Hill, on Snow Hill Street in the North End. Their kitchen was fitted out like the galley of a ship, with racks, drawers, and cupboards made by Robbie for every conceivable utensil. In this marvelously messy house one waded through mounds of books, drawings, paintings, piled on floors and tables. He gave an occasional ceremonial "feast" by candlelight. There were garlands for the heads of his guests (I can see my brother Mark with a crown of laurel leaves on his brow looking every inch the noblest Roman of them all, and Robbie himself so bedecked, the paterfamilias, fine, august and hoary-headed.) Italian wine flowed while Bach and Marx and Keats's death mask looked benignly out through the shadows at a gathering that glowed with a gaiety and warmth that I never found duplicated in Boston. One must record, in all truth, that Mrs. Chase was not included in these parties. There was the nagging suspicion that it was her hours of hard work, plodding out by subway and trolley car to Milton Academy for her tutoring classes, that made the festivities possible. If so, I'm sure no one more heartily rejoiced than she. There must have been a tacit understanding that Mrs. Chase's role was that of humble helpmeet rather than hostess. So far as that went, my parents weren't asked either. Robbie's guests were nearer my generation than his own.

After Mother's death I became the repository of the memories that never faded for him. On the birthday that was Mother's and Betty's I always received a plain little card with nothing but the date recorded on it. On Karl Marx's, the same! "Dear old Mark" loomed as the friend on whom he counted most. Though for so many years Robbie had poked fun at Father for his "religion," and though he never would have framed thoughts or words into anything as conventional as a "prayer," he wrote, when he had chosen to go and live in loneliness and exile from the friends he had so loved, that every night before going to sleep he simply held the thought of them in his mind, and wished them good things. Every year his Christmas greeting was the same—a plain white card, on which was written "Mine to you and yours."

Mrs. Chase died first. With quiet dignity Robbie then proceeded to make plans for his own exit. First, he made the rather complicated arrangements necessary for bequeathing his eyes to an "eye bank," and his body for whatever autopsy would be helpful for scientific purposes, then he simply disposed of the dear house, with all its myriad belongings which he had so lovingly put together over a lifetime, and with no good-bys took himself off to Florida. He knew that life would be easier and cheaper for him in an equable climate. He chose Sarasota because of its museum. He did not write often, but always cheerfully. He spoke of his painting, his following the changes of season, of his friendly postman and friendly milkman. The real-estate agent who found him the house became a friend. There was never a word of self-pity, or loneliness. We suspected after several years that he was ill—letters came less frequently but, again, no mention of himself. Then came a little card addressed in his own handwriting, yellow from the years he must have had it stored away. At its head were two dates, the last one filled in by another hand, with fresh ink— 1868–1956. And then these words:

Sleep after toil, port after stormie seas, ease
After warre, death after life doth greatly please.

Following it came a letter from his friend the real-estate agent, saying that on the last day of his life Mr. Chase had asked continually for his friends—Wallis and Mark Howe.

Living at their more leisurely pace my particular Gentle Americans found time to savor the joy of possessing a friend-of-the-family. Has he gone today the way of the family doctor? I hope not! Our all-purpose, all-family, friend was Mr. Hill who lived across the street, and went walking with all those dachshunds. To a far wider group of admirers, colleagues, friends—and, one must give him the credit of some enemies—his name, Arthur Dehon Hill, was one which brought honor to the Massachusetts bar as well as to himself. For three years as corporation counsel for the city of Boston, and then as special adviser to Mayor Peters at the time of the Boston police strike, particularly as to his action in calling out the militia, before Calvin Coolidge as governor of the state assumed charge, Arthur Hill had served his community well. He served the cause of justice even more notably when he risked both personal and professional popularity in accepting, as their last counsel, the defense of Sacco and Vanzetti in their long-drawn-out ordeal in the Massachusetts courts. For most of his days, however, he applied himself to his private law practice as partner in the firm of Hill, Barlow, and Homans. That practice, he wrote Father, "can best be compared to picking up pins on the floor of a dusty attic." He wrote again on "one of those days in the life of the pettyfogging attorney in which he has had hardly time to turn around and spit. I checked securities all the morning with a female executor and that is work which requires great concentration, for it necessitates both accuracy in figures and a nice adjustment to the feminine mind. I can, at a pinch, add and (with considerable effort) please a woman, but I do not like to try to do both at the same time. In the afternoon I have built a seawall at Nahant, prepared a trustee to defend his account which shows that an estate has shrunk from $600,000 to $150,000, written a letter about a dog bite, argued a case before the Grievance Committee and indulged in a number of other pastimes. All this on top of entertaining the Wednesday Club at my house, which necessitated my staying up until midnight and consuming more food, tobacco and liquor than was good for me.''

Arthur Hill was Simon-pure Yankee at its best. Son of the renowned Boylston Professor at Harvard, Adams Sherman Hill, author of *Hill's Rhetoric,* he came honorably by his wits and his wit. There was a continual warfare being waged between his tart, shrewd, lawyer's mind (he enjoyed recalling the English barrister who compared reading law to eating sawdust without butter) and a tender heart which was not abashed to spill over in writing to his "Dear Chief," as he called Mr. Justice Holmes, and say to him along with wishes for a Merry Christmas, "I wonder do we ever make you realize how much we love you and how much you mean to us? Ever since the day when, as a very half-baked undergraduate, I came to call on you (by my mother's orders or rather unwillingly) and came away with my head in a whirl and walked the streets for hours trying to realize the full meaning of what you had said, the standard you set for living has been before me in everything I've done and if ever I do any decent work it will be largely because I knew you and Mrs. Holmes.''

Add to this genuine and basic conflict another—superimposed— of attitudes: one, that of the inveterate romantic who found his happiest expression in an idolatry of the heroines of Sir Walter Scott and the other that of the world-weary cynic, disillusioned with Man and, above all, Woman. The only hitch to his striking the last posture was that anyone who knew him didn't believe a word of it!

Sandy in coloring, with a high, thoughtful brow, and something of a scholar's stoop, he gave no appearance of being out of the ordinary. It was in his resonant voice and in the smile that goes with having just swallowed a canary that the actor took over. In later years, with growing deafness, he showed no self-consciousness about letting his voice ring loud and clear with all the authority of one used to spellbinding a crowded gallery in a courtroom. I remember

one such occasion, at which Laurence Binyon, the British poet,
read his verses before a hand-picked audience in the house of Professor Paul Sachs at Shady Hill—surely haunted on that evening by
the ghosts of Charles Eliot Norton and Matthew Arnold, who had
played in the same room the roles of host and guest in their day.
Mr. Hill, surveying the academic company about him, said in a
voice which rang out into the hall, "It has always seemed to me
remarkable that in its three hundred years of history, only *one*
Harvard professor has murdered another."

Mr. Hill had served in France in the 1914–1918 war as major
in the Judge Advocate's Department of the Army, and never lost
his passionate Francophilia. He enjoyed play-acting the fantasy
that he had tasted deep of the raptures and woes of vice, as a
Parisian *flâneur*. Actually he was a devoted New England husband,
as he was a loving father and grandfather. He would utter such
dicta as "Marriage is not a bed of roses; it is a field of battle,"
with the gusto that could emanate only from an entirely happily
married man.

Father, inevitably, was the first link in the chain that tied us to
Mr. Hill. They shared membership in the Tavern Club and Mr. Hill
was a faithful frequenter of the Boston Athenaeum—two of the
strongest bonds that can unite good Bostonians—and I am sure they
met in more other ways than I remember. Once Mr. Hill crossed the
threshold of the house across the street it was inevitable that he found
his peer in wit and charm in Mother. They could together hide their
tender hearts under the thin disguise of what each accepted for the
sake of the other as cynicism. Books went back and forth along with
the darts they leveled jointly at the world about them. Then there
was a summer when both breadwinning heads of the families were
left in town, and Father went across the street to stay with Mr.
Hill. An uninterrupted flow of conversation passed their leisure
hours. Father said that Mr. Hill did a great deal of his talking
in the bathtub. They ate their breakfasts, as all Gentle American
husbands in the environs of Beacon Hill deserted in summer by
their wives ate theirs, at the New England Kitchen. I am sure they
must have dined at the Tavern Club, walking home in the summer

evenings across the Public Garden, fanning themselves with their straw hats if the night was warm or rejoicing in nature's greatest gift to Boston, the sudden saving east wind which can blow deliciously in from the sea, rolling the suffocating blanket of heat back to the Middle West where it came from—that disaster area which is the rest of the United States west of Dedham. Most of Father and Mr. Hill's talking must have had to do with politics. Mr. Hill called himself an Independent Republican. Aside from the vague, generic label of "liberal," Father called himself an Independent. As both men were capable of discussing politics, in which they were extremely interested, with affable good nature, their tongues wagged happily during those Boston summers. When there came a summer during which Quincy, too, was working in Boston—then there were three. There were other summers that followed when Father was at Cotuit, so that Quincy and Mr. Hill were in exclusive possession of the field. Then it was their turn to tire the sun with talking and send it down the sky.

When Mr. Hill appeared in the thick of the Sacco and Vanzetti fray his stock, if possible, rose even higher with all of us. Father was among those who felt doubt as to whether the men had had a fair trial. Dining one night in Cambridge with Felix Frankfurter, the latter mentioned that he had just written an article giving his arguments for his belief that the prisoners had not had a fair trial under law, and that he was sending the article to the *New Republic*. Father said to him, "I wish you would let me show it to Ellery Sedgwick for the *Atlantic*." "It would be too radical for them," Frankfurter answered in substance. "Let me try," countered Father. Father was to recall the episode, writing of it in 1957. Mr. Justice Frankfurter's letter to him at that time makes it live again.

DEAR MARK:

Thanks to Arthur Schlesinger, *père*, I read your reminiscences about the publication of my Sacco-Vanzetti piece in *The Atlantic*. You may care for the following comments.

You know what a hard-bitten and coercive editor—these are complimentary adjectives—Ellery Sedgwick was. When

he phoned me to say he had heard I was writing a piece on
Sacco and Vanzetti and that he wanted it for *The Atlantic*,
I thought I would derive pleasure from making him woo me
as he probably never in his life had to woo a contributor. The
fact of the matter is that Herbert Croly had agreed to print
my prospective piece as a supplement to the *New Republic*
and when I asked him was, of course, characteristically generous in releasing me because of the greater public value of
having it appear in *The Atlantic*. But I did have fun, as I
have already indicated, in making Ellery be more than deprecatory and almost obeisant.

Secondly and more important, about the question you again
raise regarding the propriety of publishing the article while
the appeal was pending in the Supreme Judicial Court, there
is all the difference in the world in discussing a case while it
is being tried before a jury and discussing the legal questions
of a case that is pending in an appellate court. And so while
I think I fully appreciated and respected the questions that
were raised about the propriety of publishing my article while
the case was before the Supreme Judicial Court, I never had
and do not now have the slightest doubt about the propriety
of my doing so. The final word on this aspect of the matter
was said by Lawrence Lowell in the fall of 1927, at the first
meeting of the Board of Overseers. A number of Overseers
were in high dudgeon about my conduct. They felt outraged
that a professor of the Law School should have published that
article while the appeal was *sub judice*. Several judges and
lawyers then on the Board defended my conduct, but I was
told that the devastating answer was given by Lowell. In closing the debate and addressing himself to my assailants, he
said to them: ''Would you have wanted Frankfurter to wait
in expressing his views until the men were dead?''

Whether Mr. Hill believed in the innocence of one or both of the
accused I don't know, but the fact that he believed the men had not
been given a fair trial under the law was enough for the fighting
bulldog in him to dig his teeth into the cause of the oppressed, and
not let go. The cold shoulders turned away from him at the time
in the Somerset Club only added zest to the tussle. That Father's

shoulder was anything but cold during that time is evinced in a
letter written to him by Mr. Hill, August 31, 1927:

> DEAR MARK,
>
> It is just like you to be the one person who has said the
> thing I cared to have said: when you speak of my "good
> temper." Of course my primary business was to do what I
> could for my clients but in the obligation one owes to the
> public if I could contribute anything I thought it would be by
> doing what I could to diminish the atmosphere (wording poor
> but meaning I hope clear) of violence and imputation of
> wicked motives that had come up about the case. I think one
> can fight just as hard without assuming those on the other side
> to be fiends when in fact, they are just humans. And you know
> what I tried for if no one else did. Some day we'll walk down
> the Embankment and talk it out. I'm much interested in
> Lowell's mental processes among other things. It is a good
> omen and one can learn much from good men one disagrees
> with.
>
> Curiously enough I was less tired when I finished the S.V.
> case than when I began. A good counter irritant from Oil.
>
> Give my love to your wife and deferential salutations to
> your young people.

As for Mr. Hill's own political beliefs, Quincy recalls his saying,
in essence, "I was only enthusiastic about one Roosevelt in my life.
I was a Bull Mooser, and that disillusioned me about all Roosevelts.
Franklin Roosevelt went to Groton, and no stream can rise higher
than its source." Arthur Hill's motives for voting for Roosevelt in
1940 were not those that would have held favor with the New
Dealers any more than with the America Firsters. The gist of his
feelings was, "I think the United States ought to get into the war in
Europe as soon as it possibly can. Roosevelt and Willkie both assure
us that they will keep us out of the war. I think Roosevelt is the
bigger liar of the two, and that's why I'm going to vote for him."
But that was 1940. On March 21, 1933, the frost was still on the
pumpkin when Mr. Hill wrote to Father (this was during a grueling
siege in the hospital for Father, during part of which Mr. Hill
wrote him a note *every day*):

. . . you will be interested to hear what are the principal subjects of discussion, for in Boston we never talk of more than one or two things at the same time. I think the chief feature has been the new President and the way he has taken hold, and the way people feel about it would have gratified your loyal democratic heart. Even the most benighted Republicans and the most hardened cynics admit that he has done a first rate job to date. He has been simple, clear, politically wise and extraordinarily courageous, has forced, through Congress, an economic programme which involves cutting the benefits of the Veterans to a reasonable measure, the legalization of beer, and is to be followed by bills dealing with the woes of the farmers, unemployment, etc. Better yet, he has done the whole thing with a good nature and human touch, which has made everybody like, as well as respect him. He evidently understands the profession of a politician as no man has understood it since his distant cousin occupied the White House. I do not know whether you will remember him,—few people do nowadays, but I think his first name was Theodore. Moreover, he has done a lot of gracious little things which help out. Such, for example, as calling on Justice Holmes on his birthday, March 8th, an act which greatly gratified the Justice, who has the old-fashioned respect for the office of the President, and which pleased the Liberals all over the Country. Indeed, he seems to keep in well with the Liberals while giving them very little, for his administration so far has leaned in all essentials toward the right.

As yet I am not quite sold on the man. It is too early to tell and there are some things about him which I do not like . . . but it does begin to look as if he had the makings of a first class ruler. Perhaps that is a business not entirely consistent with either the highest conception of personal honor or the most amiable type of character. . . .

Tomorrow I shall give you our second subject of conversation,—the Presidency of Harvard College. Really it ought to be the first in order of importance, but the other happened to be in my mind.

And on the next day he wrote:

Yesterday I said I was going to tell you about the choice of the new President for Harvard, but when I come to think of it there is very little I can tell except that so far as I can learn from Homans the Corporation are just as far from having made a choice as they were at the beginning. Two statements, both from entirely outside sources, that have come to me are, first, that Lowell is said to have remarked that the Corporation are all over the lot and some day he will slip in his own man. He is not said to have disclosed the name, and personally I disbelieve the story altogether, but it always gives pleasure to pass on untrustworthy gossip. The second statement is that every member of the Corporation except Homans is a candidate for the position. This, again, I disbelieve, though it is quite possible that if lightning did strike one or two of them they would not be wholly averse. In New York the other day I found a strong current of opinion that the choice was to be Elihu Root, the younger, but I can not find any indication here that this is so. . . . Tom Barbour is said to have health which requires a sojourn in the tropics every year and to be therefore ineligible. I hear no more of Merriman or Julian Coolidge. Altogether, I think it is a fair gamble to bet on anyone against the field.

In the meantime, we had a swell dinner at the Harvard Club on Lowell. Allston Burr presided with excellent taste and judgment. Nelson Perkins made a good speech, and so did Kittredge, and Lowell was more interesting and human than I have ever heard him, and convinced me, for one, of the enormous value of his presidency, although I still remain an unconverted adherent of the elective system. It was a dinner to be proud of. Very little blah, no conscious self-advertisement, and a dignity and moderation which were very striking. To be sure, I think an outsider might have felt the just recognition of Harvard superiority to all other created things, but after all why get away from obvious facts.

When Quincy went to New York to live and to make his career Mr. Hill always followed him with affectionate interest, and Quincy rarely came on to Boston that he did not find time to exchange his views of the ways of the world with his older friend. But all of

Mr. Hill's tenderness for the Howe family came, with the years, to be focused on Mark. Through their mutual friend "Felix," Mark, in time, went to serve in Washington as Justice Holmes's secretary, for the last full year of the Justice's life. On Mark's return to Boston from Washington, Mr. Hill made a place for him in his own law office. From the first there was no impediment to the marriage of those two minds. Mr. Hill spoke of him, to Father, "He is just about my age—perhaps a thought older, but near enough." On another day, "Young Mark went in with me today on his first jury case and so may be said to have lost his legal virginity." No parent could have taken more loving pride or shown more sensitive concern for a son than Mr. Hill showed for Mark's welfare and future. He gave his enthusiastic encouragement when Mark went to the University of Buffalo Law School—first as professor, later as its dean—and of course welcomed him home when he returned to nearby Cambridge and a professorship at the Harvard Law School, where his own legal life had begun. When Mark went overseas in 1945 Mr. Hill's loving protectiveness toward Mark's wife, whom he had come to love too for her own sake, was only one more refraction of the light and warmth of the friendship that played over us all.

When we were no longer living in Brimmer Street, after Mother's death, it was my turn to tune in on the share that was waiting for me. Mr. Hill used to drop in often to see me and to talk about—Mark. And so it was gradually that we, too, became adult friends. He followed my professional life, too, writing to Father about a performance of my monologues he had enjoyed, "I kept rubbing my eyes and asking myself, 'Can this be Helen-Howe-across-the-street?'"

Father's children used to laugh at his propensity for leaning on another opinion when he had a decision to make. He used to look troubled, as he said, "I'd rather like to get some advice before I make up my mind." And then, invariably brightening, he would add, "I believe I'll go and talk it over—with Arthur Hill."

I think it doubtful that New England has produced a finer example of its best breed. I am sure there was no finer in Brimmer Street.

8

PRESENCES

MOTHER AND FATHER WERE SINGULARLY FREE from the usual pressure of in-laws, to which so many American households are subject, squaring off into the two camps of HIS and HERS. Mother's only brother, living in Boston, shared her own withdrawn temperament and, except for Christmas or Thanksgiving, we saw little of him and his wife and son. For Father, the loving presence of Bristol made itself felt in occasional visits from Uncle Wallis and Aunt Molly. They seemed, between them, and in spite of the demands of their own family of six children, to sustain the town of Bristol, and much of Providence as well. "I was in prison and ye came unto me." Throw in an insane asylum or two, with a morgue here and an institution for alcoholics there, and Uncle Wallis and Aunt Molly were on hand. There seemed no human situation with which they could not—and did not—cope. How often have I heard my parents say, "Mary is a force of nature." And Father commented, "Wal is the da—ndest funeral hound." There wasn't one he missed, and hardly one that Aunt Molly didn't run. Aunt Molly was capacious of both body and heart, of bursting good nature, lusty in all her appetites, exuberantly alive. Father referred to her as the "Wife of Bristol." She produced her sixth child on the same day that her own daughter produced her first. Uncle Wal touched on this feat in verses which began,

> When aged woman stoops to folly
> And finds too late that she can bear.

[136]

His son George records his father's facing the demands of his quiverful, "I d-d-do have a varied life. Before I go to bed I've got to see that my youngest son gets his bottle, and my oldest d-d-doesn't get his."

We children loved Uncle Wallis. Perversely enough, we found his stammer—so much worse than Father's—engaging and not embarrassing. When he went through excruciating struggles to produce a word, on its final appearance it often turned out to be a mot. He had a more natural love of children than Father, and the same happy gift of rhyming, in addition to an artist's gift with his pencil. He was more of a strictly observing "churchman" than Father. First as vestryman, and then as senior warden, he served St. Michael's Church for a period of sixty-two years, not to mention the lifting of his voice in its choir. The many public buildings of his design, not only in Bristol but throughout Rhode Island, were the cause of his being, for over half a century, in the words of the president of the Rhode Island Chapter of the American Institute of Architects, "the envy of his contemporaries. . . . He has a brilliance of technique and quality of delineation that others could not hope to attain. And finally, he gets more fun out of his work than any architect we know." Uncle Wallis's essential nature was perhaps more of the artist's than Father's; his blood was hotter, he was more responsive to the charms of Woman. What feminine client could not but be charmed by an architect who, when she tried to describe a certain color she had in mind—half gray, half pink, and yet somehow with a silver tone—haltingly ventured, "I think I know what you m-m-mean. You want the color of-of-of an elephant's ear by-by-by moonlight." And yet, for all of Uncle Wallis's sensitive light touch and humor, his self-discipline—chiefly in the stoical acceptance of the crippling curse of his stammer—had touched his features with a mark of so sweet and strong a character that they finally spelled something of the heroic. Perhaps some of his strength lay simply in the saintly patience—coupled with never-failing adoring admiration—with which he learned to live with the various manifestations of Aunt Molly's vitality. He was neither henpecked nor hagridden but a willing

slave, tied to the chariot wheels of—a force of nature! Uncle
Wallis could have sung with Chaucer: "My lady and my love,
my wife so dear, I put myself in your wise governing And choose
that which to you most joy will bring."

Aunt Molly's first act on coming into our house was always to
seat herself at the telephone and place a number of long-distance
calls, likely as not to do with her antique shop in Bristol. When
she was hurriedly sent for to come to London to the side of a
traveling, ailing elderly Bristol lady, Mother wrote to me: "I fancy
her movements will have to be affected by the fate of Miss Barnes
living or dead. Father has such respect for Aunt Molly's executive
ability that he prophesies that she will see to it that Miss Barnes
is buried in Westminster Abbey! Poor Uncle Wal was practically
inarticulate with fatigue and worry on top of his household
cares . . . and he found himself suddenly at the head of a flourishing antique business, largely carried on by mail!" When a later
report told that Miss Barnes was better, Mother wrote me that "If
Aunt Molly doesn't have the fun of a funeral, she will have fun of
a less hilarious, but equally satisfactory kind in calling up all her
European friends. I can see her getting Central and saying,
" 'Please get me Tut's tomb,' " where her son George was on an
archaeological expedition. Surprisingly enough, Mother and Aunt
Molly got on famously. I have heard them together, with mingled
gratitude and amusement extol the virtues of the monogamous
Howe brothers as husbands. (Both were devoted to my Uncle
Arthur's wife, May Denckla of Philadelphia, who died suddenly
when Uncle Arthur was fifty-six years old. True to the brothers'
pattern of one-woman devotion Uncle Arthur remained a widower
thirty-eight years until his death, a few days before his ninety-
fourth birthday.) When the devoted Cal and Wal wished to communicate by telephone Aunt Molly and Mother functioned in the
roles of foreign ministers, each representing her chief of state, carrying back and forth propositions and counterpropositions, generally
concerned with the hope of a meeting. With the outbreak of the
World War—as it was naïvely called before men came to putting
Roman numerals after their wars—Aunt Molly rode its waves in

her finest hours, organizing the placing of boxes throughout the
land in which shoppers were to drop spare change for the benefit
of Belgian children. "There was no better soul than she alive."

———◆———

There were other Presences in Brimmer Street. Two were seen;
two were unseen.

One, Mother's elder sister by seven years, was my aunt Mabel
Davis. Aunt Mabel! As rich a fruit as ever graced a family tree!
How is it possible to evoke that dear ghost? Elusive enough in life,
how can I summon her forth now? The very essence of Aunt Mabel
was that it was impossible to summon her—ever. If one asked her
ahead of time for any engagement, including Thanksgiving or
Christmas dinner, she would never commit herself, but merely say,
"We'll hold the thought." So all I can do now is hold the thought of
her. She dropped suddenly into our lives as a widow in 1919, after
thirty years of living in the Argentine. Before returning to the
Boston she had left as a girl so long before, she had put in three
grueling years during her husband's last illness on his family farm
in Vermont, to which they had returned. It was characteristic of
her entrance on the scene that when she wired from Vermont the
news of Uncle Walter's death, and specified the day, hour, and
church in Boston she would like for his funeral, and her brother
and Father went to the station to meet the train they met—
Uncle Walter in his coffin. Aunt Mabel had neglected to tell anyone
that she herself was not coming—simply, poor darling, from excess
of feeling. She did appear a few days later, spent a few nights in
Brimmer Street, until she found she was disturbed by the chime
of the "Negro church," and moved to a residential hotel. From one
or another such hotel as base she was to orbit around our family,
first in Brimmer Street and then Louisburg Square, for approximately forty years.

In her heyday Aunt Mabel had apparently broken all of Boston's
eligible hearts—tall, dark (hers were the only brown eyes among
the three Quincy sisters), with a classic nose, and a soft full mouth
and delicious warm voice—she possessed in as high a degree as
anyone I have ever known the ineffable, indefinable quality of

charm. I have heard her make glancing references to Bernard
Berenson, with whom she floated about Venice in a gondola, when
the sisters along with their parents were staying there. I rather
assumed that he was her "lover," in the sense that the Gentle
American ladies used the word—that is, that he had asked her to
marry him—but I cannot vouch for this. I had the impression that
he was too small to please that daughter of the gods, divinely tall.
Mr. Berkeley Updike I know was a suitor. A widow, Mrs. Pickering Putnam, lived in the same Boston hotel with her. Aunt Mabel
particularly liked Mrs. Putnam, perhaps because she enjoyed
chuckling reminiscently over the days when she had known her
friend's husband as a young man, with special gusto recalling the
day that "Picky Put popped." (Pop used transitively—its object,
the question.)

Walter Gould Davis, whom she did marry, was a self-made farm
boy from Vermont who, first a railroad engineer, went out to the
Argentine as second assistant to Dr. Benjamin Apthorp Gould in
the Astronomical Observatory at Cordoba. There "Aunt Mary
Gould," his wife and my grandfather's sister, took such a fancy to
the stalwart young assistant to her husband that she decided there
was only one girl in the world good enough for him—and that was
Helen Quincy. When Walter Davis came back to the United States
on leave, shy and awkward, he presented himself as his boss's wife
had instructed him to do, in Charles Street where—*a-gley* went
her matchmaking schemes. One look, not at Helen but at her sister
Mabel, did the damage. For six years they corresponded, while she
continued to reject most of Boston's conventional young men, and
then confounded them—and her family as well—by marrying the
big inarticulate Vermonter. She disappeared to the Argentine, later
to live in "B.A.," as she always called it, where Uncle Walter became director of the Argentine Meteorological Service. For nearly
thirty years she enjoyed a romantically happy marriage.

Her hair-trigger nervous mechanism might quite well, after
the emotional devastation following Uncle Walter's long illness and
death, have snapped in a nervous breakdown; instead, she simply
withdrew from active participation in life. She quietly sat out the

Captain "Nor'west"
John DeWolf

Weetamoe

*"A little boy
our man was then"*

*Light and fantastic:
extraverted Bristolians
(Father second from right)*

*The Lehigh tennis
team of 1886
(Father wearing mustache)*

*The Bishop in a see
of family (see Notes)*

The Boosey Club (Father and Mother at left of picture)

Codman on "The Shoulder"—Aunt Katy's

Mother and Father as engaged couple, chaperoned by stuffed pug

The young Copeland: "No longer the quoting, literary, naught-availing person . . ."

Aunt Mabel and admirer

"The Paine That is All but a Lyman Shall Change
To the Lyman That's All but a Paine"
(Putnam Camp group in the 1880's)

"A place where the past lived on": Mrs. Fields's drawing room
in Charles Street (Mrs. Fields at the window, Miss Jewett nearby)

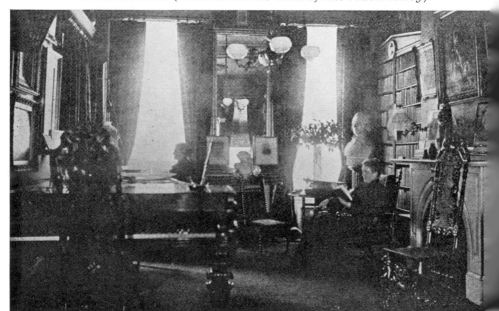

Uncle Wal

Robert Savage Chase

Arthur Dehon Hill

Naushon house party
(left to right: W. Cameron Forbes, A. Lawrence Lowell,
Mrs. *Waldo Forbes, Father, Harold Nicolson, Thomas Barbour)*

The bell-ringing Shurcliffs of Beacon Hill

Life *photo*

remainder of it, as a detached spectator, stoically reticent always about the loss she never was to recover from, but on the surface amused and amusing. Our family was the fixed Maypole around which she not so much twined herself as floated, fluttering in the breeze of her own whims—visible and invisible, at time and place of her own choosing—literally eccentric. Her telephone appearances were much like those of the Cheshire Cat: she never asked for anybody in particular, never said who she was, and never said good-by. She put her letters into the mailbox, with the stamp crooked, upside down in the lower left-hand corner. We never fully satisfied ourselves as to whether the spark of wit that flashed from her was conscious. When Aunt Helen in England took in an occasional "p.g." (paying guest), Aunt Mabel murmured concerning one, "He *p*'s but he doesn't *g*."

One discriminating friend described her as "pure poet," creating pearls within the oyster of her own nature. There was nothing literal about Aunt Mabel: everything was allusion to an inner world of her own. "Are you by chance a Pauline?" she would ask of a stranger, skipping the stepping stone of explanation that she herself was reading a life of St. Paul at the time. Her gift for rendering names slightly askew amounted to a high creative art. Hilaire Belloc became Hilary Bellaire; Henry James's "Little Tour in France" became (because she herself was taking it) a "Little Trip in Tours." She had names of her own for family and friends. Father was Abraham (to her, Father Abraham, head of the tribe). "He is avant tout, père," she used to say. Her vocabulary was dotted with Spanish, which easily modulated into allied languages. *Mi voy* was her preamble to leaving; as she left, she would say, "Au revoir-cito"—a solemn good-by was something she could not bear, and the *cito* diminished it. When Quincy became engaged to be married, she expressed her satisfaction over his choice by saying, "He might so easily have married a Soviet." Her breakfast—horrifyingly—expressed her predilection for nonconformity which she came by honestly from her father: her morning meal consisted of an egg, held under the hot water tap of her bathroom faucet, broken on shredded wheat (to her, always simply "shredded," as vegetable was "veg"), and softened with olive oil. Although she had something of Mother's capacity for an over-intense sympathy, she could, in an offhand way that was quite her own, be so sublimely unaware of other human beings—quite unlike my mother!—that she had a way of treating them as though they were not only deaf but invulnerable. Sitting with her in the theater at a matinee, I remember her patrician nose sniffing the surrounding air, as she said in her clear and beautiful voice, "I can always detect anything foot-y or hair-y. Can you, Helen?"

When, during the war, she was turned out of the Hotel Victoria when it was taken over by the WAVES, she took refuge in the far more commercial Hotel Lenox. There Aunt Mabel, with a total lack of inhibition, sailed about the lobby among the rows of leather chairs and spittoons, not only incongruously enough accepted by the traveling salesmen, who were availing themselves of both, but looked upon and looked after by an unsung hero, the manager of the hotel, with a sort of proprietary affection nothing short of chivalrous. The hotel employees, too, accepted her, even to the operator of an elevator filled with a crowd of passengers, which stopped at her floor to take on my husband and me, who had to submit to Aunt Mabel, standing in the corridor, calling out, "Drive skillfully, Leo!"

The night during which the country shifted to or back from standard time was always a storm-tossed one for Aunt Mabel, who couldn't make head or tail of the procedure. Doubtless remembering the ritual of the equator she had crossed so many times, she reported herself as calling the desk several times during the night to ask "How are we getting on?" Everything about Aunt Mabel suggested the exotic, the romantic. Her many years in a Latin country, with its easier tempo and climate, its siesta and mixed European society, gave her a vantage point from which she looked with amusement and total lack of identification at the "girls" (Aunt Mabel, in her seventies, still called them so) with whom she had grown up or come out. She was entirely disinterested in any of the "good works" with which they busied themselves. There were others who did not fit into any Boston niche. I don't know how it happened, but one of her closest girlhood friends was the daughter of Edwin Booth—to Aunt Mabel, "Edwina." Booth's signed photograph was always on her mantelpiece. Aunt Mabel told me of Edwina's going backstage to see her father after a certain performance of *Hamlet,* and asking him, "Father, what was the matter? What was wrong?" To her horror, he explained that that was the night he had *felt* the part as never before, and was sure his daughter would tell him he had given his greatest performance. He returned thereafter to his own "method," staying enough outside his part to be conscious of the means with which he achieved his end.

More than either of her sisters Aunt Mabel had fallen heir to the fatal family weakness of gullibility. If one challenged some particularly fantastic bit of lore she had picked up, her devastating rejoinder was simply, "A *man* told me so." She looked up in instinctive, feminine respect to the other sex. "How wise you are," she would purr to the least wise of men. She was anticlerical, anti-creeds of all kinds, and took an almost malicious delight in needling Father, when she considered him too conventional in either ecclesiastical or social observances. She leaned, however, on his Democratic political beliefs for reinforcing her own instinctive support of the party that had been her birthright. She turned to him on one occasion at least, in which he disappointed her. She appeared, bearing her copy of Wordsworth, marked and scrawled over as only Aunt Mabel's books of poetry could be marked. (Every morning after breakfast Aunt Mabel gave herself fifteen minutes in which she tried to "commit"—as she intransitively called it—making her own changes in the text as she went along, if it failed to please her. If a man's name was mentioned, it was automatically changed to Walter; lines that seemed to her irrelevant, or disappointing, were summarily struck out.) Standing over Father, she handed him her Wordsworth, asking him to "do better" for the last two lines for several of the sonnets. "But, Mabel, I *can't,*" he expostulated. "Of course you can." I can see him, as he must have erased his own illegible scrawl, bearing down hard as he always did with his soft pencil, truly trying to please her. After various futile attempts, he handed her book back to her, innocent of any emendations of his own. She expressed her disgust at his giving up without, as she accused him, even trying.

Aunt Mabel was patrician in bearing as well as looks. Her clothes were put together in magpie style—a black velvet ribbon around her throat, something floating in the way of a scarf, gray fabric gloves, covering excellent diamond rings, a fine sealskin coat, and cotton lisle stockings. In later years she carried a cane, and various reticules flopped at her side. She had a way of standing in the middle of the room, with her mobile mouth in its constant motion, more legato than a twitch, the back of her wrists resting in the scoop of her long back, looking about her, and uttering to herself whatever floated through her mind. Seeming in her guilelessness not to know the difference between true or false, beautiful or cheap, but still at her very core was an innate fineness that made her, in spite of all her protestations against the distinction of class or convention, essentially an aristocrat.

After Mother's death "Father Abraham" did indeed become the pivotal figure to which she clung. She never ceased to poke fun at his social proclivities, with special gibes for the Episcopal Church and clergy, but she turned to "Abraham" for counsel and support on everything that concerned her most closely. He wrote to me, "Aunt M. is busy on the telephone this A.M. and most cheerful, even asking me whether Providence, to which she is writing, is in Connecticut or Massachusetts." The last years were sad for us—thank God not for her, as a veil descended across her mind. Even in the nursing home where she spent her last few years she was a "character," and a beloved one, still capable of playing on and with words with wit and imagination when she was no longer fully aware of their meaning.

She used often, in her last days, to hold my hand, and before I would leave her, a little quavering, her last words were, "Ne m'oubliez pas." Dear, dear Aunt Mabel! Never!

———◆———

There were two unseen Presences of whose intensity of personality Father was vividly aware without their ever crossing the

threshold of 26 Brimmer Street. To Mother, one was "Amy," the
other, "Mamie." The first, to Father, was never to be anything
but "Mrs. Gray."

Mother and Father were not alone in finding Mrs. Russell Gray
of 39 Marlboro Street a very frightening woman. Father she barely
accepted with a lofty superciliousness, as a necessary accessory of
Mother's. I am sure she must have felt that he lacked the overtones
of James's *Europe*. Mrs. Gray was all *Europe*. True, she lived on
Marlboro Street, and true, the stirring of the curtains in the front
window by a bored parlor maid bore witness to its lack of passion,
and yet passionate is precisely what Mrs. Gray was, under a coating
of ice. She received the intrepid caller not in a drawing room but
in her bedroom, where she lay, reclined on a Madame Récamier
chaise longue—the archetype Permanent Invalid. No more than
one ever knew just what was the *matter* with Milly Theale did one
know what ailed Mrs. Gray. She was so beautifully in character as
an invalid that it would have seemed some dreadful dislocation of
nature to meet her plodding about the streets in hat and coat like
other mere mortals. She was, first of all, startlingly beautiful. So
far back as my own memory goes her heavy iron-gray hair was piled
up in a huge Psyche knot at the back of her graceful head. Her
nose was delicate and straight, her eyebrows and lashes dark.
There was even a faint dark down on her upper lip as provocative
as Natasha Rostov's. Her skin was as white as her thin cambric
shift with fluting at the neck. I remember particularly her exquisite long, thin hands with their finely grooved pointed nails.
There were occasions when this tableau was framed with startling
effect under a large opened black umbrella, its purpose to shade
her sensitive eyes from the light.

Though the chaise longue was her natural habitat, she manifested
herself on Friday afternoons at the Symphony Concerts, supported
by her chauffeur—hired, not regularly employed—wearing a fur-
lined Tibetan hood, and swathed in shawls. Mother had a beautiful
photograph of her, aristocratic in profile, dressed in a chiffon "tea
gown" edged with fur. I know, too, that there were occasional
dinner parties if for no other reason than that I recall Mother's

amusement over the place cards, which were simply the reverse
side of calling cards left by friends, whose names she had scratched
out. In the same spirit, when Mrs. Gray sent Mother a postcard
she was quite likely to use an order card of S. S. Pierce's on one
side, crossing out Pierce's printed name and address and adding
Mother's instead, and on the other conveying her message in a
handwriting as spidery and distinguished as she herself. Mother
always felt that Mrs. Gray's manifestations of thrift were far more
French than New England. Although it is my impression that her
childhood was spent in the Orient, I know that Spain figured somewhere in her background, whether in blood, or perhaps through
having lived there, I am not sure. I do know that as the young Amy
Heard she moved in Paris in the inner Faubourg society and became engaged—a true affair of the heart—to a Frenchman. When
her father failed in business (could it have been tea, hence the
Orient, and hence the Tibetan hood?) no dowry was forthcoming,
the engagement was broken and—she became Mrs. Russell Gray of
Marlboro Street, Boston, and Nahant. Mr. Gray was a prosperous
and highly cultivated lawyer, with a shrewd acumen for handling
his by no means negligible investments. My memories of him include
elastic-sided congress boots, a black beard, his fingers painfully
twisted by arthritis, which twirled the cigar that was lovingly caressed by his large red lips, large brown pupils set in a frighteningly
large expanse of surrounding whites, and large white teeth faintly
reminiscent of the wolf masquerading as Little Red Riding Hood's
grandmother. Mr. and Mrs. Gray were, incredibly enough, the
parents of two sons—both now distinguished in different careers
and living far away from Boston.

Mrs. Gray must have had some kind of Indian sign on Mother
because the one unbreakable engagement that Mother kept over
the years, hell or high water, was two hours of reading aloud to
her on Monday mornings. Mother used to say that it was a wonder
that her three children had not been born at Mrs. Gray's bedside.
There was a handful of other dedicated and terrorized friends,
each of whom had "her day"—and her book. Although Mr. Gray
left a fortune in the millions, Mrs. Gray never indulged in the

wanton waste of *buying* a book. Her reader either supplied it from her own shelves or got it out of the Athenaeum—on her own card. Mother's compassionate heart was touched by the frail hothouse flower, uprooted from the warmth and color that should have been her natural climate and placed in the frosty New England soil. She admired Mrs. Gray's distinction of mind and character— their reading was always history or biography—but above all, I think she was endlessly amused by a "frankness" that many people would not have tolerated and would have simply called rudeness or arrogance. Mother, who prided herself on her own "clear-sighted-ness," had met her match in Mrs. Gray. I am sure that neither ever insulted the other with a social inanity. Theirs was no salt-free diet. Almost every Monday Mother had some new tidbit smacking of Mrs. Gray's tart flavor with which to regale us.

One of the most tremendous events in my parents' lives was the annual visit the Grays paid to us at Cotuit on Cape Cod. I can't remember how many times they came, but there was always scurrying about, to try to make the simple house, with its one family bathroom, somehow pull itself together to receive the royal pair. Part of the ritual involved Mother's tiptoeing down the hall at night to remove from outside Mr. Gray's closed door the congress boots, which she polished and, like the shoemakers' elves, returned by morning!

Mother told us with relish—and it lost nothing in the telling—of a dialogue she enjoyed with Mrs. Gray when she returned to Boston in the fall after one of these visits.

Mother was greeted when she appeared in Mrs. Gray's bedroom on the appointed Monday morning with the startling command, "Close the door." There was just that edge to Mrs. Gray's voice— I cannot call it a rasp—which was more suggestive of the iron hand than any velvet glove. Her clipped, succinct speech at the best of times implicitly pronounced one guilty before being given the chance to prove innocence. These tones could reduce poor Father to a bout of stammering. Mother, on this occasion, more frightened than usual, did as she was told and came forward, prepared to receive some dread revelation or denouncement.

"Sit down. I want to tell you something."

"Yes, Amy."

"As you know, I don't believe in empty flattery, and I don't think that most people who know me would say I often use it."

"No, Amy."

"So, you are not to take what I am going to tell you as flattery."

"Of course I shan't, Amy."

"Well! I should like to tell you what Russell said to me when we came back from Cotuit. And I want you to understand that he said it quite spontaneously. I didn't ask him directly whether he had enjoyed his visit, and of course it would never have occurred to him that I might repeat to you anything he said. So what I am going to repeat to you expresses his own feelings. I felt that it would please you so much to hear it that, without asking his permission, I have decided to repeat it."

Mother, bridling in anticipation and barely able to contain her curiosity, began murmuring her appreciation in advance, "Amy, how good of you! Of course I'd love to hear it, if you really feel like telling me."

"As he was dressing for dinner the night after we came back from Cotuit, he said out of the blue—'Aren't the Howes nice?'"

Actually the visits to Cotuit consisted of more than polishing congress boots. Under the fragile *dame aux camélias* exterior was a streak not only of a passionate love of beauty but of a fire of temperament that dared express it. There was one bluff, overlooking the soft blue of the Cape water, where Mrs. Gray would sit on the warm, sweet-smelling pine needles and inhale the sights and sounds and fragrance with all the intensity of a highly intense nature. Mother christened this little promontory Gray Head. But her greatest triumph was a trip to a remote beach, shimmering in the hot summer sunshine, where Mrs. Gray, to Mother's mingled consternation and delight, insisted that she must get into the water. Stripping off everything but her chemise, this she proceeded to do.

I remember, after her husband's death, Mrs. Gray, flat on her bed, lay like a figure on a catafalque, a fragile wraith hovering between death and life. She told me most movingly of how she felt she kept seeing at the bottom of her bed her little grandson who had been tragically drowned. She went on to gasp out that life was a pure hell of suffering. But she suddenly reared up from her pillow and said in substance, "Forget that I said that! It is not true! Life is wonderful! Remember that I said so!"

In fact the smoldering fires that had lain dormant back of the drawn shades and under that opened umbrella sprang to sudden and violent intensity during her husband's long, last, and agonizingly painful illness. Then, suddenly, she left the web, she left the loom, she made three paces thro' the room and the wilting invalid, like a discarded chrysalis, was left behind. Amy Gray became not so much the ministering as the avenging angel who would brook no one near her husband but herself, in a savage sort of protectiveness and possessiveness. Night and day, in the most ignoble as in the most taxing duties, she became his devoted nurse. A wild creature would not have cared for its young with a more passionate tenderness and care. She saw him valiantly through to his painful end, and then lingered on for years, spent physically and emotionally, waiting with a touchingly increasing sweetness for her own dismissal.

After Mother's death Father used to call on Mrs. Gray. In later years she grew gentler, he grew braver about boring her, and they established a rather touching bond, founded on common mourning for Mother. I think of all her readers Mrs. Gray valued none more than Mother. Mother would have said that it was only because she was dependable, but I am sure that Mrs. Gray counted on her for much more than that. And it was this sense of the much more that helped to bridge the gulf that might otherwise never have been spanned between Father and Mrs. Gray. When, on the anniversary of Mother's death, the devoted Cotuit family who had looked after us for all the years we lived there used to send him a moist little bunch of Mayflowers, pre-eminently "her" flower, he always took a few to leave at Mrs. Gray's door on Marlboro Street.

I am sure that by the time her own end was near she had capitulated to the extent of following her husband's boldhearted lead, and would have agreed that Father was nice.

———◆———

Now for "Mamie," standing at exactly the other end of the spectrum. I don't know if Mother ever saw Mamie face to face more than once. But there remains a hamper billowing over with letters from her, in an array of handwritings that would confound an expert, as each one seems to have been written by somebody else. But there is, in them all, the indelible imprint of an amazing Jewish character, brilliant, tough, and courageous. From the day that Mother loomed over her horizon, as an unseen friend, it was to her that the faltering needle of Mamie's compass unwaveringly pointed. With the letters is a faded little penciled note in Father's handwriting, telling their provenance, and, indeed, of Mamie herself. As Father, in the language of his day, put it, she "came up from the streets" and was put in touch with Mother by a pious social worker (through what connecting link I do not know) in another city, in the hope that Mother might, though unseen, prove helpful. What could have rippled on as a conventional correspondence between the Lady and the Prostitute, condescension on one side and mock gratitude on the other, flowered instead into an interchange between two remarkable women who grew in respect and affection for each other.

I should give much to see some of Mother's letters to Mamie. They must have carried some life-giving force, judging from the response they awakened in their recipient. Father and Mother were so impressed by the quality of Mamie's letters that they showed them to Mr. Sedgwick of the *Atlantic*. His answer not only corroborates my feeling that this unseen Presence in Brimmer Street was a woman of unique gifts but it also demonstrates his unique gifts as an editor, who maintained the standards he set for his magazine:

> I have had the Mamie letters an unconscionable time, and my only excuse is that I have been really unwilling to part with them. They are most remarkable. Her clear, critical insight is highly exceptional, and, of course, quite outside of the inherent pathos of the narrative, her gift of telling a straightforward story is most captivating to a reader. After very

mature consideration, I am inclined to doubt the wisdom of
any magazine publishing the correspondence. I am led to this
decision primarily because I think the effect on Mamie herself
would be unfortunate. Among the more serious magazines, I
think the *Atlantic* is the only one which would consider the
publication of such letters, and if they were made a "feature"
of some popular magazine, I believe the vulgarization of the
whole enterprize would be complete.

That the *Atlantic* might publish a series of these letters
with great popular success, I believe to be true, and I do not
feel afraid of the venture, but I do feel that a considerable
minority would misinterpret the magazine's motives in printing the letters, and I am inclined to think (although I am not
sure) that their appearance in the *Atlantic* would be a blow
not to our circulation, but to our influence.

If the few samples I inject here seem a far cry from the Brimmer
Street or Boston way of life it is for the very reason that they
serve to highlight it, by contrast. It is teasing to think that "Little
Cunnit" might be bringing in the same morning mail a letter from
Mamie to Mother and one to Father from one of his gentle, cul-
tivated, "literary" correspondents.

After Mother had seen Father off to his office, or her children to
school, and had climbed the stairs from the basement kitchen where
she had gone to discuss the day's meals with Bertha Shea, she might
have settled down in the morning sunshine of the back parlor to
read Mamie's recollection of her time in prison:

. . . since I feel in the mood tonight, I will tell you what I
remember of it. It was such a terrible experience and I was
only past 13 years old! It was the regular prison and not the
place of detention that they use now to send Juvenile Offenders
to. I think of it but seldom—tonight I thought of it due to
re-reading the Ballad of Reading Gaol. . . .
I had left school directly after my father's death and was
put to work in the house, doing the sort of work I despised
because I had never been taught how and too because I loved
school and books and the things that school meant. I was 13

in July and in Sept., my second term at . . . high school, I was
not permitted to go back to school. Prior to my father's death,
we had a general servant in the house and a laundress and
scrub woman who came each 2 days in the week. After his
death I was given it all to do but the laundress's work and I
did it very poorly and only after receiving severe whippings.
In October or perhaps November I told a young girl who was
librarian in a City library close to my home of the reason that
I did not come for books any more which was that my mother
wouldn't permit me to read them and a book for which the
Librarian wanted to collect 80¢ had been thrown into the fire
when I had been found reading it. Of course I had no 80¢ to
pay her and I was very much ashamed of it. I think this was
my original reason for getting work in a neighborhood store to
work at night for a small weekly sum, as a "sales lady." After
this, and after a violent scene with my Mother who told me if
I didn't like my life at home that I should get out, I went to
the city and there got a regular job in a dept. store at $5.00
a week tho I was only past 13 yrs. and I was a "saleslady" and
this store to this day is quite the place for men to come during
the afternoon to make "dates" for the eve. I found I would
stay away from dinner and go along with some boys and come
home and tell some story and that it was accepted due to the
$5.00 I was able to bring home! Once there was some kind of
a fuss again and when I threatened to leave home my mother
said she hoped it was soon. Of course the inevitable thing hap-
ened. Some young chap took me to his rooms and I stayed 3 or
4 days before I put in an appearance in the neighborhood of
my home. As I neared our house a man spoke to me by name
and told me he was a "special officer," that he had a warrant
for my arrest. He took me to the Central Station which is in
the City Hall. . . . Of course I was terribly frightened but
imagine my horror when I was placed in a cell! It was a horribly filthy vile smelling hole. I cried and begged they should
send for my mother and tho they did after awhile she refused
to come. It was night time and there was no light and I could
hear the rats which I feared more than death. I was terrified
and pleaded to be taken out of there. It was only after I permitted one of the men who seemed to be in charge at the time

to take all sorts of liberties with me that I was permitted to come out of the cell and I sat up for the rest of the night. The man was perhaps 50 or even older. In the morning there was a hearing. My mother was present and I recall my Uncle was with her and he was acting with her to persuade the "Commonwealth" that I should be sent to some House of Refuge as being incorrigible. This Uncle is the same one who did me the first wrong when I was a tiny girl and had any number of times since then. It seemed that in order to prove me immoral so that I should become a public charge (without expense to my mother) it would have to be proven that I had committed a crime and the man produced. A further hearing was demanded for this as in my terror I had told the name and address of the chap and of course they were going to arrest him. I was led away to the same cell, pleading to my mother in shrieks to take me home . . . the terrible fear of spending another night there seemed imminent. . . . There was only a bench and an exposed toilet in the cell and it was as I thought terrible, at noon, there were footsteps and the jangling of keys and the cell was opened I thought for sure my mother had relented and I was so grateful. I put on my hat and coat and came out to the large room. . . I saw some men in line and I was told to get behind the last one. . . . The line moved as I did, and oh, what a lot they were. . . . We filed down the stairs and the line in front got outside and as I was last I saw them filing into a prison van, the kind called "Black Marias." . . . The ride lasted perhaps an hour. Time can never efface my impressions thru that ride. . . . One of them told me to cheer up, and said he would look out for me after he got out for he would only get 30 days whereas no doubt I'd be sent away for a number of years, until I was of age. I then knew for sure I was going to prison and oh! how I feared it. The ride was probably the worst of the whole harrowing experience.

In the prison . . . I was led away by a woman [who] . . . brought me some very coarse rough looking clothes and took away my own tho' I cried dreadfully to not have to put them on. Then they took me to another room and before I knew what they were going to do (they had combed my hair out) it was cut off to the ears. I was taken back to the cell which was similar to the one I had occupied in the central station only longer and had a pallet of straw on a black iron frame bed. . . .

It was not only past history that was poured out to Mother in Brimmer Street. Mamie's letters brought all the suspense of an unfolding drama. Sadie Thompson never had a tougher time with the Rev. Mr. Davidson than Mamie had with her would-be reformer, who was more interested in counting her soul as "saved" than in giving her the concrete help she needed for a very serious eye operation. She described a scene for Mother:

. . . First I must tell you that he greeted me very formally and until the end one would never dream that I knew him but very slightly as he was very cold and formal. I had just seated myself when he asked me to tell him about my affairs. I told him I was well, physically, which was about all I could say— then he asked about my going to church etc. and appeared to be shocked when I told him I did not go to church. I also told him that while I hadn't done anything bad since he left, I hadn't either done anything good—somehow I could not talk to him as I can write to you and I don't think he understood but rather thinks I am just perverse. . . . Among other things he spoke of his kindness to me as "works" and that in itself is exactly what makes me hate my condition so— He said as he has often said before—"you know Mamie how I am on all sides talked to by my family to keep out of this *work*." . . . Then when I told him that I simply ate and slept, he judged that I wanted more money—and said as he also has said before that he was not a rich man and that he had many calls on him and that several things he had money in had failed so his income was greatly reduced. . . . Then I told him as I did you how I despised to feel that I was living on Charity and he said he didn't see why I should feel that way when I knew it was given with affection etc. . . .

Mamie described the hat she was wearing, which she had trimmed herself:

. . . A large black shape and a bow with three loops wired and standing up and the rest flat. As I only purchased 2 yds and

½ of the ribbon it couldn't be very large (the how) and the
ribbon is black and white silk with a narrow edge of red
velvet. To me it does not look loud as I hadn't even drawn
the ribbon all around the hat but just made the bow and I
thought Mr. X. would like it as I often used to wear a red tie,
and real bright one with a white waist and he remarked how
well I looked. But just as I was dressing I decided to put on
the little blue hat but then didn't as it seemed like petty
deceit and put on the large one. Then Mr. X. remarked that I
was dressed too loud. So I said I had on only the dress you
sent—the dotted one—then he said the dress was alright but
the hat was frightful and he spoke of it again and again during
the interview. . . . It was all so terribly formal and then in
conclusion he said he hoped I would change my mind and not
"go back" . . . then he dismissed me by telling me to think it
over and opened the door for me to go without even a good-
bye hand clasp. It was all so horrible. . . . I know it will make
me seem such a dreadful ingrate for not feeling such deep
gratitude for past favors that I wouldn't dream of finding
fault but really I can't tell you what a blow this was to me. . . .
As it is, there seems but two ways open as he plainly told me.
One to submit to what I know is really a waste of time and
would only jeopardize my present good health by going to a
hospital and go under a great many operations . . . which if
I do, Mr. X. will retain his interest in me, and make it possible
for me to sleep and eat some sort of food, provided too that I
return to church-going and prayer. If I don't do that, then
of course I must "go back" for I have no other means of a
livelihood. . . . I do not know if I will get the check each week
or not—for I do not intend to submit to the operations nor do
I intend to promise to go to Sunday School and Church and
that sort of thing—but I will have to begin to look about for
the possibility of making a change, for should the check not
come I would be in bad shape and since Mr. X. told me it
would be one or the other thing and I do not intend to submit,
must begin to prepare to get away—you see even when one
lives in the other world there are different classes and the
condition of my clothes would put me among different sort of
people than I used to associate with. Of course I will "hang

on" a while longer for having been out of things for so long
a time I feel like a novice and don't know just how to start
especially since I truly loathe to do it, but really Mrs. Howe
I will have to make some sort of a break for while it will as I
know full well lead to destruction, what will this life with no
friends, no interests, no comforts, no anything else that is
desirable lead me to? No self respecting person could keep on
as I have eating the bread of charity and not even feeling
very grateful for it. I am literally all run down at the heels and
walking on the bare bricks for my shoes have holes as big as
silver Dollars in them and when I contemplate the many really
necessary things I need before I "go back" I can't think how I
will get them, so I am between the Devil and the Deep Sea. I
can't stay and I can't go. I know one thing a person can always
do and that is die and yet even that takes courage which I
don't begin to possess. . . . You know I am truly grateful to you
for your honesty in admitting you understand me. I don't
think there are many who don't, only they won't.

The letters were to continue on and on and on, in mounting
suspense through the years, in stages of hard work, self-improve-
ment (fantastically apparent in the change and development of
style of writing as well as the handwriting), a move to another city,
the decision and working out of ways to help other girls in trouble,
the meeting of a Fine Man. Should she, or should she not, tell him
of her Past? She did. It made no difference. They were married.
And lived happily ever after. Being the children of the Gentle
Generation, we children were kept in a rather hazy ignorance as
to exactly what kind of "hard time" Mother's offstage friend had
had. Alas, after Mother's death, what happened to Mamie I do not
know, and feel remorseful that I do not. It is certain that as a
woman she "lived." The shape of that living was far removed from
us not only geographically but in depth of experience. It is equally
certain that in 26 Brimmer Street she also lived—as a vital and
breathing Presence.

———————◆———————

The dislocation of mood requisite for jumping from Mamie to
"Aunt Katy" is enormous. If Mamie was offstage, Aunt Katy, as

far back as my memory goes, was definitely on. If Mamie would
have felt alien to my parents' way of life, Aunt Katy was of Boston
the most Bostonian. She was, I suppose, Mother's "best" friend.
But then, if she was your friend at all, it automatically stood to
reason she was the best. She certainly was beloved in Brimmer
Street, by young and old alike. I cannot pass on without laying a
modest wreath at the feet of her bright Presence. Mother always
said that as a girl Aunt Katy looked like a daffodil. I can believe it.
Her sandy coloring dictated the yellow and tawny colors that most
became her; her small pretty head was balanced as lightly and
delicately on a long graceful neck held erect, even at ninety.

Aunt Katy Codman, née Katy Bowditch, actually wasn't my aunt
at all. Great-granddaughter of the mathematician-astronomer Nathaniel Bowditch, she was Mother's oldest friend, dating back to the
time they went to Miss Hersey's School together, at fourteen years
old, then on to Papanti's Dancing Class, to become at last members
of the "Sewing Circle" of 1888—the equivalent of being a debutante of that year. As a girl Mother used to visit the Bowditches at
Chocorua, New Hampshire. On one such visit their neighbor William James enchanted the girls at an evening party by trying to
hypnotize them. Mother said that, for her, there was no mystery at
all when one girl after another got up and followed Professor James
around the room, as she said he was simply the most attractive man
she had ever seen, and it would have been impossible *not* to follow
his piercing blue eyes! It was sort of a dictum of the Sewing Circle
that "Katy Bowditch had more lovers than any girl in her year."

Aunt Katy was aunt in both fact and fiction to hordes of loving
young people. To Nancy Hale—speaking of fictional—she is Aunt
Katy, as she is to the three dazzling daughters of Harvey Cushing,
who was the close friend and colleague of her husband, Dr. Amory
Codman. Her tragedy, however, was that she was never anybody's
mother. As Dr. Codman was one of the earliest explorers in the field
of the Roentgen ray in 1895, it is entirely possible that he paid the
price of sterility as the toll of his dangerous pioneer work. I remember his appearing in a dark room where I, as a child, was being
X-rayed by a Dr. Dodd, who loomed in the shadows, lit by the lurid
alchemistic light of the fluoroscope, wearing gray cotton gloves,

several fingers of which were empty—testifying to the price that he too had paid in early research. I believe that Amory Codman's siege of his lovely Katy had been almost as long-drawn-out an affair as Father's of Mother. The emotional—one can certainly not name it the sex—life of the girls of the Group to which Mother and Aunt Katy belonged—as opposed to that of the generation of the 1930's—was a matter of total personal reticence. Mother told me that the first inkling she got of the seriousness of her best friend's involvement was when the two girls were walking down Beacon Street together, and, meeting Amory Codman, Aunt Katy *blushed!*

Father's motives for pursuing at the start a friendship with Fanny Quincy's best friend might have been suspect but for the fact that it must have been impossible not to wish to be in Katy Bowditch's company for her own sake. There were calls, walks, and even an expedition to Bristol. One letter begins, "Dear Miss Bowditch, When young ladies that I did not know very well have sometimes asked me to dinner, they used to say, 'Mamma wants me to write etc.—or I write for Mamma to say etc. etc.' Now though my mother is near at hand at this moment, and perfectly willing to write for herself indeed anxious to make the invitation as inviting as possible, I think perhaps I can do nothing better than to tell you this, and repeat with all heartiness every word . . ." And so the friendship continued, not having to change in essence the least bit when both were married.

Aunt Katy's spirit was buoyant with that lighter-than-air quality which goes with the human being who, at no facet of her personality, is trying to impose herself on others. Her springing step reflected this spirit—a spring still further lightened by her adherence to the technique of neuromuscular coordination, discovered and practiced by the Englishman, F. M. Alexander, followed by John Dewey, Aldous Huxley, and other eminent disciples. It was characteristic of her to champion Alexander's distinctly "off-beat" work in this country, in direct opposition, as much of it was, to accepted medical tenets. But then why shouldn't the wife of Amory Codman—known as the *enfant terrible* of the Boston medical fraternity—be as off-beat as she chose? Dr. Codman's professional love was the shoulder joint; his book entitled *The Shoulder* a standard work on the subject. Father described it: "The body of the book is *on* the shoulder. The rest of it, *from* the shoulder, is of wider appeal." It is in the introduction and epilogue that the reader finds a "frank self-portraiture of an uncompromising believer in his own views, a vigorous master of his own life, a fighter who can see something of humor through hard blows given and taken, a figure of that individual quality which is believed to flourish especially in New England." The idea which made him so unpopular with his colleagues at the Massachusetts General Hospital that he resigned his position there, to found a small private hospital of his own, was simply that of the "End Result." In those days a patient was dismissed after surgery with no "follow up." Dr. Codman fought singlehandedly against the entrenched beliefs of his time, prevalent at the Harvard Medical School as well as at the Massachusetts General. Of "the harmless ridicule" he turned on his colleagues he wrote, "If I picked at all on individuals, they were then in high positions such as President Lowell, Dean Bradford, Dr. Washburn, and Richard Cabot. I doubt if their feelings were hurt or even their self-esteem." The quixotic and often tactless methods he chose for driving home his points (one was the lowering of a huge cartoon during a public meeting at which none of his colleagues showed up showing a Back Bay ostrich burying its head in the sand; another was a statement during the 1914–1918 war that more people were killed in Boston hospitals than were killed by the Germans) made even himself wonder if he was "cracked." He went to an alienist, and was told that he was sane, only to feel a little in the position of the child who prayed,

> Now I lay me down to sleep in my little bed;
> If I die before I wake, how will I know I am dead?

It is heartening to read the resolution, passed by the directors of the Massachusetts General Hospital many, many years later, after his death and sent to Aunt Katy, acknowledging the debt that they and all other hospitals owed to this valiant crusader for the reforms which today have become common practice.

Dr. Codman and Aunt Katy—so different from my parents in this respect—were very much of the out of doors. There were occasions on which we children used to spend the day, or even an occasional night, at their camp at Ponkapoag (pronounced Punkapogg) and were there introduced to "bird walks." It happened that I spent several nights at their city house, at 227 Beacon Street, the winter that *The Late George Apley* was published. Aunt Katy and Dr. Codman were plodding their way conscientiously through its pages; he extended, as was his wont, full length on the sofa in the living room while Aunt Katy read to him. Whatever inhibitions might have prevented his participating in any kind of social talk— and *some*thing most definitely did so prevent him!—they did not stand in the way of his going serenely to sleep alongside the tea table, while Aunt Katy was entertaining a guest. The fact that for years he was in almost constant and uncomplaining pain with ulcers may well have explained the general air of exhaustion he brought home with him every day, as well as the shortness of temper with which he dealt with those who stood in his way outside it. During this visit, however, when I was with them in the evenings I could see him fighting to keep awake, Aunt Katy struggling at his side in the same battle, as they faithfully slugged it out. They were reading about Mr. Apley with as faithful attention as I am sure they gave to the heroes of any of Father's biographies, following his downsittings and uprisings, including bird walks! Aunt Katy was forced, as they approached the end of the book, to the rueful admission, "We haven't come to the *funny* parts yet."

Aunt Katy, ever a fiercely loyal wife, followed her husband into the wilds on one occasion immortalized over the mantelpiece of their house in Chocorua. There is the head of a caribou, with a sign under it, SHOT BY KATHERINE B. CODMAN. One can see that the independent Katy had a heart as well as a mind of her own in the words underneath, "I shall never shoot another."

In many ways Aunt Katy seemed an odd friend for Mother. Quite possibly in later life they might not have gravitated toward each other. I don't know whether Professor Copeland was thinking of Aunt Katy when he made the charge against Mother that she picked

her friends on the same principle that Queen Elizabeth chose her
ladies in waiting, that is, that they would make her shine by comparison. In Aunt Katy's case it was emphatically true that there was
one glory of the sun, another of the moon; the friends shone in
quite different ways, though neither excelled the other in devotion.
Aunt Katy would have been the first to insist that she was not an
intellectual; she was unsophisticated, unsuspicious, with no trace
of introspection in her makeup. Her shoes were sensible for walking, her hats could have arisen nowhere but on Beacon Street, and
her clothes were tweedy. Bricks and mortar did not suit her, as
woods and woodlands did. She could be easily recognized coming
along the Esplanade by her springy step, alert carriage, and, always
in attendance like a hostage from the country where she really belonged, a "working" English setter—Prince first, then Jennie—
who attended Dr. Codman when he went shooting. No clipped
poodles or miniature or toy anything else for the Amory Codmans!
Aunt Katy's house was Spartan and sparse in its fittings. There
were never any curtains in her bow window at 227 Beacon Street.
She looked out at the world as fresh and direct and clear as the
world could look in upon her. Straw matting on the bedroom floors
upstairs, brass bedsteads, and china washstands in the corner of the
rooms remained to the last.

Aunt Katy was the one privileged (or underprivileged?) friend
of Mother's who was allowed across the threshold of 26 Brimmer
Street on our nurse's day out. She loved children as children and,
knowing what she was getting into, was not shooed away like other
adults who were only being polite (at least so Mother believed!)
when they claimed they just loved "to see the children." I think
one of my very earliest memories of Aunt Katy must be of the day
when she sat on the sofa in Mother's bedroom and, spiritually, held
her hand because Mark had come down with diphtheria. Our nurse,
who had it much more severely, had been borne away that morning
on a stretcher to the hospital, and now, across the hall, they were
hanging up a sheet outside of Mark's room, to be kept dripping wet
with some strong-smelling disinfectant. Mother exploded into Aunt
Katy's loving ear, "That poor *lamb!*" knowing the long period of

isolation he was in for. Mother herself continued to see him once a day, allowed to go into his room wearing a mask and other mysterious garments which she shed before coming near the rest of us.

Aunt Katy was as deliciously free of ego as anyone I have ever known. This was all the more remarkable as obviously the greatest gift with which the Lord had endowed her was a tender maternal instinct. With this instinct dammed at the source it would have been understandable had there been some rough edges somewhere. Instead, the form of compensation for the motherhood denied her— and poignantly admitted to as such by Aunt Katy herself—was a flinging of herself into a variety of Causes. To glance over the list of Causes to which Aunt Katy contributed financially—filling pages, recorded in her own clear handwriting, of the little book that contained addresses and telephone numbers—is to gain further insight into her open heart and open mind (the latter so open that it caused a close relative to expostulate more than once, "My dear Katy, you are in the infancy of thought").

Am. League to Ab. C.P. leads off the list, reflecting the tender heart that shrank from committing capital punishment even on a caribou. In her gifts to Defenders of Fur Bearers, the American Forestry Association, the Audubon Society, the Arnold Arboretum, the Farm and Garden Association, and Wild Life one saw Aunt Katy against a background of nature. The American Rheumatism Foundation, the American Cancer Society, the Museum of Science, and the Seeing Eye were the concern of a conscientious doctor's wife. A sweep as large as the world included the International Rescue Committee, Near East Foundation, Spanish Refugee Aid, International Friendship League, and the American Association for the United Nations. No fellow human creature should be denied his rights so long as Aunt Katy was there to defend him through the American Civil Liberties Union, Indian Rights, Workers Defense League, the United Negro College Fund, or the United Prison Association. Save the Redwoods? Turn to Aunt Katy! Save the Children? Turn to her again! Her deep commitment over the years to the work of the Frontier Nursing Service, along with her friend

Mary Beard, and her position as the Boston head of the Visiting Nurse Association involved much more than financial support.

Aunt Katy was a close friend of Mrs. Glendower Evans, the champion of Sacco and Vanzetti, and came to know the two men as well as their wives, visiting them, and writing to them in prison. She added the perfect, unconscious touch to her own portrait when she told me she was leaving a sum of money in her will to be administered by a favorite niece, giving each year a hundred dollars to *any unpopular cause* that her niece decided would be one Aunt Katy might have liked to help! (In point of fact this characteristic impulse was never legally executed.) A close friend, who seemed wonderfully appropriate to the Codman ménage, under whose roof she spent her winters, was Dr. Alice Hamilton, first woman on the faculty of the Harvard Medical School and herself an early crusader in bringing the benefits of medical research and care to factory workers suffering from occupational ills.

The New England flavor of Whittier's lines read at the memorial service for Aunt Katy carry her purity of essence:

> For all her quiet life flowed on
> As meadow streamlets flow
> Where fresher green reveals alone
> The noiseless way they go.

> . . . Her path shall brighten more and more
> Unto the perfect day;
> She cannot fail of peace who bore
> Such peace with her away.

> . . . She kept her line of rectitude
> With love's unconscious ease;
> Her kindly instincts understood
> All gentle courtesies.

Also New England was the comment of her friend—and Father's dear friend, too—Abigail Adams Homans when she said tenderly, "Katy was a lovely feller."

9

ALL THE DEAR PEOPLE

AT AN EVENING PARTY IN BOSTON, within earshot of Father, the saintly and sentimental Miss Fanny Morse surveyed the room full of her closest friends—most of them cousins—and exclaimed, "How lovely! All the dear people are here tonight!" Thereafter, for my parents, a clearly identifiable segment of old Boston families became "All the Dear People."

As I look back it seems extraordinary that Father could adapt to this particular segment, and that they could accept him, as effortlessly as seemed to happen on both sides. In writing of Bristol he once observed that it had never been a place in which Dickens's "Society for the Prevention of Everything" would have found a foothold. Father himself, although "liberal" in general outlook, was no reformer, let alone crusader. All the Dear People were definitely concerned with improving the world. They were all emphatically Long-Tailed, made up of Boston's dowdiest, goodest, oldest (and richest) families. In recent days the country has witnessed one of this breed—the mother of a governor of Massachusetts—ready, willing, and able to go to jail for her do-good and do-*right* beliefs. My brother Mark, who went on the Civil Rights March on Washington in the summer of '63 wrote me of finding another family friend, approaching her eightieth birthday, as a fellow marcher. She wrote to Mark afterwards that it had been a surprise to her to find that two of her grandchildren had also come along on this "celestial picnic" which had given her one of the happiest days

[164]

of her life. Mark's word from home to me in New York was, "This may give you some reassurance that they still turn out the old-fashioned model in these parts. Do you remember Mrs. X?—big chin, big heart, dead husband, dead daughter. But she is still cooking with gas."

All the Dear People included a smattering drawn from the Jackson, Putnam, Lee, Cabot, Lyman, Paine, Curtis, Coolidge, Codman, and Lowell families, all thoroughly inbred and crossbred. Father was not far wrong when he sang to their own delight at one of their gatherings his paraphrase of a favorite Gilbert and Sullivan lyric, "The Paine that is all but a Lyman shall change To the Lyman that's all but a Paine." There were plenty of "other" Cabots, Lowells, Codmans, etc., who were not in this little coterie I have in mind, for the simple reason that being definitely Short-Tailed they did not wish to be. The line of demarkation could, and often did, run right down the middle of an immediate family. I have known more than one Short-Tailed brother of a Long-Tailed sister: he a member of the Porcellian Club—handsome, well turned out, hunting, shooting, and drinking, at ease with attractive women as well as men, and at home in a world of fashion far afield from Boston— while she, the sister, dowdy and "do-goody," remained touchingly ill at ease anywhere removed from the little corner of Boston or its environs in which she felt as secure as she was ever to feel any- where. One thing that All the Dear People had in common was the possession of large inherited fortunes, though to mention money would have made them cringe with embarrassment. Actually they were embarrassed with most people, except one another. The Dear People put the emphasis on the simple life, wherever they lived. "Dressing up" was an unpardonable sin. In summer, sneakers, washed-out khaki, and cotton or denim were worn in the evening, as by day. In winter one wore what one *had*, keeping a "best" dress for—well, for that occasion which perhaps never came. One didn't wear it traveling, for fear of "sitting it out." But, be it remembered, whatever the Dear People spent money on, it was not on status symbols. If, to paraphrase Oscar Wilde, they knew the price of everything they also knew not only value but values. Nobly generous toward furthering great philanthropic enterprises, which did far more toward reforming the status quo than preserving it, they did so, more often than not, anonymously. The women would have thought it a sin to buy a bottle of perfume, or a pretty hat, or even to take a taxi. A friend of Mother's, as a girl, indulged herself in a beautiful Paris "costume"—both hat and dress a becoming mauve. At a Boston party a friend exclaimed on seeing her, "How well your hat and dress match!" From the sidelines of onlooking mothers came the audible comment, "*Too well.*" Plain living and high thinking were no catchwords.

If my parents yielded to the temptation of smiling (one could do nothing so gross as laugh) at the unflickering sweetness and light of Miss Frances Rollins Morse, it was obvious, all the same, that she was Somebody whom it was not possible to dismiss with that smile. William James wrote many of his best letters to her and was grateful to receive hers in return ("They are so easy, the facts are so much the immediate out-bubblings of the moment, and the delicious philosophical reflexions so much like the spontaneous breathings of the soul, that the *effort* is manifestly at the zero-point"). His brother Henry also was one of her correspondents, as were the Holmeses, father and son, Professor Child, and Henry Cabot Lodge. Joseph Lee, one of her admiring cousins, wrote of her, "She was one of those inexorable gentle people whose gentleness is simply one more instance of their obstinacy." Henry James had already his model for Miss Birdseye, but surely he would have been able to touch with his wand of satire that "little group"—mostly cousins—which Mr. Lee so unsatirically extolled. Dr. Charles Putnam, Dr. James Putnam, Miss Marian Jackson, and Miss Morse herself were "running to and fro and seeing one another. . . . This family party on Marlborough Street . . . when they met, nine times out of ten, were discussing the welfare of their city. . . . You cannot overestimate the seriousness with which they took their task." When I spoke recently to a friend of Father's about this little band of Inner Bostonians he said, "You're talking about the people who ran Harvard College." And another friend described them as "the people who ran all the Boston charities." It was Miss

Fanny Morse who founded the organization which came to be known
as the Associated Charities.

The real heartland of the Dear People lay on Beacon Hill. One has
today to walk only a few steps from the State House, down the Hill
on Mt. Vernon Street, to see that All the Dear People once walked
that way. True, and thank God, the large double house and two of
the Misses Curtis still remain. Otherwise there are brass name
plates on the doors which might have been affixed by Aunt Katy
herself: World Peace Foundation, General Theological Library,
Massachusetts Society for the Prevention of Cruelty to Children,
United Prison Association of Massachusetts, and International
Friendship League.

The Dear People were behind many more efforts toward "Good"
than the specific philanthropies that fell under that heading. Take
the firm of Moors and Cabot, Stockbrokers. Though Charles Mills
Cabot died before Father came to know him as well as he knew his
partner, John Moors, the luster of his name should not be allowed
to tarnish. It is hard today to wring a tear from the average American on the plight of the workers for the United States Steel Corporation but when in 1910 "Charlie" Cabot appeared before the
chairman of the U.S. Steel Corporation and introduced himself "as
a damnfool small stockholder" he was making history. A New
England conscience had troubled him into inquiring into the working conditions of the laborers in the company: what more natural
than that he should feel a sense of responsibility toward the industry from which he drew his income? he argued. Having so
argued, he started an investigation—at his own expense. What he
found horrified him. Feeling that his fellow stockholders would
likewise be horrified, he requested of the corporation a list of their
names. When it was denied he brought suit against the company.
Before the suit was decided, a compromise was effected whereby a
digest of his report was mailed to fifteen thousand stockholders, at
Cabot's expense. His aim—how modest it sounds today!—was to
achieve for the workers a one-day-of-rest-in-seven schedule, and the
elimination of a twelve-hour day. He did not live to see the reforms
he set in motion, but his partner John Moors lived on to fight, if

not that particular good fight, many others. It was John Moors who headed the Red Cross relief work for the sufferers from the Salem Fire as from the Halifax, Nova Scotia, disaster. It was he, to the outrage of many of the more fire-eating elements in the community, who started relief for starving German children after the war. He and Father were in constant communion on the subject of their hero Woodrow Wilson.

I have already mentioned Judge Frederick Cabot and the Children's Court; There would have been no Massachusetts General Hospital as it is today without Jackson and Putnam doctors. The cause of the Negro was covered by one Miss Curtis, while another took on the Boston School Committee; and it is to Mr. Joseph Lee that not only Boston's slum children owe their playgrounds, but the whole playground movement in America owes its initial impetus. Supporting, or overarching, all these endeavors were the everlasting arms of Harvard. When Father was elected in 1924 to serve for his first of two six-year terms on the Harvard Board of Overseers he found many of the Dear People among his colleagues. To none of them would the story have sounded strange of the caller who, ringing the telephone of President Lowell's house in Cambridge, asked, "Is the President at home?" to be answered, "No, he's in Washington, seeing Mr. Taft."

It was ironic that in our family it was Father, and not Mother, who seemed to feel at home with such a purely Bostonian phenomenon as All the Dear People. When I say "at home" I am probably stretching it a little. Perhaps it was simply that, with Bristol in his blood, Father was not put off by large family groups. In any event he seemed more able to take in stride, and with good-natured amusement, the group gatherings, in all their breezy self-satisfaction, which rubbed Mother the wrong way. For a fellow Bostonian— I can speak here much more as Mother's child than as Father's —there is something embarrassing, something that makes the toes curl and that sets the teeth on edge, about a bounciness put on to cover up a social awkwardness that shows itself often as more childish than childlike. Like my brother Mark, I hate pleasure—at least if it is of the variety that expresses itself at a party that ends up with "butter on the ceiling." It is the same curse of the New England race—shyness—merely taking another form; and if one's own psyche bears the scars of the same scourge one is particularly sensitive to its many forms in others. Father, blissfully free of it, could simply—"relax and enjoy it." And yet I cannot advocate the other end of the New England spectrum either.

The father of a family we knew well was all but inarticulate in his Cal Coolidge-like taciturnity, a trait he had handed on to his equally inhibited children. On his deathbed he raised his head from the pillow, as his family stood around him, and exhorted them, in substance, "Don't make the dreadful mistake in your lives that I have made in mine. *Show* your emotions, *express* your feelings! Don't be afraid to let people see that you have them," and sank back on his pillow to die. His daughter, dry-eyed, stiff-upper-lipped, surveyed such an unprecedented bursting of the dam of reticence and whispered to another member of the family at her side, "Pa's nuts."

Father didn't seem to let the plain living of the Dear People worry him any more than he did either their high thinking or their social awkwardness. Again speaking as a fellow Bostonian, I suggest that some of their attitudes spring not so much from a vague and charming otherworldliness as from some basic temperamental lack. Whether this deficiency is glandular or lies in the very blood stream, it seems symptomatic of an often inbred strain that is running thin. The broad social concern of the Dear People was rooted in a sublime unawareness of Social distinctions of any kind. If discrimination with a capital *D* was unknown to them, then so was discrimination with a small *d*. There was a sense that had simply been bred out of them. They were blandly unsophisticated.

During Father's Brimmer Street years one water hole at which the genus Dear People gathered, in its most characteristic habitat group formation, was the Baldpate Inn in Georgetown, Massachusetts. Thither they repaired, for several weekends during the winter—in large family groups, including children, and if memory serves, even including the Brimmer Street trio on at least one occasion.

The Dear People were all happier out of doors than in. By day they skated energetically or coasted "belly bumps." I have the dim recollection of making the top, and smallest, part of a sandwich containing President Lowell as base and Mrs. Lowell as filling. In the evening they acted charades or Dumb Crambo or sang—with Father at the piano—to their general delight. All the Dear People were irrepressibly complacent. Everything was for the best in the best of all possible worlds, including the Evil it contained, because without the Evil what justification in life could there be for those determined to do Good?

Among this little ingrown group of devoted intimates it is teasing to wonder what suppressed frustrations or jealousies, if any, what unreciprocated stirrings of love might have smoldered beneath the stout winter woolens. The beaming smiles never left the rosy scrubbed faces of both sexes. Judge Cabot remained a handsome bachelor to the last, although I picked up from my parents the fact that he caused many heart flutterings. Actually these house parties were organized by Miss Fanny Curtis around the focal figure of President Lowell. He joined in at least one of the pencil-and-paper games in the evening. One alumna of those house parties recalls playing "Dictation." She was mortified to have to admit before the assembled company that she had misspelled four words until Lawrence Lowell confessed to nineteen misspelled, saying cheerfully that he had accepted long ago the fact that the Lord obviously never intended him to be able to spell. It is no wonder that he preferred to treat his fellow guests rather more as though they were members of the Harvard Corporation, which, in fact, some of the men invariably were. He always shared with them some up-to-the-minute inside "dope" concerning the workings of the University, and in turn answered questions. What, for instance, was he going to do about Harold Laski's political beliefs? The answer was simple, delivered to the Harvard Corporation, "If you ask for Laski's resignation you will get mine with it." Perhaps suggestions were called for as to some particularly suitable candidate for an honorary degree at Commencement—always a fascinating topic for speculation among the Dear People. Mother finally gave up even the pre tense of enjoyment of the house parties, and ended by encouraging Father to go without her. The excuse given to the Dear People was that she had lost her galoshes!

As so many of those Dear People lived on Beacon Hill, it is natural for me to evoke them in that setting—and on Christmas Eve, the night of nights for that corner of the world. Those were the days when the Hill was still a village, and "everybody" knew "everybody." Dr. Richard Cabot, his head with its characteristic tilt to one side, with a tuning fork in his hand, would lead his own group of singers, who had been rehearsing for weeks for this their finest hour. As I recall it, Father did not sing "under" Dr. Cabot but was part of a group that rehearsed in the tiny house of Miss Minns in Acorn Street. The shades of the old brick houses were all up, there were candles with their little tongues of flame in the windows, softly highlighting the pools of quiet and seclusion of the rooms within. If the Long-Tailed Bostonians were dowdy not only because they thought it more important to clothe the needy than themselves but because they did not know good-looking clothes when they saw them, their houses, like their gardens in the country, told a different story. There were taste and flair and, inevitably through such a plethora of inherited possessions, inherent beauty in the objects themselves. Father, who loved choral singing the year through, and loved Christmas even more, participated with gusto, and of course we trailed around in his wake. Today the sole survivors of the Long-Tailed Dear People are the bell-ringing Shurcliff family, who stand in a solid family group on a seething street corner of rowdy revelers with sublime unconsciousness, their hands held aloft, each with the bell ready to be rung on cue with a flick of the wrist. With breath-taking skill and precision "still their heavenly music floats o'er all the weary world."

Mr. Arthur Shurcliff, an architect and the father of the family, expressed his deep and observant love of nature in a modest and enchanting volume entitled *A Man Walks the Earth,* illustrated with reproductions of his own drawings and paintings. Indeed such a knowledgeable kinship with nature was typical of All the Dear People. Father, by contrast, was quick with an apt quotation—

Annihilating all that's made
Into a green thought,
In a green shade

—but he rarely was silent long enough to let Nature speak to him through her creatures who were not human beings. It may be said of All the Dear People that, if they were a little awkward in a strange drawing room or tongue-tied in an alien language, they were often at home in field, forest, or jungle. If they frequently were not men and women of the "world," they were attuned to the larger rhythms of the universe.

To return to the Shurcliffs—via those who are "attuned"—I have often been struck by the contrasting traits of those Boston families who, on one hand, would be too shy to ask the way on a city street, and yet at the same time, safe under the sheltering security of a family chorus in a public place, uninvited and perhaps even unappreciated, would tune up happily to disturb the peace. I remember having tea at an inn in Concord with a band of young Lowells under the wing of Mr. Thomas Surette of the Concord Summer School of Music, and I—young and self-conscious at the time—wanting to crawl under something when in a clear hum he gave them the pitch and the key—*one, three, five, eight*—and they were off on "Lo, How a Rose E'er Blooming," then a snatch of the Brahms *Requiem* or a Bach chorale. The happy Boston family choristers whom I have known have never been troubled by squeamishness over injecting a piece of "sacred" music into secular surroundings. Freethinkers all, words and subject couldn't matter less; the music alone was sacred.

Another gathering ground—indeed it might be more accurate to call it a breeding ground—of the Dear People was "the Putnam Camp." In a uniquely beautiful spot in Keene Valley, in the Adirondack Mountains, in the 1880's a handful of plain-living and high-thinking Bostonians and Cantabrigians—William James among them—bought a piece of land on the edge of the deep woods. On this land stood a modest native wooden structure called the "Shanty." The Shanty was to remain the nucleus of a settlement which through the years grew to include among an assortment of dormitories and gathering places, the "Coop," the "Stoop," the "Pen," the "Parents' Assistant," and others. Miss Lizzie Putnam, sister of two founding Putnam brothers—doctors both—laid down the policy which was to make of the Putnam Camp the holiday Mecca of this special group of Inner Bostonians. Although Miss Putnam's activities in behalf of the public weal were broad-based enough to include reform schools and bettering the lot of "wayward girls," at the camp she took steps to see that no guest be so wayward as to roam off the reservation limited to the Dear People. The yardstick she used in inviting some twenty or thirty young people to make up a house party was simply that "no one should be invited whom you would not want your son or daughter to marry." A glossary of maiden and married names, written on the backs of two photographs of the period taken at the Putnam Camp, bears witness to the success of her plan: Ella Lyman (Mrs. Richard Cabot), Anne Cabot (Mrs. R. T. Paine), Anne Codman (Mrs. Henry B. Cabot), Susan C. Cabot (Mrs. Arthur Lyman) Margaret C. Cabot (Mrs. Joseph Lee). Against the background of woods magical enough for the Forest of Arden, including a mountain brook which gurgled through the encampment, it is small wonder that cousins who were all but brothers should change into husbands who were—well, at least incestuously close. When Mark and I were eleven and twelve years old Mother and Father took us there one summer. Then, due to a death or some adult catastrophe which I have forgotten, they had to leave, and left us to the kindly—and bouncy—Bostonians.

The experience still stands out in sharp outline. There was the icy deliciousness of a brook, with its swimming pool segregated for each sex, without benefit of bathing suit, walled off behind a barrier of canvas. There were mountains to climb. Then, too, life was not lived in isolation, as it was with us at home, but in the heart of a jolly—and *how* jolly!—group. Seated in a semicircle about a campfire at night—some of the Dear People clad in costumes of other lands—songs, anecdotes, and "stunts" were in order. Those per-

forming arts are just over the horizon of my memory, but one of the
Putnam Campers of early days has left a record of themselves at
play:

> How I have been acting at breakfast today,—it makes me
> blush to think of it, —fighting over griddle cakes, egging on
> Ethel to throw potatoes at Mr. Lyman, etc. . . . Two days ago
> Dr. Bowditch took us a walk such as you have never taken.
> We had to go on our hands and knees a good deal of the way.
> It was perfectly splendid fun. I simply delighted in it and
> almost stood on my head mentally as well as physically. . . .
> Last night we grew perfectly rampant sitting round the camp-
> fire. The crowd began singing quietly, and A. Lyman with
> pipe and slouch hat reclined in silence, apart from the others.
> Suddenly he jumped up, seized a burning shingle with which
> he beat time, and shouted a chorus from Tannhäuser. That was
> the end of Peace. A full orchestra was formed, and "George,"
> who remarked at intervals that he was getting into the spirit
> of the occasion and then lit another cigarette, was called on
> by A. Lyman to sing all Wagner,—which he did with great
> vim. Beethoven's symphonies, and other classical music fol-
> lowed, excitement waxed high, and A. Lyman and Mr. Bur-
> rage only increased their shouts and enthusiasm.

More muted ghosts undoubtedly still haunted the pine forests:
reverberations of philosophical discussions (Dr. James Putnam and
Dr. Bowditch discussing psychical research in its relation to William James and his "tiresome" Mrs. Piper), faint echoes of faint
proposals of marriage (if hand-me-down stories were to be believed,
some of them even emanating from the hopeful female to the elusive male) hung in the still mountain air, to be picked up by the
proper psychic antenna. It was not hard to believe that James's
great friends Josiah Royce and Richard Hodgson had been guests
here, as had Dr. Osler and James Bryce; it is much harder to
envisage Sigmund Freud and Carl Jung among the genus Bouncy
Bostonians. It is fascinating to wonder what mysteries of the New
England psyche were penetrated or remained unplumbed by either
or both of these explorers into the hinterlands of personality. If
either guest was late arriving in the dining room for a meal he

would have had brought down on his head the lusty singing of
"Popsy Wopsy."

> Little Popsy Wopsy, Chickabiddy Chum,
> He shall have a pysie-wysie and a sugar plum,
> He shall yidey-pidey in a coachy-woachy too,
> All ayound the parky-warky
> With a cockle-doodle-doo!

My own memory which serves as the blackout picture of the Putnam
Camp is seeing them lined up, as they always did, to speed a parting
guest, like the front row of a chorus, with their arms over each
others' shoulders. I see with special clarity Dr. and Mrs. James
Putnam (Marion Cabot)—she, white-haired, he, white-bearded,
in Tyrolean costume—kicking up their legs diagonally across their
knees, and singing, "We'll dance like a fairy, and sing like a bird,
and so while the hours away!"

I cannot let this vision serve as the final tableau before the curtain is lowered on All the Dear People. I must try to evoke the
flavor of one more clutch (although clan is the literally appropriate
word) of them—the Long-Tailed Forbeses. Although in winter most
of them lived on Milton Hill, twelve miles from Boston, the Forbes
fortune (amassed in the nineteenth century through railroads by
John Murray Forbes, whose son married Emerson's daughter)
was managed from State Street in Boston. Father crossed the paths
of the Forbes men at many points. It was, however, chiefly on the
beautiful island of Naushon—some seven miles of woods and fields,
beaches and inlets just offshore from Woods Hole—that the clan
carried on its traditions, rituals, ceremonies, and feast days as their
Highland chieftain forefathers must have done in Scotland.

Although the Long-Tailed Forbeses could certainly be numbered
among All the Dear People they had marked distinctions of their
own. The mere fact of *place* was one. Naushon Island offered a backdrop for their family activities and characteristics which would be
hard to duplicate anywhere in American life. The one unmentioned
and unmentionable guest among them all—and yet omnipresent—
was $. Although they all adhered to plain living and high thinking

and were on the side of the angels—how could they be on any other,
with Grandfather Emerson's blood in their veins?—still they were
less definitely reformers and crusaders than many others among the
Dear People. Father's particular friends in his generation were
two brothers. One, William Cameron Forbes, one-time Governor
General of the Philippines and American Ambassador to Japan, a
lifelong bachelor, was Uncle or Cousin "Cam" to generations of
young Forbeses. Father's other friend was Edward Forbes, director
of the Fogg Art Museum, whose features are the most Emersonian
of the whole clan. There seemed to go with those features in all of
the family who bore them not only a placidity of temperament but
a benign acceptance of the inbreeding with which Naushon
abounded. Indeed such a recognizable type has emerged that a
stranger arriving on the island for the first time has difficulty in
making out any individual name, and gets small help from his hosts
who tell him when he asks, "Who is that sweet-looking girl?"
"That's Ellen's Amelia," and on asking the same question about
another pretty girl is told, "That's Amelia's Ellen."

I remember seeing Mr. Edward Forbes wander into a formal
wedding in Milton, with disheveled hair and mud on his heavy
boots, and a fading bunch of wild flowers in his hand, with that
vague, seraphic, Emersonian look of another world which made one
wonder if he himself was quite sure he was not settling down onto a
log stump instead of a pew of an Episcopal church. And yet this
same dreamer as a young man had been so impressed by the potential value to Harvard College of the property along the Charles
River that, when he could get none of the authorities to listen to
him, raised the money, much of it, one suspects, out of his own
obviously deep pocket, and presented the land to the University. It
is on this property that today some of Harvard's houses stand.
Mr. Forbes, at Naushon parties, accompanying himself with a
guitar, seems to have a boundless supply of old songs. At more than
ninety today he admits that in a recent illness, to pass the time, he
sang words and music to himself, interested to see how long he
could keep on going, and did so for nine hours, when he fell asleep.

The rules and regulations in force in the ugly Victorian pile

from which "Cousin Cam" reigned, and where Father used to stay,
had been laid down by Emerson's daughter. Smoking was allowed in
only one room, cocktails were never served, and wine only at a
Hunt Dinner. On that occasion even the ban on cocktails was lifted.
After the first one downed came the toast, introduced by "Charlie"
Coolidge, "Thank God I feel more like I do now than I did a while
ago!"

One Naushon ritual is the "sheeping"—which occurs both in th
spring and in the fall. At those times the whole island is "driven"·
and the sheep brought into a pen. Until about 1940 the drive was
done on horseback; now there are more "footmen" than horse-
men. With so many deer on the island to be thinned out before
winter, the high point of the year, however, is the Hunt, rounded
off with the Hunt Dinner. Its ritual includes singing, the recital of
verses, and the reading of a passage of a hundred years before from
the "Island Book." As one turns the pages of this book—vintage
American—a unique door swings open. A non-Forbes, who has been
generously offered a peek inside its pile of volumes finds it guarded
in the inner sanctum sanctorum of the office of J. M. Forbes and
Company opposite the old State House in Boston. Jarndyce and
Jarndyce were never housed in a dustier, fustier, less ostentatious
setting. In fact the whole effect is so understated, so noncom-
mittal, that one feels there must be a catch somewhere. Are
the old John Murray Forbes moneybags stuffed away under a
loose plank? A Forbes emerges from his modest cubicle, his Cabot
mother's rosy cheeks still fresh in spite of his surroundings. One
exclaims how different it all looks from a New York office. His
comment is succinctly made: "They've got a lot of plush down
there. We don't need it." He disappears into the recesses, where
the right touch is applied; a vault opens, and out comes the mound
of volumes making up the Island Book.

In it are preserved autographs, drawings, prose, and numberless
rhymes and jingles set down by the stream of visitors, entertained
by hospitable Forbeses, since Washington Irving was among the
earliest. Barrett Wendell once said that the nineteenth-century
Boston custom of celebrating social and civic events in verse "has

probably produced an amount of ephemeral metrical composition, sometimes avowed doggerel, sometimes aspiring to be poetry, more than equal in bulk to the entire lyric and dramatic poetry of Elizabethan England.'' The Island Book of Naushon contains a giant's share of that output. Many of Father's own efforts are there along with those of his masters, surely the ''happiest in expression of them all Oliver Wendell Holmes.'' The variety of contributors to the volumes is pellucidly Forbesian, which is to say pellucidly literal-minded. Many of Father's Gentle American outdoor friends appeared to share an affinity for unadorned statistics. Forbeses liked to measure the girth of their trees; Putnam Campers, the distance between two points on their walks and climbs; Father's friend Mr. Allston Burr, with whom he went on a trip to Jamaica, recorded in a little pocket notebook the number of paces of the hotel swimming pool, and the time of departure for and return from any expedition during their stay. For what *reason* he recorded these statistics Father was never to discover.

In the Island Book each contributor, regardless of relative merit or fame, is immortalized lovingly, seriously, and impartially. There are lines wrung from the heart of a four-and-three-quarters (!) year-old little Forbes girl:

> The summer days are passing, passing
> The summer days are far away
> I feel so sorry that we've got to go.
> We can't pack the sea
> We can't pack the house
> And we can't pack the clouds
> But we can come back next summer.

There are also lines from Ralph Waldo Emerson, and these from Ogden Nash:

> I could go on and on
> About Naushon
> But it would take the stylus of a Diogenes
> To do justice to the gratitude felt toward the Governor
>   by myself, my wife,
> And my two rightfully ecstatic progenies.

The Book records a dinner on July 27, 1941, in honor of the captain and navigating officers of the British battleship *Rodney*, which had played a major part in running down and sinking the German battleship *Bismarck*, with the same emphasis that it records "Ralph's Bird List." "The Thirty Mile Ride" and the "Lily Lock" known to the *Brushwood Boy* were no more magical than are the familiar and loved "The Siamese Twins" on "Glen Elvo Path," "Don's Hill," "Ram Cat Alley," or "Beetle Gate Wall" to the Forbes clan.

They were as out-of-door oriented and as energetic as the rest of the Dear People but perhaps they indulged in their sports with a little more sweep (or is "sweep" only a circumlocution for money?). Mr. Edward Forbes, at ninety, excused himself to a lady for not getting out of his chair as he admitted he was rather tired, having just come in from playing polo. Governor Forbes had in his winter house at Norwood, Massachusetts, what he called his "pony parlor" for his favorite polo pony. He composed the epitaph for one of his beloved Naushon horses:

> Leap Year
> Lies here
> Sans fear
> Sans peer

Indeed the listing of Forbes horses, through the generations, is as dear to a Forbes heart as listing relatives is supposed to be to most Bostonians: Katydid, Peg, Greylock, Countess, Zita, Iolanthe, etc. Perhaps there is as much pietistic fervor for the memory of boats the family has owned and sailed. As Naushon has been dotted with other Forbeses and Emersons of succeeding generations, so have the Buzzard's Bay waters been dotted by the shapes of the *Merlin*, the *Azalea*, the *Kalinga*, the *Black Duck*, and countless schooners, yawls, ketches, cutters, sloops, and catboats, in addition to the *Puritan* and the *Volunteer*, bought by John Murray Forbes from the syndicate of which he had been a part, after their victories as Cup Defenders.

One can only surmise what future Forbeses will think, as their history books tell them what the autumn of 1939 brought to Europe

and the world, to read an entry at that time which reveals Father
playing his role, along with the other insulated innocents.

At the Hunt Dinner in 1939 we were privileged to have as
distinguished guest Mark Howe, the poet laureate of the
Tavern Club, known for his standard biographies, felicitous
verses and delightful singing. In his repertory are numbers
of Gilbert and Sullivan's masterpieces which he sings to his
own accompaniment. As the interpreter and student of Oliver
Wendell Holmes he had delved delightedly into the early
Naushon records. Examination of early records show that
Holmes's song "No More the Summer Floweret Charms" was
written to be sung by himself to the tune of Jock O'Hazledean.
Mark Howe is also authority for the fact that Dr. Holmes who
was very short was lifted to the table to sing his hunt songs.
For two consecutive years now Mark has delighted guests at
the annual hunt dinner by singing Holmes's Hunt songs.

The one most in favor at the feasts was:

> You sportsmen of New England
> Who bear the rusty guns
> Your fathers shot the redcoats with
> And left them to their sons
> With all your firelocks blaze away
> Before the deer are gone
> As you aim
> At the game
> In the woods of old Naushon!

The account continues:

This year, on the centenary of the original delivery of one,
Mark, in singing Ye Hunters of New England to the tune of
"Ye Mariners of England" added this new verse:

> One hundred years have vanished
> Since first this song was sung
> And Old Naushon is older
> But never yet more young
> While youth by years unmeasured
> Still lives in Cameron

Every guest
Still is blest
On the shores of Young Naushon
Where the host is youngest of them all
On the shores of Young Naushon!

And in the fall of 1964—with the battle for racial justice still not won—it is moving to learn the fate of the Beau Sabreur of the Lowell family, in a none-too-legible Victorian handwriting:

On the 20th of October 1864 our Flag was hoisted on the new hickory staff in honor of Sherman's victory of the day before which was kindly announced to us by Mr. Richards on the American telegraph Co. We little knew then how dear the victory had cost—but going up the next day on the car we learned that Charles Lowell had fallen in the final victorious charge—after having been wounded in the early part of the day and refusing to leave the field—: When he mounted for the final grand charge he was unable to give his orders aloud, but nevertheless charged at the head of his Brigade. He lived a few hours—fully conscious and able to send messages to his friends and family and to arrange many business affairs with his usual clearness. And so fell the young and beautiful and brave. First in college, first everywhere, first in the deadly charge!

Among the list of distinguished visitors through the years—Presidents (both Roosevelts), the Crown Prince of Japan, General George Marshall—are names quite as modest as mine as a schoolgirl in the 1920's. The occasion of my presence was the dedication of a tree in honor of General James J. Harbord. With that Forbesian imperturbability in the presence of rags or riches, enthusiasm or boredom, the children of the island presented a pageant for the delectation of General Pershing, who was on hand to witness this tribute to his AEF Chief of Staff. As I recall it, the theme was simply America's entry into World War I. There was a pack of Forbes boys, who went on all fours, submerged in heavy gray camping blankets clasped with safety pins, representing the Dogs of War. My role was—the South. My one speech, "We are all, all with you!"

Is it any wonder that Father, with his interest in New England's
past, with his inbred Bristol love of the sea, with his penchant for
"occasional" versification, his pleasure in family singing—let
alone a natural inclination toward enjoying meeting new and interesting people, of whom there were always at least a few under the
roof of the Mansion House (he particularly enjoyed an occasion
when Harold Nicolson was a fellow guest)—is it any wonder that
his visits to Naushon were something quite special, as they must
always be, to any guest of the Forbes family?

It was difficult (for many of Governor Forbes's family and
friends it was impossible) to see any excuse or excuses for the visit
he paid to Spain, along with Mr. Ellery Sedgwick, as the guest of
Generalissimo Franco in 1938. Mr. Sedgwick expressed his own
feelings when he wrote, on the publication of Father's autobiography in 1941, "I who once rejoiced in 'liberalism' have learned with
bitterness that it has lost, utterly lost, its old beneficent quality and
significance and has made our United States a congeries of selfish
groups that have no national will, no national patriotism, and no
national sense." I do not know what were Mr. Forbes's rationaliza-
tions.

Here is Father's dearly loved and tenderly loving friend, the
artist Charles Hopkinson—of the same "liberal" stamp as Father
himself—making his effort to cling to all that he could still love in
his old Forbes friend:

> I was asked to go down to Naushon to help celebrate Ed-
> ward's 75th birthday last Friday, so down I went and my
> heart was warmed by Cam's hearty and affectionate welcome,
> sitting there in his chair where he has to stay most of the time.
> There was a characteristically Forbesian "play" with the
> delightful singing of verses to an old tune that Elinor [Mrs.
> Hopkinson] had brought back from Naushon forty years ago,
> and a charming atmosphere of innocence and good. I forgave
> Cam some amazing inconsistencies. At breakfast Sunday morn-
> ing he told us all that with the help of the Germans and the
> Italians Franco was fighting for civilization and twenty min-
> utes afterwards was telling me that Hitler deserved the epithet

of *"Fiend"* more than anyone ever on earth! So when I left I practically embraced him with a very warm feeling of friendship for he has, as you know well, a gallant side and he is a Forbes after all.

Father himself was entirely out of sympathy with his friend's political proclivity but he, like Mr. Hopkinson, found much to be fond of in Cam Forbes. Chiefly, for him, the image that outshone all the others was the childless old gentleman who loved and was beloved by the swarming brood of oncoming little Forbeses that surrounded him. As "the Governor" drove about the sandy roads of the island behind his pair of Toronto mares to wait while a little great-great-nephew would hop out to open a gate for him to pass, the old gentleman would bow respectfully from his seat aloft, saying, "As a gate-opener you have few superiors and no equals."

Today there is no "Master of Naushon." The Mansion House is closed, and the difficulty in staffing it makes one wonder if it will ever open again. Two thirds of the other houses on the island are now occupied during the summer months by non-Forbeses.

The Long-Tailed Forbeses were unique in certain of their manifestations, but they shared nonetheless many characteristics with All the Dear People. Even in Father's lifetime their world began to show signs of giving at the seams. During the twenties the children of many of them were experimenting with sex and alcohol. The fact that the experiments, for the most part, were made with a certain flat-footed seriousness, as something that "should" be tried, was simply part of the heritage of serious living that was their birthright. The provenance of the gin might be a laboratory of the Massachusetts General Hospital and taken neat, as might the first cousin found under the same blanket on a sand dune. Both approaches lacked the aesthetic sensitiveness that looks for nuances of pleasure. (I hasten to confess that this is purely hindsight on my part, and that during those same years I was nothing but a frightened little prig, using derisive laughter to cover up my own sense of inadequacy.) These sexual experiments among the children of All the Dear People ended in more neo-incestuous marriages, the only difference between them and their parents' being that a large number of these marriages cracked open into divorce. The second marriages that ensued were almost always contracted with someone whose blood stream was more richly fortified.

The Dear People were quite free of prejudice. Where they were *not* liberal (and herein lay the Achilles heel that makes them open to the charge of smugness) was in condemning any other than their own narrow mores. Conduct and principles were of prime importance. It was far harder to accept as daughter-in-law a girl who "made up," or even who "dressed up," than one whose name proclaimed another ethnic background.

They are all gone now, and, for myself, I know that, whereas once I reacted violently against what seemed to me their narrowness, I have lived to see far more poisonous narrowness elsewhere. There truly was something dear about these people. Their hearts were as gentle as their ways, and yet they were undergirt by a stamina of principle and belief.

All the Dear People had character.

10

THE MIGHTY MAIDENS

JOHN JAY CHAPMAN SAID that a man from Mars would learn more about life on this planet from Verdi's operas than from Emerson's essays, because he would at least learn that we have two sexes. If Verdi had ever visited Boston he probably would not have chosen it as a setting for his *Masked Ball*. In the city of my parents' day there lay a vast no man's land between the sexes, dedicated not to passion but to *friendship*. The friendships which flowered in this asexual arena would hardly have offered the necessary ardor to fill the lungs of an Italian tenor or soprano, but they were strong and vital and enduring nonetheless.

Mr. Arthur Hill used to speak of certain of the frequenters of the Boston Athenaeum as the "fierce virgins." Perhaps a kinder phrase for one of the species was Henry James's "that mighty maiden." Did such friendships exist in other parts of the country at the same time? Or at the same time in other parts of the world? Or have they ever existed at other times, anywhere in the world? I do not know.

Most of these maidens belonged to the world of All the Dear People, dedicated to a Cause, or to one or more of Boston's Associated Charities. They wore heavy, serviceable clothes, were bluff and hearty in their manner, unless they belonged to the terrified twitchy fringe. I do not wish to give the impression that all unmarried ladies in Boston belonged to this category. Indeed there was another breed—which seems to have no counterpart in succeeding generations—which one might call the Romantic Maidens. There were Miss "Alie" Haughton, Miss "Sattie" Fairchild, Miss "Mamie" Williams, to name only three strikingly beautiful and fascinating women who remained mysteriously unmarried, in spite of continuing charm for the opposite sex all their lives. The charm for the opposite sex—at least as represented by Father— exerted by the Mighty Maidens, however, existed not in the realm of romance but in that of good fellowship. Father gravitated to those who were bright, and who shared at least one of his interests— books, politics, or Harvard College. A mere Cause was not quite enough for Father. These single ladies liked him for the same reason that so many other Bostonians liked him—simply because he made them feel at ease.

Mighty Maidens often came in families: two or more sisters, living on in the big family house where they had once revolved, like dutiful satellites, around a mother who had been more beautiful than any of them, and certainly more selfish. One of the sisters would be powerful and dominating, the other yielding, gentle, and given to intermittent lapses into delicate health. In some cases there was, offstage, a married sister around whose household the Maidens revolved. This wife and mother had once been one of them, but by a freeing act had hacked her way out of the smothering shelter into the independence of marriage.

We have seen that the Putnam Camp afforded the backdrop for such romances among All the Dear People. A bride on almost any terms was certainly more fortunate than one Boston maiden lady of my parents' vintage who, living with her hearty unmarried sisters, lapsed over the years into the martyrdom of "sick headaches." Whether she herself ever faced their cause as lying in the breaking up of a secret engagement in her youth through the derision of her family, I do not know. If the man had belonged to a dark-skinned race the freethinking, "broad-minded" family would have taken him in stride. What they could not tolerate, however, was the fact that he was not only a clergyman—ridiculous enough! —but that he was an *Episcopalian*. Better a life extended on a sofa

than falling for any such poppycock as that! But for the sisters
not fortunate or brave enough to achieve marriage the recognized
substitute for love was either a Cause or Charity—not the brand
preached by St. Paul, but that practiced in Boston. It did not
bring the release of true *agape;* there was something sad and still-
born about it.

The Mighty Maidens were daily confronted with the insoluble
problem, what to *do* with one's deepest emotions. To express them
aloud, in words, was unthinkable. To sublimate them through the
beauty of religious ritual was impossible to temperaments frost-
nipped by the cool winds of Unitarian self-control. One must never
give oneself up simply to feeling. One must act. One must *do.* Even
friends, and the loss of friends, could be made to serve a useful
purpose. One Mighty Maiden of my acquaintance formed the habit,
after the death of a loved friend, of saying, in substance, to her
sister, "You know Emily had all those perfectly good sheets and
pillow cases. It seems a pity they should go to waste." As the same
routine was repeated after several deaths her linen closet became
stocked with slightly worn sheets and pillow cases, with different
monograms. Stark New England thrift was obviously part of the
motive force behind such a move, but even more was the instinct
in the face of emotion toward doing something *practical.* To count
over the contents of dear Emily's linen closet was a distraction
from the painful realization that one had lost forever dear Emily
herself.

I know another family of maiden sisters whose ranks were
thinned by the death of one of them. One of their nieces told me of
the comic-pathetic dilemma of her aunts who didn't know what
to do with the urn containing the ashes of their beloved sister. This
niece was appalled when one day, at their country place, in a sort
of garden room used mainly for dead (!) storage—picture frames
made from seashells, a broken toaster, kerosene lamps someday to be
wired for electricity, piles of boxes stored for next year's vegetables—one of her aunts suddenly said, "Right under your hand,
there are Aunt Virginia's ashes," then helplessly exclaimed, "We

don't know what to *do* with them!'' The niece, with sensitive understanding, saw at once that the dilemma was not physical, centering around the added entry to the storeroom, but that it was emotional. Her aunt, in substance, was pathetically asking, What do we do with what we are feeling? Seeing that she would somehow have to come to the rescue of the discomfited sisters, the niece organized a little family gathering of nieces and nephews, to be held outdoors on the porch, at which, with easy informality, each member of the family would tell something nice that he remembered about Aunt Virginia. Things started off swimmingly until a competitive younger sister of Aunt Virginia's got the bit in her teeth and began reminiscing about her own exploits. The niece, who had been forearmed, reached hastily for her secret weapon, Emerson. From his works she read to the assembled family his poem on— Berrying. (The spelling is correct. The poem concerned the lesson to be learned through being ''caught among the blackberry vines.'') Whereupon she and her husband buried Aunt Virginia's ashes under a laurel bush and, I am sure, in the words of the staunch survivors, that was that.

Father moved among some of Boston's Mighty Maidens with serenity and affability. Of a Sunday afternoon he himself became a ''caller''—as often as not on one of them. Father enjoyed their society, quite oblivious of the psychological undertones that had made them what they were. I submit a few of them, in loving nostalgia, for an extinct breed.

''F. G.'' CURTIS

When I lived alone with Father after Mother's death, and would answer the telephone to hear an unmistakable voice, I did not need the speaker on the other end of the wire to identify herself, as though she were Chairman of the Board of a large corporation, ''This is F. G. Curtis.'' In a sense she *was* chairman of a board, and that board was *the Misses Curtis*. It consisted of ''F. G.'' (Miss Fanny), Miss Isabella, Miss Harriot, and Miss Margaret. As a family the Curtises were strong on nicknames: the sisters were known as Fan, Bog, Hat, and Peg—or Pedge. One sister, Elinor,

who married the painter Charles Hopkinson, founded another
dynasty—"The Hops." One of Miss Fanny Curtis's Causes was
adult education, known familiarly as "Adult Ed." Their five nieces
were the "Tads" (short for tadpole). The large family place on
the rocks at Manchester, north of Boston, was "Manch." (When
the Hops went abroad as a family Mrs. Hop took her children
through a tour not of the Lorna Doone nor the Pickwick, but of the
Peter Rabbit country.) By the same token I can assert that the
Misses Curtis lived in the very heart of All the Dear People
country. On Upper Mt. Vernon Street the worn brass mail
slot still dimly shows the name *G. S. Curtis* outside the large
double brick house where Father went so often to have tea
with the sisters assembled. He wrote: "For a long time it has
been the Boston home of a remarkable family, established by
Greeley Stevenson Curtis, a distinguished officer of the Union
Army in the Civil War, and his wife Harriot Appleton, a
half-sister of Mrs. Henry Wadsworth Longfellow. . . . The four
[unmarried] daughters for many years have occupied . . . the
house together, making it a focus of friendship, intelligence and
countless good works." Around them, within spitting distance,
are the houses, already mentioned, of erstwhile Dear People now
taken over by the organizations they helped to form.

On opening the door, what do we find in the vestibule inside?
A tumbledown stroller. Not for a baby. No. This stroller was spied
by one of the Misses Curtis on the sidewalk outside a tenement on
the neighboring "backside" of the Hill, thrown on a heap of discarded rubbish. Recognizing a bargain when she saw one, she
dumped into it the heavy bags of flour and sugar she was carrying
in her arms. It is cheaper, even if one is over eighty, to carry one's
provender from the supermarket than to have it sent by a fancy
grocer nearby. Let it not be thought that the Misses Curtis could
not *afford* to patronize any store in Boston they chose. It is simply
that they have always put into practice the values in which they
believe. Self-indulgence is a weakness. The Curtis sisters have not
only always been morally vigorous, they have abounded in greathearted and anonymous generosity toward the Causes in which they

believe. Miss Harriot Curtis, at one time Dean of Women at Hampton Institute, Virginia, has spent a lifetime involved in the fight for the rights of the American Negro. How often have I met any one of the sisters, puffing up Mt. Vernon Street, in her sensible groundgrippers, head bent forward under its Boston hat (the same for at least a decade at a time), drooping bag filled with tracts and pamphlets concerning the worthwhile Causes for which she has poured out herself as well as her money. If one of them had so far indulged herself as to wear a fur coat, be sure that it was shabby, and that it had been bought cheap in a rummage sale. Taxis were taken only under acute provocation. One's own feet or public transportation served the purpose very well.

I don't intend to give the impression that there was something dour about F. G. Curtis and her sisters. The reverse was true. With their scrubbed rosy cheeks, hearty laughs, vigorous hand-shakes, and forthright manner they were like four jolly Brothers. As they pushed their chairs back from the dining-room table one would proclaim, "Cut square and eat all!" They possessed the masculine vigor to do both. But they were gentlemen of the old school, with a high sense of civic, national, and international respon-sibility. After Mother's death Father rented a summer cottage from them on their place at Manch, and enjoyed the society of the Curtis sisters as much as though they had been members of the Tavern Club. There was a something in their presence that gave off the subtle sense that they *were* graduates of Harvard. Miss Peg Curtis, standing before the open fire in the old Victorian stone mansion in which they lived—legs apart, puffing on her little pipe—would discuss with Father some mutual friend in the terms commonly used between Harvard graduates. "It's my impression he is a ninety-niner" (pronounced *ninah*), referring, of course, to the date of his graduation from Harvard. One was aware of being in the presence of a forceful American; no wonder that, based on the able work she did for the Red Cross in France during the First World War, she was recalled to Greece in 1921 to assist in bringing relief after the Armenian slaughter. There was no feminine backbiting or frivolous gossip at Manch. The topics Father and his friends discussed were those that concerned the public weal. They had to be, because Father was left far behind in another great interest of two of the sisters—the world of sport in which they both excelled. Miss Harriot Curtis was National Women's Golf Champion, followed by Miss Margaret, who won the title three times. (Their best medal play scores were: Miss Harriot, in 1908, 85 and Miss Margaret in 1909, 86). Miss Margaret was also three times National Champion in women's doubles in tennis. What delight they must have brought to their fans on the occasion described today by Miss Harriot. It was a local golf tournament in which "Peg started at the top of the draw and I started at the bottom of the draw. And, by gravy, we ended up in the finals!" adding modestly, "Peg smeared me."

The house at Manch was a bastion in which the Curtis sisters stood fast against the world. It was there that they had been shaped, as daughters of a veteran of the Civil War, to look upon him and their brothers as gods, but gods who needed mothering as well as worship. Other men, beyond the compound, were, in a sense, the Enemy.

There is a memory of Miss Peg Curtis, an Amazonian vestal virgin, keeping at bay twenty-five men from the local Fire Department, who had come clanging into the family woods to extinguish a blaze. When they began unrolling their efficient hoses she shrieked at them through the tumult, "My brother foresaw this in 1890!" Pointing to the heart of the forest, "There is the hydrant he installed! USE IT!" "Lady, we've got water right here, with us. Get out of the way." All but force was needed to brush aside this *maitresse femme,* sovereign of her own domain, fighting to protect the will of her half-god brother, who, indeed, owed his very godhead to his sister's stamina. Perhaps it was not the flames of Götterdämmerung licking high at her back, which she was trying to keep away from her door as much as the archenemy who had come to extinguish them—*Men!*

If Father and Brother were idols in comparison to whom other men were pygmies, the Curtis sisters at least showed a kindly indulgence toward one male relative, a bachelor cousin, William Sumner Appleton, founder and secretary of the Society for the Preservation of New England Antiquities. "Cousin Apple," or "Cousin Sum," as he was known in the family, lived in the same apartment house on Louisburg Square to which Father and I were ultimately to move. I knew him only as a rather fussy and boring old "fuddy-duddy," as Father would have called him, with a Caspar Milquetoast mustache, who terrified me by asking me if I would like to go out with him some evening, to *dance!* I did not in those days know of his other pastime of table tipping at spiritual séances, or of his belief in his own former incarnation during which he had enjoyed the favors of a Roman empress. Only recently have I learned of the annual family Christmas dinner at which Cousin Sum, in the spirit of good will to men, was allowed free rein for the expression of his quite special tastes. After the family had cut square and eaten all, the white tablecloth was bared to receive the array of presents which he had brought for the five nieces of his cousins, which he was allowed to arrange in a display. It consisted of a full "line" of every kind of intimate feminine apparel, chosen and bought by him—panties, brassieres, girdles, chemises, and nightgowns. Whatever deviation this offshoot from the stout family tree may have shown, "Cousin Apple" could count on the kindly, healthy, rollicking amusement and delight of his cousins, Fan, Bog, Hat, and Peg.

Christmas Day was not the only day in the year in which the Curtis sisters engaged in fun and games among themselves and with their nieces. An endless supply of costumes in the family attic was available for Dumb Crambo, charades, and singing of old ballads. For these games, as for the family reading aloud, there was a wide and vast reservoir of cultivation to draw upon, rooted exclusively in the Anglo-Saxon tradition. The hilarity that accompanied the family hijinks had its tradition, too. It was that of the Boston that made Mother so shrink into herself: the whole family was aggressively "sure." Whether coasting "bellybumps" with All the Dear People at Georgetown or stuffing herself out with sofa

cushions and adding orange peel teeth in "dressing up," a Curtis
sister felt that her posture in the world was impregnable. I have
heard one of them, for instance, taking Mrs. Pat Campbell to task
(to me, not to Mrs. Pat) for her pronounciation of the word
"tired." "She says *tahd*," protested the sister, "as though she
were talking about a macadam road. Everyone knows it should
be *ty-ud*." By the same token Father, to all the sisters, as to most
of his Boston friends, was *Mahk*. Though the Curtis family faced
the outside world with a united front of solidarity there was,
within it, an undercurrent of competitiveness. Christmas Day
afforded one opportunity for it to come to the surface. Hat and
Peg, with their rooters, gathered after the family feast into two
opposing teams, and would vie with each other in seeing who could
successfully pop into a distant wastebasket the highest number of
secondhand tennis balls, collected during the year for just this
purpose. Tradition ruled that it was a member of the winning team
who had first choice of Cousin Sum's dainties. This same spirit
of rivalry showed its head even in their acts of charity. When
the most loving and demonstrative of "the aunts" offered to one
of her nieces a fat check to cover the outire education—through
private school and college—of a daughter named for herself, saying
with emotion, "I know I've picked a winner," the Corporation
moved. "*We* shall educate the great-niece. The check will be a contribution from *all* of us" was the ruling. The Curtis sisters were no
exception to the rule which decrees that Puritan charity be dispensed with a certain flatfooted gracelessness. In the kindness of
their joint hearts they gave to an "underprivileged" friend a
holiday in the Caribbean, who admitted to being almost ashamed
by the packages that followed her from her benefactresses—worn,
secondhand books wrapped in greasy, crumpled paper, tied with
odd bits of knotted string. This object of the family charity was
feeling in a not altogether charitable frame of mind herself when
she opened an envelope (probably crumpled too!) from one of the
Ladies Bountiful, containing a scrawled note, saying in substance,
"Hi! Since you're down there, why don't you stay a little longer?"
and enclosing a check for three hundred dollars. "Praise to the

face is an open disgrace," and Boston maidens will choose brus-
queness rather than risk being thanked.

These Mighty Maidens were like others of my parents' friends
who acknowledged on the fringes of their family existence at least
one "lame duck"—so called. (It was a matter of general complaint
during Mother's growing-up years in Charles Street that if one
opened any bedroom door in her father's house some lame duck of
my Aunt Helen's was likely to be taking a nap on the bed. Her
lame-duck-in-chief was the blind daughter of a lighthouse keeper.
Aunt Helen was so busy trying to strike a spark between this luckless girl and a visiting Englishman, James F. Muirhead, that she
was utterly confounded when he chose to ask *her*, instead of the
lame duck, to marry him. It was only by dint of a stern talking-to
from her younger sister Fanny that she ruefully abandoned her
attempt to serve as matchmaker, and herself became Mrs. Muirhead.) One lame duck of the Curtis sisters they called Hiram.
Hiram was a woman who had come to Boston from the back country
somewhere, because she had felt a deep concern for the fate which
could overtake a friendless girl in the city and had become a
member of Boston's police force. It was on her beat in the Boston
Common that one of the Curtis sisters had first made Hiram's
acquaintance. From that day on, into her impoverished old age and
illness, she was never allowed to want by the Curtis sisters. Another
lame duck was a Miss Lutie Pleasants from Richmond—called
genially by the sisters, in their New England accents, Loot. Although Loot lacked a palate, she was not short of either breeding,
courage, or liveliness. F. G. Curtis somehow set her up in the
genteel occupation of hand-painting trays which became the standard Curtis wedding present.

Loot was a friend of "Nannie" Astor, from Virginia girlhood
days. When Loot and Miss Curtis—also a friend of Lady Astor's—
visited her together in England they went off one afternoon on an
expedition to Hampton Court. As the two American women came
out, prepared to walk down the long driveway, it was pouring rain.
Nice weather for ducks, it may have been; but not for a lame duck,
if she happened to be rather fragile, and also happened to be under

the sheltering wing of F. G. Curtis. She, spying a Rolls-Royce with a chauffeur at its wheel waiting for the owner—probably a duchess at the very least—strode up to the car, opened the door next to the driver, and popped Loot in beside him. Before there was time for expostulation she explained that her friend was not very strong and she was sure the owner would be happy to give her a lift down the driveway. Turning on her heel, she herself strode off into the British rain, satisfied that her lame duck would not have to do the same.

Most of the generosity dispensed by the Curtis sisters, however, was on a larger scale. It was this generosity which, more often than not, was back of many of their petty economies, and such economies merely were part of what appeared as a proper scale of values. It was such a natural reflex to the Curtis sisters to practice economy that even the two athletes practiced it in sport. At a National Women's Golf tournament, played on the nearby Essex links, the admiring public which followed one of the champion sisters was incredulous when, between holes, she stopped to gather mushrooms in a small basket which she had brought along for the purpose. A handy way of getting one's supper—free! Even now, at over eighty, Miss Peg Curtis, on her way to the village post office, still believes in picking up other people's golf balls, which she captures in a small wire cage, attached to the end of a stick—an invention of her brother's. She prefers, however, to rely on the sense of touch rather than of sight, and, if possible, puts into practice her favorite method— which is rolling on the ground! The expertise evinced in both these methods bears fruit in the collection of more than five hundred secondhand golf balls kept on the top of the piano at Manch.

Though Father was on friendly terms with the whole Corporation—particularly during our summer at Manchester—it was the Chairman of the Board who was his special friend. For one thing, they had Harvard College in common. Miss Fanny Curtis—again in her unconscious role as Harvard graduate—must have been the only woman on record to attend football games in the Stadium unattended by a male escort. Ticket procured through brother "Jib," she would arrive, with a steamer rug for her knees, and plant herself to witness the game with an air of serene authority suitable to a member of the Corporation—and I don't mean Curtis Corporation, I mean Harvard Corporation. In 1913, when Miss Fanny ran for election to Boston's School Committee, she asserted to the members of the press who had come to interview her, "You behold a candidate who does not know fatigue." She served on this committee for thirteen years. At the annual meetings when cigars were passed out to her fellow members, there was always "candy for Miss Curtis." With the sublime self-assurance that was a mark of the breed she entered the race for nomination as Mayor of Boston in 1925, an occasion which served as a springboard for one of Father's happiest verses, read at a small gathering, to wish her godspeed before leaving for a trip to Greece, "Mayor of Athens, ere we part . . ." It was F. G. Curtis who, with Mrs. James Storrow, joined in founding Boston's Women's City Club, and was its second president. Three successive governors of the Commonwealth of Massachusetts appointed her a member of the State Board of Charities. Her interests were not only local, but included the Chinese Industrial Corporation and the American School at Athens. There was one occasion when F. G. Curtis became exercised over the bad sanitation at the back of Beacon Hill. Wishing to improve plumbing conditions for the newly arrived immigrants, she conceived the idea of creating some sort of communal laundry. Knowing, however, that if she were to appear before the State Legislature asking for what she wanted she would be waved aside as a henheaded woman, she repaired to the Massachusetts Institute of Technology where she took a course in plumbing so that she would have—as I am sure she did—all the answers. Where she learned carpentry I don't know, but I do know that on the first day of Father's tenancy of her cottage at Manch, when we found a window sash that was jammed, we called the big house to ask if there was a handyman on the place who could attend to it. F. G. Curtis herself, pushing eighty at the time, appeared with not only hammer and nails but a stepladder which she mounted, and proceeded to do the job forthwith. In keeping with the athletic tendencies of her sisters, F. G., as Father put it, "became early an expert horsewoman.

She was, moreover, a vigorous skater, and spent many a Sunday
with her friends, John F. Moors and Joseph Lee, in skating all day
up and down the Concord River. The civic interests of these friends
were very much her own.'' Father neglected to mention that Miss
Curtis's present to herself on her seventy-fifth birthday was a new
pair of boot-skates.

Father's friend, Charles C. Burlingham in New York also valued
Fanny Curtis's friendship, and often wrote to Father of the exploits of their mutual friend, to whom he referred as ''Old Fan.''
One of these was a visit to him in his large Park Avenue apartment,
just before Miss Curtis's ninetieth birthday. On her arrival—by
daycoach from Boston—as soon as the maid opened the door Miss
Curtis strode through the large hall, back into the kitchen, opened
the icebox door, and popped in a sandwich. As she did so she explained to the cook that her Margaret, back in Boston, had made it
from the Thanksgiving turkey (of several days previous) for her to
eat on the train, but as she ate only half of it she would save the
other half for the return trip, in two days. She must have taken this
hardy remnant with her to the matinee performance uptown at the
Ziegfeld Theatre of *Antony and Cleopatra,* which she attended
along with her niece Isabella. That five-o'clock train back to Boston was not forgotten for a moment during the performance.
As her niece described it, ''Just as Cleopatra was about to apply
the asp Aunt Fan said, 'Come on, Isab.' '' She rose from her
seat in the middle of a row, down front, pushing her way to the
aisle, and thence out of the theater. A brisk walk from Seventh
Avenue to Madison brought her to the bus stop which she had
in mind. When she boarded the bus her niece reported a great
deal of fumbling over the exact change, which she protested she
could not find. In fact, Aunt Fan made such a production of being
penniless that a fellow passenger was moved to give her a penny—
which she accepted. Once arrived at Grand Central Isabella
escorted her to the train—daycoach—and before watching it pull
out said comfortingly, ''Aunt Fan, your car is next to the diner
so you'll be able to get dinner easily.'' It was at this point—

pooh-poohing any mention of the diner—that she produced from some hidden recess of whatever reticule she was carrying, the veteran sandwich.

Looking back on a life in which she had so often fought the good fight on the side of causes which were unpopular at the time, it was a matter of pique to F. G. Curtis that she was *not* called on to testify at any of the McCarthy hearings. She, as her sisters at her side, had spent a lifetime in the tireless zeal of the truly dedicated public servant, with largeness of heart and breadth of mind. When Miss Curtis, confined to her room with what seemed only a minor complaint, died with unexpected suddenness Father, in writing to the Boston *Globe* of her activities on her last day, rounded off her portrait. "The note [actually received the day after her death] now before me alludes to the enjoyment she was finding in 'going through' Emerson as she had not hitherto done, and by finding out precisely what Lincoln said at Gettysburg." He rounded off his appreciation of her by saying, "Since the death of Henry Lee Higginson in 1919 there have been suggestions from time to time of men who might take his acknowledged place as First Citizen. . . . Stopping to consider the value and variety of her contributions to the life of her city, over a period of about 50 years, one may well ask who deserves more the title of First Woman Citizen?"

It was superfluous for Father to qualify the title F. G. Curtis had won. Whatever else it may have been, frailty her name was not. Concerning her, Nature might stand up and say to all the world, "This was a man."

ELIZABETH GASKELL NORTON

Lest I appear to give the impression that Father was the center of a blindly adoring circle of friends and admirers, "all kneeling," let me here introduce a Mighty Maiden (the fierce virgin version of Mrs. Gray, if one so dare name her) who I am sure held him in something approaching thinly concealed disdain. All the same— being Father!—he did, though with a certain trepidation, oc-

casionally on a Sunday afternoon present himself at the front door
of 19 Chestnut Street, behind which sat Miss Lily Norton. She
was one of the three daughters of Charles Eliot Norton, Harvard's
one-time famous Professor of Fine Arts. Known to the world as
the translator of Dante, he himself undoubtedly did not know that
his daughters were to his students Paradiso, Purgatorio, and Inferno. Miss Lily was Purgatorio.

Miss Lily Norton was emphatically *not* one of the Dear People.
It is only the stark truth—which she herself relished—to state
that she was not dear at all! Not, at least, by the time I—or Father
—knew her. It was rumored, however, that she, as well as Paradiso,
her beautiful sister Sara, in her youth had received a generous share
of offers of hearts and hands— some of them attached to distinguished British names. But both girls automatically turned down
all proposals of marriage for the simple reason that the applicants
did not measure up to their father's high standards. Mother, a girlhood friend of Lily's, used to visit her in Ashfield, Massachusetts,
and assured me that she had been attractive and lively when she was
young. Mother described the torture of sitting through meals during
which the suave, Anglo-veneered father sadistically made Inferno,
his youngest daughter, Margaret, not favored by good looks, squirm
as he laid down the stricture that a woman was nothing if she was
not beautiful. Father used to tell that when the intrepid Margaret
set out alone on a journey to Europe some friend of the family
raised the question, in Henry James's presence, as to whether it
was quite safe for a woman to travel without a chaperon, to
which Mr. James offered his reassurance, "I should think that
Margaret Norton was probably . . . [pause] . . . the *safest*
woman in Europe." Plain or fair, it was in the heart of Inferno
alone, appropriately enough, that smoldering fires burned. Indeed
they generated enough heat to blast open the family prison. Margaret achieved a life of her own, and increased her happiness by
adopting two children. Miss Lily Norton's account of her own interview with one of these girls became, for us, a family classic. The
lecture began, "You were a *pauper*, Harriet, when my sister was

good enough to take you in," and ended up, one can only imagine after what tongue lashings, in her most British-inflected tones, "No teahs, Harriet! No teahs!"

The two sisters worshiped at their father's shrine. Father told of walking as a young man with Professor Norton in his garden in Ashfield, and talking to him about his hope that there might some-day be an "American Men of Letters Series," and suggesting that, since the English series numbered sixty, it might be reasonable to expect that the American might run to something like twenty. Father enjoyed imitating the bleating more-Oxford-than-Oxford tones as Norton wearily sighed, "I think not more than thr-r-ee." There was a young man under discussion between Father and Professor Norton whom the latter sadly dismissed: "I am afraid that he is a very *artifissial* young man."

Whenever Father did ring Miss Norton's doorbell he could give himself courage by the thought that, quite apart from Mother's long-standing friendship with "Lily," he had, on his own account, literary links with the family. Credentials or not, however, speaking for myself I can testify that I never met Miss Norton "Attended or alone, Without a tighter breathing, And Zero at the Bone." There was a chill about her which made it clear that *she* would have welcomed no guest from Hampton Institute, and I am sure that when Father was brave enough to venture into her presence and inevitably got into a bad bout of stammering, he felt her condemnation of his weakness would have been expressed with one of her favorite words, "deplorable."

I have already referred to the nod of condescending encouragement offered to Father at the start of his biographical writing by Professor Norton and his sister Grace. That awe-inspiring bluestocking, incidentally, was a friend of Mother's family and made history in it when she gave to Aunt Mabel as a wedding present a set of books—my impression is that it was Montaigne—which showed, on scrutiny, that she had been through the volumes with painstaking care and glued together those pages which she considered did not make appropriate reading for a young girl—not even on the eve of becoming a married woman. When Professor

Norton himself died, however, Father was enough in favor with
the daughters to be selected to edit in 1913 the *Letters of Charles
Eliot Norton,* with his daughter Sally as collaborator. Her dealings
with Father were Paradise enow, taking the tangible shape, in
addition to whatever he earned, of a comfortable armchair from her
father's library which she gave to Father, and in which he sat
till the end in *his* library. Coping with daughters and widows is
for a biographer a tricky business at best. One gets a whiff of what
Purgatorio might have been. In a letter written by her to Father
many years later she referred to a request she had received from
"a certain Professor R. L. Rusk (unknown to me)" to grant access
to the Norton-Emerson correspondence at Harvard. The request
that had affronted Miss Norton's sensibilities was for the "actual
date of my parents' engagement!" To request so intimate a detail,
she felt, was "such as my Father would have felt to be almost an
impertinence."

In some areas—notably the Fine Arts—Miss Norton must have
felt that Father was culturally deficient, and would certainly have
found Reading, Pennsylvania, in his background deplorable. The
air she breathed was permeated with England. One could hear it,
sniffed through her nose, which tapered at its tip to a sharp point.
Miss Norton's astringent conversation was punctuated by sniffs.
Coming into the drawing room of a house in Washington in which
my parents were spending the winter, she looked about and exclaimed, "What a hodgepodge!" An entirely affable smile added
piquancy to the sneers that fell from her lips, apparently as unconsciously as from the mouth of that fairy-story princess from which
popped out toads: "I hear that the Howes are to have some painting done—at last." But then who had a better right to sniff or
sneer than the daughter of the great Professor Charles Eliot Norton, she herself named after his friend Mrs. Elizabeth Gaskell, the
author of *Cranford?*

A mutual friend has told me of witnessing a painful scene at the
Somerset Club where Miss Norton, lunching there with a friend,
discovered a cockroach on her plate. She rose, amid bowing waiters,
to say that she could not possibly remain to lunch, or indeed ever re-

turn again to the club. The news was broken to her: "The Somerset Club kitchen has been fighting a losing battle with cockroaches for years. If you want to lunch at the Somerset Club, you must accept the possibility of a cockroach." Miss Norton chose—the Somerset Club.

Professor Norton is said to have prefaced his opening lecture each year at Harvard by sighing wearily as he said, "I suppose that no one in this room has ever seen a gentleman." Lily and her two sisters had been brought up to believe that since Matthew Arnold had visited the family at Shady Hill they were Britain's cultural hostages in the United States, and were taught to shudder at the vulgarity of everything American. A Sedgwick cousin of the family has told me, though I am not sure that the anecdote has been substantiated, that on the same day that Professor Norton wrote in his diary: "Dined with the dear Carlyles," Carlyle wrote in *his* diary: "Goose N. came to dinner."

In the early days of the New Deal Mother was amused at the distress of Miss Norton, who certainly had been born into this world alive as a little conservative, when she was contemplating her annual visit to New York to her old school friend Sara Delano Roosevelt. Franklin had been President for several weeks and there was nothing about his performance in office that Miss Lily Norton did not find deplorable. She would truly have liked to cancel her visit but, ever a stickler for tradition, felt it would be going back on an established custom and might moreover hurt her old friend's feelings. She confessed to Mother, however, her perplexity as to what she could possibly *say* to her about a son who had "let down the class" and thus disgraced his family. She spoke as though he were serving a term in Sing-Sing, rather than the White House, and had decided, after much thought, to meet the delicate social dilemma by not referring to the black sheep at all!

My own picture of Miss Norton, in her last years, was that of a formidable, but not negligible, relic of a world and set of values that had passed her by. The very name of the father on whose altar she had sacrificed all that might have been spontaneous or life-loving was only a faint echo in the ears of a few of the elect. It is true that every year the first move made by the visiting professor to Harvard from England, brought over as Charles Eliot Norton Professor of Poetry, was to dine in Chestnut Street. What T. S. Eliot, Sir Laurence Binyon or C. M. Bowra made of their American hostess I should like to know.

I am sure that they saw her most agreeable side: it was her old friends, and not these visitors, whom she excoriated with her caustic tongue. When one went to call on her at teatime in the forbidding dark house on Chestnut Street, the curtains in the downstairs room were apt to stir—as behind Mrs. Gray's window on Marlboro Street—as one glimpsed a wistful parlor maid hoping for an arrival of a caller. Then upstairs went one's card and, presently, oneself after it. There, in a room encrusted with heavy gold-framed paintings of her father's period (a Burne-Jones? a Constable? a Turner? I can't be sure), she sat behind her heavy silver tea service, before an open fire. On a settee in the corner lay her only companion—a stuffed dog. For her dinner she dressed and went down to the dark, high-studded dining room, where a place was set opposite her for symmetry, complete with napkin, silver, and water glass. A friend suggested to her once, "When you're alone, Lily, why don't you have a nice cozy dinner on a tray in front of the fire?" Her answer was simple and firm, "It lets down the class." When cataracts on her eyes made reading impossible she carried on her life according to the same stern set of rules of behavior that she demanded of others. She did not utter a complaint. She and her stuffed dog sat it out together.

Aside from the two credentials of her father and my mother, Father always felt that he didn't cut much ice in Miss Norton's drawing room. She was not one to cater to guileless egotism. She cuttingly snubbed him for one of his annual Christmas verses, saying in essence that it must be a pleasure to *him* to write them, as it was to an old lady of her acquaintance who lived in Cambridge who enjoyed doing the same sort of thing. The intended snub was not lost on Father; but he simply sent her another the next year! I find, however, one late letter from him, when the years perhaps had brought some mellowing, in which he says, "To break my

solitude went to call on Lily N. Lily was of a sweetness quite disarming and lent me, for reading, a box of Lowell's (J.R.) letters
to her.''

I am sure that, looking from across the gulf of generations, I
must have missed some essence that, at least once, had been appealing. If Miss Norton felt that demanding the best, and scorning
anything less, was a worthy goal in life, she achieved her goal. If
there was loneliness, there was courage to meet it. If she was ever
disturbed by any self-questioning, or asked herself whether beyond
the confines of her own world there were riches she had not tapped—
even so close to home as the great Fine Arts Professor Paul Sachs
who had bought Shady Hill, but whose threshold she would not
cross—if, in short, the breath of the tragedy of *waste* brushed her
in flashes of realization, or if she faced the fact that the world she
had lived in and for was finished, at least she never belied that
world by lowering its or her own standards. If ''noblesse'' was the
climate she chose, her obligation to its code was paid in full measure.
She did not let down her class.

MARY CABOT WHEELWRIGHT

As it is part of the Anglo-Saxon tradition to produce sons and
daughters with affinities for other races and remote parts of the
world, so, too, the Boston breed can spawn its own venturing spirit
that vaults over restrictions of time and place. That spirit, furthermore, is not always limited to the terrestrial plane any more than
is its British prototype. To this species—part mystic, part voyager—
our next Mighty Maiden belonged.

Mary Cabot Wheelwright. Even her name suggests her. There
she stands. Foursquare. No frills. No nonsense. Her figure is gawky,
her coloring sallow, her nose flat. I have heard more than one man,
susceptible to the charms of the opposite sex, dismiss her with a
snort as unattractive. An uncompromising Boston porkpie hat on
top of her slippery straight hair, which did little to soften features
which to a fellow Bostonian were recognizable as unmistakably
Cabot-y. Comfortable walking shoes, and good tweeds. But look
again. Those tweeds are not only good, they are handsome in color

and texture, and put together with scarf or jewelry by a knowing eye. The large reticule she carries is obviously handmade, the beaten silver and turquoise ring or bracelet is unmistakably Indian; those handsome heavy prayer beads, are they Chinese? are they Syrian? There is not only originality here, and knowledge; there is flair. Mary Wheelwright had an air; one looked at her twice. If her face was unmistakably that of a Cabot, one was sure that the hazel eyes, with a milky white penumbra about the pupil, had scanned distances far removed from the bricks and mortar of Boston.

Sure of herself and her opinions, not stopping, or stooping, to explore with any gentle probing of tact the sensitiveness of any interlocutor, she frequently irritated and alienated those who crossed her path. A cousin who was devoted to her was prompted by the insistence with which she propounded her opinions to call her "Cousin Mary Wheelwrong." It is almost impossible to reconcile the image projected by the middle-aged Miss Mary Wheelwright with the portrait by Frank Duveneck which hangs in the Brooklyn Art Museum, entitled simply "Mary Cabot Wheelwright." Velásquez might have used the same little girl as model for a Spanish Hapsburg Infanta (there is a line of Cabots that looks like Hapsburgs)—in her long white dress, blue sash, and doll held in the crook of her arm. As remote from the Mary Wheelwright I knew is the photograph of the little forlornity of later childhood, with huge frightened eyes, dangling her spindly legs in heavy black stockings and all but cowering in a deep high-backed armchair, too big for her, like a small prince on a throne that he knows he will never have the strength to mount. The throne in this instance was a well-buttressed Victorian background of both family and fortune, and delicate dyspeptic Mary its sole heir apparent. She told me once that her father had fallen in love with her mother at first sight, across a room at a party "before he knew who she was." Implicit was the assumption that had the name "Cabot" been spoken aloud it would automatically have cast an aura of enchantment around the head of the unknown.

The rest of my parents' Mighty Maiden friends I knew only as children generally know adults, surveyed remotely across the great

gulf fixed between the generations. Mary Wheelwright alone I
came to know in later life, and to call by her first name, as a friend
of my own. When I knew her first, through Father, I nearly disliked her and certainly laughed at her. I ended by not only admiring but truly loving her.

Sailing was Father's "bond" with Mary. I must have been about
eighteen years old when "Miss Wheelwright," as she was known to
me then, asked Father to bring me along on a cruise, on board her
schooner *Lyria*, out of Northeast Harbor down to the eastward,
along the Maine coast. In the early 1900's her parents' yacht, the
massive and beautiful *Hesper*, had been a punctuation mark against
the pointed firs of Northeast Harbor. On board the *Hesper* Mary
had learned not only the love of the sea that was bred close to her
bone, with a firsthand knowledge of the Maine coast, but the funda-
mentals of navigation, through fog and storm. She could read a
chart and steer a course by compass, without benefit of power, under
sail, like the true salt that she was. Even better, she could read the
portents of nature itself in wind and cloud, current and tide, moon
and stars, sea bird and seaweed.

Back in Boston during the winters of her youth the young Mary,
like other gently nurtured girls of her time, studied music. She told
me that she used to play four hands at the piano at 82 Charles
Street with my grandmother Quincy, of whom she was very fond.
Mary also studied singing; if the time and the place had been
different, she might have left home to pursue her studies profes-
sionally. As it was, she became the Victorian daughter whose delicate health indicated that she stay close to her parents, and then,
after her father's death, remain attached to her mother's apron
strings. When I told her once that, in looking back on my own life, I
felt I had made a mistake in remaining at home with Father after
my mother's death, she said, with the sublime certainty that was
her birthright, "Rubbish! There was a need to be filled, and you
filled it."

After her mother's death, however, this Elizabeth Barrett of
Beacon Hill, without the benefit of a Robert Browning, simply rose

up from her sofa, flung aside her lap robes, and decided that it was time to begin to live. First, she made up her mind that she was missing a great deal by being shy, so, with strong-minded Yankee practicality, decided not to be. Then she set out to see the world. And see it she did! She had already, inevitably, been to Europe with her parents. Now she struck off the beaten path. She cruised the Greek Islands before it was the chic thing to do, explored the prehistoric paintings in the caves of Southern France, motored through Spain; she bought a house in Majorca. Then came the Far East—a trip by mule litter into the interior of China, as well as travel in Japan. But during all these years the lodestar of her interests and temperament was New Mexico, and the history, lore, and present plight of the Navajo Indians. There, in Alcalde, she bought an old Spanish ranch house and flung herself into learning all that she could about the myths and rites of this people for whom she felt such a deep affinity. She formed a friendship with an Indian medicine man (it used to amuse me to hear her flat Boston rendering of his name—"Klah"). She recorded stories he told her, she attended the ceremonial dances of the tribe, and she delved into the symbolism of their sand paintings. The tangible memorial to her love and interest stands today in the Museum of Navajo Ceremonial Art at Santa Fe.

I suppose when I went on that cruise on the *Lyria* Mary must have been in her mid-forties. I only know that to me she seemed as old as God. The unceasing yackety-yack that went on (in all candor one must admit that Mary's voice was not pleasant) on subjects of no possible interest to youth, seemed part of a conspiracy on the part of my elders to bore and irritate me. On top of it, Mary Wheelwright's, to me, embarrassingly kittenish baby talk, her announcing that she was going to get the giggles, and then, horribly enough, doing so, her giving a nickname to everything—stove, frying pan, spoon, as well as to her good Maine captain—"Cappie"— only finished the work of plunging me into a self-absorbed sulking. I was not such a total dud as to remain impervious to the glories of the Maine coast, dropping anchor in a still black cove at sunset, getting the sails up with the first breath of wind in the morning, but I took to sitting alone before the mast, or lying face downward on the forward deck, watching the waves part as we cut through them, thinking about—eighteen-year-old me, me, *me*. I must have come very near to ruining everybody else's pleasure (*si jeunesse savait!*). A merciful veil of forgetfulness has concealed just what words transpired between Father and me; I can't even imagine what the interchange must have been between him and our hostess. I only know I was put ashore at, I think it was, Cutler, to make my way home alone by train. More than thirty years later when, from time to time, I asked Father, in a mood of self-flagellation, if I had been really awful, all I could get out of him—and how characteristic it was of him, neither to dwell on what was unpleasant nor, on the other hand, to deny a misdemeanor—was "You did not behave very well."

Father, actually, didn't relish Mary's giggles or Mary's Indian moccasins any more than I did, but he had a benign way of not letting unimportant traits stand in the way of what was to him important in his friendships. He was, in point of fact, no more attuned to the Far East and the American Indian than he was to Mary's good work on behalf of the South End Music School in Boston. In fact, sometimes I wonder exactly in what common ground Father and Mary's friendship and affection for each other did flower. Mary was no better a listener than Father to conversation concerning a subject that bored her. She liked to talk about what interested *her*, as he liked to talk about what interested *him*. During any given dialogue between them, each, with not well-concealed impatience, was obliged to wait out a monologue from the other before returning, more determined than before, to the attack. They agreed on politics (it added zest to any stand Mary took to revolt against the conventional Boston of her upbringing), they were fond of music and of poetry, were apt to have read any new British or American writer of interest, and—as I have said—they both loved sailing and the sea. I think, however, more than any of these bonds, along with a solid bedrock of character, they shared a positive, outgoing attitude toward life.

Mother and Mary Wheelwright simply didn't get on. As I came to know Mary better in later years I was aware how much each had missed in not doing justice to the other. In Mother's eyes Mary was overbearing, "sure" (that sin against the Light!), opinionated, and insensitive. There was, for instance, the friend to whom Mary said, "Why have you never let me meet your husband?" "Because I don't think you would get on" was the answer. Mary insisted. The introduction was made. At the next meeting Mary's verdict was handed down, "You were right. I don't like him." And yet I have heard Mary refer to Mother as "cruel"! Mary, as opposed to Mother, belonged to the same school of broad-gauged aristo-demo-cratic Gentle American which I have touched on among the Dear People, lacking a satirical sense. (Is it not true, for instance, that Eleanor Roosevelt lacked the same sense?) People were *people,* unilluminated by nuances of wit or perspicacity in the eye of the beholder. It was too bad that Mary and Mother never found each other out, because Mother would have followed Mary's explorations into the religions and philosophies of the East with far more sym-pathy and understanding than Father who, I rather think, reached for his pouch of Ehrlich tobacco blend and began filling his pipe when she started to talk on such subjects. All the same, before Mary sold her handsome high-ceilinged house on Upper Mt. Vernon Street, on a Sunday afternoon Father would say, "I believe I'll go and call on Mary Wheelwright." In later years, when my husband and I bought a house at Mt. Desert, Maine, Father followed with pleasure, not unmixed with ironic amusement, my own change of heart as his friend became my friend.

By this time Mary herself had cut the Boston knot, selling the large house on Mt. Vernon Street and even disposing of her parents' rambling old-fashioned house at Northeast Harbor. Allowing her-self to keep only such possessions as would fit into a snug little sea captain's cottage—the White Hen—built some hundred years ago, she settled herself on Sutton's Island, about a mile offshore from Mt. Desert. There, with only one Maine woman for company, before the few other "summer" families arrived, or after they left, Mary, unperturbed and unperturbable, lived as one of the only two occupants of the island, with a few ospreys and herring gulls for company. In winter she would take off to whatever corner of the world beckoned most temptingly. We knew that the next year we would find her, sails furled, riding happily at anchor back in her home port, ready to share the richness of the experience she had brought back with her.

I loved the fact that her passport simply read "The Cranberry Isles." To be Miss Wheelwright of The Cranberry Isles, U.S.A. seemed quite as splendid and every bit as authentic as to be the Dame of Sark of the Channel Islands! And yet it would have distressed her, as much as the Forbeses in their Naushon version of plain living, to hear emphasized the fact that some less fortunate people have to lead more conventional lives for the simple reason that they have not the money to live on an island—with a captain, a boat, a cook, and a massive stone dock. All of these prerequisites of the simple life she accepted as naturally as the wild lupin blooming in a field behind the house or the osprey's nest on one of the rocks.

The heart of the White Hen seemed to beat most intensely in the tiny bedroom (surely once it had been the captain's and his lady's) with its dormer windows looking out to sea. There was the little porcelain stove rescued from the *Lyria* before she was sold, and there was the rocking chair in which, back in a Boston nursery, an English nanny had rocked in her arms the little Boston Hapsburg Infanta with the large brown eyes.

Before I returned to Mt. Desert as a married woman the *Lyria* had been sold. When news reached Mary that the engine, which its new owners had insisted on putting in, had caused an explosion sending the beautiful schooner to the bottom, she broke the news to "Cappie." He spoke for them both when he pronounced the epitaph, "She's safe now." In her later years Mary chugged through the beloved waters in a converted lobster boat, with a Cappie the Second at the wheel. Sadly she would survey a yawl or ketch of a friend, saying, "They've told me they were going to ask me sailing this summer, but they haven't." The goal of a day's excursion was one of the countless islands that dot the coast, and the attraction of that island generally consisted of a great variety of stones along the beach. Alongside of Mary's selective eye for color, shape, and texture the responses of her companions showed as crude and uncontrolled. They staggered on board ''Cappie's'' little boat with burdens almost heavy enough to submerge her while Mary's slender long fingers serenely and gently caressed the one perfect object of her search.

On the outbound trip she would stand, alongside Cappie, peering through her field glasses at a dauntless little guillemot riding the waves or at the wet nose and melting eyes of a seal watching us woefully as we chugged past. Once landed, our picnic lunch invariably followed the same pattern: Mary, like a queen who has taken possession of her kingdom, would sit authoritatively on a stump of log, or warm rock in the sun, or hillock of squashy moss and, surveying her domain, pronounce with satisfaction, ''Nice world.'' Then she would uncork her thermos bottle, pour out her hot drink and repeat the same incantation, ''Soup of the evening, beautiful soup!''

When Mary and I were alone we talked with the intimacy of true friends, but neither of us ever mentioned that disastrous faraway cruise on the *Lyria*. In the intervening years, it is true, she had been kind to me—always, I felt, simply because I was Father's daughter. Her house in Northeast Harbor was one of the first in which I did a program of monologues at an evening party, and she came to another recital of monologues in London when I appeared in the little Mercury Theatre, and (I am ashamed to say, embarrassing me all over again!) turned up, by way of dissipation, with a long glass of ginger ale in the shadows of the rather *louche* atmosphere of the Blue Angel, where I was performing—her first taste of a New York nightclub!

As Miss Fanny Curtis announced herself as F. G. Curtis, so Mary Wheelwright spoke of herself in the third person as M.C.W. What M.C.W. lacked in humility, she possessed in *authority*. With the habit not unusual in a woman of means living alone, M.C.W., to put it bluntly, could be bossy—to the poor relation or other dependent female companion who happened to be in her train at the moment. All the same, there was a touching craving for human affection behind the façade. She was uninhibited in using terms of endearment to the friends whom she loved. "Pet" and "Duck" fell trippingly from her tongue. I was appalled as one can only be in the presence of a senior, when the façade cracks: Mary broke down once before me, and cried, remembering the pain she felt in having to give away a beloved little dog. Dipping down in the early morning from the pinnacle of the Notch Road, as a curtain of fog parted in a shimmer of sunlight to reveal the boats riding at anchor in Northeast Harbor, Mary exclaimed in gratitude for the memories she had of early mornings during her cruising days, adding, in substance, "When a married friend mourns for a husband who has died, I want to say, 'But you have *had* him.' " Only in those few words did she ever lift to me the curtain of reticence covering what must have been moments of acknowledged sadness.

For all her travels over the world there remained a pristine lack of sophistication; it did not seem to occur to Mary that part of her power lay in the depth of her pocketbook. She was not imaginative about realizing that dollars and cents didn't just naturally line the pockets of others. There was an occasional man—or an excuse for one—attached to her suite. I have heard Father speak of at least one of them as a "little brother of the rich." What hothouse bachelor, with aesthetic responses and a taste for comfort, would not have happily joined a cruise on Mary's schooner, or motored through Europe, or explored the Greek Islands, as her guest? Perhaps I am wrong, and she may have known exactly what she was doing. Even her giving of financial "charity" was done with her own touch, representing a personal, even idiosyncratic, interest. There were not only the Navajo Indians but the isolated inhabitants of many of the islands along the Maine coast, with many of whom Mary enjoyed personal friendship, as well as helping the ministry, on many levels, of the Maine Seacoast Mission.

As definitely as she knew what did appeal to her she knew what didn't. She simply didn't like Mexico. Albert Schweitzer left her cold. She liked to discover her Causes herself, and didn't care to take them at second hand. The Navajo Indians were "hers." There

was a royal sweep about the pronouncements she handed down. I
myself cowered under them more than once. Of my writing she
said with firmness, "I don't think you're a novelist, dear," and
we left the matter there. When she tore down her family house in
Northeast Harbor the purchaser of the property started to build a
new one. This lady, who did not know Mary Wheelwright, one rainy
afternoon was directing carpenters and contractors, following
her architect's plans, when a limousine rolled up to the door, driven
by a chauffeur who let out a tall lady wearing a sou'wester and
rubber boots. She advanced on the owner of the house saying simply,
"I've come to see if I approve of what you're doing." As it happened, she did. And the two owners, past and present, spent an hour
in congenial conversation. If Mary's displeasure was aroused, she
could dismiss with a word. At the Cosmopolitan Club in New York,
where she spent many winters and became something of a land-
mark, holding court in the lounge—she rose from an audience,
crowded into the club library listening to a young poet read from
his works, and left the room, pronouncing audibly as she swept
out the one word, *"Bumbly."* Of Cleveland Amory, who had
ventured to write of Boston and Bar Harbor, she said with
decision, "He should be boiled in oil." I witnessed, however,
the weapon of the one-word shaft turned toward her own retreating back. My husband and I, driving with Mary in a
New York taxi on the way to a concert, noticed that the driver
kept turning around to eye the *rara avis* in the back seat who was
delivering herself of various fruity opinions in firmly stated terms.
"Beethoven is like a deep massage. Mozart is like a light massage
with the fingertips." "I've never liked Vivaldi" was one of her
dicta, expatiating further by adding, "His music is twiddly." She
got out of the cab first, and as my husband collected his change the
driver looked past him to the entirely oblivious Mary, and with all
the mingled irony, incredulity, amusement, and plain scorn of
which a New York taxi driver is capable, uttered the one word
"Twiddly!"

Mary, actually, was rather remarkable where taxis were concerned. The same sixth sense that guided her judgment of tides and

winds and migrations stood her in good stead in the whirling currents of New York. She explained that, coming out of a concert at Carnegie Hall, or a Broadway theater, she saw that the thing to do was to get upwind of the taxis. So, when the stampeding theater public flung themselves on a stream of uptown traffic, the wily and agile Mary Wheelwright, springy of step as on the pine needles of a Maine island, crossed the avenue and pounced on her prey coming the other way, while bands of old ladies—actually her contemporaries—tottering on unsure legs and clinging to each other, waved futile white gloves and beaded evening bags at the full cabs that whooshed past them.

' In New York, Twelfth Street and Cherry Lane knew her quite as much as the more conventional Broadway theaters. If there were dancers from Bali, Japan, or Greece, there was at least one receptive pair of eyes out front. The Musica Aeterna concerts at the Metropolitan Museum and the Vedanta Center on Ninety-fourth Street were part of her New York life.

' Such artists as were friends of Mary's she picked before they became lions, and not afterward. Her friendship with Rachel Field was the natural outgrowth of their common love for Sutton's Island, where they had been neighbors. Mary actually had told Rachel Field that she was going to leave her the White Hen in her will, little thinking that the much younger woman would predecease her by many years. I don't know how or where Mary had known Sarah Orne Jewett, but remember, as we sailed past the burying ground on Big Gott's Island, windswept and yet strangely cozy and self-sufficient, Mary's telling me that Miss Jewett had said she would love to be buried there. The writer Henry Beston and his writer-wife Elizabeth Coatsworth were friends who lived the year round in her beloved state of Maine. Mary followed with proprietary interest any poetry on which her friend Abbie Huston Evans, inherited from Rachel Field, was at work. Mary did not live to know that Abbie Evans won the Loines Award for poetry from the National Institute of Arts and Letters in 1960. The English artist and writer Clare Leighton was a friend who returned Mary's appreciation. She wrote after Mary's death:

Our friendship was always so respectful—each of the other
—towards our separate works and concerns. . . . I hate to say
it, for it sounds horribly pessimistic, but it seems to me that
in the death of Mary there lies also some terrible passing of
most important and valuable verities: the sense of humble
duty to life, as well as the feeling of wonder— To me, as a
European with an almost extinguished trust in American
values, Mary stood staunchly as a vindicator—as a supporter
of what I had hoped. . . . For I am serious when I say that she
passes, with such as Santayana, as a challenge to what we
have to put in her place.

"Of all the wonders that I have yet seen, it seems to me most
strange that men should fear," could have been spoken by Mary.
Most strange—and, to her, most tragic. I remember her telling me
of talks she had had with her friend Mrs. John D. Rockefeller, Jr.,
whom she had come to know at Mt. Desert. Mary quoted this remarkable Abby Aldrich Rockefeller as confessing to concern about
her two oldest children. "It has *got* them," she said. "The others
will be all right, but it has got them." "It" was simply the curse of
fear, branded into their natures by the possession of great wealth.
Mary, taking pity on Mr. Rockefeller himself, whom she felt to be
suffering under the same excommunication from freedom, suggested
that he might find refreshment, as she had, in sailing. "Get a nice
Maine captain, shove off from shore, and go sailing" was her salty
advice. "How do I know I could trust the captain?" was the
answer, which might as well have been spoken in a foreign tongue
to the dauntless M.C.W.

When Mary went to live alone on Sutton's Island conventional
friends exclaimed, "I should think she would be afraid. Suppose
something were to *happen!*" The essential quality in Mary was that
she was unafraid—and that quality she shared with Father.
Through all the years, Mary never came to Boston without coming
to see "Your blesséd Pa," as she always called him to me. They
exchanged Christmas cards—Father's of his own composition,
Mary's always bearing some beautiful, little-known quotation
which she had discovered during the year. She came to see him when

he was staying with us in Maine, the summer in which he reached ninety and she herself was pushing eighty. She and Abbie Evans had been spending the night nearby, and came to breakfast with us. I remember Mary's exclamations of delight in the morning sun pouring in the windows, and gleaming on meadow and cove. "Everything about this house faces east," she said, "including your blesséd Pa." The amazing and unexpected thread that ran through Mary's nature was a shaft of mystic illumination. She said to Father on that visit, as each protested to the other that he/she did not feel old, "I'm glad to say I'm still not too old to know ecstasy." As she grew older she relaxed some of her Unitarian prejudices against ritual and was able to cross the threshold of an Episcopal church without a bristling of her Yankee spine. Of Boston friends who could not do the same she said, "They're afraid of it." The last summer of her life she was sharpening her intellectual and spiritual appetite on the whetstone of Jung's massive *Psychology and Religion: West and East,* and was working on a memoir of her own, *Journey into Understanding.* During that summer she seemed to be responding to an instinct to lighten the load of earthly impedimenta as she began giving away, with no dramatics, more and more of her possessions, saying simply, "I want to keep only what I can use."

The thing that might "happen," which her friends had so feared, occurred as an act of simplicity and dignity. On an August day, excusing herself from the table at lunch, saying that she was not hungry, Mary went to her little bedroom, with its dormer windows looking out to sea and distant islands, closed the door, lay down on her bed, and quietly died.

It remained for Abbie Evans to paint a poet's picture:

FOR ONE WITHOUT FEAR
(M.C.W.)

Struck down. No warning; no quarter. As should be
For one without fear.
Knew she the end was toward, was on her? Did
Illumination grant a blinding minute?

Did ecstasy companion her (God grant),
Her old friend of the road at utmost need
Coming at call?

How now, unhoused, let abroad?
Dispersed past knowing, or still
Indestructibly one,
In what guise and whither now courses
Down what trajectory new
The unspent force that was she?

Left back in time
Along with us
The things she knew:
The fog, the sun, the desert, and the sea;
In the long-loved, swift-relinquished room
The shut book lying, and the Hittite seals.
With its dead-honest word
The worn and handled pebble speaks of her.

ALICE BACHE GOULD

And did you once see a Bluestocking plain? If you saw Mother's
first cousin Alice Gould you did—even, alas, to the plain. Not just
as an uncompromising or uncompromised Boston maiden so often is,
a little dreary, but almost to the point of caricature—to the
point of ugliness. She bore a startling resemblance to the Mock
Turtle. She lacked a chin, she didn't do anything about her hair,
her figure was dumpy, her hemline uneven, her clothes dowdy. There
was about her the impression of sagging and spilling over; manuscripts overflowed bags that wouldn't retain them, just as strands
of loose hair straggled from under her hat. She could manage to
exude an air of martyrdom at the same time as implying that oneself was responsible for the fatigue, disgust, or simple disdain she
was suffering. Her little piglike nose, flat at the end, turned up in
the air, could give off a condescending sniff (she, too, sniffed); her
little brown eyes gleaming with intelligence were almost constantly
suffused with tears, of either amusement or sentiment. All the same,

Father often said simply, "I think that Alice Gould's is the most brilliant mind that I have ever known."

Indeed Cousin Alice's tragedy lay in the fact that the clear mind of a brilliant man was housed in the nature of a sentimental, difficult woman—and that woman ill favored physically. ("As I told you once," she wrote Father, "membership in the Phi Beta Kappa and in the Tavern Club, both impossibilities to me, are the two impossibilities that I most resent at the hands of Fate.") Torn in two emotionally, she nonetheless possessed wit and humor. Both crackled with classical and literary allusion. Her memory for quotation seemed bottomless. Her brilliant mind came to her through her father, Benjamin Apthorp Gould, that scientist whose name is most associated with charting the stars of the southern heavens at the University of Cordoba in the Argentine. Cousin Alice graduated from Bryn Mawr, in its first class, intending to become a mathematician. To that end she did graduate work at both M.I.T. and the University of Chicago. Only such a Mighty Maiden as she would have been nothing daunted to find herself, during the first war, teaching navigation to U.S. gobs at the Great Lakes Naval Training Station! In 1903 a visit to Puerto Rico not only revived her childhood knowledge of Spanish but fired the dormant passion of a born researcher. Like the desperate heroine of a fairy story, working against the dreadful odds of failing health, lameness, and pain, the aftereffects of a sunstroke, and the Spanish Civil War she completed—almost—her Herculean task (eleven articles in Spanish printed in the Bulletin of the Real Academia de la Historia, referred to by Samuel Eliot Morison in his *Admiral of the Ocean Sea* as "the most important piece of original Columbian research yet done in the present century"). In *almost* lay the flaw. Like the last sleeve of the last shirt the princess was making for her brothers who had been turned into swans, there was a twelfth paper left to be finished by the director of the Archives of the Indies in Seville.

During those years in Spain Alice Gould achieved unique recognition for a woman—and a foreigner. Known throughout the country as "La Mis," she lived to see in Simancas a street sign proclaiming the "Plaza Alicia B. Gould y Quincy," to receive, on petition of the Real Academia de la Historia, of which she was a corresponding member, the Cross of Alfonso XII, and to have pinned on her black silk dress by the Minister of Education that high symbol of Spanish approval, the Cross of Isabella the Catholic.

Father kept in touch with Cousin Alice during all those years. He did so not only for the interest and affection he felt toward a remarkable—and remarkably difficult—woman, but because the relationship involved Mother at a most sensitive point. There had been a highly charged intimacy between the two clever teen-age cousins, living on the family place in the remote country—as Quincy, Massachusetts, then was—when the elder returned from South America with her family. One of the indoor sports with which the girls entertained themselves was a running competition in writing the worst possible verse which still would be accepted for publication by the local Quincy *Advertiser* ("Long may'st thou continue, Thou ablest of sheets, Whose arrival on Thursday, Such gratitude greets" is a sample). For this performing art the girls used a variety of pen names. I still have a scrapbook, bequeathed when they were fourteen and sixteen years old, to the first daughter of either of them, bubbling with rhymes, drawings, and stories that obviously served as a safety valve to the sizzling energies of two talented girls. As I reconstruct it, Mother, by far the prettier of the two cousins, was the object of something approaching a sentimental "crush" on the part of poor Cousin Alice (come to think of it, I don't think I ever heard my parents refer to her in any other way than as "poor Alice"). She—like Margaret Norton—had been made to feel by her brilliant father that she had failed him on two counts; one, by not being a boy; two, by being an ugly girl. Then in Cordoba at the age of six she had lived through the traumatic experience of witnessing with her mother the drowning of her two twin sisters. She was unhappy at home, and had boundless senti-mental devotion to offer—to somebody.

If a bond of humor united the young girls in the first place, I am sure that their final separation was caused by Cousin Alice's Achilles heel: in a letter to another cousin she speaks of herself as "sillily, slushily, goo- and coo-ily sentimental." She placed friend after friend on the pinnacle of her adoration and, in time, inevitably when, to her eyes, feet of clay appeared—crack! went another friendship. It was after Mother's marriage that the inevitable happened. Mother was always reserved on the subject, and I could see that the mere mention of Cousin Alice made her unhappy. Somehow, unwittingly, she had managed to hurt the hypersensitive feelings of Alice. In any case, henceforth Alice placed herself merely on the fringes of Mother's life, remaining the aloof martyr.

Though Father was to murmur over and over again, "Alice can be very trying," it was he who served as go-between, correspondent, consultant, and sympathizer-in-chief with the self-estranged Alice. She reported back to him of her doings, and always saw him on her trips to America. There was not a little irony in the fact that Father was elevated to a rank worthy of her friendship. She had made it abundantly plain from the start that she considered that Mother, by stooping to a simple Howe of Bristol, Rhode Island, was tarnishing the sacred Quincy scutcheon. An English friend, about to visit America, asked Alice Gould, shortly before her death, if she had messages to send to anyone in Boston. "No," she replied, "but if you visit Quincy, fall on your knees and kiss the earth for me."

If there was a passionate love for the spot where she had been young, and where her forebears had lived, it was overlaid with a crust of such grotesque snobbery as to be more ludicrous than pathetic. That any descendant of the Quincy family was not automatically royal, and the rest of the world his inferiors, was sublimely illustrated when, on my return from entertaining with my monologues at a private party in Detroit, Father told her of my disappointment that Mr. Henry Ford had not been there as I had been led to hope that he might be. "Would Henry Ford [upturned nose in air] be at the same party as *Helen?* I should have thought that he would eat in the kitchen." It was she who, on first hearing that Father was the son of a bishop, delivered her withering one-two, "Methodist, I suppose?" The joke on her was that she came not only to accept the Bishop's son, but—more extraordinary still—

the pious wife of the Bishop whom she deigned to describe as a "rubricated version" of my grandmother Quincy.

Actually, aside from the bond of Mother, Father and Alice Gould, in quite other circumstances, would have found, in spite of her cloven hoof of snobbery, that they spoke fundamentally the same language. The vocabulary of that language consisted in literary and historical references, quotations (including Greek, Latin, *and* the Bab Ballads), interlaced throughout with humor. At random, here is a montage of some of her exchanges with Father:

> I am getting on decently well in health, though the sudden spurt of October last has withdrawn itself (Does a spurt withdraw?).
>
> ... Oh, my dear Mark, *do* you know somebody's Psalm Book just after the Revolution or during it, editor Billings? If not, make its acquaintance without delay. ... Whence the small tag Credat Judaeus—let the Jew believe it if he can? The little gnome in my head says, Satires of Horace; but he doesn't say it with deep conviction. I could walk straight to the shelf [in the Athenaeum] (4th floor, to the left ... where are the dictionaries of phrases and quotations in every sort of language). I find myself using the phrase as my sole commentary on a most elaborate theory of Columbus naming islands in the Hebrew tongue. Little Latin tags are vulgar, but this one fits. But unverified tags are dangerous. ... Dear Mark, Thank you so very much for the Credulous Jew; it seemed a good deal to ask of anyone to go on such a silly hunt; you did it *primorasamente, opiparamente*, and please give my thanks also to Miss Wildman, toward whom I feel a "lively sense of favors to come." En cuanto the decoration, I am *Comendador* like the Statue in "Don Giovanni." ... I miss the possibility of comparing notes with you on things true sense of that word, though seldom funny—things like the plums in the batter of an essayist—that are scattered through all sorts of miscellaneous books. ... I find I am continually trying to place things, and they sometimes come to me out of the ether. ... I will bet you heavily that you don't know Vicente Turturetus, on whom I have been battening; You have not missed much, unless you

expect in the next world to be a monarch—the crowned head
is the one for whom Lipsius wrote nice little maxims—Machia-
velli in syrup I call them. . . . There is no news to give you.
Archive publications would leave you more than usual ca'm.
. . . Here it is at last spring. In my head rings the characteristic couplet—

> "Spring beckons
> All things to the call respond—
> The trees are leaving and cashiers abscond."

(I hope you recognize it.)
. . . This reminds me to offer you a passage I ran across in a
quotation by Ruben Davis from an utterly (to me!) unknown
essayist, a Nicaraguan? which seems to me worth the best
essayists there are. Of course, the Spanish is more succinct
than my translation. "To make man in his own likeness and
image, it was necessary that God should make him also a
creator. The creation of Man is the world of books. Man makes
the book in his own image, he breathes into it the breath of his
own life, and it becomes a living soul and leads its own independent course." On which note I end affectionately.

When Cousin Alice used to come to see us as small children she
seemed to find open only two possible avenues of approach: one, to
teach; the other, to gush. I know we preferred the former, although
it was irksome, to say the least, to see her lips move in instinctive
correction, framing a *shall* or a *should* as a running accompaniment
to one's own ungrammatical *wills* and *woulds*. Her demonstration
with the skin of an orange, illustrating the principle of great circle
sailing, held, to be sure, a certain fascination, although today I
have completely forgotten what that principle was. It was harder
for a normal child to take in stride a note scribbled for his benefit—
as it was for mine—found on the front hall table when I came in
from playing, reading simply, *Didums was*. As we grew older we
found her tactlessness grew no less. On any piece of work accomplished—book written, recital given—she felt her first duty was to
criticize. This duty, always unasked, she always faithfully performed. Torn—as usual!—between heart and head she wrote Father

on the publication of his autobiography, "In fact, dear Mark, it moved me too much for me to be able to criticize."

She would send a message to Mark, already a professor at the Harvard Law School, "Tell him that I am always begging people to dot their I's, and that it is a pleasant variant to ask him to I his dots. A colon is not equivalent to the letter I." Praise or censure, she withheld neither. Her verdict was law. "The notice of Mark Jr's book is so good that it consoles me. . . . You sent me shorter notices before—I don't see— barring the *would* for *should* which you had so thoughtfully corrected!— how it could be better. And I point with pride—I point all over at the new writer in the family. Of course it was a very special chance, but the fact is that it is a better first book than any one else in the family has put out. And to be a Dean at his tender years! vamos!" She had the temerity to pass judgment even on her peer Samuel Eliot Morison. "Your excerpts about the Morison voyage are welcome. . . . I was still in the north when his party was in Seville, and am very sorry to have missed them; they would have been most refreshing. Some of his implications are certainly misleading—for instance, he makes it sound as if that very celebrated Virgin of the Navigaros was neglected and thrust into a casual cellar. It was waiting in a safe place its return to Seville, where it arrived in state two days before I got here, and was installed in the chief's office at the Archive with every government formality. And 'in Columbus' lifetime!—oh *dear* me! It was probably painted in 1536, or close to that date, CC had been out of his trouble some thirty years." In another letter, "I have not yet written to Sam Morison, but of course I mean to do so. It amused me to think how much his compliment in his *Admiral* has helped me to keep a stiff upper lip; I owe him very much though I ought not to care for any approbation but my own." Skipping any such conventional preamble as "it seems to me" or "do you mind if I make a few suggestions?" Cousin Alice would go right to work on her victim with "The trouble is," or "You make a mistake to. . . ." It must in fairness be said that the intelligence of her comments was a match for the didactic spirit that prompted them. Here she is, writing to Father on the subject of my freshman (and only) year at college:

> Cousin Alice, probably because she had such a norful time going to college herself, cannot get over the idea that college is of transcendant importance—and wants to know, most tremendously wants to know, just what courses H. is finding satisfactory, and what dubiously so, and how she is planning to go on next year if, etc. etc. The piece of advice which I hand out again would run—choose your professor rather than your subject! (within limits of course). Get yourself taught anything by first class men, rather than a special thing by riffraff. And in recognizing your first class teacher, I trust a great deal to undergraduate opinion. If a man has the reputation of being interesting, it is more to the point than that he trails the alphabet after his name in older society.

Before we hear Cousin Alice on other subjects here she is once again riding her favorite hobbyhorse—college education for women:

> . . . nothing and nobody can give [a girl] material to live on and by. She must get it herself, and through her own character. But—here is my special message—the longer I have observed women the more sure I have become that this eager reading this providing the grist to be ground is *not enough*. The self-educated well-read lady does not feel the difference between what she knows and what she only half knows—it needs talent which amounts to genius to arrive at the standards which four years of college work are sure to give . . . and only the student who has toiled over trifles and passed examinations, is properly fitted to go on with her education herself for the rest of her life. . . . Do not, DO NOT oh *do not* encourage her to go for a year and then stop, or for two years and then say she has had enough. You want her for the testing, and the degree as receipt for work accomplished. You asked me once if I did not think half a course enough—I tell you that the whole is not twice the half, it is twenty times it.

When Mark and Quincy were living as bachelors in New York there was an occasion on which they both had been summoned (none of us dared disobey one of her royal commands) to see her off on a steamer to Spain. They dutifully did so, and as they drove downtown together with her, their taxi was stalled in traffic outside their favorite speakeasy in the West Fifties. Mark described the look of sentimental yearning on Cousin Alice's face—eyes swimming— as she looked at Quincy, on whose face was duplicated the same look, as *he* yearned through the window of the taxi toward the door of the unattainable speakeasy. No sooner had they waved good-by than they returned for a drink.

She felt so passionately involved with the lives of the younger members of her family that when a beloved niece was facing divorce proceedings Cousin Alice's impulse was to cross the ocean from Spain to be at her side. There was nothing lurid in the situation, but in Cousin Alice's melodramatic imagination it drove her "wild" to think of the younger woman "facing curiosity derision and shame with no older person beside her." In justifying by reason the impulse which that same reason would never have been able to control she went on: "When it comes to barging in where one might better fear to tread, it is the more frequent mistake for older people to insist on meddling, but it is the greater, oh by far the greater mistake if they are defaulters when wanted."

In this instance, as in so many others, she was not wanted. In another context she summed up the pattern which was to repeat itself over and over: "I am really afraid that I unwittingly gave pain where I was trying to be affectionate." When that same niece was to remarry, her aunt Alice appeared in Boston from Spain, to supervise—unasked of course!—the proceedings. I am sure she was convinced that her physical presence would lend a certain respectability to the occasion. She lectured the bride-to-be, who was trying to carry off the occasion with simplicity and dignity, on the importance of seeing that the groom and his best man apply shoe blacking to the *soles* of their shoes: it could be very distressing to see glaring new soles as they knelt before the minister. Her orders were duly obeyed. It was fortunate, however, that the harassed bride who had bought her own slippers at the last moment in a suburban sale, could not see the horrified gaze of her aunt Alice as it fell on the soles of the bride's shoes—on which was stamped in large letters for all to read : REJECTED.

The heart of Cousin Alice's tragedy lay in a temperament which was forever preventing her achieving the very thing she wanted. "I too valued Berkeley Updike's friendship highly during the short time that I possessed it; I lost it (very justly) when I burst into tears during a social call, at a time when I was under what looking back now I think could be called a mild sort of shell-shock." She was hardly on speaking terms with her only sister, but when that sister died she was bitterly offended with those who did not write her letters of condolence. This same temperament, expressed in a total lack of order or system, was her undoing as a scholar, and thwarted her in the accomplishment of her life work. The straggling strands of hair, the dripping manuscripts, and dipping hemlines were only part of an all-pervasive messiness about which she could laugh when she did not despair. It is to Father, as usual, that from Spain she opens her heart:

I believe that it is only here in presence and touching distance of the original papers that I can finish the lagging book. It was like a derisive gesture on the part of Fate—that the last time that I wrote you naturally (and I don't even remember the date) I should prematurely have announced that the end was in sight. I really believed it, and was correspondingly elated. Well, I am today just exactly where I was then, except that I am facing such a mess of accumulated disarranged and half-forgotten papers as ought not to exist. Whatever my unpleasant characteristics may be, I am *not* an old maid, and to whoever accuses me of it I have only to say, "Go look at my top bureau drawer." But oh how fervently I now advise those who bring up children to insist on the habit of putting things in order at regular intervals—such as either bedtime or at worst Saturday night. My pitfall has always been that my high sense of the value of time has made me wait after getting papers out until I could be sure they wouldn't soon be needed again—and . . . the result is that my despacho might well be called a Chaos if it were not for the total absence of any Brooding Dove. I believe that all my vices are the seamy side of the corresponding virtues; I am late to appointments because it would be so dreadful for me to waste a minute or two in being early—etc. etc. ad infinitum et ad nauseam. But there comes a time when Satan sends in his bills, and I am now paying them. Do you know or remember that book of the last generation called "Happy Thoughts"? It was very familiar to Fanny and to me in our flippant childhood together, and today I have been thinking of the hero and the scrap he found in his notebook, 'Snails; why? who?' My haycocks of notes on different archives, concerning different friends or enemies of Christopher C are very like that.

Apropos of a special piece of paper she was looking for in her "paper haycock" she wrote, "Not a month ago, I saw the tail of it in some pile of stuff, and today I can't find it and I am reminded of somebody's receipt for dressing a baby: 'Get hold of a button and watch until the button-hole comes round.'" Her sagging spirits must have lifted, as the same letter closes on a different note. ". . . I am doing full work and giving seven hours a day to my desk and the Augean stables of hay in the drawers thereof. I repeat my dear, SEVEN HOURS. . . . Congratulations are in order! For the first time since I wrote you some fifteen months back, I am seriously dealing with the possibility that I may live to finish the Magnum Opus all myself. But I can't yet report on its condition, for I haven't yet got hold of it again. When the reins are really in my grasp, I shall feel its mouth and ride it on the curb." But she was soon writing again: "I seem to get worse and worse in disorderliness, and now being again (a year later and more) at the point where I cannot bear the confusion any longer, I am again clearing up and I would wager heavily if anybody would take me up, that I shall again stop before the task is completed." One letter to Father breaks off in the middle, and is picked up three years later. She ruefully admits, "I seem to have confounded Time and Eternity."

One of the deepest conflicts of her makeup was the continual war between the mind of the bluestocking scholar and the heart and blood of the natural creature.

. . . the older I grow, the more important I think the weather, so do I give more and more importance to the joys of what I call "rolling on the grass." In the days when one did it literally, one enjoyed it fiercely enough but still was always looking for some other joy to come along that would be better still; and now one knows that nothing is any better. But, I suppose my psychology is like that of most people, one does always want someone else to share with. "Could thy dear eyes in following mine," etc. etc. Believing that nothing dries one up like lack of enjoyment, I try hard to get some *conscious* enjoyment into each day; not always an easy task. Do you know, I think I was made more than ordinarily dependent on companionship; and certainly my life has been more than ordinarily solitary. All of which sententiousness may lead up to the simple statement that I went out today to clear my brain, and wandered under the glowing almost luminous canopy of the leaves in the Retiro, and saw the lovely rose-garden which every time I see it seems like a little bit of Seville, and too good to be true. I have been in city pent all through this spring; and have missed the best of it. The Retiro is kept in the horrid Spanish way, pulling up every blade of grass and raking the bare earth very neatly between plants when they want to be effective, but in this glorious burst of spring the workmen can't keep up with Nature, and they have agreed to let the grass grow in certain parts, and those I most affect. And the songs and the smells! the acacia trees are loaded with bloom and nothing ever smelt better than Spain in spring. The anger and bravery of the colors when you really get to the south is almost tropical. . . . I leave for the sea again tomorrow morning early; having spent three very hard-working weeks at Simancas with very little effect—the discovery is always round the corner. . . . I go under the wave seventy years old, and I come out again aged only thirty.

In wartime Spain, with its inevitable food shortages, the tug of home was particularly acute, but the tug to finish her work was stronger.

Let us leave the Deluge and speak of Mme. the Duchesse d'Angoulême. (I rely on this expression but I declare I don't know whence it is quoted.) No, my dear, don't waste ink in suggestions that I gather material and go home to write. That cannot be. This sort of work can only be done in situ; but there is no use in explaining this to those who have not worked with original documents. One can only bow and thank them for their happy suggestions. . . . At Thanksgiving, instead of drinking toasts to my health I wish you would have me in remembrance when you take a hot bath—and when you have afternoon tea with cakes. But vamos! if I deliberately go and live in a tiny village of adobe like houses on the upper plateau, I can't expect the service I might ask from the Ritz. At any rate I am thankful that I am where I am. Remember me most cordially to the turkey, and tell him I shall be thinking of him.

She wrote to a beloved cousin, "Ah, my dear, I believe, though it sounds as if I didn't, that the strongest help is across the ether and without contact; as for instance dear brave soul that I find you to be, have often and often helped me when you knew nothing about it. Don't cry, don't explain, and carry on! are my three commandments that I don't keep. . . . This is a week of anniversaries for me—no less than four of them, three of the profoundest import to me, and it is always a hard week to live through." She closed the letter: "If I ever get this book finished, I think I shall put on the title-page the slave's inscription on his oar, 'Oft was I weary when I toiled at thee.' . . . P.S. Damn."

That *damn* must have been wrung from her when she felt, for the thousandth time, the prick of her same old conflict. In a lucid moment she could write: "The Law School, and (mirabile dictu) the Business School are two institutions I should like to attend if I could be born again in proper shape." Since the shape into which she was cruelly born was a woman's, it was natural that she should have been a militant feminist. Even in her researches she was quick to take up the cudgels in the cause. "A day or two ago I ran into the name of the wife of a man known to fame only because he signed on in June 1492. The world will know from me that she was already a widow in—I forget the year and month, but she went and drew his pay, and *got it;* I rejoice with her across the centuries."

When Mother's sudden death felled us all, Cousin Alice's grief was compounded with the bitterest remorse. For the rest of her life she was to cling to Father with touching devotion, not only as a remaining link with Mother but for the particular quality of unruffled steadiness and sweetness that he was able to offer her. Her letters became more and more affectionate: "Mark dear," "Mark dear-*dear* Mark." She always wrote to him at the time of Mother's birthday in April, for which day, each year, even before they were engaged, he tried to get a bunch of her favorite Mayflowers. "Day after tomorrow—the 14th—there will be Mayflowers on sale in Boston streets, as we both remember every year." When my brother Mark's second daughter was named Fanny, "Yes, I know how you feel about the name. I feel the same way."

Father, on his side, played the role of a sort of faithful, long-suffering Hound of Heaven, never quite letting Cousin Alice slip entirely over the horizon, in spite of the vagaries of her temperament that would have made it all too easy to do. She wrote: "I am really thoroughly ashamed of my long silence. You have been so good and so persevering in writing, and your letters have meant a great deal to me." She knew she could turn to him, no matter what her mood. "I enclose a scream. Adding a trifle of ordinary letter, would say: I am of course not very well, but when I look back upon today a year ago, when I could have sat for a portrait of the Moon herself, craters and all, I do feel the gratitude I should. I suppose it is time we both accepted the fact that we are old. . . . Dear Mark, excuse my screaming aloud at you; I know one ought to consume one's own smoke, but you do it better than I do." The intensity of her affection for and dependence on Father deepened. "I hope my dear that you won't think yourself at liberty to die now that you are eighty, for you are one of my remaining anchors," and "I love you my dear—try to love me! Is there anything you especially wish me to do (or not to do)?"

Father was eighty-two when I became engaged to be married, and Cousin Alice's first thought was of him:

   I was once told that my natural attitude was that of a mother-in-law. I mean that her point of view always occurs to

me first of all. If not quite true, it is true enough I realize that
I look at your side of it more than is intrinsically just or wise.
You, and how much more I, don't any longer matter in the
making of such decisions. . . . This neatly finishes your work
as head of a family; now retire and try to contemplate this life
as if you were looking through a hole in the clouds already,
and had never heard of responsibility or of doing your bit—
all that belongs to the Past.

Cousin Alice never wrote to me, any more than she ever referred
to any of my books, which I am sure she must have loathed. But
when I went out to be married in Los Angeles—a city in which I
knew nobody—there were flowers on the altar of the small church
in which the ceremony was performed. Afterward the card told
me they had come from Cousin Alice, cabled from Spain. If she
was not thinking of me personally, she had not forgotten the
daughter of my parents.

As the date of my marriage was approaching she had written to
Father: "My dear, this goes by sea not by air, but even so I hope
it will go slowly, for I don't want it to arrive just at this im-
portantest date that is left you (except one)."

That other date, mercifully, Cousin Alice did not live to see, so
that her wish was granted that Father not "go and die first."

Let him finish her story:

> Oppressed in her later years with deafness, lameness, and
> excessive fatigue after brief periods of work, suffering a sense
> of frustration in having to commit to other hands the conclud-
> ing pages of her monumental work, she was yet able to draw
> with her own hand an admirably lucid last will and testament
> only twelve days before her death on July 25, 1953. On the
> evening of that day she was sitting in the garden at Simancas
> between the castle containing the Archives and the Research
> Residence in which she was then living. Feeling chilled, she
> asked her faithful attendant, Maria Zamora, who seldom left
> her side, to fetch her a coat from the house. Maria charged her
> mistress not to move during her brief absence. When she
> returned she found that Miss Gould had risen and fallen on
> the near-by bridge leaning across the moat at the Archives.

Women carried her to her bed-room where a doctor, immediately summoned, pronounced her dead from cerebral
hemorrhage. The day of her death was that of the Feast of
Santiago, Patron of Spain. Her body, accompanied by Maria
Zamora and the Mayor of Simancas, was taken to Madrid
under arrangements made by the American Consulate, and
buried there in the British Cemetery. The Spanish press
recorded her death and work as if honoring a national figure.
If not at her beloved Quincy, the beloved soil of Spain would
surely be that in which she would have chosen to lie.

No allusion has been made here to Alice Gould's religion,
which I take to have been like that ascribed to the sensible
man—a religion about which he does not talk. Brought up a
Unitarian, confirmed in middle life in the Episcopal Church,
decorated finally with the Cross of Isabella the Catholic, she
may be assumed to have cared more for deeds than for creeds.
It would have been hard to obtain her consent to quoting
from a letter, written when she was 82, a passage of "thinking
out loud." Yet I venture to give it here as a declaration of
faith not made for shouting abroad but revealing a spirit
comparable with Schweitzer's "reverence for life," and no
less to be held in remembrance than the labors she performed.
"All that I have to say sums up to the acknowledging of affection, and of its preponderating importance. But one can't
enjoy any real friendship, nor any deep affection, without
sharing a central underlying, all-motivating belief in the
existence of right as opposed to wrong—a distinction really
existing in this bewildering world. But as for details—for
judging any particular act or belief as belonging to either
class, that does not matter at all! I fancy that you and I
would in general tend to classify right and wrong in the same
way—but I have intimate friends of whom this is not true, and
it does not (Heaven be thanked) affect the intimacy. I am
much attached to some religious (or irreligious) fanatics, to
some of utterly different social placing, to some whom I
humbly acknowledge as my superiors, and some whom I think
silly and ignorant, and I love them all with exactly the same
sort of love. I suppose it is the sense that we are fighting under
the same banner even though our inmost objectives are differ-

ent. Shoulder your duds, dear Camerado, and come along to the next world, be it a conscious world or not."

There seems something ironically out of drawing in the fact that this amazing woman and distinguished scholar and born writer, if ever there was one, left behind just one small published volume— a life of Louis Agassiz—which appeared in the series of "Beacon Biographies" edited by Father. Appearing in 1900, the year of Quincy's birth, it was dedicated "To Q. H. Parvum Parvo." As a human being, her impact was unforgettable, but there, too, she was overtaken by the same fate, embodied in the word *manquée*— courageous, sentimental, brilliant, impossible, loving, lonely—she was a most unhappy woman. R.I.P.

11

VOICES

IN RECALLING CERTAIN HUMAN LANDMARKS on the Brimmer Street and Boston scene I have written only of those I myself knew. But Father, like other breadwinning family men was answerable to voices which came to him from beyond the circle of family and friends. His response to their call may serve as a chink through which we catch a glimpse of the daily round of one Gentle American of the Boston of fifty years ago.

During all his Boston years no voice was to speak to Father with the ring of clearer authority than that which came to him from Harvard. It spoke to him in the summer of 1913 in a letter from President Lowell:

> William Phillips writes me that they are urging you to take the editorship of the Harvard Bulletin. I hoped they would do this, for although it is not my business,—the Bulletin being conducted by the Alumni Association, of course it comes very close to me, and the paper has to be conducted in intimate relations with the University authorities. I am writing, therefore, to say that it would be a great pleasure to me if you should take the place; and that I believe you would do it to a turn. I have no doubt also that you would enjoy the job.

It has been said by a contemporary critic that "Boston and Harvard are two ends of one mustache." Father was to give himself up to the enjoyment of wearing just such a mustache. He used to quote the aphorism that the Harvard Corporation is "a government by seven cousins." To indulge in a little social, if not sociological, hairsplitting I see the hard inner core of Harvard's governing body, speaking the language of State Street with overtones of Wall Street, as definitely Short-Tailed. It remains one of life's mysteries how that small group of inevitably limited men has managed to create and maintain at the same high level an institution which C. P. Snow, for one, sees as "in many ways the most splendid university" in which he has ever set foot. Surely the Long-Tailed scholars, teachers, graduates, and undergraduates, with an occasional member of the Board of Overseers, have helped to make the University what it is. It was unquestionably with the latter group that Father found his reward during the years he spent as part of the Harvard family. Actually he was editor of the *Harvard Alumni Bulletin* for only six years, though he was a member of its editorial board for more than twenty-five. Long after those years were past there was a group of men, then scattered in their various literary callings— Brooks Atkinson, David McCord, Ralph Barton Perry, Edward Weeks among them—who continued to remember with nostalgia the Friday lunches, held at the Colonial Club, when subjects for editorials for the next issue of the *Bulletin*—and many subjects of far more widely ranging interest— were discussed.

During the years 1913 to 1919—the span of his term as editor of the *Bulletin*—Father was inevitably insulated from participation in the war behind the barrier of his years. The swath cut by the nation's wars through the generations of one family is as capricious as history itself. In the Civil War my grandfather, then over fifty, along with his friend Phillips Brooks and other clergymen of Philadelphia, shouldered shovels to make earthworks of defense for the city when Lee was invading Pennsylvania. His attitude toward the whole drama seems today as outmoded as the earthworks themselves: "It was a grand period in our Nation's history, and I have always regarded it as an occasion of personal Thanksgiving that I had my time of being cast at that period, and my residence fixed in Philadelphia, the patriotic city.

I saw many of the regiments that were on their way to the seat of war, march through the streets, and whenever I met them I stood uncovered until they had passed by. I not infrequently heard them chanting to their music to which they kept step, 'John Brown's body lies a moldering in the grave.' '' In spite of the fact that Father and his two brothers lived into their nineties, none of the Bishop's sons were involved in any of the nation's wars. But the Bishop's grandson, son of his daughter Elizabeth, Alfred Reginald Allen, a brilliant neurologist in his early forties, living in Philadelphia, with a distinguished career ahead of him as a pioneer in the opening new field of psychiatry, rather than joining a medical corps along with his confreres, was so fired in World War I with crusading zeal in his passionate adherence to the cause of the Allies that he enlisted in the Army. As a major in the infantry he was killed on his first day at the front in September, 1918, in the Meuse-Argonne offensive. And in the Second World War it was the turn of the generation who, without benefit of conviction of living in any "grand period," were struck down with an even more poignant gallantry by the onslaught of history. In the Howe family the sacrifice was paid by the Bishop's great-grandson—Uncle Arthur's grandson—Alder Blumer Howe, who, at twenty-four years old, was killed in 1943 at Guadalcanal.

Even without the barrier of years Father's impaired eyes would have kept him out of active participation in the war. He could not but have agreed with Emily Dickinson that "war is an oblique place." And yet for all that was oblique about his involvement with the great drama of his time Father touched it (or was touched by it) through the voices of the young Harvard men who fought and who lost their lives in its battles. These voices came to him in their letters. First, came his editing of *Harvard Volunteers in Europe,* published in 1916, confirming his belief that any man can write, provided he has a story to tell. This book led ultimately to five massive volumes (three of which Father edited singlehanded, two with collaboration) *Memoirs of the Harvard Dead in the War Against Germany.* Considering the two hundred and thirty-four biographical sketches which he wrote himself (two thirds of the total number published), it is not surprising that he took more satisfaction in this achievement than in any other work he ever performed.

The life of one son of Harvard touched Father's with particular poignancy. And a son of Harvard is quite literally what Lionel de Jersey Harvard was. Young Lionel, a collateral descendant of the founding John Harvard, was brought to Cambridge in 1911 by a group of interested alumni. Father, who had played a role in ascertaining his very existence, met him on the evening of the day of his arrival, and the foundation for the affectionate friendship that was to blossom was laid forthwith. Lionel made a name for himself not only as a student but in countless college activities, winding up as winner of the first Boylston Prize in elocution, class poet, and writer of the Baccalaureate Hymn. Father recalled, "At the afternoon exercises of the 1915 Commencement there was nothing finer or more memorable than the straightforward, manly speech of this youngest alumnus." When Lionel returned to England in July of that summer (not having been accepted the year before when he tried to enlist) he wrote to Father, "I can never put on paper, of course, how much I owe to you. To you, probably more than to any other man, is due the happiness—and I think the profit, too—of these last four years of mine." Letters continued to come to Brimmer Street—first from the Chelsea Barracks of the Grenadier Guards, in which outfit Lionel had been given a commission.

"It all seems so natural in a way, and Cambridge seems such a tremendous distance off, too real for a dream-world, but almost as remote. I often think of all the friends and haunts there, and look forward joyfully to the time when I can come back and show them all to my wife, and show her off to them. . . . Give my very kindest regards to Mrs. Howe, and in fact remember me to America."

He was invalided home in 1916 and later returned to the same regiment in which his brother had been killed a few months before. He wrote to Father in June, 1917, "I hope Mrs. Howe and your boys are well. I can imagine Quincy thirsting for khaki!" On April 11, 1918, he was killed in action. I remember Father's sadness, some of which crept into his official words in the *Bulletin*: "His hope was to serve his generation as a medical missionary.

Instead he has laid down his life of rare promise—a life peculiarly embodying the joined sacrifice of England and America to the common cause. Thus he has repaid all that Harvard gave him, and left, in overpayment, a fragrant and noble memory.''

It was owing to Father's connection with Harvard that Brimmer Street enjoyed yet another foreign infiltration, this time with a happy ending. The French officers! Father had brought home for the scrutiny of Mademoiselle photographs of the five officers of the French Army due to be sent over by their government to train the R.O.T.C. at Harvard. Naturally, with me jumping up and down beside her, we had to decide which was ''le plus beau.'' The decision was made. Came a big parade in their honor the day the medal-bedecked officers arrived in Boston. I stood with Mademoiselle in the window of the house of a family friend in Beacon Street. As they passed our window, Mademoiselle spotted ''her'' officer, and called out the name she had memorized, loud and clear, ''Vive, Giraudoux!'' He turned, enchanted to be thus personally welcomed among strangers, and waved and smiled. Jean Giraudoux.

He came subsequently to the house along with his companions. One of them was André Morize, who continued to come to see Mademoiselle, and who was to stay on after the war in Cambridge to charm future generations of Harvard undergraduates—and of susceptible Boston ladies. As for Giraudoux—I wish I could remember more than an attractive presence. Naturally, he was forgotten by me when Mademoiselle became engaged to one of his fellow officers. Up to the last she said to my mother in private of her prospective bridegroom, ''Le Capitaine a très mauvais caractère.'' Mother wrote to a friend: ''The whole performance is very un-American,—'Made in France' is the label on this marriage. Mademoiselle is entering matrimony so free from illusions that she can't be disappointed. . . . It will be at Emmanuel, and a little reception here will follow. Mr. Howe will escort her up the aisle, and Helen and [Mademoiselle's niece] will be pink crepe-de-Chine bridesmaids. Little Mark is the color of a cucumber to think that he is to have no official position in a wedding at which blue-clad French officers with raised swords may figure!'' So we lost Mademoiselle, and Kiss. And so, in fairly short order, did le capitaine. He lost her to his lieutenant, whom she subsequently married—and with whom she lived happily ever after. Could the Brimmer Street verdict be anything but ''How French!''

Welcoming French officers was by no means the only way Boston showed its war feelings. ''Don't sit next to Mark Howe. He's tainted.'' So spoke a fellow member of the Tavern Club, seeing an empty place next to Father at the club table, and knowing of his admiration of Woodrow Wilson. Father merely tainted himself further by heeding his own inner voice of gentleness and moderation at a time when many members of the same club were turning their backs on an erstwhile friend and long-time fellow member. He was a German portrait painter, Ignaz Gaugengigl, affectionately known as ''Gowgy.'' This sweet modest artist had been tenderly loved and humorously teased for the heavy German accent which he had not been able to shed after more than forty years of living in the United States, and had attained in the club the status of a sort of neo-mascot. When war feelings ran high, incredulous that men he had believed to be his friends could turn on him, Gowgy rarely went to the club, remaining alone and heartbroken in his studio, near us, in Otis Place. Mother and Father made one wartime Christmas dinner memorable for us by including him in our family party.

Father and Major Higginson and other like-minded trustees of the Boston Symphony Orchestra were terribly unhappy when Karl Muck was apprehended as an undesirable alien, and forced to leave his post as conductor. At Harvard there had been whispers of suspicion leveled against Hugo Münsterberg, Professor of Psychology. Before the matter could be settled to anyone's satisfaction Professor Münsterberg tactfully solved the problem by dying of a heart attack while teaching his Radcliffe students.

Even the Armistice, bringing the cessation of hostilities to the battlefields of Europe, did little to dampen the fever pitch of emotion in Cambridge, Massachusetts. Father was caught in a crossfire of infighting Harvard alumni. At a meeting of the Harvard Corporation in November, 1916, it had been voted to ''establish at

Harvard University a fitting memorial to the Harvard men who
gave their lives in the European war of 1914, at such time and in
such form as shall later be determined.'' Among those who were
to do the determining were President Lowell, Major Higginson,
Cameron Forbes, and Father. Then followed a stream of violent
letters to the *Bulletin*. Some expressed horror that implicit in the
resolution of the Corporation was inclusion in a Roll of Honor men
who might fall fighting for Germany; others, equally violent, gave
vent to the opinion that if a man gave his life for his country—no
matter what the country—he was worthy of a memorial, along with
his fellow sons of Harvard. After America's entry into the war
there were those who preferred to forget that official Harvard had
ever taken a stand so *audessus de la mêlée,* and Father, as editor
of the *Harvard Alumni Bulletin,* who had merely reported the
official resolution, came in for as much blame as though he had
instigated it.

Perhaps this tempest in the Harvard teapot was one of many
reasons which made Father responsive in 1919 to the voice of his
old friend Ellery Sedgwick, who invited him to return to the *Atlantic*—as vice-president of the company, and editor of the Atlantic
Monthly Press.

Father used often to say, ''There are two Ellerys. One of them is
the nicest, most warmhearted fellow in the world.'' It was that
Ellery with whom Father went on a camping trip in the Canadian
Rockies one summer, who appeared to give us children his blessing
in Brimmer Street of a Christmas morning—all rosiness and glowing Yuletide cheer: between Father and that Ellery there was a
lifetime's affectionate friendship. Mr. Sedgwick's brilliance as an
editor verged on genius. The fact that, during his years as editor
of the *Atlantic,* the circulation of the magazine paid for itself before
counting any advertising returns speaks for his magician's or Midas
touch. As actual business colleague—and Father's were by no
means the only findings on this subject I have heard expressed—
the ''other'' Ellery could cause both dismay and uneasiness. I
should not be recording honestly if I did not recall that there was
more than one occasion when my parents emerged with worried

faces from a colloquy behind closed doors, concerning the "other" Ellery.

One of Mr. Sedgwick's great gifts was to manage to keep the cauldron of drama and excitement continually on the boil in the *Atlantic* offices at 8 Arlington Street. One of these dramas exploded around the "Lincoln" letters. I have been told by an eyewitness of the great day on which Mr. Sedgwick gathered his staff about him to tell them he was about to receive a recently discovered packet of love letters written by Abraham Lincoln to Ann Rutledge. My informant laughed in remembering the way Father received the announcement (repeated on the day when the letters arrived and Mr. Sedgwick was so overcome with emotion that he had to withdraw to an alcove alone to give vent to his feelings)—with a smile, and a slow shake of his head. In spite of that smile and that shake the letters were published in the *Atlantic*. Whenever the inevitable publishing disaster that followed was mentioned Father used to say, "The truth is Ellery *wanted* to believe the letters were real." Nobody that worked in 8 Arlington Street—least of all Father—ever complained that working in an office dominated by Ellery Sedgwick was dull.

Aside from the perennially mounting pile of manuscript of whatever was the work in progress at home (in 1919, he published *George von Lengerke Meyer: His Life and Public Services* as well as *The Atlantic Monthly and its Makers*) his daily concern was the care and feeding of authors in his role of bringing them to bed of a book to be published by the Atlantic Monthly Press. One was Lord Charnwood's *Lincoln*, another was James Truslow Adams's Pulitzer Prize-winning *The Founding of New England*. A volume of essays in which he took especial interest, as he did in everything that came from his pen was *Letters and Religion* by John Jay Chapman. The voice of Chapman both as writer and as friend was one which was to boom in Father's ears in unique tones.

———◆———

Although that name is even yet not known to the wide public it deserves ("in his fiery incompleteness and buffeted integrity

he looks like some of his predecessors from Poe to Melville
and the elder Henry James, or like his contemporaries Adams
and Mencken''), his unique genius expressed itself not only
in some of the most brilliant letters written by an American but
in ''the most miscellaneous of miscellaneous writings—two books
on political reform, essays on Greek genius, on Emerson, Whitman,
Balzac, Shakespeare; sketches of his contemporaries; translations
and moral and religious speculations; a life of William Lloyd
Garrison; and numerous attempts at original plays—for adults and
for children—on such native themes as Benedict Arnold and John
Brown.'' A Gentle American Chapman was not—either in his
feelings or in his expression of them. A crash of thunder, a bolt of
lightning were always to hand in his writer's arsenal. He said of
himself, ''I hate and despise respectability. I am full of poetry and
blood.'' Although Chapman's rage was often brought down on
Father's head, there was something in the very way he let it rip
more suggestive of a protectively tender older brother than a God
of Wrath. After the friendship was under way, all of his letters to
Father were signed ''Affectionately, Jack.''

Here is Father's impression of his friend:

> One saw him approaching on a New York street, perhaps
> Fifth Avenue, and felt at once the nearness of a notable figure.
> Tall, with the commanding presence to which a prophet or a
> poet might lay claim, bearded in his later years, and then of a
> grizzled grayness, with small, piercing, friendly eyes, and
> clean-cut features, bending slightly forward as he walked
> with shorter step than most men of his height, dressed with
> something of the sweet neglect that sits best upon either the
> well dressed and well formed, wearing a woolen scarf about his
> neck and shoulders in almost all weather, and singular above
> all else through the lack of a left hand.

Chapman, who, to expiate his sense of sin for having struck a
friend, had burned off his own hand in a live fire, was literally
seared by his recognition of evil and violence in himself as in
others. He seemed to feel an obligation to shelter the guileless Mark,

pointing out to him that the world really was not the sweet and secluded garden he took it for. Father, for his part, savored his friend's extraordinary capacity for righteous indignation, shot through with a divine sweetness. Chapman made him think of the man in an epileptic fit, whom William James recalled as described by a witness in a trial "pleasant like, and foaming at the mouth." Each of the friends was true to his own essence.

Chapman wrote to Father in June, 1918:

> I noticed that you were made a scapegoat of by the Corporation—in the Roll of Honor business. Serve you right for playing with that bunch. They're the biggest bunco men in American life. . . . As I understand it, the Harvard Bulletin has not anything to do with Harvard—nor is it in any sense a *Bulletin*, but just a sort of sheet that M.A. DeW.H. gets out once in a while and puts in anything he happens to think of— it's just the cries and joyous chatters of an idiot boy—and one day he was saying "Roll of Honor" "Roll of Honor" to himself— and he acknowledges—they say he admits that he meant nothing at all by it—but only as if he were saying "Goo!" Serious old drulers shake their heads at me and say, "Ah, Chapman, you were misled by M.A." etc. It appears that the rumor all arose etc.
>
> Your masters are not only liars but cowards or they'd have been interested in *excusing* your very natural error (if there was any)—due to their own past course of conduct. This would have cleared them from future suspicions.

To Father, as editor of the Atlantic Monthly Press, he wrote:

> . . . Ellery has been so wonderfully good and taken so no end of trouble over my books that I don't want to bother him; but you see I *must* offer it to him. It would be indecent not to and I shall not be surprised by his not wanting it. It is strange that MADeW etc. should be able to hold Ellery and me together. You must be a rare amalgam to equalize such different conductivities.—You can't be pure gold or he'd put you in the safe deposit.

A little over a year later:

I know perfectly well that your own desire is to publish the essay as soon as possible and, of course, know that trade conditions next autumn, Ellerys's health . . . anything you like, may arise to make the Atlantic Press not desire when autumn comes to put out more money in such a slow-returning of profits enterprise as this essay of mine. But—remember this also—that the Universe is groaning for that essay and that it ought to come out next autumn at the latest, and that it would be rather a weak answer to the Universe for me to say that Mr. Sedgwick regrets that his financial ventures do not make the new essay look "attractive" etc. I should really blush to answer the Universe with such rubbishy talk. . . . This outcome for me is due to your exceeding conscientious honesty (as to which I have never known another man—let alone publisher—who approached your standards) which has caused the truth to sift into my mind that I might be getting into a position of helplessness as to the time of appearance of that essay—for *you* may die, Ellery may go mad etc. It would be truly a great consequence flowing from a small matter if your death or Ellery's madness delayed that essay's publication. . . .

As to Ellery, I believe Ellery is half converted and day after tomorrow will find he's glad to have printed it and damn the sales. I believe in miracles. . . . I am damned grateful to Ellery and am . . . against feeling that we've led him on unconscionably. Why, man, mightn't we to care about his immortal soul?

For Father's Gentle Americans the very words "*Atlantic Monthly*" were sacrosanct. Invigorating breezes from Chapman's home on the Hudson blew all cobwebs away, very nearly blowing the *Atlantic* along with them.

I:— What shall we do with this dreadful *Atlantic Monthly* that keeps piling in? It depresses me to see it about.

My wife's sec'y (Miss Montgomery): Why not send it to Mr. Crosby the Clergyman at Red Hook?

(Red Hook is a doghole 100 miles from N.Y.—with nothing

in it—no human beings ever—only the descendants of Dutch farmers—about 500.)

I:— But wouldn't it be cruel to add the *Atlantic* to Mr. Crosby's miseries—like poking in cornstalks through the bars to a dog?

Miss M.:—No, I think he'd like it.

I:—You mean *read* it?

Miss M.:—Why yes.

I:—Well, do as you like.

The explanation seems to be that the *Atlantic* is the skyey messenger to the shut-ins. One must be intellectually marooned—dying of starvation—in America preferably—but perhaps anywhere . . .

If Chapman exaggerated his own feelings of derision for the subject matter printed by the *Atlantic* that was only because Chapman, on his own account, was every bit as explosive and emotional as Ellery Sedgwick. Though he was to continue to heap objurgations on Father's head over the years, Father could be sure of an affection which did not waver. When he declined an invitation which had been given to him and to Mother to visit the Chapmans in Barrytown, New York, Chapman wrote: "I'm only afraid that you've got so used to being tied up that you tie yourself up unnecessarily and forget to scatter in a bit of leisure—so that the remaining years of your life may show more of it than the early ones. . . . Now—unless you are resolved to die in your shell—I shall leave it to you to suggest yourself and don't forget that you're growing old; and old people become stuffy and immobile and it's very bad for them."

He knew how hard Father worked, and respected the economic necessity back of much of it. In speaking of one of his own sons he wrote: "I wish he had a hard working New England father like MADeW. Howe—and *no money*—and were obliged to run about and do errands and learn hardness. . . . Do punch his head if he needs it." Though Chapman's translation of Greek plays was published by Houghton Mifflin, he could write to Father, employed by a rival firm: "I wish you would write the *Transcript* or *Atlantic*

review of my Gk plays *yourself*. These professors and Greekists are
jealous and narrow minded. Just see if you can't do it, and if it
wouldn't be a good change from your everlasting Biography." And
then, "I am delighted at your kind remarks and only surprised that
a man of your experience, penetration, age, refinement and sagacity
shouldn't perceive the kind of hair-pin I am anyway."

————◆————

There must have been some magnetic substance in Father's
makeup destined to attract hairpins. Perhaps it is not a fair description of the ascetic, suffering Gamaliel Bradford, but he, too, was
an offbeat as well as an offstage voice. One can even fancy these
voices of Bradford and Chapman as emanating from behind a tragic
and a comic mask at either side of the proscenium arch which
spanned Father's time, both parochial and universal. In actuality
the flesh which embodied them could not have presented a greater
contrast: Chapman, bearded, robust, and arresting in any company; Bradford, pale, emaciated, so withdrawn in temperament as
to be virtually an invisible hairpin.

Does the reading public today remember the popularity of
Gamaliel Bradford as the author of a "new" brand of biography?
Preceding Lytton Strachey, as H. L. Mencken pointed out, Bradford introduced to America a form of sketch which he called a
"psychograph." I remember Father's quoting Lawrence Lowell,
in discussing biography in general, as saying, "I don't care what a
man *is*. I care what he *does*." Gamaliel Bradford's interest lay in
exactly the opposite direction. Father had come to know Bradford
when he was writing unsigned editorials for the *Youth's Companion* and had been canoeing with him on the Charles River.
Then came encounters at the Examiner Club and the Saturday
Club, as well as at meetings of the Library Committee of the
Boston Athenaeum, which, incidentally, Bradford loved as much as
Father did, saying he wished he might be laid out there in death.
The discovery that he was a distant cousin of Mother's provided an
added "bond" and we children were asked to call him "Cousin
Gam" on those very rare occasions when we saw him in what passed
for the flesh. Any such appearances in Boston were to become less

and less frequent for him, except when by Herculean effort he was able to achieve attendance at a Symphony Concert, or a professional baseball game!—as invalidism, probably largely psychic, kept him confined to his home in Wellesley Hills. Father felt that "never . . . was there a more gently considerate soul, condemned to the tortures of his own sensitive spirit—and never a more sympathetic friend . . . he fought the long battle between weakness of body and strength of spirit to a triumphant close."

As early as 1919, having discovered that he could use a type-writer, Bradford wrote to Father:

> I suppose you are thinking a great deal about the vast issues the world is debating. So am I, of course; but they are too big for me, so I mostly take refuge in the past, where issues that seemed equally weighty have so often been debated with equal passion and have then vanished and been utterly for-gotten, along with the other trivial affairs of trivial mortality. Leagues have been proposed and battled over and tossed aside, politicians have advocated universal panaceas, and innocent souls have fought for them and died for them. And where are they now? Which does not mean that we should ever cease debating, or fighting, or dying; for that is the only thing that makes us know we are alive. Only, when you are shut up day after day within four walls, it all gets to seem a little remote and insignificant, and the struggles of a thousand and two thousand years ago seem quite as real and quite as im-portant and unimportant as the furious noise and tumult of today.

The fact that Father had not only written a life of Phillips Brooks but clung to his memory as sacred did not prevent Gam from pouring out his own intense New England protest. He had been considering the possibility of writing a sketch of Brooks:

> . . . Well, the queer thing was that when I came to read for Phillips Brooks I couldn't make anything out of him at all. . . . There seemed to be this magnificent, inexhaustible fountain of golden, infectious, spiritualizing speech. But ap-parently it flowed through the mere human instrument as if

it were the direct gift of some divine effluence, which acquired
its power and richness precisely from the complete negation
of the human personality which received it. I couldn't make
anything of a man of that magnificent physique who yet was
perfectly indifferent to all athletics and sports of every kind.
I couldn't trace any human passion in him, any love or hate
or ambition or despair. I couldn't find even any real religious
struggle. Everything seemed to be accepted naturally and
happily as in the preordained order of things. Then when I
came to the little touch in your book about his indifference to
physical pain, I gave up. I said, a man who is not human
enough even to feel pain is not a subject for me.

Bradford was no more rewarded by the Unitarian Dr. Hale:

There must be something constitutionally wrong about me
which makes me quite incapable of appreciating or understanding ministers. . . .
It may be that only men who have no intense, personal, passionate life of their own drift into the ministry, and again, it
may be that the ministerial habit itself tends to foster such
impersonality, to crush out all the intense, riving, tearing im-
pulses that make the essence of the lives of most of us. . . .
And then I turn to the study of James Gillespie Blaine, and
what a contrast. Plenty of humanity there, oh, plenty, humanity surging out and bulging over, all sorts of mixed motives and passions and ambitions, some noble, and some
dubious, but all so fiercely and gloriously human that it is a
delight to write about them, and the only trouble is to con-
dense one's material within reasonable limits.

Bradford seemed to feel that he was speaking to a mind and
spirit to match his own when he wrote to Father, apropos of Hamlin Garland:

Oh, Mark, do let us beware of getting fossilized and petrified
(you are not in half so much danger as I, with my horrible
habit of living to myself)! Let us look upon these eager,
furious young radicals with all the sympathy we can, and
only wish we were as young and as furious. To be sure, their
ideas are mostly as old as the world, but they rejuvenate them

by believing in them with such splendid ardor. And it is glorious to believe in any thing, even in the Virgin birth, even in oneself, perhaps most of all in oneself. It is the radicals who make the world go, after all, while we miserable conservatives (that is, I, not you) just sit on the brake and hold it back. We should let them have their way and give them at least our affection, so long as they do not trample too much on our gouty toes.

Concerning the power of the Roman Catholic Church one of Father's offstage voices took up antiphonally the refrain of the other (Father, incidentally, the link between them, was a supporter of Al Smith for President):

DEAR MARK:

I must write a line at once to say how wholly, heartily and enthusiastically I agree with every bit of Chapman's verses, without any reservation whatsoever.

I have always loved the Catholic Church as a tradition. For several years I attended its services, and was long tempted to consider identifying myself with it. To me it is the only form of Christianity that really counts, or ever will.

But as it is today, and with my Puritan habits and legacy, I hate and dread it like the devil. If I were inside, I should adore, but so long as I am outside, I detest, as wholeheartedly as Chapman. I utterly disbelieve in its tolerance, which does not exist, and cannot. It would burn you and me at the stake tomorrow, if it could, to save our souls. The whole of South America is the living witness of what we shall be taking a step towards, if we elect Al. Smith.

If I had the courage of a rat, I should come out and say all these things in print, and that is where I most of all agree with Chapman about the degrading subjugation of Boston. The sole thing that keeps me from taking this stand is, as he says, fear, of the howl of vulgar abuse that would overwhelm any one who ventured to criticize the Catholics even as mildly as one might dare with the Christian Scientists, or the Unitarians, who are fair game for everybody. If you see Chapman, tell him how grateful I am to him for saying what I feel. Boston has become a slave-city. . . .

We enjoyed having you so much. If only, as with the angels,
the charm of your visits were not matched by their rarity.

Yours,

G. B.

———◆———

An aftermath of the war for the gentle as for all Americans was
the racking debate over America's participation or nonparticipa-
tion in the League of Nations. To both my parents "Henry Cabot
Lodge" were three ugly words—in spite of the fact that both were
susceptible to Senator Lodge's social charms, and that Mother always spoke affectionately of his wife, "Cousin Nannie," her father's
cousin. After his wife's death in 1915, Senator Lodge wrote to
Father, asking him to "give my best love to your wife, for
whom Mrs. Lodge had a great affection." In 1923, when Father
was editing a collection of Barrett Wendell's letters, he wrote to
Senator Lodge asking for any which might be in his possession.
The answer showed a shrewd awareness of the gulf which separated
him from his correspondent: "Of course, my dear Mr. Howe, I quite
understand that Barrett's views, which he expressed in his most
characteristic manner, in regard to me and some of my writings
and speeches will not find agreement with you, but they are part
of Barrett's biography and I send them as they stand because in any
other way they would be meaningless." A year later, Mother, writing to me in Europe, showed where my Gentle Americans stood
vis-à-vis world affairs: "Now that Lodge has joined Wilson in
Heaven (which will become Hell if they should meet suddenly
around a cloud) the possibility of our joining the L. of N.'s seems
nearer. . . . We are hoping so much [Herriot] can stay in and
really accomplish some of the good things he and Ramsay Mac-
Donald planned."

Father himself has recorded his and his friend Bliss Perry's

> . . . one foray into politics [which] had to do with Wilson at
> the time of his ill-fated request for the election of a Democratic
> Congress in the autumn of 1918. . . . Wilson had enunciated
> his Fourteen Points, but had not yet begun in Paris his fight
> for the League of Nations. He wanted and greatly needed the

support of his own party in Congress. There were those, not
natural adherents of David I. Walsh, then running for the
Senate, who found themselves responsive to Wilson's plea.
Accordingly, they signed their thirteen names—more impec-
cably Bostonian in general than Perry's and mine—to a
political advertisement in the local press on November 4,
1918, under the conspicuous heading, "President Eliot and
Other Independents Ask the Voters to Support President
Wilson by Voting for David I. Walsh for United States
Senator." Beneath these words appeared in three paragraphs
a specific "Appeal to the Citizens of Massachusetts," to join
the Independents. I do not remember that we claimed the distinction of having elected Walsh. But there he was, securely
seated for what proved to be a long time.

The scorn and horror with which many of our more respectable friends regarded us at first, must have been mitigated a
little later when Walsh abandoned the very stand the Independents had expected of him, and joined Senator Lodge
as an antagonist of the League. The Boston *Evening Transcript,* hitherto as intense a foe of Walsh as it was a friend of
Lodge, closed an editorial when both the Massachusetts senators arrayed themselves definitely against the League, with a
triumphant declaration that here they stood, shoulder to
shoulder, two noble sons of Massachusetts! A happy day for
the *Transcript,* but with sobering implications for the Independents who may, all innocently, have contributed something to the creation of a new Castor and Pollux! Perry and
most of the rest of us were cured of meddling in political
affairs.

In the mention of Bliss Perry we come to one of the most loved
voices that ever spoke to Father. I have often heard him say, "By
and large, I believe I prefer to any other group the *best* of the
academic." If not among the scholastic giants of his day, this beloved Professor of English Literature at Harvard—and his brother
Lewis, Headmaster of Phillips Exeter Academy—surely stood
among the *best*. Bliss Perry's magnetic power as a teacher lay in his
own contagious enthusiasm for the finest in English writing. His

brother Lewis wrote: "I think Bliss was the most modest man I have
ever known. He accomplished a lot, and always seemed to be finish-
ing things. He had them finished before he began talking about
them." From the earliest days of Bliss Perry's and Father's careers,
as each came to Boston from the outside, their paths crossed and re-
crossed, always with such mutual pleasure that at Father's death
Professor Perry's son assured me that his father considered *my*
father his best friend in Boston. Yet, for all that they had so much
in common, were very different. Father himself could pinpoint some
of those differences when he wrote:

> All outdoors beckoned him. He collected butterflies. He
> learned early, and continued through life, the joys of a fisher-
> man. A notable baseball player in college, he turned in the
> course of nature to golf, and enjoyed it till he could no longer
> stride the links. One detects the budding sportsman in a story
> of his boyhood—that the possession of his first shotgun so
> delighted him that he took the weapon to bed with him. Such
> tenderness could be offset by righteous indignation, as when
> he saw a bully on a ball field tormenting one of his younger
> brothers, and felled him on the spot with a furious blow on his
> temple. The lithe, athletic body, more than six feet in height,
> which he carried well poised through life, gave an impression
> of capacity to hit hard blows. Yet there was something in the
> handsome, serious face, the twinkling eyes, the sympathetic
> voice and friendly smile which gave assurance that his real
> strength lay in the ways of peace rather than violence.

It was characteristic of both friends that neither was irked by any
sense of strain which would have been apparent in more competitive or aggressive natures, when they found themselves in line for
the same position. When Father was once referred to in print as
"Editor of the *Atlantic*," a position he had never held, Bliss Perry,
who *had* held the position, wrote that "this is just as it should be;
and would have been, I believe, if your eyes had not failed precisely
when they did! Later on I blundered into the picture, knowing
nothing about how the Fates had drawn the lines."

When Father was made editor of the *Harvard Graduates Maga-*

zine in addition to his position on the *Bulletin,* Perry wrote him: "All that I fear is that you may be swamped with so much routine work on a single field. . . . I hate to think of you as wholly absorbed in recording Harvard activities. Perhaps if I were a Harvard man or had more real enthusiasm for President Lowell's leadership, I should feel differently. Very likely it is only jealousy for the intellectual freedom of a good friend whom I see in danger of passing under an inexorable yoke!"

When that yoke was shaken off and Father returned to the *Atlantic,* I am sure he would have mourned if he had thought his leaving Cambridge meant he would see less of Bliss. But, after all, did Bliss not also operate on a Harvard-Boston axis? Was he not the beloved president of the beloved Tavern Club? And in the Tavern Club surely the voices of all of Father's friendships were raised into one united chorus to beguile him with as seductive strains as ever sirens used to beguile Odysseus.

The Tavern Club, as I look back, seemed to contain everybody whom Father knew and liked—or, to put it another way, there was not a member of the Tavern whom Father did not know and like. *Meum est propositum in Taberna mori:* so runs the first line of the club hymn. (I have heard Father say more than once that, considering the number of gray heads, his own included, visible at their revels, it often looked as though one of the older members were sure to get his wish.) Impossible, and unseemly too, for any woman, let alone a daughter, to follow a man into that last bulwark against the opposite sex—his club. Since her view would have to be from the outside looking in she might be tempted to ask: smug? absurd? running rather more to obstetricians and trustees among its members than to the "artists" whom those members continue to believe burgeon among them. I come, however, not to satirize the Tavern Club but to let its members speak for it. To the tune of "The Vicar of Bray" Father used to sing every year the verses he wrote to the song he called "The Presidential Range" in which he rehearsed the names and exploits of the presidents who had ruled over the club since the reign of William Dean Howells. One of the verses, celebrating "Dan" (Owen to the world) Wister, ran:

> Now who comes next? What shining star
>   Shall glitter in the answer?
> One sought in Beersheba afar,
>   But found right here in Dan sir.
> And Philadelphia—somewhat slow
>   But charming Quaker sister,
> Who stole Ben Franklin long ago—
>   Cries, "Quits—here's Owen Wister!"

It was that same Dan Wister who describes not only the beginnings but the essence of the Tavern Club for its members:

> Observe: one painter asks a doctor, another goes recruiting in State Street; so did the various recruiters work, gathering miscellaneously as to vocation; guided very slightly by such definite adjectives as prominent, important; somewhat more by such adjectives as talented, clever, promising; guided most by the happily elastic word, sympathetic. . . .
>
> No Tavern Club could be made from a set of Rotarians. No group, whose only interest was money, or golf, could make one—but it could spoil one. Nevertheless, we have found that civilized geniality without talent is better than talent without civilized geniality; we never sank into Bohemianism on the one hand, we escaped commercialism on the other.

Jack Chapman was another out-of-town member who spoke for what the club meant to him:

> I shouldn't wonder if more unforgettable dinners have been given at the Tavern than in any other club in the world. The club-house itself had a good deal to do with this influence. . . .
>
> For many years I have used the Tavern as a nest, a secret habitation, a refuge in times of crisis, tragedy, or fatigue. Everybody welcomed me, nobody bothered me. I have been part of the place, and the place of me, and its rooms are full of memories—scenes with my sons when they were at college— some of them almost tragic, many jovial. After Victor's death I stayed at the Tavern for ten days and read Plato's Republic, and in the intervals resorted to the Public Gardens and took tours in the Lohengrins. In more recent times when I have had some particularly hard job on hand, something that re-

quired an astronomical abstraction of mind varied by the re-
laxation of familiar faces, cups of tea, pipes of tobacco, and
no appointments to keep, I have moved on to Boston and
roomed at the Tavern.

Over the years there was a succession of feasts in honor of visiting notables—none surely more thrilling than that in December,
1930, in honor of Paderewski, who, to quote Father, "made a
speech that for sheer impressive eloquence has had no superior at
any Tavern feast. What more need be said of it than that his
passionate tribute to President Wilson won applause, however
reluctant, from hands that had never been stirred before by the
war-president's name except in opposition? (There is no place but
a footnote for the reported remark of an anti-Wilsonian whose enthusiasm excited surprise:—'Oh, hell, I thought he was talking
about Hoover.')"

But it was at its Christmas dinner that the Tavern Club felt
itself come most gloriously into its own. First there were carols, as
Langdon Warner put it, "to lift the rafters and make the candles
gutter," then a march up the winding staircase behind the boar's
head, to the low-ceilinged room with its one long table, Christmas-
bedecked, and the singing of "Meum Est Propositum" before the
moment of sentiment and comradeship expressed in the toast (orig-
inated, I believe, by Winthrop Ames): "To the Absent—the Living
and the Dead."

But always, under the siren voices of friendship, Father's ear
was tuned to the obbligato coming from that stern daughter of the
voice of God—Duty. And with Father duty took the form of
plugging hard work.

Looking back on two of his books of this period Chapman wrote
Father:

> Your productivity and extraordinary power of digging out
> and marshaling facts and putting through some dogged job,—
> and then appearing as halfway through the next one, as-
> tonishes me always. . . . I don't really think that Mrs. Fields
> and Barrett Wendell afforded any biographer a chance. Mrs.
> Fields, though she was so charming and so impressive in her

natural surroundings, and her voice was so remarkable wasn't really anything in particular, and Barrett was a figure for fiction rather than for biography,—for he was fictitious.

When Mrs. Fields died, making Father her literary executor, she told him to do what he liked with her papers, and with the proceeds to "buy a trinket for Fanny." What he was able to do— before turning over the papers for the final resting place to the Huntington Library—was to make a book, *Memories of a Hostess.* It is my impression that Father's *Memories of a Hostess* sold more than any other of his books, and certainly was greeted warmly by the press. Jack Chapman, however, was not to be so easily won. He must have sat down to pencil and paper and let rip to Father, and then decided that the medicine might be a little strong—even for Father. Years later, when Father came to write his friend's biography, he came upon the letter and, with the humility and humor which were characteristic, felt it was much too good to keep to himself, and printed it in his own autobiography.

November 28, 1922

DEAR MARK:—

. . . In endeavoring to lengthen out a lonesome meal I dipped into Mrs. Fields—and looked at the illustrations. Well, I must say, Mark, I never saw a book on first glance seemed to have less venom in it. People will read more uninteresting facts about deceased authors than they can bear on any other sub- ject—a weakness which you have preyed upon, you villain. Now, please do what I say—and I'll write a memoir of you. Get a big pine box and put in it the contents of your waste- paper basket the day you receive this (the mail of the master craftsman) also a piece of your shaving soap; photograph of the view from your back window; some verses you were ashamed—even you—to print—which were written by Thomas Bailey Aldrich on a pancake; this letter; anything you find on Brimmer Street on your walk to the Atlantic Monthly Press; a pen and ink drawing of Ellery Sedgwick posting a letter containing a cheque to a contributor (the cheque is in- dicated by Ellery's heroic expression) . . . a visiting card left by a man you didn't know—very old-fashioned—this to be *mounted* on a full page and entitled How our ancestors did it—and—you see the idea;—but *fill the box.* I will write the letter-press. I think I should call the volume [word scratched out and undecipherable] and O my! if I don't give you a send off! . . . I think I shall call the volume "Whiffs of literature." . . .

Yours affectionately,
JACK

P.S. It just occurs to me that the *letter-press* of your book may be good.

As for *The Life and Letters of Barrett Wendell,* which came out in 1924, Bliss Perry (the very antithesis of Chapman!), on rereading it years later found that

> a fresh perusal confirms my faith in your exceptional mastery of the art of biography. This book deserves all the praise it won. I call it perfection.
>
> I never liked Wendell and he certainly never liked me, but I think that I understand him now better than when he was alive. His physical make-up played him false from boyhood on. He could not help his nervous irritability. Some of his mannerisms were no doubt cultivated, but that was a part of his physical curse.
>
> You had a tender understanding of his weaker side, and could forgive him when I can't.

After ten years of commitment to an office routine, on top of—or rather undergirding—his own steadily growing individual output Father was beginning to harken to the most tempting voice of all—that of independence. The *Ladies' Home Journal* was paying him well for two series of articles—one published as a book *Causes and Their Champions,* and another, *Classic Shades.* Since 1924 he had been working on a part-time basis at the Atlantic Press, allowing himself time for another biography, *James Ford Rhodes: American Historian.* I know, too, that there were tensions for him at the *Atlantic* office in the realm of dollars and cents. As it became clearer that he was slowly withdrawing from active participation, Ellery Sedgwick wrote him: "Well, Mark, I feel as if

this gradual withdrawal of yours were a sort of slow death of the
life that is still within you. You know I hope that I retain and always must something more than the bond of how many years is it
together? Affection respect and confidence—knits a triple chain
hard to break.'' And when the break became final, it was the voice
of friendship speaking. ''If I seem to you in any way inconsiderate
it is my manner and not my heart that is to blame. Affectionately
always. E.S.''

When Father did finally take the leap into freedom—and risk—
he left behind two positive contributions. His first was his introduction to Mr. Sedgwick of Edward Weeks, of whom he had been told
by Frederick Lewis Allen of *Harper's* when he went on an ex-
ploratory mission to New York in search of an assistant for Mr.
Sedgwick. The other was a brain child—conceived on a train between New York and Boston by him and Alfred McIntyre, the
president of Little, Brown—a merger between Little, Brown and
the Atlantic Monthly Press. Organized and executed by other
capable executive hands it flowered into the Little, Brown-Atlantic
Monthly books so successful today.

There were still years—how many!—of hard work ahead for
Father and creditable recognition too. The heyday of publicity
which any American author is human enough to value if it comes
his way came for Father in 1924 with the publication of his
Wendell (surely far from being his best book). He was in England
with Mother—come to fetch me home from a stay in Paris—when
he received a characteristically succinct cable from Quincy. Its
message consisted of the one word: *Pulitzer*.

III

The Underground Spring
That Fed You All

12

MOTHER—THE PRINCIPLE OF RESISTANCE TO BOSTON

LEAVING THE PERIPHERAL FIGURES on Father's Boston horizon, I turn back to the center of his—and, indeed, of all our lives. As I peer down into the waters of childhood memories, it is Father whose reflection grows blurred in the surface ripples. It is Mother who rises clear from the very deeps.

Father's attributes were all the basic ones—faith, hope, and charity: his outlines corresponded with any archetypical Father Image. Clearly Professor Whitehead saw Mark Howe in general terms when he nominated him ambassador for nothing less than the human race. Mother's qualities, on the other hand, were "counter, original," in many ways the antithesis of Father's more obvious ones. "Reticence" was a word she often used, a quality she invariably practiced, and a virtue she admired. To free myself now from its grasp and dare to lift the veil that covered her averted face is an act that marks a milestone for her daughter—for good or ill, I hardly know. But because I believe her features were so remarkable, I cannot keep her memory to myself. Furthermore, how tell Father's story without her?

Where to start? Where, indeed, to end in suggesting the complexities in a nature compounded of depths and lightness, acerbity and warmth, aloofness and passion, sensitiveness to the suffering of others, and an icy barrier of reserve around her own? She named the one novel she wrote (being Mother, anonymously) after her favorite stone—*The Opal.* Actually, the heroine she depicted would have been better called the Chameleon, taking on, as she did, the color of anyone to whom she was exposed. The great difference, however, between the friable stone and Mother lay in her diamond core; or perhaps it was a subtratum of granite from the quarries of her native Quincy.

Something of its spirit of nonconformity stirred in Mother's blood. Her temperament made it easy for her to pronounce a resounding *Amen* to one of Henry Adams's strictures: "Something was wrong, but he concluded that it must be Boston. Quincy had always been right, for Quincy represented a moral principle—the principle of resistance to Boston." Growing up in Quincy—then, the remote country—until she was in her teens, she led virtually the existence of an only child. Some sense of her insulation from the currents of the time is revealed in the fact that her parents would not allow her to read *Little Women,* as the people it depicted were so "common." Mother's father—of whom more later—was a gentle, scholarly recluse, gullible for fads. My grandmother, daughter of a judge in Hadley, Massachusetts, was born Huntington, a family known for generations as "stouthearted men of action, with established religious convictions, faithful to church and state, upright in morals."

The vital elder Henry James could not have written to her as he did in 1878 if he had not been aware of a spirit as lively as his own on the receiving end:

MY DEAR MRS. QUINCY:
   My wife said to me, after her visitors had gone away, "Didn't you give that book to Mrs. Quincy?" "Yes," I replied unhesitatingly from my inner consciousness. "Why do you ask?" "I thought," she replied, "that I heard Mrs. Quincy say something about soon returning it." "So doubtless you did, dear wife, for in fact I forgot the form of giving, and went through the substance only. The truth is I never meet Mrs. Quincy however casually but I feel myself so blessed by the sight of her flowering and abundant womanhood, as to make it something of a feat for me to assume the attitude of a

giver towards her. And that is the reason why—although I got this book for the very purpose of giving it to anyone that liked it—I never thought of going through the actual form with her. But I'll do it tomorrow morning."

So you see my dear friend if you do not accept my poor book you will seriously embroil me with my domestic angel, whose estimate of you does not fall behind mine. She is a real wife to me, so much so that I am sometimes foolish enough to imagine that [there] are few better if as good. But then with all my partiality for her, I can't help confessing her inferiority to my friend Quincy's wife in one respect: that while the latter makes equally a most real wife to her husband, she suggests to all his friends the ideal wife also. Perhaps he doesn't know this. I give you leave to tell him, from me, that every word of it is true, and will always go on to be more so doubtless.

Believe me dear friend

Yours affectionately
HENRY JAMES

Even through such a warm nature as that of Grandma Quincy ran the deadly vein of New England morbidity which, to a certain extent, scourged us all.

Infant mortality in Mother's family had struck, as it had in Father's, but only once and with shattering psychological after-effects. Over the mantelpiece in my parents' bedroom in Brimmer Street there hung a large crayon drawing of the little sister Violet who had died at four years old, before Mother was born. This loss was catastrophic to my grandmother, so that when little "Fannette" was born all the intensity of the mother's broken heart found its focus, and a bond was forged that was the strongest emotional tie in both their lives. Writing to her mother-in-law in Bristol, after my grandmother Quincy's death in 1904, Mother said:

I can hear of no one's grief now without a rush of sympathy that ends in a burst of futile tears. . . . Here things go on the same. . . . I am attacking Mamma's closet shelves and locked trunks. . . . The sight of a dress or a ribbon that she has lately worn upsets me pretty completely, and I was much overcome on finding a box containing the little dresses and

shoes which had been worn by my little sister who died, which
Mamma had tied up to be gently dealt with after she had gone.

There was still another reason for the mother's attachment to
her little Fannette. A tiny scar on Mother's forehead—the result of
a minor operation performed by a country doctor, and invisible in
later years—was magnified to my grandmother's morbid view so
that, in her eyes, her child was doomed to go through life disfigured.
It is pitifully characteristic of what must have been the climate of
that childhood that the pet name of the little girl, after a popular
book of the day, was "Little Sorrow."

When Mother prided herself on her "clear-sightedness" it must
be admitted that she generally looked on the negative side of any
picture. It was an attitude which perhaps she took to offset Father's
positive, *couleur de rose* view of the world. Father wrote to a friend,
"I have been remarkably well, though 'going on seventy,' as Fanny
keeps reminding me since I turned sixty." How often have I heard
Mother say that the only reality in life is unhappiness—the stretches
of happiness between being only parentheses. She used to say that,
whereas Father expected a check in the morning mail, she expected
a bill. Optimist and pessimist, believer and agnostic, serve only to
indicate, not define, the width of the gulf that separated my parents
in temperament. I remember their talking about the death of Miss
Fanny Morse, and Father saying, in effect, "If there *is* a Heaven,
we may be sure that Fanny Morse is in it." "How do you *know?*"
was the question Father could not answer.

The weapon with which Mother met the world that would otherwise have overwhelmed her was a glancing wit. If it was more often
than not turned on those closest to her, her motivation was twofold.
Though she loved us with an almost terrifying intensity, there was
about her an inherent "sort of elegance of humility or fine flame of
modesty," as Henry James had said of Sarah Orne Jewett. This
self-depreciation spilled over onto us in the form of downright de-
traction. Why should the world find charm or merit in anyone who
belongs to *me?* was her inner reasoning. But, more important, it was
her very doubt of life itself that made her dread its hurting us. Half

consciously, I think, she hoped to build up in us an immunity against those far more cruel blows than the flick of her wit which she was so sure would inevitably be dealt us. Father came in for his share of her defensive-offensive shafts. She hoped to restrain the ebullience which set him talking about himself or what particularly interested him, thus sparing him a possible snub. Coming back from Europe, the last night on the steamer I remember her admonishing him not to talk about his trip to his friends, assuring him that nobody is ever really interested in anybody else's travels. I am sure it was Mother's warning attitude that enabled him to write a jingle about "The Bore":

> Why did I find him the full-blown flower
>   On boredom's bounteous vine?
> He talked of his ills and his bills for an hour
>   When I wanted to talk of mine!

This weakness, actually, was not Father's. He did not wish to talk of his ills, but of his pleasures and enthusiasms. "He's a confounded bore," I've heard him say often, and he had pretty well learned to sidle away from such a menace—or simply to talk him down! Mother, on the other hand, used to amuse herself by wondering what it would be like to give an all-bore party and see if any of the guests noticed anything! The Bab Ballad "Emily, John, James, and I" was a point of family reference. Every verse ended with an irrelevant piece of information about the narrator. One of them was:

> The Derby Day sun glittered gaily on cads,
>   On maidens with gamboge hair,
> On sharpers, and pickpockets, swindlers and pads
>   (For I, with my harp, was there.)

If Mother, using the family "little language," murmured the words, "I with my harp," Father took it as a warning he could ignore only at his peril. She used, also, to reprimand him for not concentrating enough on other people. There was a famous evening in the family annals when Father and Mother were driven home by their dear friends the Bentley Warrens, who had just returned home after an absence from Boston of several days, occasioned by the funeral of Mrs. Warren's aunt, Miss Hatch. Father, all affability, leaning back in the car, asked, "Where is Miss Hatch spending the winter?" Mother's kick in his shins came too late. It must, however, have been redoubled when the *next* time he saw the same friends he asked—again, all affability—during the course of the evening, "What do you hear from Miss Hatch?" Though there followed profuse apologies, "By jove, of *course* I knew she had died. I don't know what I could have been thinking of," etc., the harm was done—and he was not allowed to forget it.

Though Mother's self-control was of iron, she was subject to a variety of fears—kerosene lamps, candles on a Christmas tree, and the sea, to name only a few. Unaware of whatever psychological implications these fears may have revealed—implications which she herself would have hotly denied—she met them by making fun of them. Planning to come with Father to bring me back from a winter in Europe she wrote (pasting onto her letter, as she often did, a few words clipped from a newspaper), "I am performing various last rites, assuming that, of course, I shall die at sea. I fully expect to be found [clipping pasted on] DEAD IN BERTH ABOARD LINER from fright, if not by shipwreck!"

It was Father who made the decisions for us all, he who administered the ultimate punishment, who awarded the final accolade. The little darts from Mother's tongue directed in his direction enchanted and amused nobody more than him. She was first and foremost—perhaps I should say second and hindmost—his wife. When she wrote an invitation to dinner with a couple the better half of whom was known in Boston for her lively charm and conversation, Mother invited her friend "to dine with the Mabel Welds." Mother and Father were unmistakably the *Mark* Howes. Like other Gentle Americans of their time the Mark Howes had their own family whistle. Father, the assertive male, seeking out his mate, either in a crowd or a deserted landscape, would give forth with the four opening notes of Beethoven's *Fifth*. The passive, acquiescent female would answer with the same pattern, repeated a step lower. This antiphonal give and take was the very leitmotif of their marriage; it was Father who stated its theme, Mother who echoed it, with variations. Quincy unequivocally says that he has not known a more happily married couple, laying stress on the fact that they were different in temperament but alike in tastes. Among Mother's papers were a few lines of verse which must have expressed, for her, her basic devotion and utter dependence on Father's qualities:

> 'Tis human fortune's happiest height to be
> A spirit melodious, lucid, poised, and whole;
> Second in order of felicity
> I hold it, to have walked with such a soul.

Indeed her dependence on Father was one of her fears. How often did I hear her say to him, "You must promise not to die before I do." Her view of the role she—or, indeed, the average wife—played was part modesty, part cynicism. She used to say, "If I should die before Saturday, you will find your symphony tickets in my desk drawer." She was quite sure that there did not exist the husband who could not be consoled. Whenever a friend was left a heartbroken widower, she would say, "I give him a year," or, in special circumstances, "Perhaps it will take him two." Because Mother could lean on and turn to the solid actuality of Father and his devotion she could amuse herself by playing with his small framed photograph that stood on her desk in the back parlor. Over the unblinking features—steel-rimmed glasses, Harvard-Boston mustache and all—Mother used to insert other photographs that she clipped out of the paper. I remember in particular the exquisite features of John Cowper Powys, and the dramatic locks that surrounded the romantic face of the pianist Percy Grainger. Eugene Debs reigned temporarily for other reasons.

My parents read the same books, they liked the same people, Father merely liking more of them, and they shared political beliefs. Yet, although Mother participated in Father's Boston life, there was some inner wellspring of her being that remained uninvolved. She read the books that Father read, and the magazine articles too, but she had her own private store of reading that he did not touch. As she looked at life and love she treated them both, on the surface, with *"de la gaîté pour s'en moquer."* Ruefully cynical about the brevity of human devotion she was equally so about the enormity of human egotism. Favorite lines of hers were William Watson's

> Momentous to himself as I to me
> Hath each man been that ever woman bore;
> Once, in a lightning-flash of sympathy,
> I *felt* this truth, an instant, and no more.

She herself found it possible to carry on a friendship without ever mentioning herself. I remember walking with her on the street and meeting a friend of hers whom she had known some seven years. The friend was thunderstruck to see *me*, not knowing that Mother had any children! She had none herself, so Mother's excuse was simple: "I didn't think she'd be interested." She impressed on me firmly that the one, and only one, social asset for a woman was to be a good listener. And she meant a really good listener, not paying just the perfunctory lip service of a languid "Oh, really?" or "How fascinating!" dropped while one's own ear is cocked toward a more interesting conversation being carried on at the other end of the table. She meant the gift of tossing back the one most flattering question that showed you had been listening with intelligence as well as attention to what was being told. (Come to think of it, I was reared in the school of hard knocks, as my stern older brother Quincy always impressed on me that any woman who talks consecutively for more than one minute is automatically a bore. Perhaps it is not surprising that I, with a penchant for monologue, was driven to seek captive audiences beyond the confines of Brimmer Street.) Mother's capacity for listening manifested itself preeminently in various friendships in which she was the one to extend the ear, while the other offered the tale of woe. In one of her published essays she wrote of the woman who "in the large leisure of quiet home-staying, —[was] always ready to lend a sympathetic ear or to share the wisdom of an experienced heart." It was Mother's experienced heart, pouring itself out in intense compassion, with the added elixir of intelligent advice, that her friends counted on.

Mother was not involved with a round of committee meetings, or the organization of benefits, or the running of community campaigns. It was the "single Doe attempted of the Hounds" who found shelter with her. Several of her more affluent friends kept her supplied with a small fund into which she could dip, when heart and head told her there was need. But even her kindnesses were done with characteristic lack of sentimentality. Like all other families of the time we had in our orbit a "little woman," around the corner, who emanated the actual odor of stale poverty. Poverty and failure, always perking up or bogging down toward some imminent disaster, were the theme of the monologue, delivered in a thin whine through a mouthful of pins that accompanied the activities of her fingers with their dirty broken nails as they fumbled with a hem. "Poor Mrs. G. . . . has been evicted, and the house at 81 Charles Street has been sold. . . . She can't find a thing she can afford, so has taken a flat that she thinks *I* can, and will occupy it for a month till she finds something worse. Her situation is a real tragedy, and I feel myself getting caught in its financial coils."

Although Mother shrank from boards and committees, she was so sensitive to the suffering of the world around her that she picked herself, characteristically, just one "cause," and into that poured time, thought, and energy. It was the same South End House already known to Father. Mother was chairman of its Women's Committee for many years. Various of the resident social workers who lived in the Women's Residence in Union Square came to visit us in summer. I know that to them all——as was testified in the inevitable tribute in the *Transcript* after her death—her judgment and level head were as invaluable as her compassionate heart.

It was to her living interest in the South End House rather than any association of Father's remote involvement with the work there that I myself became involved in a one-day-a-week volunteer stint during my winter between school and college. I have always been grateful for the ineffaceable experience of firsthand exposure to the abject slum poverty of Boston's South End. I climbed the rickety stairs of dismal overcrowded tenements on my rounds to pick up children to—often gory—visits to a dental clinic. I can still evoke the mingled smell—atrophied in the air of a freezing Boston winter —of blood, dirt, and urine which emanated from the howling little victims committed to my charge, always gloveless and always handkerchiefless. By contrast, pure joy was my first taste of holding an audience by myself, as I did with the telling of fairy stories to a constantly swelling group of children in the library which they visited in the afternoons. Mother was much gratified by a letter from Mr. Woods, prophesying a future for me in that field if I would stick with it. The fact that I did not do so was part of the inevitable break between home and a daughter of the twenties determined to fling herself into the competitive world waiting beyond the city limits of Boston.

Mother herself certainly never dramatized her role at the South End House into anything bordering on the Lady Bountiful: "Last night while the boys went to a movie, and Father to the Tavern Club play, I went to one of those delightful South End festivities! . . . 1500 dirty people (minus one clean one!) watched 50 South Enders at their pathetic revels! . . . several of your feeble-minded little charges expressed the wish to go to the bathroom periodically during the performance! Mr. Woods is quite ill with a bad heart, but it did not prevent Mrs. Woods from leading a chorus of Wassailers in a carol pitched two tones above the accompanying piano!" . . . She attended "one of those terrible South End parties of workers, volunteers, and committees. There seemed to be no representatives from the Back Bay but myself and I had to stand up to be looked at after dinner, as if I were the tattooed man in the side show, and I could think of nothing to say except that I should never know one of them again if I saw them, and I hoped they would not know me. Awful as the women are, the male of the species is more deadly than the female when it comes to social workers." Mother *was* good; in the presence of those who *do* good she was not happy. "Last night we dined with that reckless libertine Miss Fanny Morse, before adjourning to John Moors to hear two pacifists speak. . . . [They] were convincing but irritating, —no one is more of a pacifist than I, —but I don't like my kind."

It was part of the complexity of her nature that Mother's talent as well as her kindness was hidden in as deep an anonymity as she could achieve. I cannot explain this streak in her nature, I only know it was there. Although Mother and Cousin Alice as girls started their anonymous writing as a joke, when they grew older and Cousin Alice urged her cousin to try her wares on more lofty publications than the *Quincy Advertiser* they still went out under a variety of pen names. The furtive Fanny had to face the pleasant surprise of discovering that almost everything she sent out was accepted. Pasted into the scrapbook which the girls kept are not only many of the actual stories themselves but bits of correspondence from editors, giving a sidelight on the way they (and the authors!) conducted their business. One letter from the *Youth's Companion*, rejecting a manuscript, teaches the young neophyte a lesson. " 'The Diamond Pin' is an amusing little story, and might have received greater consideration from us had it been written on only one side of each sheet of paper.'' Mother must have had the intestinal fortitude to sit down and rewrite the pages because later in the scrapbook, along with a note enclosing forty dollars, is written in handwriting a P.S.: "It gives us pleasure to add an especial word of thanks for this clever and entertaining story; and we beg to express the hope that we may see more of your work. We shall always be glad to read it!" The nom de plume Mother used most most frequently was Wilmot Price. A story that appeared in *Harper's* elicited a letter from a sheet entitled *The Writer*, addressed to "Dear Sir" and asking for "information both about yourself and your literary work." Certainly no such figure as a literary agent was on the horizon of those innocent days. The *Saturday Evening Post* wrote: "Your price of thirty dollars ($30) is satisfactory," this following a letter asking the author what price she would set for her story! It is gratifying to see that without benefit of agent the checks rose to a hundred dollars. *Harper's Monthly, Scribner's*, the *New England Magazine,* and others published the stories of *Wilmot Price*, sometimes transvestized into *Catherine Russell*. It was inevitable that a novel come next. And the anonymous *Opal* was published in the early years of her marriage.

On one occasion during the Brimmer Street years Mother's han-

kering for anonymity was expressed with impudence and won her a
moment of triumph. On a certain St. Valentine's Day there was a
party at the Tavern Club. For the celebration each member had
been asked to send, anonymously, a contribution of verse. Father
went off to the party to serve as one of the judges. When he came
home late that night Mother asked him which poem had won first
prize. Father told her that *he* had voted against the one the other
judges thought the best and, further, that neither he nor they knew
who was its author, as no one present had confessed to having written it. Mother asked just enough more about the poem to be able to
say presently, "I wrote it." Today one of my most treasured possessions is the present the club gave her—a large silver cocktail shaker,
with the Tavern Club coat of arms, and Mother's name, bearing the
legend THE DRINKS ARE ON US.

With her husband at work all day, her children at school, her
household run by servants, it is not surprising that Mother's gifts
and energies found another outlet than the more obvious ones open
to the "lady of leisure" of her time and place. She returned to the
occupation of writing, finding in the "Contributor's Club" of the
Atlantic an appreciative audience for the lively little essays which
preceded the taste for and the taste of *The New Yorker*. These
essays were ultimately to appear in book form: first was *The Notion Counter:* its subtitle was Notes About Nothing by Nobody.
Successor to *The Notion Counter* was *Small Wares*. The subject
matter contained in these two small volumes was as feminine as
their titles: flashes of Mother crackled through them. Confronting
a baby: "I wanted to say, 'What a grotesque head it has!' but, instead, murmured, 'Isn't he the image of his father?' " *My Wife's
Address Book* (purportedly written by a put-upon husband) revealed Mother's own methods of recording addresses. Cynthia, the
wife, calls out to Algernon, reading his paper in the next room to

"Just look in my book of Social and Domestic Emergencies
and tell me Nora Mahoney's address. It is something River
Street." . . .
I turned to the N's, remembering that Cynthia had once
dropped the remark that very few of the people she had ever

employed seemed to have last names. There was no Nora among the Nightwatchmen, the Nurses, the Nellys, and the Neds. "Is your name M or N?" I murmured as I abandoned both initials and turned to L for Laundress. Again I was thwarted, but my hunting blood was stirred. . . . [Cynthia takes the volume and mutters] "Let me see now, would it be under W, for Washerwoman? No. Perhaps it might be under G, for General Housework—don't you remember, Algernon, how cleverly Nora was always able to do things that we didn't want her to do? Here are the G's,—let me see,— . . . Oh, here we are! General Housework! Oh, no, that isn't housework, it's General Houston—don't you remember that delightful man with the military moustache we met in Virginia? . . . so here he is,—just where he belongs—only, where is Nora? . . . I always used to think Nora's name was Agnes, it's so exactly the same kind of name—and I probably put her down under A, thinking that is where I would look for her. Oh, yes, here she is! She leads off the A's, like Abou Ben Adhem. Nora Mahoney, 18 Brook Street—just what I told you, except that I thought it was River Street.''

Mother's little books sold so well that she took in tidy royalties (they, like all aspects of my parents' finances, were never mentioned, so I don't know what they amounted to). The money went into the general family coffers, as I know she never spent a penny of it on herself. The two tangible objects she bought were: one, a large comfortable sofa for the library—the only piece of furniture I remember my parents ever to have bought as, aside from wedding presents, everything else was handed down from Bristol or Quincy —and, next, a sumptuous fur-lined coat, not for herself, but for Father! I remember the moment of her giving it to him as she so far departed from her usual undemonstrative ways as to embrace Father in my presence, telling him how much she wanted him to have something to keep him warm!

Gradually, with encouragement from the editors, Mother's writing began to appear in the body of the *Atlantic*. (Anonymously, of course.) Living through the postwar years when flappers and bathtub gin and petting parties were causing an outcry, she chose the younger generation as her subject and Mrs. Grundy as her pen name.

I am sure that Mother's most intense inner life came into focus when she was seated at her desk—placed between the two windows of the "back parlor." It was seated there, her own straight back not touching the back of her chair, that she poured herself out in letters. If war was an oblique place, it could send, all the same, its shaft of suffering into the depths of Mother's intense nature as, during the 1914–1918 years, she lived in a torment of helplessness over the anguish of my Aunt Helen in England, who was to lose her two sons. How often did Mother sit down at the same desk at which she wrote her anonymous little essays, or at which she wrote to Mamie, saying, "I must get off a letter to Helen." Mamie wrote shrewdly to Mother, "Goodness, I don't know why you want to bother with my small troubles . . . I believe I couldn't be so kind to you for if I was happy and the positions were reversed I'd spend all my time enjoying my happiness." Mother's temperament was slanted far more toward feeling the sorrows of others as though they were her own. It was at that desk, too, that Mother wrote her manuscripts, working them over painstakingly in her clear, handsome writing. Her habit of writing must have been much like that of Jane Austen. Seated at the crossroads of the life of her family, the moment there was a demand from any of us, she quietly closed the portfolio in which her pages were neatly tucked away, and her attention was focused entirely on husband or children.

Then, for no apparent reason, she all but gave up this secret occupation, and nobody could induce her to return to it. Mr. Sedgwick, writing to Father, added a P.S. "Would Mrs. Howe care to review a novel? She can sign it by any name she wishes, if she does not care for the glint of her own name in print." A letter from Mr. Sedgwick to Mother herself, a few months before she died, bears witness to his opinion of her talent. He must have been rejecting a manuscript, sent surreptitiously: "I am shamefaced about letting it go back to you. I know the incident will confirm every mistaken opinion you have of your own writing. I am quite honest in saying that one of the troubles of the *Atlantic* of late years is that we have been worrying along without you."

Speaking of Mother's writings in his autobiography, Father wrote:

I refrain from saying all I should like to about them. . . . A story I remember hearing Miss Jewett tell seemed to have its bearing upon this aversion from notice. It was the story of an old woman in London so reduced in circumstances that she was obliged to sell sprats on the street. To this end she posted herself where few could see her on the sidewalk of a small, dark street, and there, in a faint voice, kept saying, "Sprats, sprats, —I hope nobody will hear me!" . . . As Jane Austen wrote of Anne Elliot, "It was a great object with her to escape all enquiry and éclat." For myself, I could never cease to admire the wit, felicity, and understanding that marked the best things she wrote. Of course the best was not always; but in everything she wrote, from her many postcards to her few books, there was a strongly individual quality, always distinctive, sometimes distinguished—if distinction lies in an intelligence, grace, and compassion rarely encountered in the common run of human beings. In this opinion I am sure I was not alone, as possibly I am in seeing, in a small photograph she gave me long before our marriage, the face that remained unchanged in my eyes to the end of her days.

Poor Father! Even late in his life, looking back, he used to say, "I am sometimes afraid that it was my fault that she gave up writing. I encouraged her too much." From what deep subsoil sprang the roots of Mother's cringing in the face of attention, let alone recognition, I cannot say. In a way, Father was dreadfully right: his very enthusiasm as he would say, "The truth is, Fanny, you're da—ned good," caused her to take a kind of revenge—on herself?—by ceasing to compete in the public market altogether. In trying to probe further I must recognize in her an instinctive penchant toward failure rather than success, a glorification of sacrifice as opposed to fulfillment. She knew much of Emily Dickinson's poetry by heart not only because it was beautiful poetry but because the figure of Emily herself—wry, secret, intense—attracted her. If the pallid symbol of a vestal cloister held attraction for her, I cannot quickly enough add that there was nothing "die-away" about Mother. She had, for one thing, too much physical vigor for that. The gasps and cries of mingled pleasure and protest in her ice-cold bath every morning (Father, too, started his day with a cold bath in the zinc-lined wooden tub), her firm step walking along Brimmer Street, recognizable to the ear from the library on the second floor, her paroxysms of laughter over the Marx Brothers' movies—all bore witness to vitality.

This same vitality flowed out in a passionate ardor of appreciation of what was beautiful in nature and in art. As children, returning from the Putnam Camp in the Adirondacks and crossing Lake Champlain there was a spectacular sunset which caused Mother to exclaim: *"Look* at it! Drink it in! *And never forget it!"*—so that I never have. I can see Mother now, when she came to visit me in New York, in the twenties, leaning forward in her seat in Carnegie Hall, wearing the little white "bunny" fur coat then so prevalent, her head tilted up rapt with delight as the music of her favorite Brahms Third Symphony poured over her. Europe had been an actuality in Mother's life as it never was in Father's, thanks to her two years' stay abroad with her parents. When we children had childhood illnesses, we were tucked into bed by day in my parents' double bed and given a mound of magazines, *Masters of Art,* to look at in the hope that we might lay the groundwork for some knowledge of the great painters.

When it came to people, she instinctively warmed to any visiting stranger. *Not from Boston* was a recommendation, in her eyes, on any passport. After all, it had been on Father's! No, Mother was no ascetic. She loved good perfume and good soap, and enjoyed pretty clothes, and bothering over her appearance if she went to a party. She might fasten around her neck an opal pendant, to match the little opal earrings, or a graceful *parure* of seed pearls, which had belonged to her mother, saying as she did so, "These will be yours someday, when I am under the sod." Then there were the days for the dressmaker, several rungs farther up the ladder than that on which the "little woman" precariously clung. The dressmaker could be either one of two Canadian MacIver sisters—both loved and loving through the years. The talk, with Mother chiming in, concerned patterns, colors, materials, and style.

There was a special flutter in the dovecote the winter of 1929 when Mother accompanied Father to Washington, where he served as Consultant in Biography at the Library of Congress. That one winter seemed to disprove everything I have said about her, and everything she believed about herself. The lid of her Boston cage having flown open, she stretched wings which at home were tightly furled: with the background of a charming rented house, and an excellent cook thrown in, she gave herself up with almost light-hearted pleasure to a gay and social winter. Her wit, her sympathy as a listener, and her pleasure in her surroundings obviously made a hit at the dinner and tea tables of Washington. All the same she was glad when the golden coach turned into a pumpkin and she found herself back in Brimmer Street once again, and anonymous. The boundaries of the "Boston" she had spent a lifetime resisting would not have shown on any map. Her problem was not so simple as that she was trapped "inside Boston." It was that "Boston" was trapped inside *her!*

One of the many paradoxes of Mother's nature, and one recognized over and over again by Father himself, was that it was she, in a self-flagellating New England conviction that to harbor any religious belief was to yield to an unallowable self-indulgence, who was far more concerned with eschatological and metaphysical speculations than Father. She did not belong to the breed of Bouncy Bostonians: her mind had far more in common with Henry Adams's, which disdained "the mental calm of the Unitarian clergy. . . . For them, difficulties might be ignored; doubts were waste of thought, nothing exacted solution. Boston had solved the universe . . . so thoroughly as to have quite ceased making itself anxious about past or future, and should have persuaded itself that all problems which had convulsed human thought from earliest recorded time, were not worth discussing."

There was a class of those who rubbed Mother the wrong way whom she dismissed as "irritators." It was made up of those whom I have already identified as "sure," whose self-satisfaction proclaimed that they were intellectually, spiritually, socially, or politically emancipated. Only those who knew Mother well were aware of her "tragic sense of life." Isak Dinesen wrote that "the true

aristocracy and the true proletariat of the world" understand
tragedy as "the fundamental principle of God," adding that "the
bourgeoisie of all classes" deny it, because it represents "un-
pleasantness."

I have known unhappy women since Mother, but all of them had
a pedestrian—not to call it bourgeois—streak of discontent or envy.
Mother had neither. The questions that haunted her were deep as
her sights were high. A piece of paper in her handwriting, with the
word "Ecclesiasticus?" was tucked in a desk drawer.

> O Death, acceptable is thy sentence unto the needy, and unto
> him whose strength faileth, that is now in the last age. . . .
> Fear not the sentence of death, remember them that have been
> before thee, and that come after; for this is the sentence of the
> Lord over all flesh. And why art thou against the pleasure of
> the most High? there is no inquisition in the grave, whether
> thou have lived ten, or an hundred, or a thousand years. . . .
> We are born at all adventure, and we shall be hereafter as
> though we had never been; for the breath of our nostrils is as
> smoke, and a little spark in the moving of our heart—which,
> being extinguished, our body shall be turned into ashes, and
> our spirit shall vanish as the soft air.

Mother would have repudiated the implication that she had any
firsthand knowledge of God. She was born too early for Tillich, who
might have told her that "if you know that God means depth, you
know much about Him."

In casting about for light to throw on whatever mystery Mother's
complex nature contained, perhaps her eldest son came nearest
when he said to me, "Don't forget the law of dialectics, then remember that Papa was in a sense the classic optimist-extravert;
Mamma, the classic pessimist-introvert. But each contained its own
opposite. After Mamma died, I became convinced that she really
had more pride, and ambition, and drive than Papa. But she so
feared disappointment for herself and those she loved that she never
let it out completely." Perhaps Quincy is right. I don't know. I
always felt she wanted, above all, to shield us from being hurt.
Perhaps—who knows?—there was an undercurrent, unacknowl-

edged to herself—a fear of failure. Somewhere there must have hovered the shadow side of her modesty. However hooded its features, I only dare to wonder now, might not its name have been, after all, Pride?

I suspect that if this is so the family from which she came could be held accountable. If Father's native Bristol supplied a backdrop of conflicting worldliness and piety, Mother's family offered a mingling of public achievement for eight generations, warring against a transcendental withdrawal into the inner life. Furthermore, the tribe of Howe was rolling on, on all sides, in the oncoming generations. The Quincy family was about to come to a standstill. I am not sure that the entire lexicon of modern psychiatry could fully explain the resulting inner tension which existed in Mother— a tension as to whose causes I should not have the temerity even to guess.

13

THE ARTICULATE QUINCYS

"To F.H.Q.H. MY BEST HERITAGE from the city of her fathers." So ran the dedication of Father's "big Boston-y book." The irony of the relation between dedicator and dedicatee was that it was the outlander who saw his wife's family in a certain historical perspective. Mother herself was most emphatically not one of those Bostonians who suffered from the complaint of the city, "Grandfather on the brain." She could not, however, save herself from the hereditary birthmark of Grandfather *in* the brain. "Family characteristics last a long time in the old town of crooked streets and politicians." So wrote the perspicacious Ferris Greenslet of Houghton Mifflin when he reviewed *The Articulate Sisters,* a collection of journals and letters written by Mother's great-aunts during the years 1829 to 1849, when their father was President of Harvard— and edited by Father. So far as I know the only time that Mother's veil of anonymity as a writer was ever lifted in public was when Mr. Greenslet, after expressing his pleasure in the writings of this sprightly quartet, went on to say, "They are of interest, too, for the student of inherited traits." These he saw in Mother's "perceptive, very feminine essays with a teasing sub-acid flavor, typical of the family temperament and talent."

Mother's own shrinking from any emphasis on ancestry sprang from the bellyful she had received in youth from her great-aunt Susan Quincy, the eldest of the Articulate Sisters. Though clearly a remarkable woman in her many gifts Aunt Susan seemed to have

outdone Lady Catherine de Burgh in snobbery. "What would Aunt
Susan say!" was a part of our family's little language. The energies of this redoubtable woman were poured out in large part in
recording the exploits of her family back into times so remote that
one wonders where serious historical research left off and a high-
flying imagination took wings. If Mother could fulminate at having
to listen to Aunt Susan's carryings on about the great days of the
Quincys, Mother's daughter finds a certain fascination in contemplating Aunt Susan as a useful sort of telescope, mounted on a
swivel. Looking in one direction we see the oncoming world containing Mother and her brother and sisters, as it appeared to the
eyes of a formidable old lady; turn her about, to look the other way,
and the scene shows not just one family but glimpses of American
history itself—including memories of her father entertaining Lafayette on his two visits to America, both in Boston and in Quincy,
her brother serving as his aide, and the family's friendship with
their neighbors the John and the John Quincy Adamses (so named
because of a marriage between the families).

In Brimmer Street we could not help knowing that there were
such things as Quincy ancestors, simply because one of the walls of
the dining room was lined with photographs of family portraits
(alas, not with the portraits themselves) from earliest colonial
days. Chester Harding, Copley, and Stuart had perpetuated themselves and their sitters. In Mother's line there were six Josiahs in
direct descent, following three Edmunds before them. The first
Josiah—like his father before him, Colonel in the Suffolk Regiment
—was part owner of an armed merchant vessel during King
George's War (1744–1748) which captured a Spanish treasure ship.
Although the family had had private means since their arrival on
these shores in 1633, this exploit afforded him "the prosperous
occasion of his withdrawing from business." His own and three
ensuing generations were thus painlessly supplied with what
amounted to a large fortune. There were in particular four of these
Quincy men, each of whom left behind him a sharply defined image,
characteristic of his age, as well as injecting a distinctive strain
into the famly bloodstream.

What American family is not proud to claim a Patriot? We had ours, dying in 1775 at thirty-one—Josiah Quincy, the Patriot. With his friend John Adams, at the time of the "Boston Massacre," he followed the unpopular course of defending Colonel Preston and his British soldiers. Then a hush-hush mission to England, in spite of health which was showing signs of a "decidedly pulmonary character." The young wife he left behind him—Abigail, nee Phillips, the mother of his two small children— in her turn played with fortitude the role expected in all times, in all lands, of the wife of a Patriot. For a year and a half there were secret meetings with important friends—and foes, too—of the American cause, the results of which were poured out in a stream of letters to his wife, whom he promoted from his "bosom friend" to "my political confidant." On March 1, 1775, his journal records: "On this day I had about an hour and a half of private conversation with Dr. Franklin, on the subject of the present situation of American affairs, and what course America, especially New England, ought now and during the spring and summer to hold. I wish I might with propriety enter his discourse." Two days later, the day on which his journal abruptly comes to an end: "This day being the day before my departure, I dined with Dr. Franklin, and had three hours' private conversation with him." The Patriot had recorded a few days previously, "It is a good deal against my own private opinion and inclination that I now sail for America." Small wonder! He was struggling against rapidly worsening symptoms of consumption.

It is a moving experience for a pampered twentieth-century descendant of this Patriot to touch the faded parchment and read the illiterate writing of the seaman to whom the young man dictated his last words as he recognized, after five weeks at sea, that he was dying. The letter is headed, *At sea. April 21.* The shot fired at the Battle of Lexington and Concord twenty-four hours before had not yet had time to be heard round the world, let alone by the ears of the dying man, still hoping to pass on his messages to Samuel Adams and Joseph Warren. One can see the poor struggling sailor, shoving his reluctant quill over the paper, his brow furrowing as he spells the words the best way he can, to express "the Last Desire of a Dying Man the last Request of Expiring Husband that [my most Dear belove wife] may lay by my side at her Death to this Purpose I am willing to be Inter anywhere and Pray that my Request may not be denied because sum People will think it Wimsical . . ." That wife was at the moment preparing to flee from Boston with her three-year-old boy. Her little girl had just died. When the boy grew up (he was to live to be ninety-two) he buried his mother, more than twenty years after the death of her husband, in the "tomb of his ancestors." It was John Quincy Adams who wrote the inscription for their monument.

Sacred
To the memory of
JOSIAH QUINCY Jun.
Of Boston, Barrister at Law
Brilliant talents, uncommon eloquence,
And indefatiguable application,
Raised him to the highest eminence in his profession
His early, enlightened, inflexible attachment
To the Cause of his Country,
Is attested by monuments more durable than this,
And transmitted to posterity
By well known productions of his genius.
He was born, the 23 of February, 1744
And died the 26th of April 1775,
His mortal remains are here deposited, with
Those of Abigail, his wife, daughter of William Phillips Esq.
of Boston,
Born the 14th of April 1745. Died the 25th of March 1798

It was for Benjamin Franklin to say the last words. Writing from Passy, in 1783, to the father of the Patriot, they include a few of the most famous uttered by our First American.

. . . How admirably constituted was his noble and generous mind. Having plenty of merit in himself, he was not jealous of the appearance of it in others. I shall always mourn his loss with you, a loss not easily made up to his country. . . . We are now friend with England, and with all mankind!

May we never see another war! For in my opinion, there never was a good war, or a bad peace.

Adieu, and believe me ever,

my dear Friend,

Yours most affectionately,

BENJAMIN FRANKLIN

Our Patriot ancestor shone—and continues to shine—in the glow that must always surround the young martyr to a high cause. His son, the next Josiah, as President of Harvard represented much more the archetypical ancestor. Honored by the "Establishment" of his day, he was the very figure of it as we children were taken to see him on the walls of the Boston Art Museum, painted by Gilbert Stuart, with the Faneuil Hall Market, built during his term of office as Mayor of Boston, serving as background. His young Patriot father would have repudiated the notorious Federalist activities of his son and namesake. This Josiah did at least, through sheer vitality and character, live ninety-two years to do honor to the heroic young mother who had to bring him up singlehanded. He lived to serve as State Senator, Representative in Congress, five years as Mayor of Boston, and for sixteen years as President of Harvard. At his death, John Motley, borrowing "the expression of our friend Wendell Holmes," spoke of him "as the type and head of the Brahmins of America." James Russell Lowell, in the midst of a flowery encomium entitled "A Great Public Character," added one vignette, "During his presidency, Mr. Quincy was once riding to Cambridge in a crowded omnibus. A colored woman got in, and could nowhere find a seat. The President instantly gave her his own and stood the rest of the way, a silent rebuke of the general rudeness. He was a man of quality in the true sense,—of quality not hereditary, but personal."

The son of this Josiah was another Josiah, Mother's grandfather, and another Mayor of Boston. It was through his fingers that the family fortune began to trickle away, revealing a fatal Quincy weakness where money was concerned. His brother Edmund was a more interesting character.

John Jay Chapman, writing of the Abolitionists, said, "The man who could have stood a volume was Quincy; who was a wit—and every letter of his in the Garrison life casts as much light as a bush-burner on the queer crowd of enthusiasts he spent his life with." Father dangled him before the Massachusetts Historical Society in a paper he entitled "Biographer's Bait." Father found the epithet "Come-Outer" was tailor-made for Edmund Quincy who, once having tasted the heady wine of reform, added to his agitations for abolition of slavery the causes of woman suffrage, temperance, and nonresistance. But Quincy was a Come-Outer with a difference. "Among his fellow reformers he stood virtually alone in the possession of a lively wit and a broad cultivation."

Edmund took himself somewhat more lightly. "I have been called the Prince of Bigots, His Anti-Slavery Highness, an aristocrat, a hyena, and a squash: and have possessed my soul in patience."

The sharp little needle of irony wielded by Mother was surely a splinter off the stiletto handed down from her great-uncle Edmund. Writing to me in 1926 from Cotuit, "President Eliot has at last died, and Father went up to his funeral yesterday. Rudolf Valentino's death appealed to a different audience." Edmund, on another funeral in 1859, wrote:

> We are not done with poor Mr. Choate yet. . . . You know we were a whole week burying the poor man—as long as it took to create the world in the beginning. From the moment the telegram came announcing his demise, the resolutionizing and slang-whangery, and half-mast flaggery, and bell-tollery, and ninth-gunnery, and all the rest of it were going on in one form or another. . . . One thing at least was very certain, that there was no possibility of its being a case of premature interment. For, if Mr. Choate had not been very dead indeed, he must have been recalled to life by hearing the names of the parties who took the initiative in his posthumous honors by the Bar of the City. . . . So that it is a proof of his being dead beyond resuscitation that he lays quietly under the galvanic battery of their eulogy. I believe you republished a part of Dr. Nehe-

miah Adams's Funeral Discourse, which, if your readers did not find entertaining reading they must be dull fellows indeed. We looked upon it as one of the most diverting performances of recent times and were as merry over it as mutes after a funeral.

In my grandfather Quincy we can claim our family Transcendentalist. In the midst of the stilted unreality of the family portraits on our dining-room wall the photograph of his beautiful head was as arresting as a trumpet blast. It showed a high forehead, deep-set eyes, burning with poetic intensity, an arched, patrician nose, and a silky beard, cut à la Zeus. The English photographer—Miss Julia Margaret Cameron, well known in her day—must have covered his front with a cloth as there is no collar visible around the throat, so there is nothing but a black background against which this head of the prophet stands out in brilliant relief. The effect was such that an English visitor, looking at it, asked, "Was he beheaded?" Though that head was never served on a salver, it did present very real problems, as perpetuated in a plaster death mask. The sinister box, once sacred to Father's "pop-up" opera hat, in which it was kept, confronted us among other family white elephants when it came time to make a move. We would open it, peer inside with mingled awe and helplessness, and then close the cover again—the problem unsolved. The occasion of his death stands out in my memory with a painful clarity: Mark and I at four and five years old come to the breakfast table. No Mother—a terrifyingly upsetting of the natural order. Enter Father. Lugubrious. *More* terrifying! Then, very portentously, "Children, your grandfather died in the night." Our response? Agonizing *laughter!* Agonizing, because it *must* be suppressed, like the kind which could sweep over one in church. The simple fact was that we were embarrassed.

This grandfather, as a once dreamy young man, might well have been depressed by the expressed wish of his grandfather (the President of Harvard) that he would "live to be a blessing not only to his parents, but to his country and race." It was an irony that he had the same handicap of stammering to contend with as Father, although in a much milder form. But so different was his specula-

tive, introverted temperament that he felt himself to be banned
from participating in any kind of public life. Father wrote of his
father-in-law's "devotion to privacy," wondering whether it was
due to this physical handicap or "how far it was the direct result
of an habitual state of mind, speculative rather than executive and
unworldly to a degree most rare in any time or place." One might
have guessed the way the tree would incline, considering how the
young twig had been bent. As a child he attended the famous
Bronson Alcott school for children where the following statement
was recorded: "Mr. Alcott, we think too much about Clay. We
should think of Spirit. . . . If we should go out into the street and
find a box, an old dusty box, and should put into it some very fine
pearls, and bye and bye the box should grow old and break, why, we
should not even think about the box; but if the pearls were safe,
we should think of nothing else. So it is with the Soul and Body. I
cannot see why people mourn for bodies."

Small wonder that Emerson recorded in his Journal of 1836:
"Little Josiah Quincy, now six years, six months old, is a child
having something wonderful and divine in him. He is a youthful
prophet."

If ever Child was father of the Man, my grandfather was that
child and that man, the typical Boston Transcendentalist of his
period. It is easy to see why the senior Henry James was his friend.
Like his uncle Edmund before him, he was a member of the Massachusetts bar but did not practice law. He was enough a member of
his family to have lively political interests, and his writings on
matters of public concern were abundant—frequent contributions
to the *Anti-Slavery Standard* among them. Antislavery and elec-
toral reform were all very well, but Mrs. Piper and her spiritualistic
trances were of far more interest to him. His freely flowing pen
poured forth on a variety of subjects which give a little of the flavor
of his interests: "Cotton Mather and the Supernormal in New
England History," "Dreams as Factors in History," "The Limits
of Reliable Memory." In the *Unitarian Review* he discussed an
amplification of Froude's dictum that "real belief is necessarily
intolerant."

Poetry and fiction were not neglected. At the annual meeting of Phi Betta Kappa in 1867 at which Emerson delivered his second oration, Grandpa was the poet of the day. "Psychology dramatized," the *Transcript* described it. His novel *The Peckster Professorship* was published serially in the *Atlantic* before appearing between covers in 1888. Its theme, "a satirical treatment of intellectual and academic society—for readers with some intimacy with and sympathy for psychical research." A satirical treatment of the novel itself could come all too easily to present-day readers. Its stilted dialogue serves merely to expound the "way out" speculations of the author, stifling all resemblance to any human beings, living or dead. But in its day it received two pages of commendation in the London *Spectator*. Grandpa Quincy knew whole plays of Shakespeare by heart. Did I say Shakespeare? Being Grandpa, one of the bees he carried in his bonnet was his conviction that Bacon was his man. Whoever the author, Grandpa was his faithful student, publishing "Manuscript Corrections from a Copy of the Fourth Folio of Shakespeare's Plays."

As a human being, and a father, his family found his prototype in Mr. Woodhouse, Emma's father. Addicted to fads in foods (like Mr. Woodhouse's gruel), he smoked five-cent cigars and wore celluloid collars. His daughters had to restrain him from buying a motorcycle which I am sure he would have driven as recklessly as Mr. Toad. Quincy remembers his doing setting-up exercises to the strains of a music box, clad in long underwear.

Father put his finger on the essence of his father-in-law when he wrote that "between the outward show of this sheltered existence and the inward reality the divergence was broad. Of external adventure Mr. Quincy was peculiarly innocent all his days. In mental and spiritual adventure he was undaunted and untiring."

Although to all of his children he passed on something of his special qualities, perhaps the philosophical cast of mind and temperament were particularly manifest in my Aunt Helen. Father, when he stayed with her in London, was as amused as appalled by the offhand way in which she introduced to him her friend Evelyn

Underhill, murmuring absentmindedly, "The leading mystic in England." With his characteristic naturalness Father was hardly surprised to find himself presently talking with the great religious seer about tennis!

Aunt Helen's was not only as noble a soul as I have ever known, but the freest. When she was trying, during the First World War, to call upon all the resources of her deep nature to see her own anguish against a wide backdrop, she spent one night—alone!—among the wind-swept ruins of Stonehenge. Aunt Helen was ever on the side of youth and change; although a true intellectual herself, the vitality of her spirit put her in revolt against an "intellectual" approach to life. Speaking of the oncoming generation she wrote that "in the ability and courage of that new generation no one has greater confidence than I. Personally I feel that La Farge was right when he said, 'Henry, you think too much!'—a malady of a later generation I opine as well as of Henry Adams." Mother was acutely aware of the difference in temperament between herself and her older sister; she wrote me when I was visiting Aunt Helen in England· "How good it is for you to be with a person like Aunt Helen who closes her eyes to all that mine seek out—and who so genuinely believes in and enjoys the best in everyone!"

As with other American families, individual Quincys, like individual Howes, were called on, each in his own generation, to make oblation on the altar of history. There was the Patriot dying on the eve of the Revolution he had helped to bring about; in the Civil War there was Mother's "Uncle Sam" Quincy—who lived with the family in Quincy and of whom his nieces said many times, "Poor Uncle Sam was never himself after the war." Was it their way of saying he took to drink? Today his plight would be called battle fatigue. The heading of one of his letters, "In hell, *alias* the *Libby* prison," gives a hint of the source of his psychic scars. A Captain of the Second Massachusetts Regiment of Infantry, he was wounded at Cedar Mountain and from the battlefield was ordered by a surgeon who "came along" to be sent to Rapidan on the box seat of an "avalanche" (ambulance) : "and an awful 'avalanche' it was,—four men with legs and arms off inside. It was eight miles over rocks and through rivers, and generally such a drive of damnation as never entered the heart of man to conceive.''

In the years 1914–1918 it was Aunt Helen's turn. The first mortal wound was delivered through the loss of her firstborn, Phillips Quincy Muirhead, at twenty years old, Lieutenant of the 40th Howitzers, 43rd Brigade of the British Army. We children had been thrilled when this English cousin—a big, handsome schoolboy—had visited us during the Christmas holidays in 1913. The next summer Aunt Helen, her daughter Mabel, and her youngest son, Langdon—Langdon, the dreamer, the poet, who played the violin—visited us at Cotuit. While they were with us war was declared. My parents recalled afterward the look on Aunt Helen's face as she said, ''Phil will go.'' For my part, I remember the look on Mother's face, during the summer of 1916 when the Battle of the Somme was raging, as she came out the screen door onto the piazza at Cotuit, holding an open letter in her hand, and said, ''Just what we have been dreading. Phil has been killed.'' It was in the fall of 1918 that I see again the look repeated. We are at the breakfast table in Brimmer Street. This time Mother breaks the news, ''Langdon is wounded and missing.'' That pronouncement, against the fever chart of false hopes and sinking fears, up to and even long after the Armistice, was never to be repealed. Phillips was a man—what am I saying?—a boy of action. (''There was a big attack. It was fine watching the infantry on a ridge just in front of us. . . . Streams of wounded were passing down the road. . . . The Germans are using chlorine gas, following it up and making sure with their bayonets. Rather beastly isn't it? . . . I had my serge jacket, shirt, and undervest perforated. This would have been O.K. if I had not been in them.'') Langdon was a boy—he, too, died at twenty—who already showed Grandfather Quincy's speculative turn of mind. At nineteen, when he reread a fragment of his own authorship, *On Reading Plato,* he found it ''perfectly hopeless . . . but I resist the temptation to tear it out, because it does represent in its awkward and ungainly way something which, I think, I really felt on that and some few other occasions.'' We discover a touching kinship with that nature in which Emerson had seen something wonderful and divine in the youthful lines,

> I was reading Plato. I read and thrilled;
> Great thoughts, enveloped in a mist,
> Half seen, half unperceived,
> Swept darkly through my mind . . .

Though Aunt Helen's tragedy hung heavy across Mother's heart, she suffered another and quite particular pain through her only brother Josiah, the sixth and last of the line. There must have been much about Uncle Joe which was a throwback to his Patriot great-grandfather: the impulse toward public service, the marked ability which fitted him to make it, and a lofty disregard of public popularity, as well as popularity with the privileged few among whom he had been born. There was also a destiny written in his stars which spelled tragedy. To us children Uncle Joe was an austere figure, seen on Christmases and Thanksgivings—handsome, tall, and stiff (today I know the word is "shy"). To the public he was known as a man of brilliance through his participation in civic and national affairs. He was the third Josiah Quincy in direct descent to serve as Mayor of Boston, having already made a name for himself as an able lawyer in manifold activities for the Democratic party. These culminated in his accepting, at thirty-three, the post of Assistant Secretary of State under Cleveland.

Through the eyes of Beatrice Webb, in her *American Diary, 1898*, we see something of the manner of man he appeared to be:

"When he is not a practical politician he is a visionary" said the precise and correct young Charles [Francis] Adams Mayor of Quincy of "Jo" Quincy Mayor of Boston. Both belong to the blue blood of New England; both alike are of sufficient means to devote themselves in the English sense, to politics. . . . To us [Jo Quincy] is distinctly attractive. He is, to begin with, remarkably good looking—tall and slight, well-shaped head and features, deepset brown eyes, sensitive intellectual expression—irreproachably dressed, quite the hero from the pages of a novel. In physical type he is like the Balfours—especially Gerald Balfour. . . . It adds a certain

romance to his personality that in spite of his aristocratic
aloofness and stiffness, and a total absence of good fellowship,
he is the Boss of the Democratic machine; and has complete
mastery of its inner workings. In short he is the "Parnell"
of Irish Boston, substituting for Home Rule, Fabian Collec-
tivism as the goal toward which he is working. . . . "How far
do you consider it necessary to consult the Ward Politician in
your appointments?" I asked. (Quincy is a man it pays to be
direct with.) "Well," he jerked out looking straight in front
of him, "in the unpaid Boards not at all. In appointments to
these unpaid offices I consider exclusively personal fitness.
With regard to the highest paid officials I give political ex-
igencies a certain consideration. . . ." The cross-examination
has not been, however, exclusively on our side. The many
hours we have spent together—a long drive in the Parks on
Saturday, an expedition down to Manchester-on-Sea on Sunday—have been quite as much occupied by questions from him
on London government, on the theory of municipal administration, and on Trade Union activities in England as by questions from us with regard to his administrative work in Boston
or his political associations with the Democratic Party.

It was in 1912 that Uncle Joe's tragedy came—when he became
involved in a public scandal and trial. He was indicted in that
year with a group of men in the Federal District Court in New York
for using the mails to defraud in connection with "Canadian mining
schemes." Taking its name from one of the men involved, Julian
Hawthorne—son of the novelist and himself the author of more
than fifty books—the mess was blazoned across the newspapers as
the "Hawthorne Case." Actually the court had struck out five
counts against Josiah Quincy, leaving only one—conspiracy in
allowing his name to be used in promoting the stock. For four
months the accused men heard such epithets hurled at them by
the prosecuting attorney as "bunko steerers" and "swindlers."
After nine hours of deliberation there was no verdict from the
jury, who were then sent to the Astor House for the night. The
next day the verdict was announced in the leading headline of
The *New York Times:* CONVICT THREE IN HAWTHORNE CASE. Julian

Hawthorne and Dr. W. J. Morton—the son of the discoverer of
ether—were found guilty on seventeen counts each. Albert Free-
man was found guilty on twenty-nine counts. All were sentenced
to the Atlanta Penitentiary. The two words QUINCY ACQUITTED—
of the only charge which stood against him—brought what relief
may be imagined to those most deeply concerned.

In retrospect it seems clear that the intensity—even morbidity—
of nature shared by Mother and her sisters magnified the proportions of the trial beyond what they merited, so far as their brother's
public standing was concerned. After all, in spite of all the painful
publicity, he was found guilty of nothing but extreme gullibility
and a total lack of financial sense—a weakness which has appeared
in the family in other generations. A contemporary researcher of
the period and of my uncle's historical reputation—"virtually non-
existent"—holds the opinion that his career was broken long
before the trial took place. He was a "remarkably enlightened
politician, a virtual municipal socialist as Mayor of Boston, ahead
of his time in ideology and beyond the sympathies of most of his
contemporaries." Working with the Irish—Honey Fitz and the
like—blackened him in the eyes of Harvard and the Back Bay, and
yet rising young politicians like Martin Lomasney, jealous of their
own ethnic power, resented him too. "His misfortune was to have
played the political game the way the New Dealers would play it,
but in an era when the rules of propriety were set by the likes of
Grover Cleveland." The trial was an excuse for his enemies to close
in from both sides.

There is a painful irony in the thought that perhaps his sensitive
sisters contributed to his imprisonment behind a barrier of social
and human isolation, although he walked abroad a free and guiltless
man. Suffering both personally and vicariously, instead of asserting
stoutly both his brilliance and his innocence, they closed themselves
up in an agonized New England reticence—the same reticence that
enclosed him. Articulate as the family had always been—in public
life, as through the written word—when it came to personal suffering they simply closed their mouths, and remained inarticulate.
The sixth and last Josiah Quincy died at sixty, a man broken

in health and spirit. Mother cherished all her life a letter that came to her at his death from Bentley Warren, whose own high probity as well as his adherence to the most conservative Republicanism made it the more striking:

I think you know, without my repeating it, how I have always regarded him since my first acquaintance with him in the Legislature of 1891 . . . already a statesman, to whom I might safely look for guidance. . . . In the more than a quarter of century that has passed, I have seen no reason to modify this judgment. On all such matters he was extraordinarily sane and clear-headed, neither an unpractical radical nor an obstructive reactionary. His apparent failure, on the practical side of life, in improving his material personal condition, and safeguarding it, has always seemed to me the conclusive proof—if any were needed beyond acquaintance with him—of the peculiar purity of his character and of the very superman-ness of his nature. He was so honest himself that he could not for a moment believe anyone else was dishonest. . . . When we are all weighed by a Judge little influenced by mundane standards, the Josiah Quincy of our generation will be in the Abou Ben Adhem class.

The following interchange of letters between Father and Mr. Brooks Adams shows Father in an altogether unaccustomed light. For once his role is neither benign, kindly, nor even conciliatory. His hand is on his scabbard, as he confronts an older and distinguished adversary.

Dining at the table of Mr. Adams, along with Aunt Mabel, and hearing his host, who had forgotten the relationship to Uncle Joe, make some slurring remark about him in connection with his recent death, Father sat down that very night and wrote:

Dear Mr. Adams,
    As a guest at your table this evening, and out of a strong desire to spare my hostess pain, I refrained from answering your unprovoked attack upon my brother-in-law as it should have been answered. I can only hope that for the moment you had forgotten that you were speaking to one of his sisters and the husband of another, and in terms which they could

not fail to resent and cannot easily forget. Joe's memory calls for no defense at my hands, but I am not content to leave in your remembrance even a faint impression that members of his family can give any acquiescence whatever to your characterization of him.

The answer was:

MY DEAR MR. HOWE—

I have your note asking for an apology from me for my stupid blunder yesterday. I humble myself at once. My only excuse is that your brother was a public man and like all public men was much in the newspapers. I should have had the relationship in mind. I did not—that is all there is about it. I am seventy-four years old. That is my excuse. I should be shut up. Men of my age have no business to live—but they won't kill us,—nor let us kill ourselves. What can we do. I see no way out,—unless you are prepared to do me that service. All I can say is that your brother had better luck. He died young. Can I say anything more to mollify you? If I can I will. Only tell me what to say.

Very truly yours,
BROOKS ADAMS

Father's answer to the answer shows him in more characteristic vein. And a true Adams answers the answer to the answer. (I am sure Father must have been glad to call it quits.)

DEAR MR. ADAMS,

I wrote in some indignation last night. Tonight I have to acknowledge your forthright reply to my note, and should like to do so by suggesting that, since you speak of having failed to bear in mind a matter of relationship, we shall endeavor to forget the episode which has led to this correspondence. I appreciate heartily the frankness of your note to me, and am,

Sincerely yours,
M. A. DeWolfe Howe

MY DEAR MR. HOWE,

I am pleased to see by your note this morning that I have, to a certain degree, succeeded in assuaging your wrath against me. Suffice it to say that I am a very objectionable old fool.

There are lots, at my age, as bad as I.

Nevertheless I would like to draw your attention to one side of our little trouble on which you do not dwell. Perhaps you are not religious! No more am I. Still for the sake of argument, I assume that God created the world, and us. If so, he has a certain responsibility which he can't escape. Why, then, did he make men to grow old? It's a devilish torment! You don't feel it as yet—but you surely will. You can't escape more than I. Happy are they who die young—for those the Lord loves. He don't love me! I don't blame him, for that, but why did he ever let me be born? Why were my brothers born? They were little better than I. Maybe no better. And I am sure my mother meant no harm. She did her best. So, I think, I have done my best—bad as it is,—but God is greatly to blame. Think it over! Am I not right.

Sincerely yours,
BROOKS ADAMS

The repercussions of Uncle Joe's tragedy on Mother's sensitive nature can be imagined. Eventually she and her sisters were to derive much happiness in watching the growth of Uncle Joe's son Edmund as a painter. Father, I daresay rightly, always felt that her suffering on Uncle Joe's behalf was in large part responsible for her turning away from the world as much as she did. The company of those from whom she shrank as "sure"—smug, self-satisfied and respectable, many of them publicly committed to high-minded causes of reform—only rubbed salt in her open wounds. Even the laying aside of her own sprightly pen may also have been prompted by the same shrinking from attention. Pride in the contribution that her forebears had made toward the public good, mortification for past silliness and snobbery that had expressed itself in a certain vaingloriousness in some of them, fear that her own gift might fall short of an inner standard she set herself, and a passionate loyalty to one of her own flesh and blood who had suffered, and a stinging sense of humiliation that the suffering and disgrace were public property—all played a part in the tangle of emotions that warred beneath her unyielding self-control. It was no easy thing to have Quincy blood in one's veins.

14

COTUIT—THE CALM OF THE OYSTER BEDS

"THE CALM OF THE OYSTER-BEDS on which I look out from the attic-study in which I am sitting is emblematic of our existence here." So Father wrote to Copeland from Cotuit. For him, as for all of us, our summers on the southern sandy shore of Cape Cod represented the happy flowering of our year. Cotuit was unsocial to the point of being antisocial. The lethargic climate blurred all incentive to activity. Each family curled in upon itself and its own resources. Santayana, who had visited Cotuit in his day, recognized that on Cape Cod "Nature here seemed to breathe very slowly, and to have fallen asleep." "Dead Neck," a sandspit across the mouth of the little harbor with its warm, nearly soupy waters, enclosed us in lives as sheltered and tepid as the harbor itself. The sight of children tipping over under a strong southwest blow in a sailing skiff (ours, the *Flounder,* invariably finished last in the races of the Mosquito Yacht Club) offered no fears to anxious parents on shore; likely as not the children were within a few feet of the sand bar where they could stand happily, waist-high, until rescued, in the warmth of that all but fetal fluid. And how that southwest wind could blow! It alone, in the sleepy monotony of the trance that lulled us through August dog days and nights, sounded a note that was restless, disturbing, vaguely dissatisfied, urging us to break the bonds of adolescence and to get up, get out, get going. This poltergeist southwest wind manifested itself about the house in

the flapping of the Audubon bird charts on the landing of the
stairs, the banging of screen doors, and the blowing over of rocking
chairs on the piazza. The piazza was the vantage point for a family
spectator sport which consisted in watching Lassie engage in a
mysterious game of solitaire. (Lassie was a capacious English setter
who saw us through our teens, following on the heels of our childhood Brownie, and preceding Mingo, the poodle of my twenties, and
after.) At low tide Lassie entertained herself by wading very
slowly in water deep enough to submerge her legs, wagging her
tail, with a foolish smile on her face as she looked down at—what?
We never knew. She never seemed to try to catch anything. For
an hour or two at a time she just waded, wagged and smiled.

Of all the inhabitants of Cotuit who passed the summer months
in a state bordering on somnambulism only two groups were active:
the small children and the Harvard professors. Each professor had
his own little shed or shanty in which he spent many hours a day
absorbed in his own particular scholarly pursuit. President Lowell
called his "The Caboose." Father's workroom was the attic of what
had once been one of the "oyster houses," more of which still existed
close by on the same shore—modest shanties used by the local oystermen at the start and close of each day's haul.

On looking back at the routine to which Father held himself, I
recall the sense of excitement with which each new biographical
subject fired him. He would join us at lunch or dinner, bubbling
with some good quotation he had just come across or an amusing
incident, generally ending up, "I have a feeling that this is going
to be a da—ned good book." It was never cockiness about his
own prowess as a writer, but enthusiastic interest in a new human
being whom he was coming to know better. I do not recall his ever
tearing his hair in the fine frenzy of creation or losing an hour's
sleep over any technical problems in his path. It is easy to say that
he did not dig deeper into the psyches of the subjects of his biographies than he dug into his own. He adhered simply to the conventional format—"Life and Letters"—prevalent in the days of his
youth. He wrote every word in longhand, and I cannot imagine—
though I do not know for sure—that he ever did more than two

drafts, if indeed as much. He wrote with painstaking care, and I think did little revision after his first draft. In those Cotuit summers, along with a great deal of other writing, he produced *Portrait of an Independent—Moorfield Storey, The Children's Judge—Frederick Pickering Cabot,* and *Bristol, Rhode Island—A Town Biography.*

My parents never gave a name to our place, letting it be known simply by the name of the region and the little brook that ran through our six acres—much of them marsh—Little River. Our point of land was at the end of Little River Road, so no one came down our driveway of crushed clam shells (how proud we were as children when our bare feet were tough enough to run on it without flinching!) except to see us. The house itself was a strange architectural phenomenon for Cape Cod, made of stucco, with the antlerlike beams of a Swiss chalet at its gables. My parents bought and furnished it in 1910—and it looked it. We lived our life by day on the comfortable piazza that ran around three sides of the house, all of them looking out on the harbor. In the evenings when the inevitable dead flat calm descended and the sweet whistles of "Whip-poor-will" and "Poor-Bob-White" could be heard from the pine woods at our back—the mosquitoes and the "midgies" drove us indoors. In the early years there were kerosene lamps in the living room, and candles in the upstairs hall to be carried into the bedrooms. There was one bathroom for our family of five plus my great-aunt Mary Huntington and her nurse-companion who spent the summers with us. Aunt Mary, adored by Mother, was a sweet old lady; but no matter how sweet one's wife's aunt may be, nor how unassuming her companion, the average husband might be excused for not welcoming her presence in his household. Not so Father! He was fond of her for her own special qualities, but memories of "Cousin Lizzie" and "Cousin Virginia" under the roof of Weetamoe established a precedent for such a member of the household.

Aunt Mary and Miss Butler, after eleven in the morning, were permanent fixtures on the piazza. Mother had been puttering in her flower beds—sometimes succeeding in getting Mark and me as children (it was only Quincy who took care of a modest flock of hens, and was allowed his own rabbits) to do a little reluctant weeding. Or perhaps we were given an assignment of picking peas or beans in the vegetable garden, sometimes rounded off by gathering a bunch of sweet peas, smelling delicious in the summer sunshine. Then I joined Mother and Aunt Mary for reading aloud, while one of us shelled peas. It was there and thus through my teens that I read all of Jane Austen for the first time and, in my early twenties, much of Henry James.

Swimming was the event of each day in which we all joined at whatever hour the tide was high. I can see Father, holding his nose and jumping off the end of the pier, exclaiming as he surfaced and shook the water out of his ears, "Bully!" or "By Jove, that's nice!" Mother approached her swim much more cautiously, shoving off with the breast stroke from the steps at the end of the pier, clad in a home-made bathing suit which billowed into voluminous bloomers; on her head was a bathing cap which she said was the result of an alliance between Minerva and a sponge bag. Sailing, however, was the pastime that offered Father, as well as his children, the fullest recreation. Aside from the small skiff sailed by us children there came first the chunky, comfortable catboat, the *Viking*. Later, as the boys grew older, the family expanded into a larger catboat, the *Venture*. Her original tiller was changed to a wheel, thus offering Father more authority as skipper as he sat, legs astride, pipe in his mouth, with the mildewed, green-lined canvas hat on his head that Franklin Roosevelt made his own trademark—entirely in his element. Quincy through college and after took to commandeering the *Venture* for cruises with his friends. The climax of every summer occurred in his cruise over the Labor Day weekend, either to Martha's Vineyard or to Nantucket. Perhaps it was in obedience to some equinoctial law that on Labor Day afternoon a veritable gale howled across Nantucket Sound so that Father was worked into a state of apprehension about "those wild men" when late in the day the *Venture*, low in the water, heavily reefed and yawing dangerously before the wind, blew or rather was blown into port. If there was an occasional lurch in the gait of any of the crew the rolling of the waves had not been solely to blame. There must have been times, such as the occasion when one of the desperadoes fell overboard as they were trying to shoot for the pier, when Father's room would have been more appreciated than his company. But all of Quincy's friends seemed to feel at home with—perhaps because they were so genuinely welcomed by—"Mr. Howe." Here, in later life, is one of Quincy's Cotuit boyhood friends speaking: "Your father was probably the nicest man I ever knew. He always had friends, real friends, everywhere. . . . He was such a very good man in a boat, too. I think he had as much feeling for sailing as any man I have ever known. But where in the world did he learn to be such a terrific gentleman? I mean how does any man become such an all-around, consistent gentleman?"

There was nothing self-conscious about my parents' circle at Cotuit; it in no way smacked of an artists' or writers' "colony." Each household, revolving around its particular man of letters or learning, went its own way. I never heard of a businessman at Cotuit. We could set our watches every morning by the sight of Edward Channing, McLean Professor of Ancient and Modern History, who lived opposite to us on Grand Island, rowing across the harbor in his little black rowboat to pick up the morning mail at the Cotuit post office, and then returning with little short strokes, taken over his round paunch, stern first. Another seagoing professor was Kirsopp Lake, Winn Professor of Ecclesiastical History. I can remember Father's mingled horror and delighted amusement at witnessing this spellbinding classroom magician very much out of his element in a borrowed catboat, making a landing at a pier by the simple expedient of crashing into it, full tilt, with sail spread, before the wind! From atop his sandy wooded bluff in the part of Cotuit known as "Highgrounds" Professor Frank Taussig, Henry Lee Professor of Economics, could look down at his children, almost always victoriously competing in the sailing races. How could he, or any of us, have imagined that his sneakered, middy-bloused daughter Helen would achieve world fame as a doctor at Johns Hopkins and her discovery of the cure for that form of heart disease that manifests itself in "blue" babies?

Another member of my generation who was to make a name was Otis Barton. Mark, as a little boy, along with his friend Henry Hitchcock, used to be willingly drafted by Otis, some eight or nine years their senior, for the purpose of lowering him by means of a rope to the bottom of the harbor, bearing with him a homemade diving helmet, and then responding to a tug of the rope to send down air to him from his also homemade pump. This fearless, untamed boy was to grow into the inventor of the bathysphere, who, along with his colleague Dr. William Beebe, explored waters a great deal deeper than those of Cotuit harbor.

President Lawrence Lowell of Harvard manifested himself on our children's horizon in the shape of a periodic Sunday afternoon call. We would sight him approaching on foot, across the tiny wooden bridge that spanned Little River, in his Sunday blue-serge suit, low white stiff collar, and large-bowed bow tie, head under its white leghorn hat bent forward, and leaning on his tall, rough wooden staff that would have done credit to Wotan. He was followed by his reigning cocker spaniel whose trademark was a waving plume of unclipped tail—first Mowgli, then Phantom—and by his wife (who was also his second cousin), Anna Parker Lowell Lowell. Mrs. Lowell was a gentle lady whose soft brown eyes had much the same expression as those of Mowgli and Phantom; her long white skirts and sunshade were appropriate to the generation preceding hers. (Clothes at Cotuit, unless they actually wore out, were never thrown away, even if it meant spanning a generation to keep them in sensible use.)

Mr. Lowell's calls always caused a sort of electric excitement, with his crisp, hard-hitting approach to every subject he touched. When he arrived on the scene there was an atmosphere of action. I always resented the fact that the wives in his presence were treated as definitely second-class citizens. Mrs. Lowell, in a modest little murmur to Mother, would embark on topics of purely domestic or village interest, as if there were no possibility of her being able or expected to understand the conversation of the men—concerned almost exclusively with politics, academic and national. Lawrence Lowell had a way of galvanizing his listeners to attention by pointing his finger directly at them, as though telling them to drink Moxie, and saying, "You know the story, don't you, of the man who . . ." I remember his saying to me as a child, "You know how to keep track of your dog in the woods, don't you?" Of course I didn't. "Make him feel it's his responsibility to keep up with you. Don't keep calling him unless you really want him."

Inevitably the Sacco-Vanzetti case was Topic A for discussion during the time that President Lowell was so closely involved with it. The fact that Gardner Jackson, the prominent crusader on behalf of the men's innocence, also spent his summers at Cotuit only added to the intensity of feelings already running high. For all of Father's respectful admiration of Mr. Lowell he held firmly to his own opinion that the men had not had a fair trial. He could not help being impressed, however, by the fact that Mr. Lowell not only had backed Professor Frankfurter against his opponents but had talked, *before* he was involved personally in the case, as though he tended to believe in the men's innocence. What Lowell later decided, as one of the three-man commission appointed by Governor Fuller, is history. Whatever evidence it was that convinced him of what he had not been expecting to believe, from the moment that he had made his decision Father had the impression that Mr. Lowell never looked back or doubted for one instant that he had been right. Judge Grant, on the other hand, whom Father also knew well, never failed to bring the subject up, and always with an attempt at justification which seemed to Father to be wrung from a man who continued to be deeply troubled by the part he had played in the drama.

Quincy recalls, "I never heard in my life a more effective speaker. . . . Nor had I ever met anyone who was so sure that he was always right, and yet was so often wrong. Through his advice, in large measure, I went to Harvard when I was sixteen. I think it was a mistake. But Mr. Lowell knew better." Quincy, in characteristic tart and ironic vein, says that, as he has grown older, he has come more and more to admire "the rigid Boston-Harvard type . . .

because [it] is so sure that it is right that it is very liberal and very willing to let any other point of view be heard. Of course they're perfectly certain that the other viewpoint is wrong, so it really doesn't matter. . . . I did feel that in many ways he was awfully sure of himself and not always right. . . . But I do think one must give him enormous credit for his tolerance and his living up to a creed of liberalism which many who call themselves liberals don't even begin to approach. That is, he tolerated the other person's point of view. So many so-called liberals are liberal as long as you agree with them, but for anything that just isn't suitable to them they don't have much use.''

My own memories are not on that level. They concern Mr. Lowell's driving of an automobile. On rare occasions he came to see Father sitting at the wheel of a car. The accomplishment caused stirrings of envy in Father's breast. If Lawrence Lowell could drive a car, then, by Jove, so could he. Father's shrilly articulate and none-too-even-tempered children, who took a dim view from the start, were not the best teachers. We used the family Model T Ford (Quincy's Stutz Bearcat being his own sacrosanct private property), shrieking at him, "No, Father!" "I *told* you that was the accelerator, not the brake!" "Look out!" The fact that it was well known that President Lowell was a menace to life and limb on the highways of the community made no impression on Father. He was frankly envious. The incident that comforted him—and sped the day when he finally of his own accord abandoned the attempt to drive—occurred when President Lowell offered to drive Father to some spot they wanted to visit together. Father joined him at his house, climbed into the front seat beside him, and watched a little wistfully his more accomplished friend go through all the checking of equipment which is demanded of a good pilot before take-off, with a loud revving up of the engine. Then, as they both leaned back, satisfied that all was in order, and prepared themselves to face the wild blue yonder, with a jolt and a shiver the car shot off down Mr. Lowell's driveway—backwards.

The name of Lowell at Cotuit was not associated solely with A. Lawrence. There was also his cousin "Fred" and his family who lived, invisible to us, in the beautiful pine woods at our backs. The gulf separating the natures and talents of Fred Lowell from Lawrence Lowell separated their wives as well. In any room of men discussing politics Isabel Shaw Lowell would never have sat silent in a corner! The blood of the Abolitionist Lucretia Mott had not run thin in her exuberantly, delightedly nonconformist great-granddaughter. Mrs. Lowell, however, was not a "reformer" who joined committees; she was too nonconformist to do that. She was an amused and amusing parlor rebel, who enjoyed discussing the latest *New Republic* or *Nation* and the issues they raised, and made stimulating company for the young who agreed with her—Quincy was one of them—and got under the skin as an irritant to her Boston contemporaries who didn't. Where she parted from the genus "reformer" was in her orientation to the world of the arts. Not only was she herself a first-rate pianist— Harold Bauer would not have bothered about her as a pupil if her talent had not warranted it—but it was she who gave the moral support and courage to free her artist husband from shackles which might, but for her, have held him a lifelong prisoner. Fred Lowell had a heaven-sent gift of a lovely tenor voice, most beautifully expressed in the singing of German Lieder. But it was neither voice production nor musicianship—both of which he possessed—which made his singing unforgettable—it was an X quality (not quantity) which brought tears to the eyes of the listener. Another talent, however, lay slumbering under the surface of the State Street trustee who, by an act of manly strong-mindedness, at about the age of fifty, threw off his Boston shackles and betook himself to the Rue de Lille in Paris, with his gifted family at his heels. (It is obvious that his connection with State Street had made the *beau geste* possible.) In any case the result was a production over the next ten years of water-color paintings, which won both public and private recognition of the fact that Fred Lowell was an artist.

My parents' social life at Cotuit was as mild as the waters in which they swam, its few engagements rising and falling as gently as the tides. As for dinner parties—once a summer Mother and Father walked along the beach at low tide, or through the woods at high, by the light of an electric lantern, to dine with the Lawrence Lowells approximately a mile away; and once a summer the Lowells dined with them. The same exchange of hospitality went on with the James Ropeses (he was Hollis Professor of Divinity, and she was Fred Lowell's sister) and the Hitchcocks, our nearest neighbors and closest friends. (Judge Hitchcock miraculously lived down at Cotuit the fact that St. Louis was his home and that he was a Yale graduate.) Any one of the couples would be the *pièce de résistance* when my parents dined with the others. For these functions Mother kept one dress sacrosanct, summer after summer. It had been made originally by one of the sisters, Marion or Etta, and was as dressy as what today would be called a "spectator sport" dress, of plain silk or print. Father put on his white flannel trousers for these outings. It was rumored that the Wadsworths from Geneseo, New York, had a butler who brought the first and only dinner jacket to Cotuit.

Every Sunday Father, minus Mother, and with such of his children as he could muster, attended either the Congregational or the Methodist Church, as did the Lowells, the Ropeses, and the Hitchcocks. They all felt that they owed it to the community to "stand for" churchgoing, and they rarely faltered in putting their beliefs into practice. When the roof of the Methodist Church had to be reshingled, and its members all pitched in to help, there was President Lowell, an ardent chopper of wood in his spare time, with hammer and nails on the rooftop, along with the rest of the village. If because of bad weather, or some reason of health, church was out of the question, Father read us the Collect, Epistle, and Gospel for the day at home. And at Cotuit, even more than in Boston, there was hymn singing on Sunday evenings—often with the Hitchcocks for company—ending up, more than likely, with Gilbert and Sullivan! There was no club at Cotuit—yacht, country, or golf; there were no cocktail parties and no lunch parties. Mrs. Lowell made it gently but firmly clear that she felt that even the serving of afternoon tea was not quite in the "spirit" of Cotuit.

Father's masculine companionship was chosen almost exclusively from the Cotuit bill of fare, although in 1926 Mother wrote me,

"Mr. James Truslow Adams is staying with us for a few days, so Father has a playmate at last." The popularized American histories —*The Adams Family, The Epic of America* among them—written by this friend of Father's whom I never knew—were record-making best sellers in their day. Professional success, however, had not immunized the author from finding himself caught up in an emotional tangle. In trying to extricate himself from it he turned to Father during this visit as confidant and counselor. "Jim" Adams, as he was to Father, recovering from an operation, had fallen in love with his trained nurse and, wanting very much to marry her, was putting himself through psychological torture because his unmarried sister disapproved of the step. A letter from Father written to his friend in the fall of that year gives us a glimpse of both men:

10 October, 1926

MY DEAR JIM ADAMS,

Since you have treated me with the confidence of a friend, I have come to feel that I should not be fulfilling my part in the relationship were I to withhold something that came to me as a sort of illumination as I journeyed to and from Newport yesterday. It involves some plain speaking, but I am sure our relation has grown to be such that you will not take it amiss.

What I have seen, in the new light of reflection, is that instead of laying your troubles before a mere friend of the laity, you should have consulted a wise, up-to-date doctor. I am sure he would now be telling you that you have worried yourself into a pathological condition calling for the opinion and advice of a psychologist. You happened to come to me instead of to him, but I believe the advice I have to give you is just as sound as any doctor's—provided only you will think it so.

You must shake off the habit of deferring to another member of your family, and make a definite strike for personal happiness before it is too late. No state of mind brings greater unhappiness than the consciousness that one has not had the courage or the independence of thought to follow one's own instincts. You may remember my saying something of this very sort to you in Cotuit. Even an unhappy marriage of one's own choosing would bring less mental suffering than that of impotent regret. The illumination I have seen tells me, however, that the marriage you have been contemplating would not be unhappy. Accordingly my earnest advice—which I wish you could regard as a psycho-medical prescription—is to stop playing Hamlet at once, stop thinking, stop analyzing, stop wondering and worrying, and marry the girl you care for as soon as she will let you—this very week if possible. My firm conviction is that, acting on this advice, you will never regret the Declaration of Independence I suggested as we walked up the Embankment.

If you doubt the validity of all this go at once to such a doctor as Riggs in Stockbridge or Adriance in Williamstown. I believe either or both of them would confirm every word I have said—and that you would be wasting time and money in asking their opinion.

Forgive me if I have gone too far, but is not a Father Confessor expected to talk back? I have done so only because I have the genuine concern of a friend for your permanent welfare, and should never forgive myself for sitting silent when a timely, honest word might effect the issue out of all your afflictions.

Very faithfully your médecin malgré lui,

M. A. DEW. HOWE

The happy postscript to a correspondence which burgeoned on this subject must record that the self-questioning Hamlet who was trying to live out his American Dream married the girl of his choice, and went to England to live for several years. There he became a great friend of Aunt Helen and her husband. Through Aunt Helen's letters, as well as his own rather ponderous and humorless animadversions, Mother was to enjoy, across the miles, what she pleased to call "The Education of Mrs. James Truslow Adams."

Another writer, who was in time to become one of Father's dearest friends, spent a summer with his family at Cotuit. But this early introduction to Van Wyck Brooks occurred just as the shadows of the mental depression of which he has himself written so movingly were gathering around his gallant head, and my own memories of him at that time are both shadowy and sad.

An annual ritual at Cotuit occurred with the first stirrings of spring, generally over the 19th of April holiday, when we walked in the thawing, wakening woods in the hope of finding trailing arbutus, always called by its colloquial name of Mayflower. The same excitement was reborn each year as we uncovered the shy, fragrant little blossoms hiding under the dead leaves of winter. "Known to the Knoll," they grew in one sunny clearing in the woods to which I could find my way today. Mother always quoted Emily Dickinson, "Pink—small—punctual, Aromatic—low," and for Father it was a photo finish every year to see just *how* punctual Mother's favorite flower would be, as he combed Boston, looking for the first bunch to give her on her birthday.

It is difficult today to recall, in the vernacular of present-day real-estate agents, how "restricted" Cotuit was. Race, creed, color, or national origin were not even contemplated as problems to be faced. The worst bogies that Cotuit feared were represented by the neighboring communities of Hyannis and Wianno, filled with "Middlewesterners" and "people from the Newtons." As for any Irish-American family who played touch football, spent large sums of money that *showed*, belonged to some summer club or clubs, and went to a Catholic church—the Cotuit clan would have been no more likely to rub shoulders with them than with the few remaining Indians in the little village of nearby Mashpee. I knew one little Boston boy in Cotuit who was invited by a little Kennedy girl to a party at her house in Hyannis. His mother wouldn't let him go because she had heard there was a soda fountain in the house.

It was only shortly before our own span at Cotuit had run out, in the early thirties, that the first Jewish summer visitor bought property—and a Freudian psychoanalyst at that!—and became a brilliant addition to the life of the generation that followed my parents. The fact that Father came to like the charming Dr. William Herman as he did was a triumph over prejudice—*not* concerning his race but concerning the mere existence of psychoanalysis, which caused in him an instinctive recoil as from something vaguely "slimy." Mother, more subtle, and temperamentally introspective, welcomed

Bill Herman's tangy fillip, although she, too, a true product of her period, shrank from "all this emphasis on sex."

It is certain that there was no emphasis on sex for me during my prolonged Cotuit childhood. I was six when we went there first, and twenty-seven when we spent our last summer there. Little girlhood melted into my teens, and my teens into my twenties, and still Cotuit remained the frame for summer after summer. When I see mothers of today lashed to the wheel of a car, hauling the children about to swimming classes, outing classes, treasure hunts, club tournaments, or fetching and carrying them to and from evening parties, it appears as though my parents were not at all concerned about my social or psychological—let alone sexual—development. They thought boarding school in Milton covered all of my expanding possibilities. There seemed to have been rather different steps taken about the boys. For Quincy, there was a summer working on Aunt Mabel's farm in Danville, Vermont, and another summer in the shipyard at Bath, Maine. For Mark there was summer school in Madison, Wisconsin, and an archaeological expedition to New Mexico. But for the only daughter there was—Cotuit. I feel now as though I must have dreamed all those years away, by day as well as by night. On a summer evening I would go out onto the balcony off my bedroom and watch the moonlight falling on the silvery gray water, throwing into relief the three erect little cedars which stood at the foot of the lawn. I always saw them in fancy as representing Quincy and Mark and me. When we grew up, what was going to *happen* to us? Everything seemed to be holding its breath. Nothing ever changed. I would sleep ten hours at night, and then on the blustery summer afternoons sit in front of the mast on board the *Venture,* with my bare legs dangling down either side of the bowsprit, or lie along one of the decks and listen to the mild water *plash, plash* under us while Father or my brothers steered. Even sailing was subject to the same monotony—and the same charm— as everything else. Once we got out of the harbor we would sail straight out the channel, with sandy shoals on either side, to the "Rock." Even this one jagged reality in a world of haze and sand and tepidity lay hidden out of sight under the buoy which marked it. Then we would come about—and sail home again. How hard to think that this was the "Roaring Twenties," when, at other summer resorts, my contemporaries were sailing and swimming in crowds, and dancing, if not petting and necking, in twosomes. Cotuit afforded me nothing in the way of "beaux." Brothers of my friends, and friends of my brothers, would have rated me lower than the fiddler crabs which rustled in the eel grass under the pier at low tide, and I certainly never found any of them in ther adolescent years as fit subject to wear an aura of romance.

I don't think that Father ever fully took in the difference between his youth in Bristol and ours in Cotuit. Aside from the fact that his children were far more introverted than any of his own brothers had been, the sheer size of the family in which he grew up automatically had made each meal, without benefit of guests, into a social occasion. All activities—including reading—were engaged in on a communal scale. And then all those "swells" from Newport, and New York! Cotuit boasted not one. And Mother, thinking of her own far lonelier girlhood in Quincy, thought of me with brothers and boats and movies to go to and a telephone to talk on, and at least a few friends, as heiress to all the excitements of modern twentieth-century living.

All the same there were forces in me burrowing toward the light —even in Cotuit. After a year of Radcliffe, a year studying in Paris, a year of teaching school in Boston, my parents had indulged me by sending me for the winter of 1925–26 to the Theatre Guild School in New York. It was there that I was encouraged to make a profession out of the writing and acting of my own character sketches. This more or less double-jointed outlet for whatever gifts I had was eventually to prove far more rewarding than I had dared to hope. At any rate, from the summer of 1926 on I had a thread on which to hang my energies, and my time. In a cubicle—I suppose about four feet by six—of our tiny bathhouse every morning I treated the sleeping oyster beds around me to auditions of my struggles. All of life seemed to come much more sharply in focus. I was readier to enjoy some of the new arrivals in Cotuit. Bill Herman and his wife were among them. There was a visit one summer from

Eliot Cabot, who was starring at the Dennis Playhouse with Edith
Barrett in *Romeo and Juliet*. This talented rebel Cabot shone for
me as a beacon on the path I would follow. ("Sallie Cabotte" and
I had spent a winter together in Paris with the same French family.
Here was a friend's brother around whose swarthy, incredibly
handsome head one *could* throw a romantic aura!) Had he not cast
off *his* shackles to shine on Broadway as a real star? Probably today
he is remembered most for his performance opposite Helen Hayes in
Coquette, and for his playing of Gatsby in *The Great Gatsby*. Eliot
was a great mimic and we entertained ourselves by carrying on
imaginary conversations in the Boston accents of our mothers'
friends. We were both experts in the field. Both my parents liked
him, though they knew him only slightly, and even took in stride
the theatrical late breakfast and postmidnight snack—at *Cotuit!*
After all, they both loved his mother—as who didn't who had ever
known that dear and witty woman—and he was a Cabot, and the
run was only for a week. Tragedy and early death were waiting for
him in the wings, but there was only high hope and gaiety and
laughter onstage that summer.

It was a year or two later that our Cotuit fare was further enlivened by the arrival of John and Christina Marquand, who were
to become part of our lives. Father, in response to his younger
Tavern Club friend, in search of a mild climate for his four-year-old
daughter recovering from pneumonia, agreed to rent the Marquand
family the little cottage which we owned, next to ours. The fact that
John christened the new little sailboat he bought the *Electric Bond
and Share* places the summer as 1929.

John Marquand was much nearer the age of Father's children
than of his friend, Father himself. Actually, he was the only one
of Father's younger Tavern Club friends who persisted in calling
him "Mr. Howe." There was nothing about John, in those days
when he was still a shy thirty-five, of the hail-fellow-well-met back-
slapper, any more than when he became one of the most successful
of American novelists. He was only seven years older than Quincy
and yet somewhere in those seven years fell the dividing line that

separated two generations: John belonged, recognizably, to the war generation, Quincy to the postwar. Mark and I immediately recognized in the new arrival a potential candidate to go onto the pedestal where we had placed Quincy alone. John encouraged us to laugh *at*, not merely with, the world that surrounded us. He and Quincy egged each other on in mordant comments on mutual friends, the national scene, and Cotuit neighbors. The hazy if pleasant blur which had up to then hung like a mesh of scrim over the local scene lifted: outlines became sharper, the light that illuminated them shining from the eye of the beholder, and that beholder, pre-eminently, a satirist. I myself, now a couple of years into a career as a monologuist, was particularly sensitive to this light of satire which served to intensify a slant in my own vision. I look back upon the sails, the Sunday lunches, the dinners (by this time cocktails had arrived in Cotuit!), and my ears ring with incessant talk and laughter of Marquands and Howes in happy counterpoint of minds, spirits, and temperaments.

The full orchestra at such gatherings generally subsided to pianissimo, to let John's solo part emerge from stage center where he found himself, certainly never by design but simply because his natural gift for anecdote put him there inevitably. Mark Twain said that "The humorous story depends for its effect upon the *manner* of the telling; the comic story and the witty story upon the matter. . . . The humorous story may be spun out to great length, and may wander around as much as it pleases, and arrive nowhere in particular. . . . The humorous story is strictly a work of art—high and delicate art—and only an artist can tell it." John Marquand was that artist, and we were only too enchanted to serve as the audience that any gifted teller of tales must have. His general demeanor, in those days, was much less assured than when he added weight, rosiness, and a mustache- -*and* when he cut his hair. He was Samson, in reverse: in his days of diffidence he wore his hair so long that he almost caricatured the "Private Secretary," with the part down the middle and the long sleek sides flattened down under a wet hairbrush. Gluyas Williams, in a Tavern Club poster for a Christmas play, has caught him perfectly in this period. Those were the days of white linen plus fours and long woolen golf stockings. There was about his stance and expression a disarming sort of whipped look, partly feigned but expressive nonetheless of his true inner lack of self-confidence. Never then, any more than during the time of his subsequent success, was there anything of the stuffed shirt about him. His brows puckered despairingly as he recounted some moment of mock tragedy—generally laid in his own household. His gray-blue, blue-gray eyes—keen, quick, appraising— narrowed so that his face twisted into a mask of misery as he grasped the back of his neck with his left hand, in a seeming effort to hold his head on, while he waved his right hand about, perhaps holding a cigar, after dinner, in his sensitive artist's fingers. Those same fingers when disengaged made quick little motions, opening and closing, in accompaniment to his words. Then suddenly the sun shone, and his face was illumined with a flashing smile that was all invitation to join his own amusement.

Mother blossomed whenever the Marquands were with us, each helping to bring out the light of wit from behind the bushel where she was so apt to keep it hidden. In spite of her pleasure in their company, Mother nonetheless fulminated as a hostess over the lateness of their arrival on each and every occasion that they were invited to the house. She tried all the subterfuges that a beleaguered hostess must try—telling them that lunch or dinner was scheduled for an hour earlier than was actually to be the case—all to no avail. They rolled up to the door in the family Maxwell—I think—talking at once as they walked up the steps, apologizing, expostulating, and each blaming the other for the delay. Mother, behind their backs, quoted her favorite "Modern Love" sonnet of Meredith's, calling them "that ever diverse pair." We all felt the same way; it was possible to understand, even to sympathize with the cause of the seeds of discord between them, and yet to love them both. If John brought delight and entertainment to all the Howes, so in full measure did his lovely, his enchanting, his indescribable Christina. Her brother "Shan," known to readers of the *New York Times* through his by-line signature of A. C. Sedgwick, wrote of her as I can think of no literary or even literate brother, short of a Henry or a William James, writing of a beloved sister : ''Hers was a unique flavor and God was in His best mood when he concocted it. She was, I think, a stroke of imaginative genius, inspired and an inspiration —adorable on all the manifold facets of her being and therefore adored.'' In the hierarchy of saints there is, I have read, a St. Christina the Astonishing. Surely that patron saint would have moved over to make room in her niche for Christina Sedgwick Marquand.

How describe that combination of Texas Guinan and *La Princesse Lointaine,* with a little Dorothy Wordsworth thrown in? Slender, light of foot, with a prettily turned ankle on touchingly coltlike legs, blue eyes under hooded lids, fine gold hair and delicate complexion warm with a soft apricot glow. About her shimmered that indefinable penumbra which was more than distinction or breeding. There was marked beauty of line and texture, but there was the subtler beauty as well, for which the outward and visible sign was only the symbol: Christina shone with an inward and spiritual grace. There was nothing about her that was ordinary, either in the sense of the usual or in the snobbish social sense in which my parents used the word. She knew the English poets as only a young woman of an earlier generation knew them; her general cultivation was inhaled in her parents' house in Stockbridge—inhabited by the Sedgwicks of nine generations, where she was educated by governesses when she was not being exposed to Europe, yet I doubt if she could have passed a college board examination. When she became engaged to John Marquand in Rome it was her outline that surely suggested the mold for the archetype Heroine into which he was to pour the clay of his own future creations.

Yet the picture of Christina I have so far hinted at is only a fraction of what she was. Put her down by herself on a cruise ship to the Caribbean and, against a background of paper caps and balloons she could roister with shoe salesmen, dress buyers, and Texas ranchers. I remember one of the oystermen at Cotuit saying, ''I like Mrs. Marquand. She's real common.'' She bubbled with an exuberant gaiety, was entirely without ''side.'' Catching her off guard in a moment of reverie one felt, looking at her dreamy,

beautiful face, that she was hearing echoes of some magic fairyland
forlorn. Then, in the next instant, she was, vociferously—*plunk!*—
living the present moment with gusto and abandon that made the
rest of us seem shrinking violets by comparison. The unheard
melodies which an instant before had transformed her were translated into her own piercing whoops of amusement, her mouth wide
open, a dress off at the shoulder, and hairpins flying. She said once
that she was planning to be a "jaunty" old lady—and indeed she
would have been!—John, characteristically, groaning at the prospect. Part of her jauntiness would have sprung from a helter-
skelter, if disarming, approach to the ordinary minutiae of existence. I remember lunching with her at a restaurant when she picked
up, without comment, the *three* gloves she somehow seemed to have
about her. One met her on the street, twirling a leash, but unaware
that she had left the dog at home. This pervasive lack of practicality
about "coping" caused her, in the household, to play the role of the
perennial child wife—or, at least, it suited John's psychological
needs to see her in the role. The writer, doing his work at home, performed it against a background of long, shrill conversations on the
telephone, invitations lightheartedly given or accepted (Christina,
like Father, liked almost everybody!), and a general vagueness
about just what particular work of John's *was* in progress. Christina got thoroughly on his nerves. He all but snarled her name as
he hurled accusations and complaints at her head, as the source of
all the irritations that made his life intolerable: "Christ*eena*
doesn't seem to understand that I have to earn my living"; "Chris-
teena was so busy feeding Johnny an ice cream cone that she drove
the car into a tree instead of looking where she was going"; "Chris-
teena thinks it would be so nice if I came in to say how-do-you-do
when she has her lunch club to the house," etc., etc. An onlooker,
concerned for both, could not but see that many of John's accusations were founded on fact, at the same time admitting that the
sweetness and good temper of Christina's nature would have made
a retaliatory snarl on her part impossible. The mingling of amusement and imperturbable remoteness off which glanced any expressions of hostility was part and parcel of the very quicksilver quality

that had evaded his grasp when (as she told me herself) she had broken her engagement to him fourteen times. The fact that her frame of literary reference blandly ignored the standards of the *Saturday Evening Post* only enhanced her Princesse Lointaine quality. She would have been elusive enough for any mortal man t try to grasp and tame; but she was to prove a fatal will-o'-the-wisp to a complex New Englander who was unable to shake off the sense that he himself belonged in some lesser realm, located on the other side of the railroad tracks.

Why John was dogged by this sense is a psychological irony. His own New England forebears were quite as eminent as Christina's; certainly no Sedgwick in the field of letters made the name that John's great-aunt Margaret Fuller had made. It was not lack of blood, or character, or gifts that John felt in his own background. My reading of him—and I fully realize that it is only one of others equally possible—is that what cut deep was simple lack of money. And perhaps that lack was not so simple, perhaps it scarred the young John with a sense of downfall and humiliation following his father's financial failure and the family's return from Wilmington, Delaware, to Newburyport, where John was sent to the Newburyport High School, and, only through the generosity of a relative, later to Harvard. The only child, coming from "away," felt an outsider. His cousins, the Hales, lived next door. Years later those who knew them felt that John Marquand had brought the family to life in the pages of *Wickford Point,* pilloried or immortalized, according to one's point of view. Presented as ineffective in practical ways—in other words, as failures in a worldly sense—the fact is that the Hales were not much more affluent than the Marquands.

There is certainly a possibility that John's pain suffered through lack of money was merely a cloak covering a deeper need. The sensitive, lonely boy may well have smarted under the denial of the riches of warmth and humanity that come from being part of a lively, funny family. (For another slant on John's life in the big Hale family of an earlier generation take a second look at Lucretia Hale's *The Peterkin Papers.* Essentially, the family was the same.) In his own life it seemed as though John was driven by some inner compulsion to buttress himself financially against the sense of inadequacy he was never wholly to lose. Years later, through his own successes as a highly paid writer, and in another marriage, he attained much of what would have given another man the comfortable sense of assurance that he had "arrived." If he found both a wry amusement and a secret satisfaction that he had become brother-in-law to John D. Rockefeller III, he could still succumb to a sense of frustration in recognizing that he was forever doomed to be cast in the role of Poor Relation.

One did not have to be long in John and Christina's company before it became apparent that John felt painfully sensitive in his relationship to his Sedgwick in-laws. Rightly or wrongly he suffered under the sense that they looked down on him both socially and intellectually. "Uncle Ellery," after all, *was* the *Atlantic,* and what was any niece of his doing, married to a man who wrote potboilers for the *Saturday Evening Post?* "Uncle Harry," the author of exquisite "literary" essays surely could not have recognized the existence of a mere Mr. Moto. I remember with what relish John sharpened his stiletto when Uncle Harry asked Christina, as he was wont to ask some niece, real or adopted, to accompany him one spring on an automobile trip in France. Rolling the psuedo-literary phrases under his tongue John began, "We called ourselves *Ninon* and *Ninette.* We called our old Ford *Sancho Panza . . .*" All the same, Christina took the trip.

We had, at Cotuit, ample opportunity for observing the Sedgwick-Marquand design for living, with Christina's parents close by at Marstons Mills in a rented cottage, which John promptly, and understandably, christened Heartbreak House, called, for short, by all of them, "Heartbreak." Later the Sedgwicks bought the house and gave it to the Marquands, when the name came to fit with a dreadful applicability. Many years and one marriage later Christina, defying the laws of nature (as only she could), passed from the stage of butterfly, through suffering nobly borne, to the plane of heroism as she suffered her last illness of cancer at fifty-three. It was under these circumstances that she wrote me, speaking of her son Johnny: "He is so darling and full of feeling really. I told him Tina [his sister] and I had revisited Heartbreak and it nearly killed us, and his eyes filled with tears and he said, 'I don't see how you could.' "

In those early days, however, the very word "Heartbreak" was spoken with a laugh. Mr. and Mrs. Sedgwick were both "characters." When they first arrived on the Cotuit scene in a rented cottage near the Marquands, my parents actually knew them far less well than they knew the Ellery Sedgwicks or Mr. Harry Sedgwick. The possessive parents talked incessantly of Christina ("Pussy," her father called her) and the dastardly prescription that their friend Dr. Austen Riggs of Stockbridge had made for her marriage when she—poor girl suffering under irreconcilable tensions—had been under his care. Dr. Riggs—the Sedgwicks recounted with withering scorn—considered a good marriage a "sphere" (said with a gesture to match) and he sternly forbade Mr. and Mrs. Sedgwick to impinge on its form by adding to it their presence. They had observed the stricture for an appreciable length of time —perhaps a year? I don't know—but, in their own judgment at least, the time had run out, and they were coming, ready or not, once more to participate in their daughter's life. If there had not been so much humor on the part of all the participants, the two households could not have been as full of laughter—shared by all their friends.

If there was agitation in the orbit of the Marquands there was— in Christina's own words—"the heavenly cooling of the brow" to be found always at one wellspring. And that spring was Father! It was, perhaps, natural that Christina herself should respond to Father's qualities as her Sedgwick uncles had before her. But it was, after all, John who had first asked Father about Cotuit. It was John whom Father had urged to come. When it came to the pattern of Boston life and letters were they not both "outsiders"? The difference in response to this role in which they were cast was indicative of the nature of each. As a writer living in Boston John walked more in the footsteps of Henry James (although how dif-

ferent in fiber!) : his sensitive skin could not accommodate to the
harsh winds that assailed it. Father followed the easy, genial road
of adaptability paved by William Dean Howells.

From such a small thing as membership in a social club larger
implications may be drawn. We know how serenely Father accepted
the fact that he could not financially afford membership in the
Somerset Club. John, on the other hand, in his early years in
Boston, berated the club's members in private as he did, symbolically, in print. But when his own success was established he swallowed all his words—and joined the club. A fellow member—
revealing quite as much about the mentality of the Somerset Club
as about that of John Marquand—has said to me, ''Poor John! He
had such a chip on his shoulder that we all had to go out of our way
to be as nice to him as though we had just elected a Negro!'' By the
same token, when it came to more purely intellectual aspects of
Boston life, John stood a little awkwardly at the threshold. It was
Father, interested in seeing his younger friend both happy and
recognized in Boston, who urged him to become a Proprietor of the
Boston Athenaeum, and to join the strictly professional Examiner
Club. Father, in short, took to Boston and all its ways like a duck
to water—as he took to life itself. If his path had fallen in other
places I am persuaded he would have had an equally happy life.
John, on the other hand, carried within the seeds of discord with
himself as well as with his environment. There is no question
who was the gifted artist of the two. There is also no question
who was the happier man. I think that at Cotuit each of these
different writers enjoyed a sense of kinship in the knowledge that
the other was closeted every day, only a few yards away, hard at
his own work. As Father was pleased to have for company a fellow
writer who was not writing a professor's treatise, so John, on his
side, was grateful for the interest an older and ''highbrow'' Boston
gentleman-writer showed in his stories. There was not the sense of
condescension which he felt in the presence of the writing Sedgwick
uncles when Father wholeheartedly would congratulate John on
selling, for $3,000, a story he had written at Cotuit, ''I haven't made
as much on a book in my whole life as you can make on one story.''

In those days there was a little homemade golf course in nearby Santuit. Father wrote to Copeland, "With John Marquand I am on the point of playing one of my exceedingly poor games of golf. We shall interlard our imprecations upon bad shots with duets in your honor." Father initiated John into greater expertise in sailing, and there was always a running stream of congenial talk between them concerning many tastes and opinions held in common. John even joined Father on an expedition to Bristol so that Father might have the satisfaction of showing off its old houses to the chronicler of the past glories of Newburyport.

This seems as good a place as any to mention the single word that inevitably comes up whenever John and Father are mentioned together—and that word is "Apley." It would be absurd to pretend that Father's style of writing—florid in manner, kindly in comment, often tepid in subject matter—did not serve as the model for Horatio Willing, Mr. Apley's biographer. John himself talked with Father about his idea of a parody biography of a stuffy Boston gentleman. As to the actual bones of structure on which he would create his flesh-and-blood portrait, I remember standing with John in Father's library in Louisburg Square, and removing from the shelves his *Life and Letters of Barrett Wendell*, confirming for John his choice of format. In the same way I handed him like a pebble my own memories of Naushon and the Putnam Camp— neither of which he had ever visited—around which he created the pearl that grew into "Pequod Island." As the book began to take shape John was so unaware of any cause for awkwardness in relation to Father that he brought chapters in progress for his comment and counsel. From the start Father was appreciative and amused at the brilliance of the satire. No one, then, was more embarrassed than John when on the book's publication Father's picture appeared in *Time* magazine, with the caption "The Late George Apley . . . ?" I suppose it was difficult for him to say in print, "Mr. Howe was not the model for Mr. Apley, but for Mr. Willing," and so the legend grew until poor Father used to say, "I am afraid that my only claim to immortality will be as the model for George Apley." So herewith let it be definitively stated that Horatio Willing as an

inspired literary creation would very likely never have been born
had Father not been born and written before John. But the man
whose "affability and gregariousness" Mr. Ellery Sedgwick laid at
the door of ancestors who roamed the seas far removed from Boston,
was no Apley.

The Garden of Eden aspect of life at Cotuit proved, like all other
such gardens, to be mortal. It was there that a parting of the ways
of that ever diverse pair began to threaten. Close to the ordeal myself, I shall not write of its pain and conflict here. There was a
Marquandian irony in the fact that the hero of the struggle who
had spent so many hours at Cotuit deriding the Freudian lingo of
our psychoanalyst friend to whom he always referred as "the good
doctor" was slated ruefully to seek psychiatric counsel himself.
Though it helped to swing open the doors of a marriage in which he
believed himself to be caged, he remained an unhappy human being.
One wonders if the insight of a Jung might have helped him. Jung
at least knew that "It is often tragic to see how blatantly a man
bungles his own life and the lives of others and yet remains totally
incapable of seeing how much the whole tragedy originates in himself, and how he continually feeds it and keeps it going. Not *consciously* of course—for consciously he is engaged in bewailing and
cursing a faithless world that recedes further and further into the
distance." That bewailing and cursing, however, took the form of
John Marquand's novels. Whether they would have come into being
without an inner tension within the author or whether, on the contrary, they would have gained depth if that author had been more
self-aware, raises a question I could not answer.

There was one talk, behind closed doors, with Father. After that,
the two men were never to be alone together again. Father belonged
to the generation in Boston which could count its divorces on the
finger of one hand (that was the finger, ironically, that pointed to
John's cousin, nee Fuller, who had set the town by the ears when
she left a Cabot husband and children to marry Winthrop Ames).
In John's generation there were one or two celebrated Boston
divorces where men of established reputations had left wives and
children in order to remarry. One was punished by banishment from

the Board of Trustees of the Boston Symphony Orchestra and the
other from the Corporation of Harvard College. And this was only
yesterday! I remember spluttering to Father about what seemed
to me unjust and hypocritical on the part of the authorities, in
both those cases, and, speaking for my generation, saying that a
man's private life was his own affair. Father, speaking for his
generation, said, in substance, "It's a question of *trust*. If a man is
not trustworthy in one relationship it's fair to question whether
he might not prove untrustworthy in another." It was said in no
spirit of "holier-than-thou," and Father never had recourse to the
strong line followed by some of his contemporaries in "cutting" any
offender against the code in which he had been reared.

I have a memory of Father in his very last days, sitting in his
dressing gown in the morning sunshine. With the pellucid simplicity
that is shared by the very young and the very old he said gently, "I
have been thinking over my life, and I like to think that I have
never consciously hurt anyone," adding as a happy afterthought,
"or been hurt by anyone." John Marquand could not say the
same. At the time when Father was desperately ill in the hospital,
and we did not think he would live, John—and I can see his face
as he spoke—said simply, "Your father has clean hands and a pure
heart." Whenever I saw John, as I did occasionally in the last years
of his life, he always asked, "How is your father?" And then,
"Give him my love."

I have a little note from Christina, written almost twenty years
later, scrawled in pencil in the same hospital where Father lay in
another desperate illness. She could not know that she herself, so
many, many years his junior, was to die a few months later, and that
Father was still to live another ten years.

"Darling Helen, My heart is beating with you. [I hear that]
your father is unconscious now—so he can't be suffering. I can
only send you and Mark all my love. Your father has always been so
dear and so sweet to me and I love him very much. . . ."

John and Christina's last summer at Cotuit was the last for the
Howes too. Fate was waiting in the wings, to strike us all in
different ways. John not only never returned to Cotuit; he soon left

Boston for good. Not only for Father but for all of us Cotuit seemed
the repository of our happiest hours. In it was contained summer,
childhood, family life, and for me it must always hold more poignant memories still. Father, when he was over ninety, and unable
to read, used to pass many hours of solitude recalling events and
people that had given him pleasure. He wrote down these memories
in a long, rambling soliloquy, intended only for his children. Remembering the hundred and third psalm—"Bless the Lord, O my
soul, and forget not all his benefits"—he called this running
reminiscence *All His Benefits*. Reliving a return visit to Cotuit
years after we had all left it he found

> That memories of wife and children,
> As once they were, so flooded me
> That I could only turn away
> Blinded by hot nostalgic tears.
> Here was authentic testimony
> That among all my Benefits
> Cotuit held, and holds, a topmost place.

15

MOTHER AND FATHER—AS MOTHER AND FATHER

WHO MORE EGOTISTICAL THAN A CHILD? Even if that child is middle-aged: *my* childhood was never duplicated in charm, the pangs of *my* adolescence were sharper than any other youth's, etc. Even if one does not speak the vocabulary of depth psychology one's parents remain archetypes, fixed in Eternity. It is only the fascinating unfolding child himself who appears to move through Time, passing in and out of phases, or "stages" as the parents may forgivingly call them. To this particular egomaniac it begins to dawn that my parents too—and even at the same moment as I myself, albeit on another parallel line—also were journeying through Time. It never occurred to me that they, as human beings too, were passing in and out of "phases" as they met the deaths of their parents, lost friends and loves, went through periods of anxiety concerning work, health, money, or children(!) and confronted, in their day, the fading of youth and oncoming of old age, and the abyss beyond. Now, looking at them as dispassionately as I am able, I see a man and a woman who were young when Victoria was on the throne, doing their best as parents of children who were young in the era of the First World War, Freud, and a civilization dominated by technological achievements. It is also worth remembering that Father was thirty-six years old when his first child was born. This fact meant that through his children he was drawn automatically about ten years deeper into the twentieth century than most of his contemporaries.

Both parents showed themselves in their quintessential light as parents when Mark, who had been rather a laggard student in his years at the Country Day School outside of Boston, suddenly won a three hundred dollar prize at Phillips Academy, Andover, for showing the greatest improvement of any boy in his class. Mother wrote me, "Father is now saying that Mark is going to become a scholar. Poor Father!" Alas, that she did not live to learn how abundantly justified Father's unquenchable faith proved to be.

It was far more through Quincy, as the spearhead of the oncoming generation, that Mother and Father got inklings of the brave new world that was coming. The very fact that he always referred to "Mamma" and "Papa" (pronounced mamah and papah) as opposed to Mark's and my "Mother" and "Father" only served to point up the cleavage of years which divided "Quincy—and the children," as our parents referred to us. Mother had taken hard his adolescent years. Quincy, writing during his first weeks at St. George's at Newport, showered imprecations on his parents' heads, accusing them of having sent him to "the worst school in the country." Mother vibrated between anger with him for behaving so badly and anxiety lest he be suffering too deeply. Father, on the other hand, was to repeat, staunchly, "He'll come out of it eventually. The boy's going to be all right." It was Father's turn, however, to sigh when Quincy, as a Harvard undergraduate, threw up the opportunity to become cox of the second varsity crew because he was enjoying himself more with a group of friends who were considerably more talented, though much less popular, than the oarsmen for whom he abandoned them. It was equally hard for Father to comfort himself with his oft-repeated *solvitor ambulando* when Quincy threw up, before completing it, a year of study at Christ College, Cambridge, England, which he hated, in favor of travel on the Continent and a trip to Algiers. When he came home, smuggling a copy of *Ulysses*, it was Mother who picked it up and read it, and also followed him, along with me, through Proust's recovery of past time. Mother had Mark for company when Quincy next was reading Spengler's *Decline of the West*, and the three of us were hard on his heels in his enthusiasm for *Crome Yellow*.

Mother read Cabell, Dreiser, and Lewis. I can only assume that somewhere along the line Father must have read *Main Street* and *Babbitt;* otherwise he serenely sat out the oncoming wave of new American writing of fiction, busy with his own researches into America's past.

Mother wrote to me in the early twenties, "Quincy is going to New York for over the holiday . . . to combine pleasure and business . . . and to blow in $15.00 he has just earned by writing a few 'wise cracks' about Boston for a new magazine called *The New Yorker*. It is supposed to be the last word in sophistication and modernity, and proudly announces, 'This is not a magazine for the Old Lady in Duluth!' (*sic*)." Quincy himself remembers feeling that "in the late twenties Boston just wasn't part of the universe any more." When, like so many of his contemporaries, his first stop was the advertising business in New York, both his parents viewed his move philosophically. It caused his conservative Boston mother-in-law-elect to ask her daughter when she announced her engagement, "Isn't Quincy Howe something of an *adventurer?*"

The mother-son relationship between Mother and Mark was characteristic of both. "Father and I plan to go up to Andover, and entertain our reluctant son at luncheon, and then to mortify him still further by attending the track meet between Andover and Exeter!" She wrote of him as a Harvard undergraduate, "Never do we more want you at home than during Mark's holidays! He sits by the fire, reading Dostoievsky, *never* going out or speaking, and only occasionally looking up to utter some cynical or bloodthirsty wise-crack!" She clear-sightedly recognized a kindred nature, pitched from birth in a minor key, when she said, "I get both angry and disgusted with him sometimes, just because I understand so perfectly how he feels!" And yet, threaten this problem child with pain or danger, and he evokes the pet name which Mother occasionally called him, and his aunts always: "For the discipline of my character, I am now facing an operation for my poor Marcus tomorrow."

As for Mother's relation with her only daughter—it must, in

many ways, have duplicated that of her own relation with *her* mother. We were intensely—I am afraid that perhaps morbidly is the more accurate word—close. An involvement was pretty intricate with a mother who could write, "My dearest little Helen, how *dreadfully* sorry I am to think that you felt so badly because I felt so badly that you felt badly!" or "I almost wept with sympathy at the thought of your suffering [over a burn]—and to think that you were glad I was not with you because I would have scolded you,—and because it probably would have been true!" I am ashamed to record that when I went to boarding school at Milton Academy (by prearrangement not even saying good-by to Mother when she left me at the school, as I didn't want to cry in front of all those strange girls) I actually retired to bed for two days, a victim of that most "all-overish" complaint in the world—home-sickness. And this, ignominiously, only twelve miles from Boston!

One incident occurred during my school years which pointed up a lesson I should have done well to heed. A friend a little older than I, on whom I had a fourteen-year-old "crush," asked me to go to a matinee with six girls one Saturday afternoon, when we were both spending the weekend in Boston with our parents. I accepted the invitation at once, from such a dazzling source. Then I began to go into a New England tailspin: "I am only home for two days. Someday Mother will be dead, and I shall remember that I went off with friends of my own when I might have been with her." I made some feeble excuse, and got out of the girls' lunch and theater party, and went, instead, trailing off after Mother to call on a friend of hers in Brookline. That summer the girl whom I so idolized died at sixteen of spinal meningitis, and my remorse about the lost afternoon turned around to bite me where I least expected it.

During the years when I should have been working off teen-age growing pains with boys and girls of my own age I spent most of my time, when I wasn't at school, attached to Mother. "Revenge" is too strong a word for the satisfying sense of compensation I felt when years later I made pay off in one of my monologues—my own favorite piece of work—the time I had spent in the society of some of Mother's Boston contemporaries. It was a ten-minute portrait—christened for me by John Marquand, *Off at Back Bay*—of an affable Boston matron returning on a train from New York where she had been on a "spree" with a friend. I like to believe that I managed to recreate a composite picture of the female of that particular Boston species, now all but extinct, with a touch of something more than mere photographic reporting. I was even freed from any sense of guilt when I was told that, after seeing the sketch in one of my recitals in Boston, three of Mother's friends rode home together in a taxi. One of them exploded, "I think it's cruel of Helen to have done anything so recognizable!" "I quite agree!" and "How could she!" echoed her indignation. The happy ending to the story was that each of the ladies discovered after further conversation that she recognized someone different, and, needless to say, not one of them had recognized herself.

Probably in turning to monologues—after a false start at schoolteaching—I was only sharpening up for professional use the weapon with which we were all equipped early by Mother—a defensive-offensive satirical sense. Quincy says today on the subject of the very quality of humor which he himself inherited: "H. G. Wells warned against humor as a kind of escape, a way of avoiding certain unpleasant realities. Mamma had so much humor that perhaps we attach more importance, through her example, than she did to it. Papa never let humor get in his way, blind him, mislead him, or fascinate him, and I think Mamma sometimes did. . . . I remember Mamma saying, sometime in the twenties, that she felt her critical view of people perhaps had soured us, and she regretted it. As I look back, I think her humorous view had more serious and tragic undertones than we suspected as children. Papa supplied the corrective to this."

Speaking for myself I know that the weapon of satirical attack was put into my hands too early, and that I used it not from any impregnable citadel of a sense of superiority but rather as a shield behind which I could hide an ingrained sense of inferiority. If I had dared to let a growing natural woman achieve maturity I might not have distressed my parents by expressing the desire to go to New York to study for the stage. The instinct was strong within me to harness an aptitude for mimicry to a certain gift of identification with other people. Perhaps not feeling capable of being one whole woman in myself I chose the way of pretending to myself to be a dozen other women, and thus was eventually to enter through the back door the world whose front door had always frightened me.

Father, after attending a play in which I appeared at Milton Academy had been put to it to explain a "capacity for acting," and came up with the thought that "the stage and the ministry are supposed to have something in common, and perhaps your episcopal grandfather had something to do with it. . . . I can foresee much pleasure for you in theatricals, and hope I may always be there to applaud." "Theatricals" were one thing, just as was his quondam friendship for Clyde Fitch—but his one daughter actually flinging herself into the twentieth-century competitive Broadway arena was quite another. Mother—inevitably!—was sure (a) that I was not strong enough and (b) that I would fail. My parents had given me a year in Paris (on leave from schoolteaching in Boston) which I immediately turned into an opportunity to study under a French actor at the Vieux Colombier. Mother wrote to me:

When a young person shows a creative gift, as a painter, a musician, or a sculptor, I think one takes a grave responsibility in thwarting a talent that may lead to a useful and happy life. I think that in *writing* and in *acting,* the matter is much more subtle and open to question. *Everyone* writes (that is, uses words as a medium of expression) and *everyone* acts (that is, expresses feeling or emotion in action). Writing or acting have to be of the first order to justify making a career of either, particularly acting. . . . You have not the physical strength, nor the temperament, nor the kind of character to get satisfaction out of such a career,—nor have you the *presence* to make a professional actress. Of course, as you know there is a perfect *mania* now for "self-expression" and I can quite see the fun of going to one of the best schools of acting in the world, and having pleasant things said to you by a very good actor, and being urged to throw over the life of "Service" for the life of "art." . . . You are having a taste of life, and it is like wine, after the watery diet of Boston.

When, from a safe distance of three thousand miles, I wrote of my firm resolve to throw up my job as a teacher in Boston and go to New York to study for the theater I can imagine the talks in Brimmer Street. The refrain of Mother's next letter is one which must be repeated in each generation by parent to child—when that child has asserted his declaration of independence. I look back in middle age with a stab of remorse at how blandly I accepted what could not have been easy to offer—at any level. "Father and I will do all we can,—and pay what we are able—to give you just the kind of winter you want."

This is the last letter of Mother's that I have. There were many many more in the years that followed. When I left home we wrote each other almost every day. Before I had actually expressed my wish to go on the stage Mother had once written, "I should love to have you able to be a tip top 'diseuse' "—hastily hedging, in an instinctive gesture to ward off hurt or humiliation for her young, the deadliest words then—or now—I could contemplate—"but not professional." When a profession did open up for me, not only did she become reconciled for my sake but took an active interest to the extent of collaborating behind the scenes. Years after her death it gave me a glow of happiness to hear audiences in such unlikely places as the Blue Angel nightclub or an Army camp give forth with a belly laugh at a line of Mother's!

When I went to New York to study for the theater Father was no more pleased than Mother. He wrote to Cousin Alice: "[Helen] asked our approval of her course, and, though we cannot pretend that it represents our preference for her, it seemed unwise to withhold assent to her making the experiment on which her heart is set.

What will come of it all, nobody can foretell. For better or worse, she is in for the trial she has elected to make, and we are standing by her."

Actually the psychologically prescribed revolt against one's father was hard to put into practice for us, even as small children. Father was so everlastingly hopeful about and pleased with us, and so inclined to forgive, that to storm at him ended up in the foolish posture of flailing the air. He knew, all the same, how to elicit the most writhing penitence. There was a day at Cotuit when Mark and I—I suppose about eight and ten years old—got into a violent brother-and-sister scrap sailing in the *Flounder*, off our pier where Father was standing. Shrieks of "No, I didn't!" "You did *too-oo!*" echoed across the gentle Cape waters—I, obviously, the offender. Father called us ashore and ordered me out of the boat. I was in such a fine frenzy of tears, frustrated will to power, and blind rebellion at the sentence which so clearly gave Mark the victory that I couldn't find any other way to express my general fury than by jumping overboard in all my clothes. My punishment consisted, as I fled to the house and banged the door behind me in my own room, first in the physical misery of choking on salt water and tears, both of which seemed to have found their way into my ears, and next when I was put to bed and the room darkened, Father's gentle sadness, with no word of rebuke or condemnation. To have made an utter fool of myself, to be suffering real physical distress, and on top of it not to have anybody to storm back at—I haven't often suffered more complete misery.

Al Capp is quoted as saying, "Don't be a pal to your son. Be his father," and continues his exhortation, "What child needs a forty-year-old man for a friend? And forget about teaching him the facts of life. There is nothing that a boy could discuss with his father that he couldn't discuss much more openly with his gutter-snipe friends." I recently asked Quincy if Father ever attempted a Facts of Life talk. Quincy said that he did not but—in his opinion even more remarkable for a Boston father!—he never spoke about final clubs at Harvard or suggested that the problem might ever arise. "What mattered to him much more," Quincy remembers,

Four Josiah Quincys (1772–1919)
Three mayors of Boston
Two hosts of Lafayette
One Harvard president
In three centuries of a family tree

The young Frances G. Curtis

"By gravy! we met in the finals": the Curtis champions
(Miss Margaret and Miss Harriot Curtis)

THE MIGHTY MAIDENS

Alice Bache Gould

Mary Cabot Wheelwright

Photo by Pirie MacDonald

John Jay Chapman

Gamaliel Bradford

Bliss Perry at seventy

Van Wyck Brooks

John P. Marquand at forty-three

"C.C.B." at seventy-eight

Henry Dwight Sedgwick
at over ninety

Ellery Sedgwick in his middle years

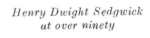

Three brothers in 1951
(Cal, Art, Wal, ages totaling one
hundred and eighty-two years)

"Mother and Father as Mother and
Father"—Cotuit, about 1911

Paterfamilias: on his ninetieth birthday,
Mt. Desert, Maine, 1954 (Mark at left,
Quincy on right)

Father en pantoufles *at 16 Louisburg Square*

His ways were ways of pleasantness, and all his paths were peace:
numbers 20 and 22 Louisburg Square

"and what he used to talk and read about when I had gone to bed, and was most impressionable, was religion, and I am sure he meant that to leave, as it did, much the deepest impression." For me, too, there are none of the old-fashioned memories of learning my prayers at my mother's knee. Prayers at bedtime were Father's bailiwick. Indeed I have one memory of kneeling at his knee, while he sat on the edge of my bed, and I opened my mouth mechanically to rattle off "Our Father Who art in heaven . . ." I heard myself, instead, inadvertently rattling off my one other parrot-like piece of memorizing: "One, two, three, four, five . . ." I was both so horrified and so impelled to laugh over my own blasphemous slip that, unable to choke down my conflicting emotions, I promptly threw up. I find it hard to explain to my own satisfaction the reaction which points to a hidden fear. Perhaps it was actually my Father in Heaven before whom I quailed, my memories of my earthly father are so consistently free of any harshness.

There was at least one attempt on Father's part to be a pal to Quincy, when Father and college son set out to sail our new catboat, the *Venture*, from Newport to Cotuit. Mother wrote:

> I wish you could see the departure which Quincy found very mortifying! In spite of intense heat and cloudy skies, Father was staggering under two double blankets, two raincoats, an enormous naval chart, a fog horn, a compass, a large lantern (which he will discover to his horror at moonrise that Lizzie forgot to fill!), also enough food and water to last two hungry men for four meals, a large traveling bag with full equipment for an immaculate toilet, and many other of the impedimenta of a recently-arrived emigrant. Quincy, sans toothbrush, razor, pajamas, or coat, carried a large new motor tire on one arm, like a gigantic bracelet,—or (what it really looked like on his nautical experience)—a rubber life-preserver! . . . I only trust that there will not be mutiny on the part of Quincy if he finds poor Father guilty of shaving or brushing his teeth.

When it came to politics it was hard for either of his sons to react violently against a father so consistently a "liberal." Though Quincy and Father agreed that Sacco and Vanzetti had not had a fair trial, Quincy was a good deal more violent in his belief in the men's innocence than was Father. There is one scene, involving father and son, which I wish a Peter Arno might have recorded. Father and Mr. Thomas W. Lamont, partner of the firm of J. P. Morgan, both top-hatted, marching side by side through the Harvard Yard in a two-by-two procession of the Harvard Overseers at the August Tercentenary Exercises. If ever two men looked respectable and conformist, surely these two must have on that day. If a *New Yorker* cartoon, however, had drawn balloons above their top hats of what they were actually saying to each other, it was *not*, "We believe that Electric Bond and Share is going to go higher still." Father himself recounted afterward with amusement that they actually were vying with each other in expressing pride in the liberal (or radical) views of their sons Corliss and Quincy, each father stoutly affirming, "The boy's *all right*, underneath."

When it came to so much faith, hope, and love I am afraid that sometimes when we should have been touched and grateful we were irritated. It was impossible to shake Father's belief in his progeny. Every year of professional effort on my part was to be my *annus mirabilis*, every recital sure to be a triumph. When I forced upon him the unpleasant truth that there were plenty of failures and disappointments along the way the pill somehow wouldn't go down. There was an occasion when some prescient instinct told me that I was in for trouble at a certain gathering of the National Book Award festivities in New York, and I wrote Father to that effect. He answered, "I realize how formidable it must appear to you. Yet your own record of meeting challenges with triumph must be buoying you up, and my confidence in your coming out on top is unshaken." When the painful contrary proved to be the case—an occasion which I am sure lost nothing in the recounting by my clear-sighted brother, who witnessed it, Father wrote: "Quincy's hard-boiled comment was a little sobering, but older brothers are not noted (perhaps so much as fathers!) for indulgent eyes."

I think all three of us would agree that in our youth the *yin* qualities of Mother held the greater attraction for us, but in later life we came increasingly to appreciate the heartening staying power of Father's *yang* attitude toward the Universe—even if we were sometimes embarrassed when it included us! At the time of Father's death an editor friend wrote to Quincy, "You and Helen and your brother must have been awfully proud of him. But he was awfully proud of you, too. The day he came to Simon and Schuster you left him in my office for five minutes and he told me so." As Mother would have said, "Characteristic!"

Perhaps a posthumous comment from Quincy on his father indicates where much of his own bounce came from.

> What Papa did for all of us—what he contributed was not so much fresh blood, or a more extroverted point of view. It was the kind of drive that old Bishop Howe has handed on to his numerous seed. . . . I noted that the British essayist, F. L. Lucas, whose lectures I attended and followed with admiration when at Cambridge, is quoted as saying that he considered energy the most enviable of characteristics. In a way it is like courage—the virtue that, as Churchill puts it, "underwrites" all the other virtues. *Mut verloren; alles verloren*— Courage lost, everything lost. Papa certainly had both energy and courage.

It is perhaps not fair to hold up Father's positive observations on his children's activities alongside of Mother's more negative ones. He lived many, many years longer than she, to see us, for better or worse, established in our various callings. He used to say, "When I was young and you children were growing up I used to hope that someday my name might be of some help in getting you started." And so, indeed, he was abundantly able to do. As Father's son, Quincy certainly had no problem about an introduction at 8 Arlington Street, where he started working for the *Living Age* and then the *Atlantic*. It was Father's friend Winthrop Ames who opened the door of the Theatre Guild School of Acting for me, and his friend Lewis Perry was able to introduce Mark to Jesse Lasky of Paramount Pictures, whose son was at Exeter, and who launched him as a second assistant director. Mark worked on pictures at the Paramount Studio, Astoria, Long Island, with the team of Clayton,

Jackson, and Durante, as well as with the late great comedian
Fred Allen. If we all started out on the longest way round—
Quincy to advertising in New York, Mark to the motion-picture
business, and I to New York nightclubs, Father lived to see
that it had been, after all, the shortest way home. Quincy has
come full circle and is now editing the magazine *Atlas* which
is a latter-day version of the *Living Age*. Mark, ironically, least
like Father in temperament (he actually *resigned* from the Tavern
Club!) is most nearly living his life in the same groove. He is not
only a member of the Saturday Club but has made a name—so
nearly Father's—as editor and biographer. (Father used to enjoy
thinking of the confusion of the librarians of the future who would
have to catalogue two biographies of two Oliver Wendell Holmeses,
one by Mark A. DeWolfe Howe and one by Mark DeWolfe Howe.)
And I, having worked the acting "bug" that Mother so feared
out of my system, find myself happier and happier with a pencil
in my hand and the same sheets of yellow paper on my knee that
I have seen Father fill with his penciled handwriting ever since I
can remember. So, for all of us, it has been rebellion—and return.
In the beginning was the Word—and for each of Mother and
Father's children it looks as though it would be in their later
chapters as well. Even in our ways of speaking that Word we can
feel the thrust and withdrawal of the *yang* and *yin* blood within us.
In our instinct for immediate communication—in television, lectur-
ing, teaching, and monologuing—we feel Father, in spite of the
irony that he himself could not express the *spoken* word. He used
often to exclaim over the "fluency" of his young, contrasted with
his own hesitancy in speech. In our withdrawals, with pencil and
paper, doubtless we feel Mother's pull, as we retreat inward, away
from active contact with the world. Perhaps there is a sense in
which we are living out part of the life which she never lived for
herself. Surely her intensity of anxiety on our behalf syphoned
off psychic energies which should have gone into a creative life
of her own. Perhaps the repression of so much of her talent may
have taken a toll in the unconscious of her progeny who, to this
day, carry its burden. For all of Father's interest and pride in us

he was fully engaged in his own life. A friend remembers going to call on him, in his late eighties, at Louisburg Square. With a benign fatherly beam he said, "This has been quite a remarkable year in our family. Each of my children has published a book." He waited only an instant before adding, with what was described as a "gleam in his eye," "*I* have published *three!*"

Although each of us, in due course, insisted on the inevitable journey from home that all children must take, no door was slammed behind our retreating backs. We were sure of being followed by shafts of light and love; the door was always left ajar to receive us home again. Come to think of it, perhaps I have overemphasized the difference of my parents' temperaments at the expense of ignoring the solidity of the front they presented as parents. Neither one was any more anxious than the other to discuss—or even to recognize the existence of—sex, as it might concern us. There we had to find our own way. "Character," "tastes in common," a "sense of values"— these were the qualities I, at least, was told to seek in any man; these were the qualities I was told to cultivate in myself. Father taught me my prayers, Father took me to church, but it was Mother who wrote me, "As you get older you will *know* that your own contentment in life comes from what you put into it, and *not* from what you get out. As you know I am not a religious woman, but I do believe that the life of your *spirit* is what counts, and that life is just a theatre for it to try itself out in—and I am sure you will act your part so well that the angels will applaud when the curtain goes down! Your devoted, bad, warning of a Mother." But preaching is not what we got from either of them. It was practice— in their dealings with us, with each other, and with everyone with whom they came in contact. A favorite word with them both was "authentic." It was one that applied to them both: they never pretended to be anything they were not. They never treated one human being differently from any other and they never made a move or said a word for the effect it might make in anyone else's eyes. In Father we had the continual example of unremitting hard work, and in both of them the pattern of self-disciplined lives, mak- ing for a household that ran smoothly, in which order, good manners, and punctuality were taken for granted, along with the sustaining love that held them and us together.

One thing more. Father used to say, "I consider one of the best things that has come out of my marriage to your mother is the relation of you children to each other." Speaking for myself, I can say that it is very easy for me to observe the third commandment. In honoring my Father and Mother I can pay them the further homage as parents by honoring, as well as loving, their two sons, in each of whom there is so much of both parents. Mother and Father belonged to "the blessed company of all faithful people." That quality of faithfulness, shining among so many others, lives on, in my eyes, in their two sons. "Their seed standeth fast and their children for their sakes."

16

A GENERAL CALAMITY

DURING THE FIRST TWENTY-EIGHT YEARS of my life I do not remember either one of my parents spending a day in bed. I realize now that they both must have been unusually hardy people. Then suddenly, in February, 1933, Father was rushed with half an hour's notice to Phillips House of the Massachusetts General Hospital for an emergency appendix operation. There followed a series of complications, with a crescendo of anxiety, involving two further operations and some thirteen weeks in the hospital. With such a dislocation in our family life, the perspective on the whole changed overnight: Father, the serene, the steady, the sunny, was ill. He was, indeed, terrifyingly ill—bottles and tubes dangling down from him, and from above into him. After his second operation there was a huge cylindrical structure which he named "Little America" placed over his middle, under which strong lights were kept, trying to force healing which would not occur of itself. We tiptoed in and out of the room. Everyone in the hospital seemed to become involved in the wavering chances for his recovery. There was the night when his nurse took home her cap, assuming the case was over.

You would be pleased if you heard how many people there are who are really fond of you and are looking forward to seeing you about again. I knew that you were a good fellow and that I liked you myself, but I had no idea how generally the fact was appreciated, and neither, I believe, do you. Everywhere I go from the Tavern Club to the Athenaeum, and even in the purlieus of State Street, I find people asking me how you are. . . . I do not telephone because I think your family must by this time hate anyone who does.

So wrote Arthur Hill, speaking for the Boston band of brothers who inundated Father's hospital room with evidences of their affection and concern for him. Not telephone? Mr. Hill was the only one who didn't; instead he appeared at the front door of 26 Brimmer Street every evening, for weeks on end, to ask Mark or me or Lizzie—without disturbing Mother—what was the bulletin of the day. Father's dear friend Allston Burr did the same (living in Brookline, Brimmer Street was way off his beat).

Bliss Perry wrote:

> Dear Mark: This is a St. Patrick's Day greeting! But I shall quote from a Scotchman, James Boswell: "A good companion, and a good Christian; which I think is saying enough. Yet it is but justice to record, that once, when he was in a dangerous illness, he was watched with the anxious apprehension of a general calamity; day and night his house was beset with affectionate enquiries; and upon his recovery, *Te deum* was the universal chorus from the *hearts* of his countrymen."

His new friend Van Wyck Brooks wrote from Florida to Mother:

> Dear Mrs. Howe, I was dreadfully shocked and sorry to hear that Mr. Howe has been so ill, and you can't guess how much I hope that things are going well with him. Can he imagine, possibly, how people feel about him who know him as slightly as I do and there must be so many hundreds of them—for never, never have I known a human being the mere thought of whom makes one happier. Do forgive me if this seems impulsive, but I have heard so many others say the same thing— that knowing Mr. Howe was one of the real privileges of living.

To Father he wrote:

> When the book came, my first thought was The crisis must have passed and you must be getting well again! And how much I hope so, and have been hoping and thinking ever since the word came that you were ill. You can't guess how much

your health and happiness mean to *one* of all the hundreds and hundreds of people who owe so much to you in so many ways.

Father's own steadiness of temperament made him not only fight for his own recovery but made him also able to face the alternative with equanimity. He said afterward that he felt Death had left his calling card, and he would feel, on any return visit, that he was greeting a friend. In fact the word "friend" was the pivotal one in Father's illness. He himself was certain that he would not have recovered had he not been buoyed up, literally drawn back to life, by the love and concern of so many of them. In illness his religion worked for him. The man who had never been interested in an abstract Oversoul but who had centered his belief in a Person now found healing coming to him in human shape. "I love doctors," he would whisper through parched lips, as one of them performed some service for him. One friend, standing by his bedside for two or three minutes, was a draught of life.

Confused through medication, yet somehow uncannily aware of the atmosphere of general calamity in the world around him— remember, the time was March, 1933—he was still sustained by a thrust toward life and hope for the world as well as for himself. Later he was to write an article, "Delusion and Reality," which was published in the *Atlantic:*

> . . . I seemed to see myself borne at a terrific speed, as if in a racing motor car or an airplane skimming the ground, along a straight avenue at the end of which rose an immense wall of solid masonry, with a bull's eye of white stone at its center. That was the spot I knew myself destined to hit. . . . There was, however, a feeling that after my smash-up I might be able to drag myself round the ends of the wall and find a peaceful stretch of grass and trees—"bright fields beyond the swelling flood"—where I might lie down and recover my strength. . . . Nor was this quite all of my vision. In the rush to inevitable disaster the impending fate of the Hoover Administration, with which my sympathy had always been limited, seemed curiously joined with my own. We were going to smash together.

Still far from being out of danger, Father's inextinguishable spirit of hope prompted him to wire Franklin Roosevelt on his election: "Even in the backwater of a hospital where I have lately undergone two operations am acutely conscious of a new spirit in America. I believe this to be your own spirit. The true democrat of the old order who has always known the new order to be a vital part of it seems coming into his own. God bless you and your Administration to the good of the whole world."

The ironic twist to the power of those loving arms of friends, which Father felt pulling him back to life, was that at the same time, in an octopus-like embrace, they were draining Mother's vitality. It was nobody's fault, except that of her own intense and self-flagellating nature, that she neither could nor would share the burdens of Father's illness with anyone. Morning and afternoon she went to and from the hospital, past 82 Charles Street where the memories of the girl she had once been must have served only to deepen the shadows of the valley through which she walked, symbolized for her by the dank, dark underpass that in those days dipped down under the roaring Charles Street traffic. "I feel as though I were never going to come to the end of this tunnel," she would say. She was in Father's hospital room all day long, taking home at night with her a sheaf of letters to answer, cards of the donors of flowers to be thanked, all to be done between countless telephone calls. With Quincy in New York, Mark and I were the only potential buffers who might have spared her. (Poor Mark! Only those closest to him know what obstacles he had to surmount during that last year of his at the Harvard Law School.) We did what we could, but more often than not we would get, "No, no. I want to speak to him myself." "No, no. I shall write the letter. I prefer to." It was impossible to offer her any alleviations without being turned down. In looking back on her self-control during that time, and her unwavering cheerfulness with Father and with those who inquired after him, her performance through such a long ordeal seems the more remarkable, as it always must in the case of those who carry on through sheer grit and determination, denied the buoyancy and comfort of a temperament to whom hope and faith come naturally. All that Father was suffering, all that she dreaded in the way of impending loss, only confirmed her in her general distrust of life. This is the way it *was,* under all the trappings. I remember her quoting to me one evening—it was the same evening his nurse forebodingly took home her cap—a poem (and how I wish I could remember what it was!) which expressed the thought that we have no right to wish anyone we love not to die, when we cannot guess what terrible fate may be in store for him, if our wish were to be granted. When she asked Mark and me coolly for an address of a distant friend of Father's we knew she was making up in her own mind a list of pallbearers. She stood up to her anxiety and grief with flintlike reserve, saying, "When you ever wonder how you're going to get through anything difficult, remember that you just have to *take it,* that's all." It was touching that under the pressure of her anxiety she allowed herself expression of a tenderness toward Father which, up to then, she had temperamentally been unable to show. (Remorse for lack of demonstrativeness in the past?) Mark and I were not the only ones who saw at what cost to herself she kept up the front. As he saw how pale and drawn she was beginning to look, Father's doctor suggested that she indulge herself in some good nights' sleep. Miraculously, considering a temperament that felt an easing of one's own misery was somehow cheating, she agreed to follow his prescription of Alanol sleeping pills.

Presently—unheard of for Mother, who was never sick—she came down with a sore throat. It became, in short order, very sore. Tonsillitis, diagnosed the doctor. And ordered her to bed. And to stay away from the hospital. On a black Friday, her own birthday, April 14—an occasion for which I had been unable to fulfill Father's commission of finding fresh Mayflowers—Father underwent his third major operation. Mother, tossing and feverish, turned with a groan of grief away from the little birthday note he had written for me to give her. The next morning she was obviously so much worse that I called the doctor—though I had told myself that tonsillitis wasn't *serious*. That afternoon, after Dr. Breed had come, and gone, and returned, he tried to explain to Mark and me that a blood count showed a very serious condition—a breaking down of the white blood corpuscles. The name of the disease—unknown, of course, to us—was agranulocytic angina. (Parenthetically, Dr. Breed afterward learned that horrifying findings showed that this disease had resulted among others who had taken Alanol. I do not know if the drug is still on the market, although I do know that today penicillin would cure the disease.) Frozen into incredulity, I climbed into the ambulance that was to take Mother to the Phillips House. For that day and the next two, Father, slowly emerging from anesthesia and surgery, did not realize that Mother was only two floors above him in the same hospital. We merely told him she was still miserable with tonsillitis. On Monday night, within the hour of the arrival of Quincy from New York and Uncle Wallis driving through the rain from Bristol, Mother died.

Understandably, I think, our first wish was that Father would follow her. Who would tell him? How could he face the prospect of recovery without her? It was wonderful Dr. William Breed who, without being asked, took on his brave shoulders the task of telling Father. Father afterward was to repeat the word "tender" for the way in which this warm friend and devoted doctor performed his task. One by one we tiptoed into the sickroom to find the figure in the bed, fragile and shaken, disguised by a white beard into an all but Learlike appearance to play the role in which he was cast. But Father was nothing, nothing of a Lear! There was no ranting, raving, or imprecations against Fate. Copeland, writing to Mother so long ago about the way Father was bearing her refusal to marry him, had said, "Mark is absolutely what a man should be under the conditions." The same verdict might have held again. Under the weight of the blow that had been dealt him, he bowed his head in a gentle, chastened acceptance. Fénelon must have known men who possessed such a quality as Father's when he wrote of *willingness:* "There is nothing striking, nothing powerful, nothing very obvious even to others, still less to themselves. If you say to such a person that he has endured bravely, he will not understand you.

He does not know how it has all been; he does not dissect his feelings. If he did there would be no more simplicity. This is what you mean by *willingness,* which makes less show but is really more solid than what is called courage."

Our two staunch uncles, Uncle Wallis and Uncle Arthur, whose presence in Boston was as good as a blood transfusion for Father, sat with us in the First Unitarian Church, to hear Dr. Charles Park read the beautiful words:

> Who can find a virtuous woman? for her price is above rubies. The heart of her husband doth safely trust in her. . . . She will do him good and not evil all the days of her life. . . . Strength and honour are her clothing . . . Her children arise up, and call her blessed; her husband also, and he praiseth her. . . . Give her of the fruit of her hands; and let her own works praise her in the gates.

If Father's friends had given him a sense of support before, it was nothing to what they did now. There was an initial moment of hush when, understandably, they were reluctant to approach him. Then, as soon as it became apparent that he wanted them, needed them, he was surrounded, enveloped. He described President Lowell, who came to see him, saying nothing of what he had been through until he stopped at the threshold on his way out of the room, then turning back, pointing his finger and saying, "You know what Macaulay said, don't you? 'Now, there is nothing worse that can happen to you.'" Some expressed their concern by offers of financial help, knowing the bills that such a long stay in a hospital must entail, and wishing him to be free from at least financial worry. Mr. Ellery Sedgwick, his most warm and generous self, was prompt with the offer of a loan, as was Copeland. Mr. Allston Burr quietly went about organizing a fund made up of donations from many friends. Letters poured in on every side. It was for Mr. Updike to express in the letter to the *Transcript* something of Mother's essence

> . . . gallant, shy, modest, warm-hearted, truth-loving . . . her genuine talent as a writer—too little and too furtively

exercised—gave real delight. But with her charming gaiety and whimsical humor, one felt that deep in her spirit there was "a place remote and islanded." . . . As the years passed she grew in grace and graces, and these were written in the beauty of her thoughtful face. . . . When the end came, as a friend said of her, "she went down with all flags flying." . . . In the splendid passage from the Book of Proverbs . . . not a word seemed irrelevant or unreal. She would have denied their application; but we, her friends, know that they were only a truthful description of a full, happy, and completed life. And for us who remain, something more is completed—a finished self-portrait, in colours that years cannot dim.

It is a mystery to Father's children why they have been unable to locate the mound of letters that came to him at the time of Mother's death. It does not seem like him to have destroyed them, but perhaps in this one instance he did something out of character. Only a few odd straggling ones have turned up among other papers. These, in addition to words addressed to me, which I have kept, give a little of the flavor of the sort of feeling she inspired. Christina Marquand summed her and us up: "Hearing first about mere tonsillitis and then nothing but this—with no intermediate stages makes it a little characteristic of your mother—just quietly and definitely dying before anyone could have any attention called to it. Words don't come easily about her, but since I've known her she's meant more to me than any other older woman except my own mother. I know . . . how terrible it must be for you and Mark, and of course your father. She was like the underground spring that fed you all."

Father's friend "Billy" (William Jr.) James said, "I think of Fanny as one of the few superlative people I have known whose qualities of character, and talent and humor seemed to me to have no limits at all." Nancy Byrd Turner could look back to her own earliest days in Boston:

For I was a stranger and she took me in. . . . Always there was the love that without what is usually called demonstration showed itself in action; always the wise understanding, always compassion. Hers was the most compassionate heart I ever knew.

Always I shall remember one ghastly winter afternoon when, returning to my lodgings after a grievous trip home, where my mother's condition had completely unnerved me,—how I opened the door of my small room and was suddenly overwhelmed by utter despair and desolation. Then turned and fled—almost running—to Brimmer Street, and there was met by understanding that seemed to kindle a flame of comfort in me. No trite arguing, not even any "words of comfort"—(which would have made things worse)—but complete, quiet *knowing*, and a bidding to go get my things and move into 26 for a few days, which I so thankfully did. And then, when she saw the worst was over, so wisely she said, "Now you should go back and face it." So I did. And the cure was complete.

Poor Cousin Alice, smitten by heaven knows what intensity of remorse for all the wasted years, made herself heard from Spain, writing to Father:

> I hope I have got myself more in hand, and can write to you. On the main thing nothing is to be said, and I could not trust myself to say it besides. . . . If I could have half an hour of intimate talk with you, it would be cheaply purchased by crossing the ocean for it. But I cannot have it. I know perfectly well that I should not get it if I crossed. I do not think I shall ever be able to talk freely. In these weeks now months I do not think I have had a waking hour without thought of Fanny.

All she could do was pour out touchingly and hugely generous offers of financial help:

> There has always been a clause in my will leaving to Fanny more than I think even these operations will have cost. You may remember—or may not—that when I came so near to dying in 1907, one of the things that made it harder for me to fix my weak forces on recovery was the knowledge that it would have been so much easier for Fanny if I had made a thorough job of it, and left her to inherit that money. I don't want to go through all that again. If I had died six months

ago you would have had this legacy to see you through the dislocation, and if it makes it any easier for you to take it, you
might reflect that it will avoid that situation again. . . .
Dear Mark, don't be obstinate and make life more difficult
than it is. Isn't it bad enough at best?

(Parenthetically, Father *was* obstinate.)

The "callers" spoke with one voice. Copeland, writing several
months later, was to say: "In those long three months of your illness, I thought a great deal more about you and Fanny than I
thought of my own affairs and when I heard of her terribly sudden
death when I had only a little while before learned that she was
ill, I gave way to sobs and tears. I wish that there were anything
I could do to honor that high, beautiful memory." Robbie Chase
to me: "I send you all my love and am yours in all the brave and
bright memories of your mother; but O how sad my heart is." John
McClennan: "[hers was] a value which pertained to the highest
and most complicated qualities of personality and yet was so simple
that no one could mistake what fineness was in that part of her
which she let be seen by those who knew her."

Aunt Mabel's heartbreak is too poignant to record. "Stricken"
she called herself, alone in the Argentine on business, when she
heard the news I had to break.

Aunt Helen, who had learned to live in and through and beyond
the sorrow her own life had brought, helped more than anyone:

> Your mother will stand out more and more as the years pass,
> just as my mother did. Her sensibility, her courage, her gen-
> erosity, her stoicism, mingled with her wit and charm made
> her a rare person that cannot be described to anyone who did
> not know her well . . . a sense of stability has gone from our
> world. . . . This blessed quality was given by a certain rigi-
> dity—and yet it was not just that else her understanding, im-
> agination, and sympathies would have been less profound and
> keen and outgoing. . . . Life will go on because it must and
> we shall accept it for the same reason as best we can and never
> know by what accident when the storm broke and the floods
> descended we were not swept out to sea. Yes, you will be dimly

conscious of some pattern in life but no one can help you make
it out or shape it to a certain beauty however austere. . . .
Your sense of enjoyment in nature and in many other things
will be shot with pain but the enjoyment must and will be
there whatever the ground bass or stringed obbligato.

It was, however, for Father to say the last words. He did so, later,
in verses he called "Afterwards":

> If you are nowhere you, or even a wraith,
> A shade unbodied, all your essence fled,
> Oh, vanished dear one of so little faith,
> And yet, all purged of self, of works so large
> What matter now the doubtings and the dread
> That shadowed many a day and night
> With fear of what might wait the dead!
> Foreboding wrought no lenient discharge
> Of fate, nor brought it on your gallant head.
> Too honest to accept forthright
> What none past peradventure could declare,
> Too honest to deny that still there might
> Be sweet continuance and renewals where
> The chosen ones of earth are gone—
> What have you found at last?
> Fain would I know who know but this:
> What was to be now is,
> Despite your vain perplexities,
> And, whether all be lost or won,
> The questionings are past,
> The answering begun.
>
> And this I know: that if there be a place,
> A lighted pleasance in the general dark,
> Where the elect are met—
> They who on earth escaped earth's branding mark,
> But in whose eye and face
> Glowed still the unseen spirit's grace,
> And they with heart and mind forever set
> On pitying thought and generous deed,
> Most tolerant of the foolish and perverse,

Constantly bettering the worse
Through sympathy and wit and wisdom freed
From every taint of a superior creed—
To such a company when you are come,
Dear vanished one, you must be welcomed home.
Your old humility
Will not avert the eyes that see,
For kindred souls will know their mate
Through self-disguises poor and thin,
And when you falter at the gate,
Will hail you, shy, reluctant, in,
One of their own immortal kith and kin.

IV

Old Age Is Like Another Country

17

A FATHER AND A DAUGHTER

THERE WERE STILL WEEKS MORE for Father in the hospital, but his forces were rallying—spiritual as well as physical. As I walked down the hospital corridor beside the wheelchair in which the nurse pushed the frail seventy-year-old man, the eyes of many of the nurses who had helped him through his ordeal were wet. They must have been shaking their heads behind us, and clicking their tongues as they imagined to themselves the darkening shadows into which the poor old gentleman was returning. What could life possibly hold for him—now? I myself felt exactly the same thing. Because, even by that time, I had not yet come to know Father!

Father never returned to Brimmer Street. Nor to Cotuit, to live. We knew none of us could face it again, so it was decided we would return, for the first summer without Mother, to the place that meant more to him than any other—Bristol. There Father lived contentedly in the center of a vast number of Howes and in the memories of his happy youth at Weetamoe. Mark and I, on the other hand, considered that we were living the life of suburban Providence, and pined for *our* happy (and isolated) childhood at Cotuit.

Before we left Boston for that first summer, we had emptied out the accumulation of twenty-eight years in Brimmer Street and set about combing the neighborhood for the right place to receive Father. Quincy was permanently settled in New York. We could all be grateful that Mother had lived to rejoice in his marriage the

[353]

previous spring to lovely Mary Post. Mark was slated to go to
Washington, to serve as Justice Holmes's secretary, so all we needed
was an apartment that would contain Father, me, and the bright
star in all our lives—Mary Lawrence. Mary, pretty, shy, and
freshly arrived from County Sligo, had come in her first position
as cook to Mother during the last months of her life. The day after
Mother's death she had gently asked me if I would like to order the
meals for the day; I waved her aside with a general "Meat and
vegetables, I guess. Oh, Mary, *you* decide." From that moment she
quietly, sweetly, and efficiently took over the running of the household, as its one irreplaceable factotum. How often had I seen
Father, when Mary brought him his cup of tea in the afternoon,
look up gratefully smiling, and say, "Mary, you must promise to
see me through!" The answer was always the same, spoken in her
gentle voice, with her own sweet smile, "You needn't worry, Mr.
Howe."

In our searches for an apartment Mark and I were led to the
spot that must have been foreordained from the beginning of
time for Father—the ground floor and basement of the charming
old Paine house at 16 Louisburg Square.

After Mother's death the Gentle Generation, with one voice,
cried in my ears, "You certainly cannot leave your dear father
now. *You* must take your mother's place." Behind the shutters
of houses up and down Beacon Hill and in the Back Bay were there
not daughters, all friends of Mother and Father, who had sweetly
sacrificed their own lives for the sake of one parent left alone? If
the merest trickle of doubt as to the wisdom of the course they had
pursued were allowed to seep into their consciousness they would
be engulfed by a desolating sense of irretrievable waste. And yet I
listened . . . It was Aunt Helen's luminous vision from across the
sea that put my particular path into fresh perspective:

> . . . if you do not deal with the many situations and complica-
> tions that must arise as your able devoted Mother would have
> done, you will judge well and follow your own star. There are
> so many ways of doing the wise thing, you must just find out

what seems to be best and not try to figure out what your wise
mother would have decided upon. . . . Your mother's delightful letters will be a very serious loss for always but you will
not be so foolish as to take on any of the jobs that you feel you
have left to you in trust by her. That must not be. She had
her life, its duties, compensations, happiness and sorrow, you
have yours and I beg that you will guide the plough to your
own furrow and not in hers. . . . Do not let the past enslave
you, especially things which live only for the passing generation who gave them blood and bones. The next generation will
not I think be able to admire the face of the finest clock when it
no longer ticks.

Today I doubt that my solution to the quandary was the right
one. It was—compromise. Inevitably, I had to leave for long trips
"on the road." Aside from such trips I spent part of each winter
in an apartment or a hotel in New York. But Louisburg Square
remained my headquarters.

Father, for his part, with the satisfaction known only to a round
peg as it settles into a preordained form-fitting hole, accepted in
1933 the position of Director of the Boston Athenaeum. He had
anyway spent most of his working hours in that beloved spot since
he had left the *Atlantic*, so it was like coming home, but now he had
a real little "office" of his own—a small, cheerful, sun-drenched,
glass-enclosed room once occupied by Barrett Wendell, off the
third floor gallery. He looked out across the Old Granary Burying
Ground to bustling Tremont Street beyond, confirming, he used to
say, his belief in Life Beyond the Grave. Over his desk hung an
oil painting entitled "The Independent Beggar," a title that
pleased him as expressing his sense of gratitude for the modest
stipend that went with his new position.

To this once-Bostonian the very smell of the Boston Athenaeum
evokes the city itself—at least as I knew it, reflected through Father.
Coming in from a hot sidewalk on a summer's day to the delicious
coolness of the lobby one asks oneself, Is its aroma redolent of clay?
or dust? marble? leather? or just an odor of antiquity, emanating

from the busts of the great and good of other days? "Here remains a retreat for those who would enjoy the humanity of books," I read on a plaque, and I know that I have come home. In winter there is quite another pleasure to be captured at the front desk, with the sun flooding in the tall French windows at its back, highlighting the vase of fresh flowers which stands there—as at other spots throughout the building. What sweeter form of immortality, Beacon Hill style, than that supplied by the daughter who bequeathed, in memory of her father, such flowers to be kept forever fresh in this world of books? Although the flowers still bloom, the ritual of the afternoon tea today, alas, is a thing of the past. But it was part of the past that Father enjoyed—the five-cent cup of tea, complete with three saltine crackers thrown in. There must be certain familiar Athenaeum ghosts from Father's time who haunt it still. Mr. Albert Matthews, with his high stiff collar, brown bowler hat, pince-nez with cord attached, and large brass ear trumpet, must be one, bending over the work that was to appear eventually in nineteen volumes of the *Publications* of the Colonial Society—a society to which, Father himself was elected in 1911. Then there was Miss Elise Johnson, who protested to Father during his tenure of office, over the infiltration of Radcliffe girls into the hallowed precincts. "Here they come to the Athenaeum," she said, "in their silk stockings, fur coats, and lipsticks, to *read books*—adding hypocrisy to their other vices!" The omnipresence in the Athenaeum of all the vintage Boston ladies is attested to by Father's story of a porkpie hat, blown loose from the head of one of these ladies, seen rolling along Beacon Hill until it came to the entrance to the Athenaeum, and, under its own momentum, turning sharp right, and up the steps.

In the Trustees' Room, with its long table flanked by busts, Father enjoyed his Monday afternoon meetings of the Library Committee as much as any social club to which he belonged. The actual business was quickly transacted, and the rest of the time, lasting till the hour of the cup of tea-cum-saltine, was taken up in pleasant discursive chat, grazing subjects of general literary or historical interest. Most of the men on that committee were prob-

ably more at home in the pages of the London *Times* Literary Supplement than those of the *Publishers' Weekly* or the *Library
Journal,* but the choice of the books on the shelves certainly did not
suffer through the absence of specialists among them. A Boston
library would not smack of the local tang if it failed to render its
own interpretation of the dictum, "Banned in Boston." Although
I am assured by the present director of the Athenaeum that there
never was such a thing as a "Scruple Room," the phrase is one I
clearly remember Father using. No one denies that there has always
been a room behind whose locked doors are kept valuable rarities.
It appears that there was a time when a few shelves in this room
were reserved for "books like Elinor Glynn's *Three Weeks,*" shelves
marked by a pharmacist's "scruple symbol." If Father, and others,
referred to the Scruple Room, at least, in Athenaeum history, it is
remembered that he was one of the two men who did away altogether
with keeping any books off the shelves because of moral "scruples."
It is too bad that that little zest, lent by the awareness that somewhere in the shadows lurked the potentiality of sin, is removed
from a setting redolent of saltines and fresh flowers.

Was the Athenaeum "exclusive"? Yes, in one sense it was. The
result, in those days, was that the library was not crowded, and
that it was always quiet—dedicated *exclusively* to concentrated
reading and serious scholarship. It is not a clearinghouse for the
current rental library best seller, with a sprinkling of greeting
cards, specializing in "sick" jokes, and crossword puzzles. A "proprietor" of the library who owns a share may extend its privileges
to any number of members of his household, and may accord
"reading privileges," on the payment of a nominal fee, to other
friends. There are also usually reading tickets available for rent to
those who apply for them. Privileges for both reading and research
in the Athenaeum have always been granted where the request is
justified in serious intent; where it is not so justified the general
public is "excluded." It was Father who initiated the happy
arrangement whereby books are sent, no matter how far afield, to
the faithful who read, learn, inwardly digest, do *not* mark, and
return them to the mother shelves.

Aside from the lifeline offered Father by a position at the Athenaeum, restorative activity came to him in the shape of his friend John Jay Chapman. Chapman, living, had always goaded him toward an intensity which was not native to him; Chapman, no longer living, and as a subject for biography, goaded him now in the shape of a challenge, offering him the most interesting subject he had ever tackled. At Chapman's death his widow wrote to Father, "You were, indeed, often in his thoughts. I think he felt that you were one of the few friends pitched in his own key. Even those who loved him most were often a little deprecatory of his trenchant forthrightness. As for your generosity and Mr. Greenslet's toward his writings, few things so sustained and encouraged him for the past decade. When he would feel guilty because the Dante didn't pay, your words of indifference toward that aspect of the book filled him with intense gratitude. You perhaps forget how often you cheered him on this score—and on many others." Chapman had once remarked to Father that his specialty as a biographer was in "cutting out the shadows and keeping the smiles—the grin without the cat." The fact that Father was just emerging from deeps he had never before touched, in addition to his own response to the fiery figure of Chapman, helped to make this his best biography. It was gratifying, in any case, that a book written after his seventieth birthday, and all that he had been through, elicited from Edmund Wilson, in the *Atlantic,* a commendation, referring to "an admirable biography of one of the most interesting and one of the most remarkable prose writers of his generation." Van Wyck Brooks, with his customary warmth where Father was concerned, wrote to him, "I seemed to feel as I read the book why Chapman was not better known. I suppose his work made no unified impression,—it needed the interpretation that you have given. You have filled in the gaps and explained all the leaps in the dark, or what looked like leaps to the uninitiated reader."

Before leaving for Washington Mark hung every picture for Father as well as doing the hundred and one other things involved in the move. None of us could have believed at the time that he was helping to create the atmosphere of the home which was to be Father's for twenty-five years. When the time came to say good-by and the door closed behind Mark, Father admitted that he broke down and wept, in mingled gratitude for a child who had so much of his mother's tender unselfishness in his makeup and sadness in knowing how he would miss him. As he was to do with all of us, however, in short order Father was enjoying Mark's new experience vicariously.

It was early in 1935, back in Boston and practicing law in Arthur Hill's firm, that Mark introduced his bride Mary Manning into the family. She brought, as playwright and novelist, not only the wit but the warmth of heart indigenous to her native Dublin. Mark and Molly's three daughters were to become Father's only grandchildren living near enough to be part of his life as little children. He had to wait until Quincy Jr. was old enough to appear on the scene as a Harvard undergraduate for one of Quincy's two children to be represented.

When, in the fall of 1933, Father and I moved into the large, comfortable rooms in Louisburg Square, they gave only a slight heave and shudder and then swallowed the conglomeration of furniture, books, paintings, and knickknacks innumerable from Brimmer Street—indeed, not only swallowed but offered them such a background of architectural grace and distinction that they took on a new luster. In the high-ceilinged living room, with its black marble mantel, we looked through the delicately tinted panes across the plot of grass in the center of the Square to the curving fronts of the houses on the other side. The ruddy glow of their bricks made Father think of a Gilbert Stuart portrait. In one of these windows stood one of the high-backed carved chairs Dickens had helped Mrs. Fields select on a trip to London. The Chickering piano seemed as much at home as in Mother's back parlor, and the handsome Lowestoft vases more so. Father's bedroom adjoined the living room and any guest had to pass through it to reach the stairs leading to the downstairs library and dining room. The old-fashioned bathroom scales were stuffed into a closet, and the only place he could find for a large Piranesi of the ruins of the Coliseum was the bathroom! A passer-by on the uneven bricks of the sidewalk outside could peer down through two windows into the basement-level library. Father had been much amused by a friend of mine who, on a first sight of the room, had exclaimed in delight, "What courage to do a room like this!" He had "done" nothing except fill the bookshelves, and every inch of available space, to the ceiling, with the indiscriminate accumulation of more lifetimes than his own.

There were relics of the neoclassical craze in America, to which my great-great-grandfather Quincy had obviously succumbed, as evidenced in a plaster-of-Paris reproduction of the Parthenon and a heavy bronze reproduction of the equestrian statue of Emperor Antoninus Pius, mounted on a marble pedestal, miraculously enough not life size. A bronze Dying Gladiator whirled about on top of the revolving bookcase which disgorged the indispensable books of reference. In heavy, ornate frames American landscapes painted by Thomas Doughty, Alvin Fisher, and John Frederick Kensett rubbed shoulders with more Piranesis, family photographs, and the reproduction of an Italian madonna, with meekly parted hair and downcast eyes, which my parents always called Lizzie Passing the Soup. Father had felt he could not afford to keep Duveneck's "Lady with a Fan," and had sold her to the Cincinnati Art Museum, dividing the profits among the grandchildren of the "lady" she had been supposed to resemble. Father still sat at his father's massive mahogany desk; Professor Norton's armchair was still the spot in which he settled to read his evening paper—alas, no longer the defunct *Transcript*. The chair was placed alongside the large brocade-covered table buried under the usual books, magazines, and pamphlets, plus paper cutters, a pipe rack, a miniature bust of Sir Walter Scott, a jar of tobacco, a brass box of elastic rubber bands, and a whale's tooth. For other family or friends there was the Spanish leather brass-studded rocking chair, at its back a high mahogany filing cabinet with green-backed drawers with brass handles which had belonged to Mrs. Fields: atop this, on a pile of books too large for any shelf, sat a bust of Dante, whom Quincy as a child, according to family lore, referred to as "the Satisfied Man."

Naturally I was always at home for Christmas, and it is impossible for anyone who knows Boston to think of Louisburg Square and not to think of Christmas Eve. And to anyone who knew Father he seemed the unselfconscious embodiment of the Christmas Spirit. So the combination of Christmas, Louisburg Square, and Father really was the time, and the place, and the loved one all together, as he sat in a cloud of Christmas cards saying, "In spite of all that is commercial and exaggerated about it, I'm free to say that I enjoy Christmas because there's a universal spirit of such *good will.*" (As a parenthetical observation of changing mores I record that my parents shuddered at any card they received with the name of the sender printed or engraved on it—a practice, they felt, only employed by tradesmen. A Gentle American bothered to write his own name, and preferably a personal message as well, to the friend whom he was remembering.) We used to laugh at Father, even as a very old man, when Mark and his wife and their three small daughters came in to open their presents on Christmas Day. He would begin, as soon as they appeared, "What time are we planning to open the presents?" Then, when the moment finally came, he became the master of ceremonies, feeling every package, turning it over, and reading the cards, "Here is one—Susan with love from Aunt Helen," and if Susan wasn't very sharp it was altogether likely that Grandpa's fingers might begin twitching at the knot of ribbon before hers.

The candles flickering in the windows of the uniformly lovely houses around the Square had been in the old days the shining crown of Beacon Hill's Christmas Eve celebration. It was natural that Father would want to follow the tradition. He began bustling about in the middle of the afternoon, preparing "Lizzie," in her role as Madonna, to be placed on a pile of encyclopedias with a Georgian candlestick on either side of her. Other candlesticks were placed in the freshly washed windows of the living room. The first

Christmas Eve in Louisburg Square, our first without Mother, was inevitably sad. Father and I were alone, and sat downstairs in his library. It is very difficult to pursue any natural pastime when one knows that one is on exhibit as a habitat group, to a multitude on the other side of the panes, who are cupping their eyes in their hands and making personal remarks which carry through the windowpanes. (*"No, it isn't a nightgown! It's a negligee!"*) I am afraid that on that Christmas Eve it is true that my Bostonian Father was reading aloud the *Atlantic* to his Bostonian daughter. In view of the fact that it was a household of mourning, Father had not asked any friends to drop in for the customary Beacon Hill "At Home," with attendant cheer. All the same I knew that his irrepressible sociability was stirring and that he couldn't help hoping that somebody might look in on him. In that unspoken hope he had put out a decanter of sherry, some crackers and cheese, with stronger reinforcements in the background. We sat and we sat. Nothing happened. Outside in the night "Good King Wenceslas" to left of us and "The First Noel" to the right, volleyed and thundered. Then, suddenly, well on in the evening, the doorbell rang. I rushed upstairs to answer it. A young man, with a girl beside him, was standing in the vestibule. "Excuse me, but as I was going by I couldn't help recognizing those drapes in the windows. I sold you the material for them at Lord and Taylor's." (Another parenthesis: Gentle Americans never used the word *drapes. Curtains* hung in windows.) Father by this time was at the head of the stairs, "Come in! Come in! Perhaps they'd like a glass of sherry?" They would, they did, and so Father had company on his first Christmas Eve in Louisburg Square after all!

Father, alas, lived in Louisburg Square long enough to witness the lovely old tradition of the Hill on Christmas Eve debased almost beyond recognition. The singing became raucous, undisciplined, and often had nothing to do with Christmas. The last song Father heard one Christmas Eve before he went to bed was "I Sober Up on Wood Alcohol"; and he woke next morning to find the statues of Columbus and Aristides, which keep watch over the two ends of the grass plot in the middle of the Square, behind

its iron fence, sporting berets! Father's expression on the subject
was "Hurricane Carol in Louisburg Square," ending with the
lines:

> There was never such an Aeolian rumpus
> Starting from every point on the compass,
> Crying to Louisburg Square "It's plain
> That you are the Eye of the hurricane!"

Mother's theory that there is no widower so brokenhearted that
he will not eventually console himself broke down with Father. I
do not blink the implications connected with the mere existence of
an unmarried daughter. If I had packed up, never to set foot in
Boston again, his story might have been different. I am not sure.
As one caryatid, there was Mary Lawrence to minister with sweetness and efficiency to all his creature comforts; the other was Con-
stance Worcester, the daughter of his old friend Elwood Worcester
of Emmanuel Church. "Connie" Worcester came to Father every
day in the official capacity of secretary. She brought him, however,
much more than that cold designation can suggest. For one thing,
she knew most of his friends, so he could always glean some local
news from her. She liked the same books and poetry and, along
with Father, when her own father was no longer rector of Emmanuel Church, she had transferred her allegiance to Trinity
Church. She not only lightened through her reading aloud the
burden that his failing eyesight was to bring him in his last years,
but offered him through more than twenty-five years the accessory
on which he always depended—a sympathetic feminine ear. In
many ways she played for him the role of daughter that I did not
play.

I do not wish for an instant to minimize the proportions of
Father's sorrow for Mother's loss or the bedrock of his unswerving
devotion to her memory. There was a touching childlikeness with
which he would perform some (for him, unusual) act of feminine
thoughtfulness, saying, "I think your Mother would like me to do
so-and-so." One such heart-melting taking on of her role was as a
letter writer, to me. An unmarried son, he had been a faithful cor-

respondent with his mother; now, as a widower, he became an
equally faithful correspondent with his daughter. Before Mother's
death I could have counted on the fingers of one hand the number
of letters he wrote me when I was away from home. But now as
I traveled over the country he told me he liked to feel he had a
girl in every port: at the front desk in hotels in New Mexico,
Louisiana, Idaho, Prince Edward Island—no matter how nearly
off the Boston map my stopping place might be—there was the
Boston postmark, and the familiar writing.

The small beer of Boston he chronicled changed little in flavor
or content. There was always the perennial British caller who
"came for tea at 4:15 (instead of the proposed 4:30 to 5) and
stayed till 6:30! He was quite agreeable—a stage director in
private life—bearded—but why doesn't a Britisher know that
enough is enough?" There was the equally perennial Tavern Club:
"On Monday evening Ted Weeks sat on one side of me at the
T.C. dinner for Sir Osbert Sitwell, with Sir O. on my other
side. . . . Sir Osbert was pleasant enough but in his little speech
made so much (as usual) of his father's peculiarities that I was
moved the next evening, here at home, to write the verses I enclose."
The enclosure read:

> Sit well—I must not say, "Sit tight"—
> Sir Osbert, on your father's grave
> Else might he rear his head tonight,
> Our next-room laughter to outbrave
> Crying "To share in all this mirth
> I must myself return to earth!"

He knew what little tidbits would amuse me, and shared them
with me: "The Authors Club dinner on Friday would have provided you with tip-top material—lady-chairman, three-named
female writers of unknown books, and all the rest of it." Lest I
labor under the erroneous impression that he accepted everyone
as equally attractive, he reported accepting an invitation over the
telephone "when I could not think quickly enough of another engagement." He found his hostess "nothing less than a parody on

somebody who exists only in books, not in the flesh—and Never Again!''

During the times I was at home I tried to play the role he enjoyed so much having me fill, as hostess at some of his parties. He would protest sometimes, ''I wish my friends would ask *you* when they ask me to dinner.'' He always wanted an audience before which he could display the charms and talents of his children! I pointed out to him sternly that I did not *want* to become part of his older circle and was happy that the hostesses who were more interested in securing a single man for their parties than in admiring his daughter were playing right into my hands. When it came to *my* wanting to give some parties of my own he automatically assumed that he would be present—for the simple reason that he enjoyed my friends so much. During those first years I attempted various declarations of independence. ''Father, I have decided that I am going to give a party on my own some evening, when you are out.'' At the flinging down of the gauntlet, tail down, ears back, he was like the same friendly dog my mother had described—only cruelly kicked. But he accepted my resolve, nonetheless, with his usual sweetness.

The warning hint for me that my plan was not going to work occurred on an evening when each guest that arrived asked— almost, indeed, demanded, ''Where is Mr. Howe?'' I explained that he was out. ''Oh, dear! Won't he come in later?''

That question I didn't dare answer for the simple reason that I didn't trust him. And how right I was! Sure enough, his party that evening was over sooner than mine, and when I heard his key in the lock I knew that it would be only a matter of minutes before he was in the living room, with me and my friends. When he came in, he shook hands all around. There were cries of obvious pleasure from my guests as they clustered around. ''Come on, have a drink, Mr. Howe!'' I am not sure that he did not quote, ''The noble gal did not decline, but simply said, 'With pleasure,' '' as he sank into the sofa, and pulled out his pipe. He stayed until the end of the party. To tell the truth I could not help suspecting that the presence of an elderly father sped that end. In any event, I am

ashamed to remember that when it was over I flew into a fit of
temper, irritated beyond bearing with his bland ignoring of the
possibility that I might not have *wanted* him at my party, ending
up with a grand exit and slamming of door. I was sleepless with
remorse, apologized the next morning, ending up with a slight plea
of self-justification of my motives, if not my manners. He accepted
my apology sweetly. When shortly afterward I had another party
my conscience began to twinge, anticipating the martyred tiptoeing
past the living-room door, and solitary trip to bed. I had reckoned
without him! With no apparent compunction whatsoever he repeated his appearance at the living-room door, to be greeted by
cries of "Come in! Come in, Mr. Howe!" He came, he stayed, he
conquered. He always did. I cannot blow him up into a poor man's
Mr. Barrett, terrorizing his maiden daughter. He simply was the
most sociable of men, as well as one of the most universally popular,
and a child didn't have a chance against him! My only recourse was
to move out—which I did. Not, I must confess, without a bit of a
tussle and a few drops of blood spilled.

I had, several years before, rented a little one-room apartment,
a few minutes away, up the Hill, on Anderson Street. I used the
room to work in, away from the telephone, as well as to give a few
cocktail parties—*really* of my own. Now, I told Father that I
thought I would actually take my clothes and move into Anderson
Street, have my breakfast and lunch there, and come down to
Louisburg Square for dinner whenever he would like to have me.
I was amazed at how hard he took it, at first. Once my decision was
made, however, he accepted it good-naturedly, and I think must
have taken a certain—I was going to say sardonic, but there wasn't
a sardonic bone in his body!—satisfaction in seeing how often I
scurried back to Mary Lawrence for meals, either to be eaten at his
table or to be put in a casserole and carried to my one room.

Since Father was the fixed object around which I orbited, and
since he was, in any case, the center of a wide circle of friends, it
was inevitable that many more of his friends came and went in
Louisburg Square than my own. Of his we shall hear more presently.

I could, however, supply a few of my own—who, in short order, became his. Among some of the rather plodding footsteps here fossilized, I should like, in particular, to indicate the passage of a lighter, quite special, tread. Johnny Ames (John Worthington Ames, Jr., to give him his full name) truly boxed the compass of friendship in our family circle, starting in the early nineteen hundreds as a schoolboy at Brown and Nichols in Cambridge with my Muirhead cousins before they moved to England to live, and ending up forty years later—with Father.

Though Quincy was three years his junior it was he who first became Johnny's friend in the Paris of the twenties where he was studying architecture at the École des Beaux-Arts. Wounded in the French Army, the loss of half his right hand presented him with the challenge of learning to execute his profession of architecture with his left. The only reference to this grim aspect of his Army years which I ever heard him make was to the French soldier in the hospital bed next to his own who muttered to himself, over and over, the refrain, "*Faut*-il, *faut*-il, *faut*-il souffrir?" Johnny succinctly said, "The answer was, 'Il faut.' "

For all his Boston years Johnny's almost nightly dining place was the Athens-Olympia Restaurant, colloquially called "The Greek's." Martinis came first, either in his apartment in Otis Place or ours in Louisburg Square. Then, after the inevitable shrimps in lemon oil, lamb en brochette, rice pilaf, and baklava, the walk home across the Common. Father, hearing our footsteps approaching along the uneven bricks of the sidewalk, and recognizing our laughter half a block away, called Johnny my "giggle-o." The French that had stuck with me from the Mademoiselle years certainly made one bond, intensified by our common addiction to Proust. We saw our Boston friends as Proustian characters, endlessly turning over the subtleties of relationships. Johnny—unlike the Dear People— was nothing if not sophisticated. His voice was part of his ineffable charm, particularly as it reflected his quick response to the mood or the charm of a woman. Indeed when it came to women—and sooner or later it always did come to them—poor Johnny did not find it

easy to adjust to the American way. How often have I sympathized
with his pangs of jealousy over the particular Albertine of the
moment who was causing him to lose sleep! It is my claim to fame—
proud or humble, I hardly know which—that among all the women
in the life of this Paris-Boston Don Juan I alone remained the one
"best friend" with whom he was never in love.

It was part of Father's formula for growing old—arrived at
more unconsciously than by design—that he made many warm
friendships with younger men. After I left home Johnny returned
from the Second World War, where he had served as Lieutenant
Colonel in North Africa. With the Tavern Club in common—of
which he was ultimately to become Secretary—Father and Johnny
found each other out as congenial, even devoted friends, meeting
at last as man to man—indeed as Johnny and Mark.

Father did not share Johnny's experience in the knowledge and
love of women. On his side, Johnny did not share in Father's instinctive sympathy for the Church. The sight of a priest of clergyman caused him to shudder as he muttered, "Gee, aren't those
Crows depressing?" What the two friends shared, without knowing
it, was an absolute purity of motive. Neither of them, in dealing
with another human being, knew what it was to have an ulterior
end in view. Each was limpidly himself—at all times, in all places,
with all people. Each had humor and intelligence and enough of the
same interests to reach out, across the gulf of more than thirty
years, to become fast friends.

There were other men who came to see the daughter of the house.
Today they would be called "dates." In my day they were called
"beaux." As usual, my heaviest competition with them came from
—Father himself. If he approved—and he almost always did—he
enjoyed sharing their society. There were even instances when he
approved more than I did myself. About the worst he could say of
any of them was "I don't like the cut of his jib." But he was out-
and-out Victorian in his disapproval of any relationship which he
suspected might have even a whiff of sex about it, and if there
was an added whiff of alcohol he became positively morose. If a man
came to take me out to dinner, and came in first for a drink, Father,

downstairs in the dining room eating his own dinner, would keep
his eye on the clock and reprove me the next morning for the time
spent before he heard me and the interloper go out. "When *I* was
young, and asked a young lady to dinner, she did not feel obliged to
offer me a *drink* first" was the gist of his condemnation, and when I
came in at night, if he heard the front door close later than he cared
for, sure that undue pressure had been brought to bear, he reminded me that " 'Tis excellent to have a giant's strength, but 'tis
tyrannous to use it like a giant."

On this score at least he was pleased when I produced a tee-
totaling young Army captain whom I had met, on my monologue
travels, on a train in Oregon, on his way home from duty in Alaska.
Later, he was transferred to Camp Devens outside of Boston. Father
enjoyed talking with the outlander whom my Boston friends
accounted for to their own satisfaction by their comment, "He's a
real *American,*" and he, in return, enjoyed Father as "a gentleman of the old school," who reminded him of Senator Norris. Father
was pleased and amused at my dismay when the young man came
to take me out to dinner at 6:30, offering me, by way of stimulus, a
plate of ice cream! We both followed his subsequent career with
interest, and pride on my part for being such a discriminating
picker-upper, when he was elected United States Senator from
Oregon, and later felt much saddened by the much-too-early death
of Richard Neuberger.

I am appalled, in looking back, at the supreme selfishness of
youth. I never gave a thought to how often the father of an only
daughter must have longed for the mother of that daughter to
"talk over" various emotional situations that arose. One in particular—involving a man already married—brought not only several
years of deep suffering to me, but more pain to Father than I care
to remember. I mention it here only because I wish to show him in
another light than that of the perennially benign and bland parent.
It was the fate of his "good little girl" to bring him the only unhappiness he was to suffer through his children. I have a clear picture of him on a gray winter afternoon a year after Mother's
death, when he and I were alone in the living room and a crisis

wrung from me the one anguished cry, "Father, don't you *know?*" From the armchair in which he was seated he opened his arms, into which I flung myself and sobbed my heart out on his shoulder. I can never hear the words of the psalm, "Like as a father pitieth his children," without thinking of his all-forgiving love at that time. He neither admonished nor blamed me. He simply accepted a fact that distressed him in every one of its multiple aspects, and, because I was unhappy, gave me nothing but love and understanding.

At long last, however, the clouds lifted and the shadows fled away; thirteen years after our move into Louisburg Square sunshine flooded the landscape when I became engaged to be married. The reluctant Harvard freshman who had found his way to Brimmer Street in that faraway autumn of 1923 was spared by a merciful oblivion any recollection of his first-half-cousin-once-removed. It was her parents only who had caught his attention. Now, in 1946, making tardy amends, he invited her to Hollywood, to marry him. When I asked Quincy if he thought that a marriage between two offshoots of the Bishop smacked of incest, he said, "It's like the descendants of Charlemagne. It was bound to happen sooner or later."

Father was so pleased with his son-in-law that he took with his usual sweetness my transference to the other side of the continent to live. After all, a daughter was only one element in his very full life. Cozily placed in Louisburg Square, was he not, after all, sitting at the very hub of the Hub?

18

SITTING IN THE LAP OF FRIENDSHIP

WHEN FATHER WROTE A HISTORY of the Tavern Club, for its anniversary, Bliss Perry wrote him, "You have not only written our songs, but set the law of friendship in our hearts." And, in another letter, "Wherever you are, on sea or land, you are sitting in the lap of friendship."

Since, aside from his family, his friends afforded Father his greatest pleasures, it always interested me to wonder why he never seemed, among so many to whom he was so devoted, to have singled out one to wear in his heart of hearts— as Hamlet did Horatio. Perhaps the fact that, in a sense, he was not intimate with himself accounted for his not being intimate with anyone else either. Not given to taking his own psychic pulse, he was not interested in taking anyone else's. If there was a twin soul among men with whom he was on deeper terms of confidence than any other, that soul was Uncle Wallis. For the rest, he moved in an easy, affable atmosphere of affection and congeniality.

I shall not attempt to tick off individually the twenty-five years as they slipped serenely over Father in his surroundings in Louisburg Square. It was inevitable that a Bostonian of Father's era and proclivities, without a wife, would find the chief constellation of his friendships in his manifold clubs—and in the clubs the Boston of fact and fiction were one. Father was only once more following in his friend Bliss Perry's footsteps when in 1943 he succeeded him as

President of the Saturday Club. He did not accept immediately the honor which pleased him so much because of nervousness about his stammering—the curse which had denied him so many pleasures over the years. But one of the phenomena which age was to bring to pass was a gradual abatement of his stammer. Actually, when he had been so seriously ill in the hospital for thirteen weeks he never stammered once. He was coming more and more to see that some pressure within himself had probably been the cause. Physical weakness was one way of easing that pressure, but there were others too. He realized—as his children could not help doing—that the absence of Mother's vicarious suffering as a sounding board for his own had removed one obvious source of strain. But he was to say more than once, and surely with reason, "I suppose it's because I am trying less hard than I once was to prove myself." In any event, feeling himself to be among such kindly disposed friends as his fellow members of the Saturday Club, he gave himself up to the pleasure of accepting this mark of their affection for him.

When Father took his friend Van Wyck Brooks to one of the monthly lunches Brooks assured him that the thought that Hawthorne, Emerson, and Longfellow had once been members did not make him think of "ghosts," as he had been warned that it might. He found "nothing of the past tense about it. . . . It was such good fun and such good company I quite forgot there was anything 'historical' about it."

The living members among whom Father sat at the Saturday Club table afforded company for whom no apology was needed. There were Harvey Cushing, brain surgeon, Thomas Barbour, naturalist, Alfred Kidder, archeologist, Karl Compton, scientist and president of M.I.T., Charles Maginnis, architect (and one of the very few Roman Catholics belonging to any of Father's clubs), Hans Zinsser, bacteriologist, Dr. George Minot, winner of the Nobel Prize for Medicine and Physiology in 1934, and Alfred North Whitehead, philosopher and mathematician. Two of Father's special friends were Langdon Warner, curator of Oriental Art at the Fogg Museum, and Billy James, artist. The two latter, in turn, were devoted friends of each other.

Langdon Warner called himself a "furious fan" of Father's scraps of Tavern Club and other writings. He wrote, "With luck I shall get into Louisburg Square and get a crack with you before we head south. . . . But in the meantime there will be Tavern evenings and Saturday luncheons. . . . In any case let's get some more golden hours." Writing to Father of the death of Billy James's brother "Alec" he gave a sense of what both he and Father felt about the James family:

> All today has been spent coming and going to Dublin where we buried Alec James. His three grand boys were all there, back from incredible adventures in open boats for days on the Pacific, torpedoings and other nightmares. The sight of their noble James heads in front of me made me feel suddenly old and horribly sentimental. . . .
>
> In these last years I never saw him, not once in three years, but when I did that meeting was not forgotten. He and Bill are the most *direct* spirits I've ever come across, and I felt mentally house-cleaned for a week after talking with Alec.

There were men of entirely mortal, even if distinguished, achievements among the membership of the Saturday Club, but they were not insulated from appreciating the presence of another dimension among them. Langdon Warner, at the death of Alfred North Whitehead, wrote to Father: "How many generations will it take to build slowly up to the birth of another like him? And why should we even try to imagine that it should ever happen? Probably some of the corpuscles and atoms of mind that came together in that individual will make up part of all future individual minds, and that's immortality Indian Buddhist style."

Let Father himself bring back "the mild because wholly native and unconscious autocracy of the luncheon table" as it shone through this one man.

> Among us like a trustful child,
> His face all wondering and mild,
> And luminous with an inner light,
> Veiled with a smile from common sight,
> He spoke, yet never to declare,

Announce, assert, but just to share
His wisdom, launched with "I submit"—
What wisdom! tinctured with what wit!

In all concerns of mind and heart,
Who could regard him and not see
The marks of immortality,
The passport into brotherhood
With the immortals great and good?
With Plato now shall he not talk,
Or beside Archimedes walk?
How could we hope to hold him here
From comrades in his destined sphere?

The talk round the table at the Saturday Club which Father always found most stimulating had to do with national or international affairs. During the war years, 1941–1945, there were visitors from the world beyond Boston who helped put things in perspective. Bill James wrote Father in 1940: "Yes, Mark, we all voted for F.D.R. in this family and I am proud to have been in the same camp with Mark Howe and a good many million others." Father actually voted for Roosevelt the four times he ran. One of the few memories I have of Father really overcome was as he sank down into a chair after listening to the news of Roosevelt's death over the radio, covering his face with his hands and saying, "I am shattered. I am shattered." With the years, however, Father participated less in matters of public concern, which meant simply that he refrained from putting his name to as many protests and petitions as he had done in earlier times.

Lunch at the Saturday Club was not the only bait Father offered Van Wyck Brooks in Boston. He had included him, along with Robert Frost, on the Visiting Committee on English for which he was responsible as a Harvard Overseer. Brooks seemed more disposed to look upon his role on that committee as a pleasure than did Robert Frost, of whom he wrote to Father, "I am getting to be almost as bad as that spoiled baby Robert Frost when it comes to writing letters." The "spoiled baby" himself wrote to Father:

Come right down to it, I am not a good person to put on committees because I want too much in this world to expect anything. But look at what has been done to English A while the old skeptic sat surlily out! And what is this about intermissions of three weeks in winter and spring to relieve teachers of some of the burden of teaching and so make them not only better scholars but better teachers? The first thing we know we shall have it granted that the best way to teach students to do original work is for the teacher to do original work himself, and in real scholarship as in art, he who lives most to himself lives most for other people, his disciples included. Then there will be nothing more to complain of in American education and it will serve me right.

My hopes and fears are all with Bliss Perry and you.

I see a glimmer of something to suggest in what you have to report about the students having taken their training in oral debate into their own hands to a certain extent. I fear I should be tempted to try if withholding on them still longer wouldn't make them take it still further into their own hands. It would be just like me sometime to try what withholding the whole subjects of writing and reading for a while would do for literature in college. You won't believe me serious—and that's why I shouldn't dare to come to your committee meetings. I don't mean I should desert the poor children entirely with poetry—for good and all. I just shouldn't be so forward with it as some of us are now. Like Cloe (was it?) I might not run away so far that I couldn't be overtaken, but I should run away. There never was anything like an artful alternation between refusing and yielding to whet the appetite.

What a long way we have come in our relations since the days when you were an editor, and I was your occasional poet.

The flowering of Father's friendship with Van Wyck Brooks was to know no Indian summer. From the earliest days of their acquaintance, when Father was "Mr. Howe" and Brooks wrote him that "I expect to have occasion to bother you with all sorts of small questions, at one time or another, about New England in the Nineteenth Century, for I always think of you as Court of Last Resort on that subject, and you are so kind in sharing all your knowledge," the two writers seemed destined for each other in a common meeting ground of literary interest. They were, furthermore, on the same wave length as human beings. The sweetness, warmth, and affection that Brooks showed to Father during all the later years of Father's life only emphasized that for him, too, friendship counted more than scholarship. The more than one hundred letters that he wrote Father must someday be part of his own literary story. Who else could— or indeed would want to—join their esoteric shop talk? "The reference to Cambridge puns in Clough's Letters ('Prose Remains,' Page 197, letter of 3 January 1853) turns out to be slight enough but indicates what the vogue was and how an outsider might have felt about it. The supper was at Lowell's house: 'Thackeray came at tea; Longfellow, Dana, Quincy, Estes, Howe, Felton, Fields and another. Puns chiefly, but Dana is really amusing.' But don't you think Clough himself was rather a dull dog?" Brooks knew he was writing to a peer when he wrote about his own work in progress, "As for Miss Sarah Palfrey, please think no more of this question. I have read that at seventy-five she took a spin on her tricycle round Fresh Pond every morning before breakfast. I take this to indicate the 'cheerful view of life,' and perhaps you will agree that this is a fair deduction. I wanted that note of relief, among several others, in a chapter, otherwise dark, on Boston in the nineties. I am making this chapter as dark as the facts permit, because, in my view of the case, another day was dawning at that moment." The shoe fits just as smoothly on the other foot when Father discussed with him *his* works in progress. The amazing record is that between the ages of seventy and eighty-eight Father was to publish, aside from his *Chapman,* a biography of *Holmes of the Breakfast Table,* his own autobiography, *A Venture in Remembrance,* the *Semi-Centennial History of the Tavern Club, The Tale of Tanglewood,* two slender volumes of New England history (immeasurably enhanced by Samuel Chamberlain's beautiful photographs), *Boston Landmarks* and *Who Lived Here?,* three volumes of verse—*Songs of September, Personae Gratae,* and *Sundown*—as well as editing the letters of the lively daughters of President Josiah Quincy of Harvard, *The Articulate Sisters*, and—in collaboration with G. W. Cottrell, Jr.—*The Scholar Friends: Letters of Francis J. Child and James Russell Lowell.*

Apropos of Father's biography of *Holmes of the Breakfast Table*, Brooks was instant with encouragement: "How splendid that you are to do a book on Holmes. . . . I fell completely in love with O.W.H., as I trust you may feel, and I think your proposed book is badly needed. He is certainly good for another hundred years and seems to me to have all sorts of aspects that people are little aware of,—at least, in the world I live in,—and they make him a contemporary author. . . . I have felt more at home with him, during the last three years, than any other writer of his time, except Thoreau, I think." If Father had reason to feel touchy when imputations of writing in too Horatio Willingly a strain were leveled at him, there was balm in Gilead when these kindly eyes read his autobiography, *Adventure in Remembrance*.

It is lovely!—and so full of yourself that I only wanted three times more of it. (Beginning with a whole book about Rhode Island and the boyhood summers.) Anything less like "Mr. Willing" couldn't be imagined, and I never could understand your feeling about this,—which Ralph Thompson disposes of in *The Times* this morning; it is all so fresh and so charming in its general tone and so brimming over with human wisdom. I loved every page of it and hold out my spoon for "more," for it all suggests the top of the wave of your writing.

When it came to other regular meetings of friends and colleagues Father was among his peers at the meetings of the Massachusetts Historical Society for which he contributed frequent "papers." I think he often, understandably, felt himself among his betters at the meetings of the Examiner Club. With Harlow Shapley as president of the club when such subjects as "Biochemical Heresies in an Atomic Age" and "Socio-Static Process in Man" were being discussed Father must have sat in respectful silence.

Father gave up the position of Director of the Athenaeum in 1936 and was re-elected Trustee in 1940, with the tenderly offered privilege of continuing to use his little glass room as long as he cared to. So it was that until he literally could no longer climb the Hill he plodded up Mt. Vernon or Beacon Street with such devoted regularity that I feel as though the worn old bricks, on which so many of his contemporaries were apt to fall in slippery weather, to break a wrist if not a hip, must bear the mark of his always slightly shabby shoes. After various bouts of ill-health or when Father was too frail to participate in large gatherings, there was often a pleasant break in his Saturday afternoon at home when friends dropped in. Bearing the flowers from the Saturday Club lunch table, singly, or together, there might be W. G. Constable, of the Museum of Fine Arts, or that most faithful and gentlest of friends and painters, Charles Hopkinson, or a far younger man, whose friendship Father particularly enjoyed—Harvard's Greek scholar and Father's successor as president of the Saturday Club, John Finley. If it was another Saturday, it would be another group of friends, still in a retrospective glow of well-being from the delights of a Club of Odd Volumes lunch—occasions which Father himself in his day relished along with the other members of this unique organization. Such a lunch held in the beautiful old high-ceilinged house on Mt. Vernon Street owned by the club, had been prepared by the legendary Mrs. Morrisey and had been planned in advance by whatever member had happened to donate on a given day a duck, a haunch of venison, or a special leg of mutton.

Mother had never been one to take entertaining easily; Father loved to dispense hospitality. It was, therefore, natural that when he was on his own he welcomed opportunities for asking various groups of men to Louisburg Square. He himself had written that membership on Harvard's Board of Overseers was tantamount to membership in a congenial club, and so indeed he found it when he was elected to a second term. In any event the committees for which he, as an Overseer, was responsible—the Visiting Committee on English and the Visiting Committee on Music—gave him an excuse for calling meetings under his roof. As he grew more frail with the

years the Trustees of the Boston Symphony Orchestra were kindly
enough disposed toward him to arrange an occasional meeting in
his apartment so that he might participate.

Father's admiration and affection for Koussevitsky (known to
his friends as "Koussy") were obviously returned, as anyone could
testify who witnessed an unexpected backstage meeting between
them in a city far removed from Boston, when the Maestro flung his
arms around Father's neck, kissing him on both cheeks, and exclaiming, "My Trusty!" At a dinner in Koussevitsky's honor at the
Tavern Club in 1942 Father celebrated his friend in verses,
"Koussy Fan Tutte":

> On the shores of the Volga
> He tied up his boat,
> And, like Pan with his pipes
> On the banks of a river,
> Set mortals a-quiver,
> Ashore and afloat,
> With the magic of music
> So sweet and so strong
> That Russia herself
> Couldn't hold him for long.
> So they bore him away
> To the banks of the Seine,
> Before the mad Fritzes,
> Those blond sons of Blitzes,
> Polluted its borders
> With goose-steps profane.
>
> By the Thames he has played,
> And by many a stream,
> But deep in his heart
> There was always a dream,
> With a word
> That he heard,
> Which kept saying, "Look here,
> You can play second-base
> (Called double-bass too)
> And there must be a place

In the land of the Bees
And the home of the Braves
For a player who waves
A baton (or bat) as you do.''

So hither he came
To the banks of the Charles
And the Tanglewood Bowl—
And waters once tame
Now ocean-like roll
With waves in control
Of the beat from the soul
Of him who turns sound into beauty,
From Mozart to Gershwin—
It's Koussy Fan Tutte!

As Father was visiting my husband and me in Hollywood at a
time when Charles Münch was conducting in Los Angeles he was
able to serve as liaison between him and the Trustees of the Boston
Symphony Orchestra, anxious to open negotiations toward his coming to Boston permanently. So, in due course, another friendship
flowered with yet another conductor of the Orchestra who also
seemed to value Father in a quite special way.

Another of Boston's "subcutaneous clubs," as Father called
them, was the Wednesday Evening Club. In Brimmer Street days
the suppers, beginning about ten o'clock, never occurred without
black tie for the guests, and at least oysters and champagne by way
of trimmings for some grand pièce de résistance, on the part of the
host. By the time Father played host in Louisburg Square a new
order was in swing—no evening clothes, no champagne—and for
fare, following Mary's supernal tiny, ethereal fishballs, there was
something as down-to-earth as scrambled eggs and sausages. "The
Wednesday Evening Club of 1777" was its full title, and the
gentlemen who founded it would, I rather think, not have started
in distress or surprise at any marked deviation in those members of
Father's time from the original prototypes of their own colonial
stamp.

It was, however, in the intimacy of the "Burr Club" that

Father's gusto for friendship came to its fullest flower. Perhaps the meetings of the half dozen friends who dined in one another's houses during the winter were too informal to record in print as a bona fide "club." They had drawn together originally out of affection and friendship for Mr. Heman Burr, a scholar and lawyer, when he was too fragile to leave his house on Chestnut Street. He had once observed that his reading of history proved to him that the Tory was always wrong. . . . After Mr. Heman Burr's death his brother Allston, also a member of the "club," attempted to rechristen it as the Heman Burr Club, but the Burr Club it still remains.

Father used to compare his beloved friend Allston Burr to Jane Austen's Mr. Knightly. His chivalry to an invalid wife, his gentle, serious courtliness, could have belonged to another century except for the fact that Father bore witness to—all but impossible to believe—that Mr. Burr could delight his men friends with a rich and racy vocabulary of profanity. Here he is, as seen by Father, on an occasion when President Conant was presenting to the city of Boston the John Harvard Mall,

a children's playground laid out on an acre of land on which the house of John Harvard is believed to have stood, and also the church in which he preached. An anonymous donor, said President Conant, had given the playground to Harvard. There were speeches by Governor Leverett Saltonstall and the Harvard historical scholar, Professor Charles H. McIlwain. These and others were on a speakers' platform.

Where was the donor? Not on the platform, but on the fringe of a standing audience. There was nothing to distinguish this gentleman, modest of mien and carriage, as an intrepid mountain-climbing member of the Alpine Club, an ardent reader, especially of Shakespeare, Trollope, and Jane Austen, or as the idealistic son of Harvard who had devoted some years to acquiring the site of John Harvard's house and adjoining properties, and to planning, with the best professional advice, the perfectly appointed playground which should perpetuate the Harvard name.

His own name, now carried by a hall at Harvard, was All-

ston Burr. There was no concealing the fact that this hall was
built from generous funds bequeathed by him to the college
for its unrestricted use. He died in 1949. . . . His memory is
entitled to a tribute to which he himself would not have
listened.

An alcove in the Lamont Library at Harvard, marked with
the name of Allston Burr, bears also this line of Tennyson's:
"O selfless man and stainless gentleman!"

I have my own special associations with the incorruptible probity
of that stainless gentleman. I was the unwitting cause of a Laocoön
struggle he passed through when he had to choose between loyalty to
a friend and strict adherence to the truth. Because of his touching
affection for Father he always expressed the greatest interest in
the activities of Father's children. Before the publication of my
second novel he bombarded Father with questions, wanting to know
the exact date of publication, its title, publisher, and so on. When
the day rolled around he was at the Tavern Club for lunch, bearing
a copy of the book fresh from the press and told Father that he was
going right home to Brookline after lunch to get into it at once.
From that moment poor Mr. Burr never mentioned the subject
again. The novel, *We Happy Few,* satirized certain aspects of the
Harvard of that time. And poor Father, too! He so loved to have
his friends appreciate his children. It would have been much
easier for him if Mr. Burr could have said, "I don't think the book
is fair" (a favorite word with that most just of men), or simply,
"I don't like it," or—better still!—let rip some of his suppressed
profanity. But because he loved Father he would not say anything
unpleasant about his daughter, and because he loved honor more he
would not perjure himself by saying something he did not mean.
Another Boston contemporary of Father's expressed, perhaps, the
sentiment of many of his friends in connection with that particular
book when she sighed, "And Mr. Howe is such a pleasant man!"

Another member of the Burr Club was Father's dear friend, his
yachting host of earlier days, "Charlie" Cummings—architect and
debonair Short-Tailed *bon vivant.* With Mrs. Cummings, as with

her sister Ethel—Mrs. John Moors—Father enjoyed one of those affectionate friendships with a member of the opposite sex which enriched the lives of my parents' generation in Boston. During our childhood summers in Cotuit there had always occurred a golden parenthesis for Father when he had left us all behind, and gone off on a cruise—generally down the Maine coast—with Charlie Cummings, and one or two other Tavern Club cronies, on Mr. Cummings's yacht, the *Avenger*.

The ice-cold martinis when the sun showed over the yardarm, the plunge before breakfast into the even icier Maine waters, a spanking northwest wind blowing out of a blue and white sky, or faces dripping in the spray of a "smoky sou'wester," the creeping into a snug little harbor as the breeze died with the daylight, and the evenings of all male conviviality ashore or afloat—all these were only memories to the Charlie Cummings and the Mark Howe of the Burr Club days. As time passed, Charlie Cummings's long, lean Yankee face on his long, lean figure grew in strength, attaining in his last years a nobility achieved through his heroic bearing of the pain of crippling arthritis. The grace and charm proved to have been only a fractional part of a nature and character that were hewn out of the very rock of New England.

Billy James, as another Burr Club intimate of Father's, defies classification. How could it be possible to label a son who bore the name and same free spirit as his father's, and himself was the vessel in whom so much of the family charm and talent was contained? When a friend asked him what it was like to be the son of such a father he was silent for some minutes with his own characteristic version of the Jamesian pause dedicated to the inner search for the right word before, on a sigh, bringing out the one word *"Devastating."* His almost pathological modesty may have prompted him to believe that he shared none of the family gifts, but how, all the same, even in a few notes to Father, the family imprint is on his mind—and on his heart! "Isn't it amusing," he asked in one letter, "that you can't refer to Emerson without appearing to 'date' yourself. What matters it who or when or where someone had a

good idea—it's the idea that is in question, not the author!" One
would know how he would feel about Chapman.

> It's a wonderful book—between the both of you—and it fills
> me with a new sense of life—inspiration. I am that much less
> dead than I was before. . . . He was a prophet. Listened in
> secret. Recognized, as Emerson did, the power and truth of
> intuition. This accounts, I think, not only for the deep truths
> that both men were able to express but for the fact that their
> utterance is freed from the ego, the pride and the self that
> pollutes somewhat the writing speech and action of the rest of
> us. This is to me the revelation of the book—sufficient to shift
> somewhat one's whole outlook on the universe. It's inconceiv-
> able that that figure shouldn't live. The critics (the only 2 I
> have read) don't see what I am trying to say and his own
> books seem to be largely out of print. And yet I believe they
> will reach those for whom they are meant as surely as if
> brought down to them, as Emerson says, by the hand of God.

I think perhaps the sweet kernel of Billy James's charm lay in
the sense that he managed to convey that you, and you alone, no
matter what the setting nor how crowded the gathering in which
you found yourself beside him, "understood" and were deliciously
understood in return.

A gifted painter of sensitive portraits but distrustful of his own
gifts, Billy James was constantly changing his style and method
in recurring fits of self-disgust. Though his every response to man
and nature—and woman too—was that of the artist, no artist ever
less suggested the Bohemian. Not only was Billy James not Long-
Tailed, he wasn't even Long-Haired. It was characteristic of him
that in his senior year at Harvard when he was captain of the
crew, he suddenly decided that he wanted to think about something
else than how to beat Yale, so he abruptly left college and went to
Paris—first to study anatomy, like his father before him, and then
to become a painter. The fine figure of the disciplined athlete remained with him, and that figure lost nothing in attraction for
being turned out by the best Bond Street tailors. In surroundings

which flaunt a defiant disregard of appearances he was a joy to look at! Speaking as a woman, I would be put to it to say which held the greater the appeal, that fine man's figure, the deep sad eyes, or the gentle, modulated voice and beautiful speech. Not British, most emphatically not Boston, but not everyday American either. Read the letters of any member of that family: he had their humor, he had their doubt, he had their humility, and an endless questioning of the workings of the universe and man's place in it. Though he was the most gentle of men (it would be inconceivable to think of his ever saying, thinking, or doing anything that did not spring from the very finest fiber of feeling for others) he was tremendously a man.

Friends, friends, friends. . . . So surrounded, the advancing years seemed to present to Father only increasing opportunities for expressing and receiving expressions of affection. He celebrated birthdays and anniversaries of his fellow Gentle Americans in an unceasing flow of rhyming. In return, in honor of his ninetieth birthday, the Tavern Club gave him a dinner, and it would seem that his younger friend David McCord spoke for the entire membership when he wrote:

> Ralph Emerson was three score ten,
> Thoreau was dead twelve years,
> A little boy our man was then
> When in the classroom he appears
> And Genius said: "I thee endow."
> And teachers said, as we say now:
> "How mark Mark Howe?"
>
> Time has a way with such as he
> To strengthen as the lengthening day
> Discloses at his apogee
> This man with still so much to say
> That we in hopelessness avow:
> "How mark Mark Howe?"
>
> Great friend, companion, Taverner:
> Historiographer who brought

The Pharaohs back to life, confer
On us the insight never sought
Until with empty words we bow.
Superlatives have failed us now—
Even the A plus, we allow.
"How mark Mark Howe?
How mark him? How?"

19

THE FLOWER AND THE FRUIT
OF A MAN

IT WOULD BE EASY TO DISMISS as both limited and pampered an old gentleman living in the charm and ease of the surroundings of Louisburg Square in the 1950's, surrounded by loving friends. Yet illness, loneliness, and the inexorable confrontation of Death pass no man by who has lived not only into his eighties but out on the other side, on into his nineties. I like, however, to catch one final memory of Father in full sunlight before the inevitable lengthening of the shadows.

Actually there were pleasures awaiting him far beyond Louisburg Square. Thanks to Cousin Alice's generosity there was a Mediterranean cruise in company with the Billy Jameses, so that he saw for twenty-four hours Rome and Athens. There was a trip with Allston Burr to Jamaica, and there were several visits to my husband and me in Hollywood. Bliss Perry wrote him before he left: "What an ungodly destination for Mark Howe! Your stay there will do something (I hope rather than trust) to save it from the fate of Sodom and Gomorrah (Though I fear I can't spell 'Gomorrah'!)." Father found it anything but an ungodly destination, and flung himself into the pleasures it offered.

When we moved back East there were visits to my husband and me in Mt. Desert, Maine. On the occasion of his ninetieth birthday there was a joyous gathering of friends and neighbors; Quincy and Mark were with us and, a few days later, all the way from Bristol,

Uncle Wallis. When the tumult and the shouting of the large summer cocktail party had died our reward for the effort we had put into it was Father's wearied sigh as he said, "I'm not sure this hasn't been the happiest day of my life."

That summer, looking across Somes Sound at the rising hills beyond, Father could see a gentle slope known locally as Little Brown Mountain. He said, "I lift up mine eyes unto the hills. From whence cometh my strength? My strength cometh from Little Brown." This mood of gratitude was engendered by the publication by that Boston firm of a volume of verses, entitled *Sundown*. That same summer, *Time* sent a charming photographer and a reporter to interview him and take pictures. Father lapped up the blandishments of both. When a none too flattering notice of his little book appeared in *Time* he merely said resignedly, "I think I should have done better to call it *Letdown*." He always found it possible to be "bucked up" by kind words. None at this time pleased him more than those written by Archibald MacLeish. "Archie," as he signed himself, wrote: "Songs for a late lark indeed—none sings sweeter. There is a thrush in the pines below the little stone house where I work who sings in the forenoon briefly and again with the coming on of dusk but it is when the dusk is truly there that he breaks my heart. How wise of you—what unerring wisdom—to put the last poems first. And what a delight to find in them new tones, new beginnings. What I love in Yeats is the old man's youth. You join him in my gratitude. Bless you—bless you."

During the many long hours which Father spent sitting alone under the trees he tried, he said, in the words of Emerson, to "contract his firmament to the compass of a tent." One friend came upon him, to find him making disastrous noises on the little recorder he was trying to teach himself to play. When she thought that perhaps—in the words of Gilbert—she could make out "something that faintly resembled an air" she was nonetheless obliged to ask him what it was, to be cheerfully told that it was Beethoven's Ninth Symphony! He set forth his struggles with the instrument in four lines:

Why blow my heart out on this poor recorder
Striving to master every flat and sharp,
When soon across the inexorable border
I may be taking lessons on the harp?

The reason that Father had recourse to his little recorder was that he had had to face the cruelest possible blow that could have fallen on him when, at eighty-eight years old, he almost completely lost the use of his eyes.

I shall not rehearse other ills of the flesh that beset him, in Job-like succession, during the last years. On one dramatic occasion his friends of the Tavern Club proved themselves blood brothers in very deed when twenty-five transfusions were made possible by the supply given out of their own veins, bringing him back, at the eleventh hour, from the shore he had so closely skirted before. This masculine solidarity of affection was enriched by the blood of one generous and loving young woman friend—May Sarton. Father told her afterward that he hoped his future work would profit by his knowledge that he now possessed the blood of a true poet in his veins. But it was two days after a cataract operation, at first pronounced a success by the surgeon, that suddenly all sight in one eye disappeared, caused apparently by the bursting of a tiny blood vessel in the head. It was clear that the risk could never be run of operating on the second eye. After a visit to the oculist, soon after leaving the hospital, he wrote me, "My seeing (left) eye has, with the new lens, only 1/3 of normal vision. Add zero to this, and divide by two and arithmetic seems to fix my total vision at 1/6 of normal." In the knowledge that that sixth must inevitably someday be obscured behind an advancing cataract, "It's a race between the cataract and me," Father realistically observed from time to time. I spent the afternoon in his hospital room the day the blow fell, when he was as near to being crushed as I had ever seen him. He did not break down, nor curse, nor evince the slightest fear, but—for him—was simply touchingly subdued. He sat with his elbow on the arm of his chair, his hand across his forehead, shading his eyes, as he turned over the possibility—which seemed to him that day more like a probability—that he might lose his sight entirely. He knew in any case that he would never be able to read again. I never found the strength and sweetness of his character more moving. Father without reading, Father without books was—unthinkable! Again the wonderful quality of *willingness* showed itself in him. The blow had fallen. There were no histrionics or attitudinizing or recrimination. He simply accepted it.

If in his meeting of Mother's death the dimension of depth had been added to a nature which had, up to then, perhaps been merely large and wide, now, in the stalwart yet quiet acceptance of this last blow, it seemed to his friends that somehow Father had touched a fourth dimension: he was more of a man than he had ever been. Certainly his friends rallied to him with a new tenderness: from Billy James in Cambridge ("and you seem to behave as if nothing had happened to your blessed eyesight") to Cousin Alice in Spain ("by an incomprehensible and logical mercy of heaven your bearing things bravely does help me. Nobody who mentions you to me but speaks of your silent courage. It puts me to shame.") Father himself, quite simply and disarmingly, always brushed away any citations of himself as "wonderful" or "an example" by saying, "I don't deserve any credit. I think I have a very fortunate *temperament* which I have inherited from my mother."

The inner core of a complex nature is hard enough to guess at but, on looking back at Father, I wonder whether such a clear nature does not present an almost more baffling problem. There seems no inner quirk, no outer excrescence of this man to which one can catch hold, which might give under assault or pressure, to reveal mysteries behind. Father himself, in his extreme old age, used to say, "On looking back over my life I am afraid that I have lacked *passion.*" It was true that the lack was there—and it was a large one—just as there were others. He lacked the gift for—as he did any interest in—abstract philosophical thought. Ralph Barton Perry, although his devoted friend, maintained his powers of incisive judgment when he found that an article of Father's which he had sent him "as it stands seems to me to have a certain flatness." Ellery Sedgwick was as much the acute editor as the friend of long standing who wrote to Father about his autobiography *A Venture in Remembrance,* published in 1941, "I like it and think others who take only a little cayenne on their oysters will like it too. . . . It's a good book and one that will make nice people nicer." The palate of his friend Bliss Perry must have craved a little more cayenne when he returned some verses Father sent *him* for advice (Father was always asking some friend's advice!), telling him, in substance, he would have done better with the same idea in prose. Father took the criticism with such affability that Professor Perry addressed his next letter to "St. Mark," 16 Louisburg Square, which was delivered, to the amusement of both friends, to the Angelican convent across the Square, St. Margaret's.

If some of his more brilliant friends missed an element in Father, it is teasing to play with the thought that he fulfilled, all the same, something of the Zen concept of "realization." "The man who has attained realization . . . may be compared with a wheel whose centre of rotation coincides with the geometrical centre. . . . The man in whom the need of the Absolute is intense . . . is touchy, and this constant excitation corresponds with the permanent activity of his subconscious emotive state and of his irritability. Whereas the man who has little craving for the Absolute is calm." If Father did not blaze across the horizon of contemporary thought like his friend Jack Chapman, he warmed many lives which touched his. Thoreau perhaps was thinking of such a makeup when he said, "I do not value a man's uprightness and benevolence, which are, as it were, his stem and leaves. . . . I want the flower and fruit of a man; that some fragrance be wafted over from him to me, and some ripeness flavor our intercourse. His goodness must not be a partial and transitory act, but a constant superfluity, which costs him nothing and of which he is unconscious. . . . We should impart our courage, and not our despair, our health and ease, and not our disease, and take care that this does not spread contagion." One indication of his unconscious effect on another life was made manifest when a younger woman friend wrote to him, after the tragic death of her young son—whom, incidentally, Father had never even met—and

of whose death he had not heard, saying in essence, "I am writing
to you because I simply like to think of you, dear Mr. Howe." If, on
occasion, he seemed sometimes lacking in "sympathy," at least what
he did give was neither cloying nor debilitating; strong in himself,
there was strength to support others.

> God appears and God is Light
> To those poor souls who dwell in Night;
> But does a Human Form display
> To those who dwell in realms of Day.

Father never ceased to dwell in Blake's realms of Day; the Human
Form had always been his greatest joy and consolation, so now
there was consolation for others in his own broad humanity.

Recalling Dr. Henry Murray's observation as a psychologist
that "the most important thing about a man who stammers is his
stammer," I feel that somewhere, somehow some inner "explanation" of Father has slipped through my fingers. Explicable or not,
it became apparent toward the end that—no matter what its
original causes—his stammer somehow had come to serve a hidden
psychological purpose. It is the fashion to denigrate any "good"
man. Psychiatry has made us painfully aware that every man has
aggressions, hostilities, frustrations. Certainly Father was no exception, but I wonder if, instead of being wreaked on others, they
had not all been siphoned off into the outlet of his stammer. In his
Commentaires Blaise de Montluc tells of Henry II, "a fiery Gascon
famous for his choler," who, in his defense of Siena against the
forces of Charles the Fifth, "astonished men by the patience and
finesse with which, through those long months of famine and peril,
he had steadied the Sienese to resist. These words are put in Henry's
mouth: "I told the King that I had gone off one Saturday to the
market, and in sight of everybody bought a bag, and put a little cord
to tie its mouth, together with a faggot, taking and shouldering them
all in the public view; and when I reached my room, I asked for
fire to kindle the faggot, then took the bag and stuffed into it all my
ambition, all my avarice, my sensuality, my gluttony, my indolence,
my partiality, my envy and my eccentricities . . . then I tightly

tied the mouth of the bag with the cord, so that nothing should get out, and thrust it all in the fire. And thus I found myself clear of everything that could impede me in all I had to do for the service of His Majesty.'' Perhaps Father's stammer served him in the same way!

The sunlight in which I recapture the very fragrance of Father's flower and fruit comes back to me as pouring in through the tall windows of Louisburg Square after breakfast. In his morning newspaper only headlines waver toward him through a huge magnifying glass. Quincy retains one happy memory which shows him Father peering eagerly through the heavy glass which shakes in his hand, as he makes out the listing of Quincy Howe, Jr., his only grandson, as graduating from Harvard, *cum laude.* This moment came as a happy ending to a rather stormy journey, which had included the grandson's abrupt leaving of Harvard, minus degree, several years before. In the midst of a good deal of adult head-wagging and tongue-clicking the young man instinctively turned to ''Grandpa Howe'' who, to the grandson's surprise, was not as disgusted as everyone else appeared to be— in fact, gave him a reassuring sense of being believed in. To have lived to witness the metamorphosis of the same young man—now with a wonderful young wife and a career of scholarship opening up before him—brought to the old man yet another gratifying justification by faith.

More important than his newspaper in the hour after breakfast was his morning mail. If the weather was mild he might even sit outdoors on the top one of the front steps. A few lines from a verse, ''Thanksgiving in May—Louisburg Square,'' reflect his mood.

> Here in the Mayday morning sun
> Trees in the Square tip-toeing into green, I offer thanks,
> First for my ninetieth spring, and then for friends.

So situated he could hail not only the postman in person, but other passers-by with all the friendliness of the village life which still miraculously pertained on Beacon Hill. ''Good morning, Mr. Howe!'' was called out to him cheerily by old and young, male and female. Indoors—the room enlivened with flowers, more than

likely from the garden or greenhouse of the devoted Cummingses
and other friends—clutching with eagerness at his letters, as a
lava flow of ashes spilled out of the pipe he put down beside
him, with risk to books and papers in its vicinity, peering through
a magnifying glass, he would enjoy the sense that ties with family
and friends still held, even at a distance. Robbie Chase wrote
from the solitude of his life in Florida: "I have counted more than
you may realize on getting a letter from you, but I must not make
undue demands on you I'm sure. . . . I do nothing but paint from
8 A.M. to 5. . . . Everything goes well here—all is green, flowers
bright and blooming, warm sun (when it does not rain), fine and
wonderful skies, birds singing—what Boston would call summer.
. . . Dear Mark, let me know if my letters are too frequent."
Cousin Alice wrote from her exile in Spain:

> I wonder if you too experience this curious sliding backward
> of time? Dreams, reveries, remembrances, emphasis, they move
> backward each month through appreciable intervals. I have
> gone further back than my European life—and in those be-
> wildered few moments of first waking I am earlier now than
> even college and university life—back in my early Quincy
> childhood with my grandmother. The palimpsest of our
> memories fades in orderly fashion but there is a simultaneous
> flickering of the present which hides that order and sometimes
> shuts out everything else. Both of us must know too well that
> early morning waking to consciousness of pain, even before
> we have the pain localized.

Uncle Wallis was still near enough, and strong enough, to be able
to bless Father with an occasional call. It seemed quite natural to
the two brothers to express gratitude for their reunion by receiving
Holy Communion together at the hands of the young rector of St.
Michael's, who had driven Uncle Wallis up from Bristol. One friend
has told me of Father's being moved to tears as he told her, a devout
Catholic, what these occasions meant to him—and then writing next
day to apologize for being so moved. But for the most part Uncle
Wallis could figure only as a correspondent. He wrote, "The days
are pretty long, and the weeks and months astonishingly short."

Even before I married when I moved up the Hill into my own quarters Father was lucky enough to find two friends, successively, to share the Louisburg Square apartment with him. The first was the painter Ives Gammell, already a congenial Tavern Club comrade, though many years Father's junior, with the added "bond" of Rhode Island roots. The next—also a Taverner—Arthur Stanwood Pier, author of books for boys, one-time master at St. Paul's School; in his case the special "bond" was the memory of the shared experience as colleagues in the old days of the *Youth's Companion*. Each of these two friends, during his time with Father, in that same postbreakfast morning sunshine, served as a sort of animated social reporter. As each was in much demand at Boston dinner tables, Father avidly absorbed the news along with his morning mail.

Quite as eagerly as letters from friends Father awaited the arrival of cumbersome packages, whose white lettering on the outside testified that they were the property of the Library of Congress in Washington, containing TALKING BOOKS FOR THE BLIND. As he fumbled with the stubborn straps that bound them, he would say, "Blessed be the Welfare State."

But though he himself had stood fast for so many years, the forest began to thin around him. Less and less was he able to turn to old friends for solace and companionship. Aunt Katy was ever faithful, but there were other terrible gaps. No more letters from Robbie Chase. None from Cousin Alice. Allston Burr had gone home from lunch at the Tavern Club, sat down in his chair, and never rose out of it. Charlie Cummings suffered long and cruelly before he was released. Mrs. Cummings followed a few years later. Arthur Hill had gone—and Copeland. Father wrote me: "Bliss Perry and Fred Allen [editor of *Harper's Magazine*] too! Who was it in the Bible who exclaimed 'I only am left'? Bliss was two or three years my senior and one must take such losses as in the course of nature. It is not so easy with the death of younger friends."

It was the amazing number of Father's younger and new friends—and his interest in still making new ones—which kept him going. Van Wyck Brooks had written him, "I really believe that

Bill [Slater] Brown is now a converted Bostonian because of your propinquity and your goodness to him. . . . You must know that he thinks the world of you." There was also the Silent Traveler in Boston of whom Brooks wrote, "Thank you for being so kind to Chiang Yee, who can surely learn more from you than from anyone else he is likely to meet." A young sailor from the West Coast, hitherto unknown to Father, had rung the doorbell of Louisburg Square during the war. He wrote afterward:

MY DEAR MR. HOWE, SIR:

My journey to Boston has been made more pleasant with the kindness you have shown a stranger at your door. For while I have valued your writings and felt I knew you through them, "I was a stranger and ye took me in." Yours has been a great trust in preserving the spirit of those former days, and you may have the word of one, however ill-suited I may be to say it, that you have done a grand and noble monument in your writings.

The friendship ripened through many more letters. From Kobe, Japan:

Our friendship is the embodiment of all my reading in poetry and biography, you have brought them all to life. Except for correspondence I may never have known that all the honest worthwhile things existed outside of the covers of a book. I shall always hold your letters through all the days ahead as a lasting inspiration to continue my searchings and longings. Please know this, that outside of all the multitude of good your life and your work have imparted to others, here is one who feels it closer, needed it greater and is more grateful than all the others. I take the flame of enthusiasm for life from you to know its warmth inside my heart always.

Felix Frankfurter wrote him in his great old age:

MY DEAR MARK,

What would I not give to have been present the other day when you went to the piano and led your children and grandchildren in "Youth's the Season Made for Joy." I share your sentiment, interpreting it, as you do, that "Youth" is not a chronological but an appreciative term!

Father left his own testament of unblemished innocence in these lines:

> Now, thieving Time, take what you must—
>   Quickness to hear, to move, to see;
> While dust is drawing near to dust
>   Such diminutions need must be.
>
> Yet leave, O leave exempt from plunder
> My curiosity, my wonder!

20

---◆---

THE OLD MEN

IT IS WORTHY OF RECORD that Father's friends did not all live in Boston; indeed many of them were not Bostonian at all. Among the visits he made away from home during his late eighties there were several to my husband and me in New York. There, with the Century Club as his base of operations, he was to embark on some new friendships. His new friends were old gentlemen like himself. Though the obvious bond that united them was that of mere survival, there were intangible links of association which were to grow stronger and more valued. Father's contact with these friends, as the years passed, had perforce to be through letters. To disclaim the charge of "filio-pietistic zeal" (the phrase used by Father about Great-great-aunt Susan Quincy) I must introduce—and, whenever possible, in their own words—a few of these other exemplars of the happy breed to which Father belonged, more cosmopolitan than local.

One friend, whom he had come to know already in New York as a fellow member of the American Academy of Arts and Letters, was the architect William Adams Delano—"Billy" Delano, though almost wholly through correspondence, a dearly treasured addition to Father's life. "My own dear Mark," "Beloved Mark," and "I shall write again soon to the man I love best—my beloved Mark" tripped sweetly from the pen of this old gentleman whose artist's sensitive touch was as apparent in his human relationships as in the

many testimonials to his professional gifts still extant. Billy
Delano's panache floated bravely in spite of increasing deafness and
almost incapacitating lameness. In writing to Father he made light
of his own dauntlessness when he echoed an old Negro who, on being
asked how he had managed to live to a hundred had answered, "I
jes' breathe."

"With you, my chief food is the sustaining diet of friendship,"
wrote this new-old friend, and "How charmingly you touch on old
age! I know it has its compensations when it can be lived well and
without too many aches and pains but I think I prefer sixty to
ninety and I feel sure you do too, in spite of your cheerful spirit."
Touching, involuntary expressions escape him only occasionally.
"Don't you find getting into and out of a bath-tub a somewhat
perilous adventure?" One quality the friends had in common was
their interest in the world around them and the quenchless desire
to participate in its doings. Billy Delano wrote:

> Your letter about Ruth Draper's nomination for the In-
> stitute has my full approval, and I am writing Marc Connelly
> to see if he would be willing to put her up, because he is more
> associated in my mind with Ruth's art than anyone else.
> Whether as President of the Institute, he will feel able to do
> so, I can't say. If he feels he cannot do so, I have suggested
> that he name the proper one. Let's hope for success, but there
> are a lot of stodgy members who cannot see beyond their own
> art. . . .
> A doctor in Harley Street and his wife gave a dinner. She
> bought some cultivated mushrooms for a savory. They looked
> to her to be rather suspicious so she gave a few to her little
> dog, who ate them with avidity and no ill effect but, when
> dinner was almost over, the butler whispered in her ear, "Your
> little dog is dead." Her husband acted promptly, took all his
> guests to his surgery and stomach-pumped the lot. When the
> guests were gone, the hostess said to the butler, "I would like
> to see my little dog before you bury him." The butler replied,
> "I don't think you would, Madam, 'e's a 'orrid sight. Both
> wheels ran over 'im."

You are still getting around on your hind legs, I learned
from Archie MacLeish, and enjoying the delights of the
Tavern Club. Archie told me last Saturday that he had been
asked to preach at the old church in Providence—his text, Job.
I'd like to be present, for Job and I have suffered much in
common the past quarter century—but home is best for

Your young friend,
WD

———————◆———————

> The Law is the true embodiment
> Of everything that's excellent.
> It has no kind of fault or flaw,
> And I, my Lords, embody the Law.

Anyone who ever heard the spirited singing of those lines by
Judge Learned Hand knew that the Judge would have been quite
as happy to embody the Stage. But what facet of human expression,
as of human lovableness—as well as of everything else that's
excellent—did he *not* embody? He had been merely an agreeable
acquaintance when he and Father served together on the Board
of the Harvard Overseers. As early as 1937 he had written from
New York to "Dear Mark Howe" about his Chapman biography:

> What a man was there! I have been reading the book aloud
> to my wife amid a continuous ululation: "And to think that
> we had the chance to know that man better—perhaps as a real
> friend—and we didn't take it! What were we doing? How was
> it conceivable we should have thought anything else as im-
> portant?" We are crestfallen, ashamed, that we should have
> passed so close to such a star and never recognized it; not
> really recognized it.
>
> This is to thank you personally. I can accept not being any
> longer an overseer—How about writing it Overseer?—without
> tears, except that it cuts me off from those I can't expect to
> see otherwise. You are one of those I really miss. Don't you
> ever come to dance around this Witches' Cauldron? Why not?
> And if in that diabolic mood, why not let me know? I can't
> add much to the rites of hell, but I'll do my best and I should
> like it.

But when the two men found themselves well into old age they entered another phase. Father was to use for the most part the Judge's nickname "B" (derived from his first-though-unused name, Billings) and the Judge, in turn, came to sign his letters to Father "Affectionately." My husband and I were blessed in counting Judge Hand a friend on our own account. How could it be possible to forget his talking of the horrors of old age which he—so much more Hamlet-like in his complex nature than Father!—so dreaded. Moved himself, there was a catch in his beautiful voice, bringing tears to the listener's eyes as well as his own, as he reverted to Stevenson's *Child's Garden of Verses*:

> Must we to bed, indeed? Well then,
> Let us arise and go like men,
> And face with an undaunted tread
> The long, black passage up to bed.

Once again, in the 1950's, Father, along with the rest of the Harvard family, was going through the pangs of uncertainty and concern as to who would be chosen successor to James Bryant Conant as President of the University. He enjoyed one little titbit which came to him through a dear friend who carried the bee in his Boston bonnet that it was the Earl of Oxford (not Bacon, as Grandpa Quincy's bee had told him) who had written Shakespeare's plays. For him there was only one burning issue on which a President of Harvard must stand firm, and it concerned neither academic standards, national politics, nor religion—and that stand was Oxford vs. Shakespeare. When Nathan Pusey's name was announced as the next President of Harvard, this friend burst out, "I knew it! I *knew* they'd choose someone on the wrong side!" Judge Hand, writing in June, 1953, was not so despairing:

> If I can ever get around to writing those damn Holmes Lectures I shall be in Cambridge next winter. And if January is to be the induction day of Pusey I shall go in anyway. . . .
> Yes, Pusey looks like a good "prospect"; but I am not so Hell-bent on the "humanities" as I have given you to understand. An education to me means convincing the man to be

educated, (they all have "ees" now, so why not "educatee"?)
that we have progressed so far as we have, by trial and error,
and that that is as true in finding out what we are in our own
dim selves, as it is about the neutrons, the positrons, the elec-
trons, and any other G.D. "trons" they may dig up to satisfy
their formulas.

And I do value the "humanities" because they are on the
whole the best way to find out about ourselves—grace the psy-
choanalysts and others of that solemn humorless fraternity.

Speaking of a subject close to his heart he wrote:

I am now struggling with painful unproductiveness to say
whatever there is in me to say about that institution, in which
we so much pride ourselves—judicial supremacy. Jim Thayer
brought up my generation to treat it with much reserve; but
the times have changed and the arising, and just risen, crop
is apparently disposed to think it the Palladium of our Freedom. If I could, I should like to nail the Thayerian colors to
my mast and go down while the band played, "That ain't no
way to carry on."

The way he *did* carry on is implicit in his own words:

I know, I know, we are both in the sere and yellow leaf; and
it can't be very long before we flutter—I hope gently—to the
ground. Still, in some ways it is the best part: I don't mean
because of its joys, but because, whether from self-deception
or not, and whether weak or not; the accidentals and inci-
dentals do drop away a bit. The mystery still is there, quite as
impenetrable as before; but somehow the outlines are to me
a trifle less misty.

When Mark wrote an unsigned review of Hand's *Collected
Papers* in the London *Times* Literary Supplement in 1955, the
Judge wrote to Father:

I am more gratified than you can realize to find that the
review which you enclosed was written by Mark. Am I free to
tell him that I know he wrote it, and how much it pleased me?

The anonymity of these articles, as I understand it, is an important part of the review, and it may be that while it is permissible for you to supply the news to me, it is not so for me to tell Mark that you have told me. I am amused at the kind way of these youngsters to us for our Nineteenth Century vintage. The idea is cropping up all about by the best and smartest of them that there is after all something in the nature of that "Natural Law" in which we, reared under the tradition of Mill, Holmes, and the like, don't believe. I am not sure that they do not also believe that the judges are in some sense a vehicle for the preservation of this kind of law, without which we should go to pot. As you probably know, fifty years ago we thought that we had laid that ghost, and our great and sacred prophet was Holmes. From what I can take in now, this is regarded as a much too easy simplification, and so we learn. . . .

Thank you for thinking of me. I often think of you.

Affectionately yours,
L.H.

Father shared his affection for and interest in Judge Hand with their mutual friend Charles C. Burlingham, better known to a wide circle as "C.C.B." Father was fully aware of the difference in intellectual attainment, as well as in matters of religious belief, between himself and the disciple of the Great Dissenter when he wrote to Mr. Burlingham a year later:

"Your remarks about B. Hand's speech in the *Bulletin* made me realize that your reading of it went farther beneath the surface than mine. I was impressed with the verbal skill and beauty of it all even as I am by the writings of O.W.H. Jr. Of course, there is lacking, both in master and in pupil, any element of recognition of something beyond human mastery. I suppose this lack in the great Justice accounts for the strong disfavor in which he is held by the Roman Church."

C.C.B. wrote to Father in November, 1957: "Learned Hand with his wife Fanny had mid-day dinner with me. . . . I told him that I had said to several knowing people that I thought his reputa-

tion was higher in the Court of Appeals than it would be in the
Supreme Court because in the S.C. he would have to consider what
eight other men thought. He made no response. Ask your son Mark
what he thinks. I asked B. another question. Who was to write his
life? No answer."

———◆———

This interchange between Father and C.C.B. is only one spark in
the steady flame of dialogue expressing the community of tastes
and interests that burned bright and warm between the two old
gentlemen for some eight years, until C.C.B.'s death at the age of
a hundred and one. At that time an editorial in the New York
Herald Tribune expressed the opinion that to call him "the first
citizen of New York became a commonplace during his lifetime.
Fiorello LaGuardia was among those who used the phrase and the
Association of the Bar of the City of New York inscribed it on a
medal in 1953. . . . Nobody is really sure who first applied it
[since the time when he] was serving his home town as long ago as
1902, when he was president of the Board of Education." His triumphant surmounting of both total deafness and total blindness
made Father's handicaps—just as his hundred and one years
dwarfed Father's paltry ninety-six—seem like nothing. I still rub
my ears as I hear the words Mr. Burlingham said to me the last time
I saw him. He waved his hearing aid toward the corner of the room
in which I was not, flashed his seraphic smile in the opposite direction from where I stood, as he waved his hand about, reaching for
mine. When finally they met, in mid-air, he wrung mine warmly as
he said, "Your father is my ideal." *He* certainly was Father's!
Actually I can't remember how they happened on each other so
late in life, but how the very thought of C.C.B. inspirited Father's
last years! Humanists, liberals, and believing Christians, they
agreed on almost every subject of importance to them.

"You are very dear to me," he wrote to Father, "and I'm thankful that I came to know you, but I grieve that I did not know you
twenty-five years earlier." When C.C.B. wrote, "A blessed Xmas
and a Happy New Year is my wish for you and I thank God for
His gift of your friendship. I wish I had the wings of the morning

that I might fly to you," he was answered, "In my ninety-fifth year
I find it a little harder to keep up with my correspondence than it
was in my ninety-fourth. . . . Please do not forget that I look upon
each one of your letters as a boon." In that same month of October,
1958, Father wrote:

> I do think—I take it, with you—that a sweeping Demo-
> cratic victory in the country at large would be the best thing
> that can happen to all of us. I keep telling myself that it is
> quite unimportant for me to know how all the problems are
> to be solved. Only, with quite a different world waiting for me
> just round the corner, I cannot help speculating on the future.
> This present world has on the whole been very good to me, and
> I shall part with it with a mixture of regret and gratitude. In
> your letters I find many expressions of the staff and buckler
> which I much need.

When the rector of St. George's Episcopal Church in New York,
of which Mr. Burlingham had been head vestryman for years, was
asked by him, "Do you know the most interesting half hour I am
looking forward to?" even his own rector was not prepared for the
vigorous answer, "The first half hour after death." To Father
C.C.B. wrote: "My favorite hymn is Saint Bernard's, 'The world is
very evil; The times are waxing late' and I think my favorite passage from the Psalms is 'Watchman, tell us of the night?' but I
don't expect any answer to the query."

There was a superabundance of "bonds" on a terrestrial plane.
It is impossible to guess which was the strongest of the many that
tied the two friends. Harvard College would be a good place to
begin.

C.C.B.: I had an amusing letter, believe that or not, from Roger
Lee, in which he said that he had tried to convince Conant that
Harvard was big enough to give sixteen honorary degrees and not
limit itself to twelve. Conant's reply was that there were not
enough superlative adjectives for more than twelve. . . . At the
Harvard dinner J.B.C. asked Gus Hand for any suggestion he might
have for the next member of the Corporation . . . so I have been
cudgelling my brains. I know the kind of man needed, but I don't

know who can fill the bill. We need a young man like you or Harry
James, who is interested in the A's and L's as well as the Sc's. I
wonder why they take to M.D.'s and how the M.D.'s come to have so
much power, *ob* rather than *con*structive. . . .

A burning subject under discussion was James Conant's successor as President of Harvard. Father, writing of his friend
"Charley" Wyzanski—"one of the very best human objects on my
horizon [who] seems almost ideally qualified for the presidency of
Harvard," found himself "not alone in regretting that the implications that go with the name of Charley Wyzanski would probably debar him."

The bond of the loss of eyesight—in C.C.B.'s case so much worse
than in Father's—helped to cement the friendship. At Father's
side there was the incessantly revolving turntable of his record
player. "I am glad," he wrote, "that your thoughts are turning
towards the *Talking Books*. All I had to do in applying for the
phonograph and the records was to request them from the Massachusetts State Division for the Blind, and ask my oculist to testify
to my eligibility for this service. You will be amazed, I think, at the
range of books for which you can ask."

Through the days, weeks, years Father listened to the reading of
much of the Bible, Jane Austen, Dickens, several novels of Henry
James and Willa Cather, Shakespeare, Conrad, and countless others,
both ancient and modern. Of the "mammoth tale" *Crime and
Punishment* he wrote to C.C.B. that it had "moved me more than
anything else for a long time. I had never expected to find myself
occasionally in tears beside a phonograph instrument." There was
irritation too. "What has afflicted me most of all is that in one novel
by George Meredith and another by Dickens the reader pronounced
Papa, *Popper.*" In trying to urge Mr. Burlingham to follow his
lead he admitted that *"The Philosophy of William James* swims in
many places above my comprehension . . . and now there is no
chance to turn back a page or two to see just what James has been
talking about." But he "enjoyed most two volumes of William
James's essays and Benét's *John Brown's Body.*" The intensity of
his pleasure in the latter he expressed in verses published in the

Saturday Review of Literature, beginning "He that hath ears to hear, now let him see!" His enthusiasm spilled over into the pages of the *Atlantic* in an article, "Books That Talk to the Blind."

(To dissipate the impression that Father lived on an exclusively highbrow diet I must record that he wrote me that just after having listened to the *Philosophy of William James* he turned to Groucho Marx in "You Bet Your Life" on the radio, and hoped I was listening to him at the same moment.)

M.H.: Korea and the U.N.! What can one do but lament and hope—and cease blaming everything on the Truman Administration? . . . Have you ever read Logan Pearsall Smith's "Milton and his Modern Critics"? My listening to that book on "Talking Books for the Blind" gives me to understand why you feel as you do about T. S. Eliot, whose criticism of Milton is devastated by L.P.S. in a way that gives complete satisfaction. For Eliot as a poet, I am afraid I was born too soon. I do find beautiful images scattered through his pages, but most of the time I have no idea what he is talking about. And Pindar—no, I have not seen or handled (as you did) Milton's copy. Perhaps you read him when you were in college. A few years later, as a senior at Lehigh, I parsed but never read him, and, with all the rest of my Greek, he has faded away as completely as that Old Soldier, MacArthur, will some day. May not the eight Republican senators who have just rushed to his defense be speeding that day? I take a Massachusetts pride in the fact that Saltonstall and Lodge did not swell the number to ten.

C.C.B.: I wonder whether any hope of peace has sprung in your breast inspired by the letter of Malik—rather an evil name is it not? I don't think the Republicans got much out of the MacArthur investigation. I had begun to think that Truman might return to Independence, Mo., but it looks now as if he were going to repeat his campaign of '48 and re-elect himself. The only hope of the R's is General Ike and who knows whether he would run.

The thoughts of the old men were inevitably brushed with intimations of another dimension.

M.H.: We, in the upper brackets of age, can hardly help turning our thoughts towards the indefinite future. For my own part, I am content not to be too dogmatic about it, but to get myself into readiness to accept the common lot, whatever that may be. I comfort myself by reflecting that, although certain things are hard to prove beyond what you lawyers call a reasonable doubt, they are just about equally hard to disprove. [I am] reading proof for a new book of mine which I regard rather confidently as my last. Yesterday, I had the strange experience of reading a chapter of it (on Sarah Orne Jewett) for a tape-recording, preliminary to an FM broadcast on Sunday evening. This is quite a pioneering enterprise for one who has been so tongue-tied as I have for the greater part of my life.

C.C.B.: Speaking of Prayer, Mrs. Howard Robbins, widow of the Dean, told me a story of a little boy who asked his mother why the minister prayed before he preached. She said she thought it was because he hoped God would help him preach a good sermon. "Why doesn't he then?"

Speaking of little boys reminds me that the other day one of the lawyers for Hiss called and told me that he had been to the prison named after your square, I should think, in Pennsylvania, three times. Hiss he found was liked by all the prisoners and by the keepers. He is assigned to the stores. His wife and his son, ten years old, visit him and the little boy wrote him a postcard, at the end saying, "Give my love to all the others."

The application to the District Judge who tried the Hiss case is being made today. They assert that the typewriter may have been rigged by Chambers. I do not think they have much chance. He will be eligible for parole in November but our maniacal witch hunters even *after* election may frighten the Pardon Board. . . . How extraordinary that you knew Robert Taber and saw him in Bristol. . . .

Herbert Satterlee and I arranged for the divorce of Robert Taber and Julia Marlowe, selecting as the site Stowe, Vermont, where Bob's Mother lived. Everything was to go through very smoothly, but Julia's maid Mary—I don't know whether you are familiar with maids of actresses—went to Vermont to testify. She thought she'd do a good job by making a strong case for Julia—so she lied it through well, saying that Robert beat his wife, threw plates at her, etc. etc. All this came out the next day in the New York papers and R. was terribly humiliated.

M.H.: I wonder if you have run across an anecdote of Gertrude Stein which I encountered in an English review of a couple of books about her? The story is that almost with her last breath she asked of those standing about her, "What is the Answer?" No reply was forthcoming. Whereupon with her very last breath she said, "That being the case, what is the Question?" Just what may be the ultimate significance of her words I do not pretend to know, but somehow I believe they will stick in my memory.

In the light of the two good nominations at Chicago the following foolish lines represent my present state of mind:

> I like Ike,
> But should not feel Badlai
> To settle for Adlai—
> Perhaps even Gladlai!

. . . By November I shall be serious enough—certainly to vote for Herter rather than Dever as Governor, and probably for Cabot Lodge against young Kennedy for the Senate—in spite of believing that President and Senate should be of the same party. The trouble with Independency is that it cannot always maintain Consistency.

C.C.B.: The Fates and Seven Sisters visited me about four weeks ago and left me with a new cataract on my better eye. I am to consult my oculist this afternoon, for he thinks he had better operate on my worse eye, and I remember your experience with some apprehension.

Did you read of one of the reporters on Ike's train, who, bored by his speeches declared "We have just reached the 38th platitude."

Nixon seems to me quite helpful to the Ds, for his impropriety may weaken the attacks on Democratic corruption.

What a pity Ike and Adlai could not both say exactly what they think and let the voters make their own choice.

I think I told you of a witticism of Arthur Hadley's, which I have just learned is recorded in a book on Yale's latest 50 years by Pierson, A.T.H. was speaking of the Academic mind and man and he said "They say what they think—without thinking what they say."

M.H.: Does it not appear to you that the public is beginning to recover from its emotional jag over Nixon's apologia—and also that the substantial intellectual quality of Stevenson's speeches, enlivened by his really humorous interjections, are making a valuable contribution to his campaign? After some wavering in its early stages, I find myself leaning strongly in the Stevenson direction. . . . Don't be discouraged by my experience with the cataract operation. The trouble that cost the vision of my right eye came about after a successful operation, and the doctors assured me that the occurrence was what the guardians against libel call "purely coincidental." . . .

C.C.B.: I am glad to learn that your hemorrhage was coincidental. I go to the hospital Monday. I have been disciplining myself to see whether I could lie in bed as motionless as a mummy. . . .

You don't have to turn to Fan for news of me. I am ready to give it direct although it is very poor stuff. My operation was a failure. Two small arteries gave way. My M.D. regrets that I am recovering so slowly and with so much pain in the eye, the forehead and the temple. But the worst thing was that I slipped in the bathroom and bruised my bones, ribs, et al. I am grateful for your sympathy of one who knows. Anything you write or may write will be a joy to me. . . . An English friend has just written me that two women were looking at a plaque in Deal or Walmar which read thus:

JULIUS CAESAR LANDED HERE 2,000 YEARS AGO.

One woman said: "Who is Julius Caesar?"
The other said, "I don't know. I think he was the father of Jesus Christ." My English friend thought that such ignorance would not be found in the United States.

M.H.: My pro-Stevenson letter to the *Boston Herald* has called forth the conflicting responses one has learned to expect. One irate

reader, mistaking me for my son Mark, urges me to read
"McCarthyism" by Senator McCarthy, and declares in conclusion
"There is only one McCarthy but Professors are a dime a dozen."

After another visit to New York in 1953 Father wrote to *C.C.B.*:
"I shall remember many of the things you said—and still more what
you were, your head unbowed. . . . If ever I discover traces of
self-pity on my own horizon I shall know to what friend I should
turn my thoughts to dissipate them all." He ended the letter by
quoting Emerson, "Nor knowest thou what argument Thy life to
thy neighbor's creed has lent." At the Harvard Commencement of
that year, "The future President [Pusey] was received with enthusiasm, and did well to confine himself to brief and modest
remarks. John Marquand enlivened the afternoon with genuine wit
that marked his speech. Does he quite qualify in your mind as a
Harvard Doctor of Letters? I must confess to a few doubts of
my own."

The creative fancy of that Harvard Doctor of Letters never conceived in fiction an interchange more characteristic of the breed
under our microscope.

C.C.B.: I was shown a little piece you wrote for the Saturday
Review of L. about Emerson—quite delightful. I think I saw him
only twice when I went to college in '76. Boston was saving the Old
South and I went in to Town to hear for 25¢ Dr. Holmes, Julia
Ward Howe, Wendell Phillips, and I seem to think Emerson. But
maybe I didn't. But in '79 at our φBK lunch Dr. Holmes presided
and Mr. Emerson came in late. That was before the odious habit of
jumping up every time to honor each and every speaker, but when
he came in the whole body rose to do him honor; and of course I
remember his ineffable smile. He was accompanied by his daughter,
Ellen, who had a paper bag from which she extracted peppermints
from time to time for Papa. . . . Is it true that he had two iron
dogs by his front door?

M.H.: I wish I could tell you whether there were iron dogs by
Emerson's front door. I consulted both Cameron Forbes and Bliss

Perry about the story of the falling pear. Cam dismissed it because
he said nobody ever called his Aunt Ellen "Nellie." Bliss told me
that nobody knew less about Emerson than his grandsons, Cameron
and Edward Forbes.

The joint concern for the minutiae of the past was often expressed
against a background of present pain and anxiety. C.C.B. wrote at
just the same time: "Will you be so kind as to tell me what you
would do if you were in my shoes or bed-slippers. My left eye is
ripe for an operation, but I suffered so much pain for so many
weeks in my right eye that I don't like to risk something similar in
my left eye. My oculist says the pain was from the hemorrhage and
not from the operation. He says I must decide. Help me Cassius."
The friends kept each other smiling. Father wrote: "You speak of
Sperry's *Jesus Then and Now*. Have you ever heard that his irrever-
ent wife, aunt of my son Mark's wife, renamed the book *Jesus Now
and Then?*" and "A psychiatrist's patient had gone to Florida for
a vacation, and after a few days there telegraphed to his doctor in
New York: 'Having a wonderful time. Why?'"
The disillusionment that many liberals of their stamp were to
know touched both old gentlemen. Father ruefully admitted that
the "Independents," of whom he considered himself one, who voted
for Stevenson had better have called themselves "Romantics."
C.C.B. exclaimed, "Poor Eisenhower! A friend of mine told me he
had an hour alone with him and he said that the President said to
him, 'You know I did not wish to run a second time, but I did and
we won, and now none of the Republican party pay any attention
to me.' As I have so often said, what a pity he ran at all," and, "At
last Allen Dulles and Bundy and Matthews have stiffened Ike. I
have almost come to the conclusion that he is not only green in politics but stupid."
When Father's dearly loved Ethel (Mrs. John) Moors electrified
her friends by marrying after eighty—Canon Charles Raven, of
Cambridge, England, Father passed on Uncle Wallis's offstage comment, from Bristol, "Quoth the Raven, Ever Moors." Only a little
over a month later Father wrote, "Many of us in these parts have

been deeply saddened by the death of her whom we had not yet
learned to call anything but Ethel Moors. . . . She leaves a broad
gap in many lives.''

Father wrote from Uncle Wallis's house in Bristol: ''Tradition is
in the air—both clerical and lay. When I take a little walk on Hope
Street, I cross four streets, named Union, Constitution, Church, and
State! You will see that I am relatively safe.'' By contrast C.C.B.'s
touch with the future draws tears: ''In the six years since I have
been blind I don't think I have complained. But yesterday I received a wonderful photograph of one of my little families—my
grandson Michael's three boys, the oldest eleven and a baby girl one
year old and I could only feel it, and how I wished I could see it.''

Bristol, however, was becoming a place of present sadness even
more than of happy associations of the past. The once apparently
indestructible Aunt Molly lay dying one summer when Father
stayed nearby. Then he went to visit his ''cruelly bereaved'' Wallis.
Uncle Arthur went next. Father, lamenting that he had not been
able to see more in recent years of the older brother he had never
ceased to look up to, confessed to C.C.B., ''I shall miss him sorely.''

In unison, however, the two friends mourned from their hearts
''Old Fan''—as C.C.B. referred to Miss Fanny Curtis in writing to
Father. When, during her lifetime, in the *Survey* of February,
1952, C.C.B. had written a tribute to her he sent it on to Father
saying, ''As Old Fan is essentially a modest woman I don't think
she will show [it to] you.'' Father felt that ''she must be taking it
I think very much like the award of an honorary degree.'' Indeed
it was C.C.B.'s Park Avenue icebox which had contained the famous
half sandwich which had nourished her on her return journey in
the day coach to Boston. Perhaps it was on this very visit that her
host had written: ''Good old Fan arrived at my house at 8:30 last
night. She had been feeding the Chinese or considering how to feed
them. She told me this morning that her sisters asked why she
came over here just to see me (I am not sure about the just) and I
told her I wondered too, but she brings me all the *dope* of
Boston . . .'' Father had written him: ''I am summoned this afternoon to 28 Mt. Vernon Street for the eighty-fifth birthday of your

old friend and mine and am arming myself with a few roses to cele-
brate the event." Now, in August, 1957, he wrote:

> You were quite right last night in feeling that I should want
> to share at once in your sorrow. But for your telephone call,
> in this time of a blackout of Boston newspapers, I should not
> have known till this morning of the death of that really great
> person Fanny Curtis. After breakfast today came a telephone
> call from Charley Hopkinson telling me about it. An hour or
> two later—of all amazing things—I received a note from
> Fanny herself, written only last Saturday [C.C.B. was to
> receive another, written on the same day]. . . . I know well
> what her loss means to you. It removes from my circle a dear
> and much admired friend I have known for many, many
> years. . . . I shall not forget your great kindness in calling
> me up—and speaking in the voice of one much younger than
> myself.

Another "bond" shared by the friends was their appreciation of
and gratitude to the wonderful Irishwomen who tended them.
When C.C.B. had a terrible fall in his bathroom he wrote Father
quoting someone who had said, "Nora is a living saint."

In January, 1958, Father wrote C.C.B.:

> The special occasion for Helen's visit was the serious, and
> I fear imminently fatal illness of my housekeeper Mary Law-
> rence, who for 26 years has befriended and supported me in
> every way. My feeling about her was expressed several years
> ago in four lines which I give you now:

> > The world is so full of a number of people
> > I could do very well at the top of a steeple.
> > But a world I should view with unceasing abhorrence
> > Would be one rolling on without Mary Lawrence.

> That is the world which I am now forced to face: . . . with
> real affection for the friend I must lose—a friend who leaves
> with me as perfect an example of a Christian life as I can
> conceive.

Father's children echoed his feelings; our loss in her death was irreparable. To us, too, the memory of Mary Lawrence will always remain that of a beloved member of our family circle.

With C.C.B. Father shared another friend whose letters also swelled his morning mail. The massive total correspondence—like the friendship itself—between Father and Henry Dwight Sedgwick, however, covered a period of some fifty years. Superficially "Harry" Sedgwick offered a complete contrast to his brother Ellery: there were the patrician chiseled features, the clear-eyed, smooth-shaven, scrubbed look of some Englishmen as opposed to the swarthy, heavily mustachioed, Ellery, with his emphatically un-Anglo-Saxon, faintly threatrical appearance of a kindhearted brigand. There were, as well, the subjects of Harry Sedgwick's books, removed from the main stream of American life (*In Praise of Gentlemen, Memories of an Epicurean, Pro Vita Monastica*) in contrast to the writings published by the editor whose prime concern was for the broadest possible human experience, recounted with the marketable magic of the common touch. But Harry Sedgwick, too, was buoyant with the same Sedgwick élan. Father wrote to C.C.B., "Leonard Bacon wrote me the other day about Harry Sedgwick who called on me, 'Did you ever see anybody enjoy anything so much as he enjoys everything?'" Sedgwick's *Short History of Spain* remains a classic of its kind, and his *Marcus Aurelius* won praise from his friend and severest critic, John Jay Chapman. Chapman wrote to Father in March, 1923, "I will endeavor to be liberal minded; I enjoyed H.D.S.'s Marcus Aurelius, but hate most of his *other* books—'mouton enragé' as somebody said of Condorcet. I'll promise to try to see if there is not some point of view from which the new cloister book is tolerable. (I must mortify my flesh *somehow*.)" And a month later he wrote:

Well, well! I'm almost ashamed to accept that big handsome book of H.D.S.'s because its contents are so unsympathetic to me. The manner is artificial,—extremely well done and yet *done,* posed—a pancake—and the substance is the essence of

all that is most commonplace—not a spark of observation anywhere—dead stuff—the kind of thing a clever chap might get
off while he was living a life of sin—and just the kind of talk
that the public will gulp down—I don't see how the same man
can write this way and write as Harry does in the Marcus
Aurelius book—almost in the same day or hour. I greatly
doubt whether Harry does really meditate. He knows the
book-theory too well—and also I don't find any mention of
our new thought saints—or of the Cloud of Unknowing man
both of whom hit me more than many of Harry's "solitaires."
Query is *solitude* the key note to the thing anyway—Isn't
solitude a result—After certain experiences it becomes a necessity—e.g. wasn't solitude really forced on all those old Johns
and Johnnies—whom Sedgwick so fatiguingly drags before
us—telling us over again what we know so well about
them. . . . The thing that makes me think that H.D.S. is not
the true article is his adopting Loyola's method of contempla-
tion—which is a rotten method. This is as if he should talk
about Michaelangelo or Botticelli and plaster away in the
style of his uncle Charles Norton—and end by handing us a
chromo. Mark my words, Henry D. Sedgwick is either a very
bad man or else a feeble minded person. And yet he wrote a
good book,—straight-forward—natural, impassioned and *most
interesting* about Aurelius. Perhaps it is merely that in this
last book he fancies himself—in the M.A. book he was simply
interested and excited.

It is possible that Harry Sedgwick's greatest gift was most
happily expressed through his letters. There is honey in each of
them. I have tasted from only a few of the later years, starting
when he is an old gentleman, living as a widower of more than
thirty years' standing, with a son in California: "I advise everyone to have 8 grandchildren per stirpes—barring raining days."
. . . "Dear Marc Antonio pio. How is it among the snows, slush,
ice, puddles, galoshes, scarves, ulsters, gloves and glittering gadgets
of winter? Have you stalactites and stalagmites in your parlor?"
He, too, had his thoughts on running Harvard College. ". . . with
Conant's indifference, or rather purposeful snubs to the Humanities,

there is little hope. D—— his eyes, can't he see that the 'soul' of
man is the most interesting thing in the universe and not hydrogen
passing into helium. . . . Do tell me how your good eye is behaving. I know how well you bear it. I should curse and swear and take
cyanide of potassium. Be sure, you have my deepest sympathy all
the time. It is with you as with that noble and luckless Athenian
general, Nicias (I think) defeated and captured by the Syracusan
on Alcibiades' venturesome attack on Syracuse. Thucydides describes him and says, 'Of all men, this should not have happened
to him.' God bless you old chap." . . . "Do you remember that
Leonard Bacon came to lunch here with you about a year ago? He
came yesterday—we missed you sadly. We drank to your health. . . .
He said, 'Mark Howe is one of those very few men into whose
mind an unkind thought never enters.' Rather nice? I heartily
assented."

From Dedham, Massachusetts, staying with another son, he
wrote: "In the first place Nobody—how delightful Nobody is you
extroverts will never know."

Then suddenly the world of the *nones*—as C.C.B. calls his
nineties—is electrified by the news Harry has to tell:

> Dear Mark—!!!! I am going to marry Gabriella Ladd—
> for 3 years I have told her that marriage at my age was un-
> thinkable. We have written for 3 years a letter to each other
> every day, over 1,000 letters each. She believed that marriage
> with her was impossible. Her friends, with whom I joined,
> urged her to marry a young man and at least, if too old for a
> child [she was in her forties], secure a companion for her
> later years. Just before Bermuda she wrote that an ideal sort
> of young man wished to marry her and she was hesitating!!
> A Volcano! I realized how deep in love I was . . .
> . . . Nothing dispute—an absolutely private wedding at
> 7:30 A.M. and off to Murray Bay for our honeymoon. I can't
> say when I can see you. A Whirlwind of Excitement—I am
> in the Seventh Heaven, doors open wide, Archangels singing—
> just like a boy of 20. I had not imagined it possible.
> Take good care of yourself Dear Boy.
>
> HDS

Father wrote to C.C.B.: "I have told him that I wanted to exclaim *credo quia impossibile,* but that he has made me change *impossibile* to *invincibile.* In point of age Harry stands about midway between us. From my lower level marriage at 92 has an astonishing aspect. How is it with you looking down from 94?" A few months later he reported on "Harry and his bride. . . . The aged bridegroom walking with two canes, and with iron braces on his feet, was otherwise the embodiment of gaiety and youth."

C.C.B. shared with Father a letter from the happy bridegroom, written several months later from the Sedgwick Mansion in Stockbridge:

DEAR CHARLEY,

I had welcome news of you the other day. Ruth Draper dropped in and said she had seen you lately, that you are very well and delightful as ever, but that you were like Homer and Beethoven, sightless. Oh I am so sorry for you—what I should do without sight, I hate to imagine—first of all, I should not see Gabriella, nor the *Memorabilia* of the late Mr. Xenophon, with which I daily wrestle, nor "Married or Single," a novel of 1857 by, in our family, revered Aunt Kitty, C. M. Sedgwick, which I have always been afraid to read, supposing I should find it unreadable, but to my nephewistical gratification, I find quite readable, with its picture of New York society before the Civil War. By the way are the Southern States going to secede again? And must I march? How about you?

. . . My two surviving classmates Sam Williston, very ill I fear, and Godfrey Cabot [known to his nephews and nieces as "Uncle God" he, too, lived to over a hundred], and I play Going to Jerusalem. I have a passionate desire to outlive Cabot for he is a teetotaler—a disgrace to the Class—and if he outlives us all he will say that is the reason. He is our Class Secretary and at our last dinner—5 of us—forgot to order any fizz—I stood up on a chair and roared "Champagne," one of us whom I had never seen, said "I am so glad you came."

Take good care of yourself, dear Boy and squeeze the flask of life to the dregs.

Father, for his part, was to enjoy the enrichment to his morning
mail that came in buoyant effusions from his happy friend whose
very pen, from which they so trippingly flowed, seemed conscious
of being wielded by a "man of letters." He writes to Father, too,
from Stockbridge:

> Gabriella is full of resources, and has provided me with two
> little tanks, miniature, of fishes with *Verdura* and snails, like
> an undersea Jap palace, which are peopled (fished?) by three
> couples. Nym and Bardolph, striped, raffish, truculent, "Base
> is the slave that pays!" kind of fish, a little less than an inch
> in length. A second couple, copper colored, silent, dignified,
> aristocratic, Castor and Pollux. The third and fascinating,
> smaller still with great violet rayed eyes that size you up in
> a most embarrassing manner, and the rest of their *bodies*
> (you could put all 6 in the bowl of a soup spoon) red, blue
> and yellow, somewhat like Harlequin and Columbine, Jock and
> "blue-eyed Jenny" (You drink *Geneseo beer,* I hope and
> learn its merits from the T.V.).
>
> Apart from the fishes—oh I almost forgot Morgan le Fay
> who occupies the second tank by himself, for he is ferocious
> or Hitlerish and will allow no rival—like Addison—near his
> throne. He is 10–20 times as big as the others and has most
> magnificent fins that he wraps himself in, like Night in The
> Magic Flute, and—mirabile dictu—when you put a looking
> glass beside him, and he sees his double, he swells, waves his
> fins like metaphors, or whatever those things are that carry in-
> formation from ship to ship. He becomes a deep threatening
> red color, and his anger permeates the room. Gabriella is very
> romantic and compassionate, and wishes to get him a mate,
> but the happy union would only last through Morgan le Fay's
> dinnertime. We named him as I thought after Marjory's—
> Ellery's wife—ancestress, but I was mistaken. Marjory's
> ancestress was La Fée Mallusine of whom I know nothing.
> Those tanks will look very well in an iglo.
>
> I hope you are doing well. I hear that Charley Burlingham
> is quite blind, but he can walk half a mile. You have all my
> sympathy on your deprivation. Is it a comfort to share it with

Homer and Milton? Take good care of your valuable self. . . .
P.S. . . . I am nearly able to appreciate what I have in
Gabriella. Put the wealth of the Indies in the other scale, and
it would mount to heaven.
P.P.S. Damn the snow

From the same Shangri-la he writes:

Stockbridge is full of possibilities, I mean in resources
against ennui. The chief of them is cook-hunting. This with
us is the open season and like the antlered monarch of the
waste our last cook made one brave bound on Saturday and
left the diggings cookless. Diana has taken her bow and arrows
from their peg, i.e., Gabriella is telephoning, advertising,
hallooing and on the point of going off to beat up the New
York cupboards when just now praise to God the employment
bureau in Pittsfield or somewhere says two does—probably
does not—are to be sighted. . . . Mary Malone and Sary
Molloy, God speed her. When Gabriella has to go to New York,
I might as well stay in bed, for when she goes, all my faculties
go on strike—I am left bargaining with the right leg, I apply
for an injunction against my left leg. I write to the Times
protesting against the unseemly behavior of my right hand, my
liver, my lungs, my adrenal glands. But all this is horribly
egotistical.

We listen to the T.V., sometimes very good, little plays full
of morality, we play Picquet and I have at last discovered
what should have been my métier, my talents as a card-
sharker. We read—Van Wyck's Helen Keller, a most wonderful woman, ranking with Einstein and Churchill, as the human
tops of this period. *The Nun's Story*—very pathetic—O Religion, what crimes have been committed in thy name! I also
am reading Clive Bell's *Old Friends*—he is very clever but
too impish for me, and I don't like his crowd, Lytton Strachey
and Roger Fry etc. Also I, having "done" the Gospels (I
like St. Peter very much) and the Acts, I start to tackle
Crito—but as I cannot master any rudimentary grammar, it
goes like frozen molasses. Still anything of Greece has a magic
touch.

His bride had been away for a few days:

. . . and to my pleasure I find 8 volumes on biographies, anecdotes of Eighteenth Century Printers (evidently they called Publishers printers at that time) and I have enjoyed— I love the 18th Century and really belong there—skipping and skimming from life to life. Did you know that Lady Mary Wortley Montague's son was a sport of the very first quality. I thought fiction writers exaggerated the type, a sort of swash-buckling des Grieux. . . . Well I must slink back into their pleasant Eighteenth Century. Come and see me there. Soyez sage . . .

It is spring, and Harry writes:

Charley Burlingham complains that he has only known you for ten years. What the Deuce! Dozens of *Dekades* lie before you. . . . Gabriella and I are released by a tremendous effort of will from bondage to Henry James. I shut Volume I *Wings of the Dove* yesterday—and, oh how salutary, how very salu-tary as Matthew—do the Marks and Matthews hobnob?—as Matthew Arnold used to say, to pick up Bleak House to read, to understand the language, to perceive a plot, and to laugh at one page and cry at another. . . . As to poesy I try to read a little Odyssey and an ode of Horace every day. I admire Homer more and more. How wonderful after 3,000 years to feel so close to classical antiquity.

But beneath the blitheness of the bridegroom and between the lines of the "literary" persiflage there hides a very old man:

. . . One of my troubles is that I cannot remember the day of the month from the time I pick up the morning paper to look and the picking up of my pen. Of other troubles at the age of 95 I have singularly few, and a great sweet-smelling nose-gay of Blessings, for which I strive to be duly thankful . . . one of my keenest regrets at 95 is that I never told so many people how much I liked and admired them. Some queer cowardice of spirit showing itself in shyness, diffidence, etc. And how one longs to see old friends and acquaintances and say "I didn't mean to be reticent, cold, fishlike, it was all diffidence on my part that prevented me from telling you how much I liked you." "Too late! too late! Thou shalt not enter now . . ."

Well, Merry Xmas, old fellow, and good luck. . . .

The New Year finds him undaunted:

> Stay me with raisin cakes
> Comfort me with apples—

Happy New Year! In my long life I have seen many revolutionary changes—slavery abolished—femine emancipation and *domination* (the very word *Domina* proclaims it)—the extinction of a servant class—and the subordination of the British Empire to the Eagle. But there is a greater revolution than those right at your elbow—let me commend it. Gabriella the Bountiful—Beautiful—comme vous voulez—has given me a half pound of flaming heather, brush, or its ancestors, from Africa, with little queer, yellow eyes that see farther into the world's mysteries than Solomon, or Merlin or Ben Franklin, and animated by an unceasing desire to learn what kind of a universe, he, Florizel, and I live in. He will soon know much more than I do. Oh, if I could make such sweet music as his purr, *sublimi side a feriam vertice.* Try it. The world will be a brave new place, all gayety, youth, joy, glee, laughter, etc.

Gabriella and I send you our love and best wishes for 1957— who would have believed that a horrid little squalling baby in East 24th Street N.Y. in 1861 would still be squawling in 1957.

> So runs my dream, and what am I
> An infant, crying in the night,
> An infant crying for the light,
> And with no language but a cry.

This kitten is named Florizel. Get a little lady cat and call her Perdita.

Don't take the trouble to write, dear Boy—Here's Howe! God bless him—and drink the toast silently.

In August, still from Stockbridge, he remembers his friend in the city:

> Gabriella and I hate to look beyond our little horizon, and sad you are alone in your city flat. I hope you are really air-conditioned and comfortable. Somebody gave me a sad idea of your perambulation. I have a good deal of limitation but I have eyes to see, and if I have to plan a course N.E. by E., for instance, I can accomplish it better than the Capt. of the Doria. Start via sofa, S.S.W. by table, etc. W. by N.
>
> Our main diversion is hunting—hunting lost dogs. For over two days our little Springer bitch disappeared—temptation rabbits I suppose—she finally was caught by some kind dog lover and taken to a Vet. where she had been a frequent lodger, but was not recognized as her appearance was most disreputable, tag gone, eyes closed, mud-clotted, etc., and she is the well certified scion of British champion Springers.
>
> By the way can you advise some good biographer or Memoir? Gabriella and I prefer fact to fiction. We have just finished the *Initials*—do you remember it? last read by me 80 years ago.
>
> Take good care of yourself, dear old fellow—Old age is like another country of alien speech and manners, and one has to get used to it.

Closer to hand was Harry's brother, Ellery Sedgwick. His occasional appearance in the flesh was an event in Louisburg Square. Father wrote to C.C.B.: "To my surprise and pleasure I have just had a call from Ellery Sedgwick on his way to the Fanny Curtis service. He was just as full as ever of energy and spirit, and after climbing my high front steps had come into the room without a wheel chair."

The same Sedgwick exuberance was recognizable in the teasing of Father—addressed as "Dear Ancient"—when George Howe's book about Bristol was published. "I have waited some sixty years to see you against your honest background. Always you have given out that behind you were rank on rank of Bishops and missionaries, and now George Howe has let the cat out of the bag and behold all the DeWolfs and Mark Antonies were Blackbirders and pirates and merry fellows generally, thus accounting for your affability and gregariousness.''

C.C.B. shared Father's feeling for and about Ellery Sedgwick. He wrote:

> Here is a characteristic letter from Ellery S. What a weird creature he is. Don't you think he writes very well? He is the only Sedgwick I have known who has got rich and he made his fortune in the old-fashioned way of watching pennies. F.G.C. will tell you a few stories or at least one of his penuriousness. Abe Flexner once told me of a talk he had with the primal J. D. Rockefeller.
>
> A.F. Mr. R., how does a great man get rich, how does he make money?
>
> JDR. I'll tell you a story. When I was young I used to lunch with my partners on Lower Broadway and we always talked of our plans and projects. We made it a rule never to undertake anything new unless we were unanimous.
>
> A.F. You must have lost some good opportunities.
>
> JDR. Yes we did, but we didn't lose any money.

In connection with a drive for funds on the part of Harvard College C.C.B. returned to the same theme:

> Ellery Sedgwick says it is preposterous for us to try to raise so much money, but you know he is pretty tight fisted. I remember Fanny Curtis telling how she and her sisters bought his refrigerator when he moved to Beverly. They sent an expressman to get it and he found it was fastened to the floor so a carpenter had to be called in. A bill for $4.00 was sent to Ellery which he passed on to the Curtises.

For his part, Father wrote:

> Yes, indeed, I agree heartily with you. Ellery is an admirable writer, whether in the printed or merely written word. He is a gifted, and also a strange bi-natured creature, altogether at his best in demonstrations of friendship. My rela-

tions with him go back more than fifty years, about six of which were spent in the *Atlantic* office in close association with him—a period of many advantages to me, but with some puzzling memories. We still count each other the best of friends.

Ellery Sedgwick himself was aware of another manifestation of a double nature when he wrote to Father:

> It is astonishing and comfortable to find how many of us, including me, are living. I myself am creating another legend outdoing Tithonus. For though the lower half of me is quite dead, the doctor says that the upper half is about 45 years of age. . . .
> Get well, keep well, drink hearty!

The response to misfortune befalling an old friend was instantaneous. After the loss of the sight of Father's eye Ellery Sedgwick wrote him an effusive letter, dwelling on the fact that his well-stocked mind would stand him in good stead. Then the façade cracked: "But, oh Mark, I am distressful at any sorrow of yours. Old age is very compassionate. . . . It remembers all that the full employment of one's powers once meant." Then suddenly Father found an unexpected deposit in his bank account which he could not explain. He asked the bank about it, and received an evasive reply that roused his suspicions. He pressed further, until he found that a deposit had been made by someone who wished to remain anonymous. Father, refusing to accept this state of affairs, finally wrested from them the name of—Ellery Sedgwick. When Father challenged him, the answer was characteristic: "Think of what help and pleasure you have given me these sixty-five years."

Mr. Sedgwick wrote in November, 1957:

> I think of you much lying there in the dark with your faithful Mary about. And your waking thoughts like mine are on the President and this terrible misfortune which has come on the nation. I have just been reading a Life of St. Benedict. He lived in a time so much like ours with Attila and Generic on the loose to balance our Knutships. His answer was Monte

Cassino and the Rule which set a standard for the Middle
Ages, while ours is to turn our faces to the wall and think of
other things.

Marjorie and I saw a remarkable film yesterday of Disney's
—no silly story but the life of the forest with every animal in
the hierarchy preying upon the creature just below him in
power of beak and claw—life not free a single instant from the
danger of instant death. The trembling rabbit not safe even in
its hole. Then comes a terrific forest fire. Every creature races
for safety to the water and in desperate common terror, the
rabbit leaps on the back of the wild cat, swimming to safety.
It was all like a parable of NATO. Every nation seeking its
own safety and when danger comes rushing to its fellows for
help.

When it became clear that Father, after Mary's death, could not
continue to live in Louisburg Square, Mark's wife—to her everlasting glory—said, "I love him, and I open my heart and house
to him." Such a gesture, in a "help" less age, was accepted by
Father and Ellery Sedgwick's generation as far more of a matter
of course than it could ever be to those who had to bear the burden
and heat of putting the gesture into practice. Mr. Sedgwick wrote:

Your faithful Miss Worcester writes me of your Hegira. I
was fearful of a nursing home and your comfortable and
natural address comes as a great relief. Family life is the
single comfort of old age and now that is all about you. "I
have not much to tell you. I see a few friends, some delightful
ones like the remarkable Miss Edith Hamilton who came to
tea the other day. At 91 she came to us because I could not
climb the steep ascent to heaven which is her stairs. She has
just accepted an invitation from the Bollingen Corporation
[sic] to construct a one volume Plato out of the best texts,
pencilling out the great Jowett's conversations as a little rough
and colloquial, and subtitling her own. Quite an adventure for
an old lady. I had been absorbed in the wonderful parallel—
Prometheus Bound and Job and what bound them together.
Nothing was of her own translation of the former. Here you

have almost identical situations and the diametrically opposing attitudes of the pagan and pre-Christian heroes oblige the reader to take his choice between defiance and humility.

Oddly enough my kind and learned preceptor Prof. Pfeiffer tells me that in the Book of Job the Hebrew does not rise to the heights of its version of Isaiah I and II and that the laxness of the text enabled King James' men to rise to the heights of their own genius.

Another visitor . . . we have taken a great fancy to is Sen. Flanders, a Yankee of the purest type. He told us this pleasant story of Sen. Goldwater with whom I am sympathetic because of his distrust of Reuther. Goldwater's Mother was a Christian and he was hurt at being blackballed for country club membership on account of his race. His plea I thought admirable. "But perhaps they would let me play nine holes."

Last night for the first time in a year I went out, enticed by a lecture on Zen Buddhism in which I have long been interested. I sat in the front row and heard not one word. So goodbye to lectures.

It was to be good-by to more than lectures for the old men. One more faraway voice in its ninetieth year rings as a last echo before the breed, as it touched Father's life, is lost to sight:

I Tatti Settignano Florence, Italy

DEAR HOWE,   Jan. 17. 54

I have received and perused and delighted in the book on illustrations of "Who Lived Here." As I have no indication of who sent it, I presume it was you. If not, it gives me the opportunity to tell you how much I admire your writing and all that you have done to keep dear old Boston alive, Boston— and some of its most interesting Bostonians. In a deep sense even Jack Chapman was one. Altho I have lived away so long, and came there when I was ten and left at twenty-two, the word "home" means "Boston" still.

Hold the fort.

Sincerely yours,
BERNARD BERENSON

Settignano, Florence, Febr. 3. 55

DEAR MARK HOWE,

Your Xmas card reached me only yesterday. The verses are as beautiful, as free from rhetoric, and as simple, legible and instantly comprehensible as if they came out of the Greek Anthology. I am saving them up in Matthiessen's "Oxford Book of American Verse."

I need not tell you how they come home. For years I have felt what you express so well, and so accurately.

How I envy you living in Louisburg Square the quintessence of the Boston I still love so much—despite 67 years of expatriation.

Every good wish for the rest of the trip.

Yours

BERNARD BERENSON

DEAR HOWE,

It is a pleasure to hear from you and of course I lap up your flattering words about my *Italian Painters*.

I wish I could see a paper I wrote on Matthew Arnold in '87. I worshipped him but I do not recall writing about him. I admired and sucked in his criticism and his verses exposed me and some others in my youth. They still haunt my memory and speak on of old.

What would I not give to see you! I fear our traveling days are over. Mine are except for toddles to Venice, to Rome, to Naples, to Palermo, etc.

Live and enjoy it.

Yours

BERNARD BERENSON

The rest of the trip for the old men was to last only a very little longer. They were yielding, one by one, their place on the American scene to their successors: "the new men" were taking over.

21

THE PASSENGER

I sit alone in a way station
On a long railroad,
Waiting for the train that will pick me up.
Nobody can tell me
Precisely when it will arrive,
Or precisely where it will put me down.
The print on my one-way ticket should help,
But it is a little blurred,
And, even if I could read
The name of my destination—
Never visited before—
It would not tell what may be found there.

Fond as I have always been of travel,
The thought of this my last journey—
For such I somehow know it to be—
Brings little comfort.
Yet let me not forget that all my journeys
Have won a crown of happiness
Through coming home.
How will it be this time?
I hear a nearing bell and whistle—
The train will soon be here,
And I shall join its passengers,
Cumbered, myself, with little luggage,
But bearing in one hand

[429]

A parcel packed with thankfulness,
And in the other a parcel of surmise
Not unmixed with hope.

Father's verses described his situation in essence, if not in actual fact. He is sitting in his own two comfortable rooms, with his white uniformed nurse in attendance, on the second story of Mark's house in Cambridge. Mary Lawrence—at fifty—has died of cancer. He has been sitting in this room for three years, since he recovered from pneumonia at ninety-three, thanks (?) to the modern sulfa drugs. Louisburg Square is only a memory. So are most of his friends—C.C.B., Billy Delano, Harry Sedgwick among them. Aunt Katy, so lame that she is almost bent double to drag herself up the stairs, still drives herself out from Boston, serenely sailing through red lights, for an occasional call. Uncle Wallis comes too on rare occasions, all the way from Bristol. Like two good little boys Cal and Wal eat their lunch together, then they take a nap in separate rooms, before parting. As they sweetly kiss each other the same refrain is repeated, "Good-by, old man," "Good-by, old boy." Then (Mark must tell him) Uncle Wallis is gone too. "Pshaw!" is his first impulsive exclamation before he reiterates in every letter he writes, "I have not only lost a beloved brother. I have lost the best man I know." With the removal of Uncle Wallis and so many others from the dimension of time, gone too are so many reflecting mirrors of different selves he has left behind. Only the heart of the old man—the "poor forked creature"—with all his outer props stripped from him "the thing itself"—remains the same.

He says often, "I have every alleviation." Aware of the unpayable debt of gratitude owed to his daughter-in-law he repeats, "I am blessed—" adding, as if for his own ears alone, "Blessed—and bored." I tell him he is like a passenger (this time not on a train) sitting on the promenade deck, unaware of the toil going on in the boiler room below the waterline. There his daughter-in-law valiantly deals with nurses' schedules, trays for them and the Man Who Came to Dinner—as he calls himself—and a brood of teen-age daughters. This Man is still himself and does not lose sleep with morbid self-questioning, saying merely, "I've stayed too long—

but what else can I do?'' He belongs to the generation which automatically housed the old—with those invaluable fifth wheels to the coach in the shape of a Cousin Lizzie or a Cousin Virginia. Because he is a man he is barely aware that the coach no longer has even four wheels. A nine-year-old Helen pops in for an occasional chat, in company with her heart-melting bloodhound, Sorrow. The future is knocking at the door of the house. Its first daughter, beautiful in a cloud of Alice in Wonderland hair, black stockings, and a black turtleneck sweater, is bride to a blue-jeaned abstract painter. Quincy's son has brought home a young wife from postwar Germany. So the vacuum fills: modern art, Europe, and other races flow in to fill it. Grandpa genially welcomes them all. (Mark, whom more often than not Father calls Wal, will himself become ''Grandpa.'') A new golden-haired, blue-eyed Fanny— her Irish heritage granting her release from the prison of the New England temperament that held an earlier Fanny captive—brings her poetry to show her grandfather. The future is here.

It is here on the television screen, with Quincy moderating the last of the Kennedy-Nixon debates. Father is wakened out of his sleep, and insists on getting out of bed, to listen. His wits are still sufficiently about him to insist on casting an absentee ballot for Jack Kennedy, hoping somehow to make amends for the vote he failed to cast for Grover Cleveland in 1888! (If Father was filled with hope and faith in the future, as exemplified in Kennedy, it is moving to recall that this young man paid tribute to the tradition of the past for which Father stood when he sent a telegram to Mark at Father's death—several weeks before his Inauguration.) Father still likes to talk politics with the friends who are kind enough to come to see him, though it is difficult for his old friends to make the long trek to Cambridge and the climb upstairs. There are wonderful Cambridge neighbors. His dear friend Charles Hopkinson lives nearby with a daughter, and comes in almost daily. Together they play the most innocent and gentle of games, grown out of Mr. Hopkinson's failing memory. ''I have just seen an old friend. What *is* his name? His father was a philosopher.'' ''Oh, so you've been seeing Billy James.'' ''I lunched with that

dear man—you know, he was Headmaster of a boys' school and
his brother was a professor." "Oh, so you've been with Lewis
Perry." And so on. To name the Roll of Honor—for so their
names stand to Father's daughter, who realizes full well that it is
so much easier *not* to go and see an old gentleman—there is Arthur
Schlesinger, *père,* Professor Fred Robinson, John Finley, Charles
Wyzanski, and Sam Morison who bothers to fit this obeisance to
age and friendship into a busy Cambridge day. Robert Frost has
not forgotten, and has climbed the stairs several times. Does he
think, as he climbs, I wonder, of his own austere lines on old age,

> No memory of having starred
> Atones for later disregard
> Or keeps the end from being hard.
> . . . Some have relied on what they knew.
> Others on being simply true.

Father has relied on the latter—on "being simply true." One
hesitates to breathe that four-letter word which of all others has
the most jarring sound in modern ears—g-o-o-d. Yet it is applicable.
Here sits a good man. But neither Oriental Dharmakaya, nor
Occidental Humanism, nor classical Virtue inspires the particular
feeling Father has called forth in his friends. They have been
attracted by a life led in the "Christian style." So much of its quality has been implicit that it surprises even Father's daughter to see
it written out, December 28, 1958—explicit in his own words—
written to his friend and minister, Ted Ferris.

The letter begins: "Your talk over the air last night made a
perfect conclusion of the Christmas Season for me. I have always
liked especially to think of what it means to live in a Christian
civilization, bringing with it many of the benefactions which we
take for granted, without realizing what it must mean to the
people of such a country as Russia which lives officially without any
such blessings." Apologizing for bothering so busy a man he goes
on to say: "If you ever find yourself in this corner of our region I
should greatly enjoy seeing [you] and receiving the Communion
again from you. I shall soon be entering the year in which—if I

live till near the end of August—I shall be celebrating my 95th birthday. I should like well to have the year begin with that symbol of my belonging to something far larger than any of my immediate surroundings, which I have enjoyed nearly all my life."

Father often tells me during this time that when he takes Communion at Ted Ferris's hands he is invariably moved to tears. Van Wyck Brooks wrote of him once, "For Mark Howe was a poet all the time." If he has not achieved it with his pen, he has achieved it in essence. There is a shimmer in the outward and visible sign of an inward and spiritual grace. If we have seen him as a river—not deep, perhaps, but clear and smoothly flowing, as innocent of cragged rocks and precipices as of treacherous quicksands—we are aware now that at its bottom there has been all along some glint which has attracted a variety of people to its margin. He has not been all things to all men; he has been one thing to all men. It is this noble metal which has given not only luster to the stream but strength and purpose as well. It knows not the alloy of dogma or doctrine. The vein is of gold, and its name is love.

On an outgoing tide our Passenger departs. "Do not go gentle into that good night," Dylan Thomas exhorted his father. I do not have to exhort mine. He goes into the night—as he has lived in the day—gentle.

John Rock, the Catholic doctor who has made such a courageous stand for the cause of Planned Parenthood, in writing of "dear splendid Mark" went on to say, "How unsparingly, and without apparent effort, he evidenced the grandeur of a good man; strong, yet gentle; kindly, yet critical; witty, yet harbless; cultured and idealistic with no chauvinism. We all loved him."

Judge Charles Wyzanski wrote:

> He lived such a wonderfully useful and interesting life,, and I hope so happy a one, that my first feeling was that this is man at his best. Oh, I am sure that he had his time of bitter disappointment. . . . But how much better than most he filled the other pan in the scales. He earned and received the love from so many of those by whom one would most want to

be loved. He raised the level of the community in which he lived. His perceptiveness of what was heroic, of what had charm and significance for civilization became the incentive for a better future.

Hollis Smith, the postmaster at Mt. Desert, Maine, wrote: "If men would only follow his creative example and contribute to the good of the world, we could worry much less about bomb shelters and mass destruction. I feel grateful for having known him, and grateful that he spent some time in this village that I am sure he loved."

The service at Trinity Church in Boston a few days later was characteristic of Father. He had, with his usual pellucid natural-ness, indicated that it was there he wished his funeral to be. We children—also, characteristic!—cringed, saying to ourselves, "With such an old man, all of whose contemporaries are dead, the church may be empty." On the contrary, it was full—not only with Proper Bostonians, but with a wide variety of people—musicians from the Orchestra, office workers, writers, students, teachers. I am sure that they were there not only because most of them had loved Father for his special qualities, but because they felt, even if half consciously, that they were saying good-by to the last of a breed that they knew had vanished from their city, as from the country as a whole.

Ted Ferris read the service with an emotion for his old friend that he could not keep out of his voice. Looking about at the all-Boston congregation who had come to pay their last homage and affection to one old gentleman who had lived among them for as long as any of them could remember, it was hard to realize that in this same church seventy-one years before a "friendless youth" had experienced his first Easter away from home, and had sent a letter to his mother describing the beauty of the service. Of the sermon, during which the rector spoke of those members of the parish who had died within the year, the young Mark Howe wrote that Dr. Brooks "declared, throwing his head back as he often does, that they had gone only 'as the quenched sunlight passes through the glass.' " But it was Dr. Ferris's voice today that was carrying the congregation with him:

> Lord, we thank thee for the life of Mark Howe; for what he said, what he wrote, what he sang, what he did, and above all for what he was. Grounded in the simplicities of the good life, he grew naturally and almost inevitably toward the sky. His body, mind, and spirit worked together for good to make something like music out of the assorted materials of life.
>
> He never thought of himself more highly than he ought to think, nor more lowly; he never lost interest in what was going on around him; nor did he ever cease to give pleasure to the people who came his way.
>
> He never asked too many questions, but rested more and more in a few ultimate answers and was willing to risk the rest.
>
> We who knew him felt that in knowing him we knew what a man is meant to be. Wherefore, as he now joins the larger fellowship of all faithful people we say, Glory be to thee, O Lord, and praised be Thy Name for ever and ever. Amen.

In the afternoon sunshine, flying back to New York—and the future—three days after my night flight in the other direction, I soared above the town of Quincy. In a corner of it, that morning, we had laid Father's ashes alongside of Mother's. The soil in which she had traced NO with her parasol—as he had traced YES on the bedrock of life itself—now contained them both.

> This quiet Dust was Gentlemen and Ladies
> And Lads and Girls—
> Was laughter and ability and sighing
> And Frocks and Curls
>
> This Passive Place a Summer's nimble mansion
> Where Bloom and Bees
> Fulfilled their Oriental Circuit
> Then ceased, like these.

NOTES

ASIDE FROM SLIGHT EMENDATIONS which do not belong in the body of the book these notes refer to (a) people not otherwise identified in the text or (b) those whose names may not be known to the general reader. The books referred to are others than those included in my list of sources.

Foreword: "Papa's Papers"

Page

xv. Van Wyck Brooks, *The Shadow of the Mountain*, New York, 1961.
xvi. The poet is Sydney Tremayne.
xvii. Alfred North Whitehead, *Immortality*, Chapter VIII, the Ingersoll Lecture delivered at the Harvard Divinity School, April 21, 1941.
xvii. Walter Lord, *The Good Years*, New York, 1960.
xvii. Henry James, *Notes of a Son and Brother*, New York, 1914.
xviii. John Glenn was quoted in the *New York Times*, February 24, 1962.

Chapter 1. Mark Howe of Boston

4. *The Atlantic*, April 1950.
5. Robert Lincoln O'Brien, edition of the *Boston Herald*, 1906–1928.
11. "The Sensation Captain" from the *Bab Ballads*.

Chapter 2. The Bristol Way

15. The family bishops were:
Benjamin Bosworth Smith, 1794–1884, first Bishop of Kentucky. Jackson Kemper, 1789–1870, Bishop of Missouri, Indiana, and Mississippi, first Bishop of Wisconsin. Frederic Dan Huntington, 1819–1904, first Bishop of Central New York. William Hobart Hare, 1838–1909, first missionary Bishop of South Dakota. M. A. DeWolfe Howe, 1808–1895, first Bishop of Central Pennsylvania.

Page

27. Ralph Barton Perry, 1876–1956, Professor of Philosophy at Harvard and biographer of William James, became one of Father's closest friends in the vicinity of Boston.

28. Marianne DeWolf married Captain Raymond Perry.

30. James Baldwin, *The Fire Next Time,* New York, 1963.

30. There is one, to me, unexpected connection between my Bishop grandfather and Nathaniel Hawthorne. The "Recollections of George W. Childs," the publisher of the *Philadelphia Public Ledger,* in *Lippincott's Magazine* for June 1889, tells of the state of nervous shock in which he found Hawthorne at the Continental Hotel, where he had been staying with his friend W. D. Ticknor, the publishing partner of James T. Fields, from Boston. Childs found Hawthorne pacing up and down the room, apparently dazed.

" 'Hawthorne,' I said, 'how are you? Where's Ticknor?' 'They've taken him away,' said he.

". . . Indeed I could make nothing out of it all . . . he seemed to me bewildered. I feared for his mind, and, going down to the office, asked the clerk, Mr. Duffy, what it all meant. He then staggered me with the information that Ticknor was dead—had died that morning. . . . Hawthorne lingered in Philadelphia with me for a few days, and then I placed him in the keeping of good Bishop Howe, a common friend, who accompanied him to Boston. There he passed the night with James T. Fields . . . shortly after he died at Plymouth, New Hampshire."

31. Ferris Greenslet tells the story of Levi Whitney in his *The Lowells and Their Seven Worlds,* Boston, 1946.

Chapter 3. *I Had Never Seen a Unitarian*

39. William James, *Varieties of Religious Experience,* New York, 1902.

40. Richard Clarke Cabot, 1868–1939, was a physician and professor of social ethics at Harvard.

42. M. A. DeWolfe Howe, "In Gratitude to 'Stubby Child,' " *College in a Yard,* edited by Brooks Atkinson, Cambridge, 1957.

45. Norman Hapgood, 1868–1937, writer and magazine editor.

45. Robert Herrick, 1868–1938, novelist, university professor.

45. H. Taylor Parker, 1867–1934, dramatic and music critic of the *Boston Evening Transcript.*

45. George Pierce Baker, 1866–1935, professor of drama, famous at Harvard for his course, "47 Workshop." He went to the Yale Drama Department, 1925.

49. Francis Boott, 1803–1904, musician and composer.

Page

Chapter 4. *Tragicomic and Triangular*

54. The late and immortal Bobby Clark sang of "Roger the Roué of Reading, Pa. . . . A gay bon vivant who knows his pommes de terre."

55. James Bradley Thayer, 1831–1902, lawyer and Professor at Harvard Law School.

55. Louis D. Brandeis, controversial Boston lawyer, appointed Justice of the Supreme Court of the U.S. in 1916.

Chapter 5. *The Little World of Boston Letters*

77. Charles Eugene Flandrau, 1828–1903, jurist, soldier, author, known particularly for his *Harvard Episodes*.

77. John Macy, 1877–1932, man of letters, editor.

79. Bertram Goodhue, 1869–1924, architect, partner of Ralph Adams Cram.

79. Margaretta Wade Deland, 1857–1945, author, known particularly for her *Old Chester Tales, The Awakening of Helena Richie*, etc.

84. As Miss Jewett's letter is not dated I cannot identify the book to which she refers.

Chapter 6. *We Were Neither Long-Tailed Nor Short*

108. The sculptor of the bust of Judge Frederick Pickering Cabot, in Symphony Hall, was Korczak Ziolkowski.

Chapter 7. *Callers*

122. Nietzsche's *Thus Spake Zarathustra,* Chapter XVlll, "Old and Young Women."

127. The lines are from Edmund Spenser's *The Faerie Queene,* Canto 9, Stanza 40.

129. The Parkman-Webster case was a cause célèbre not only at Harvard but nationally when, in 1849, John White Webster, Professor of Chemistry at the Harvard Medical School, murdered Dr. George Parkman.

134. Robert Homans, 1873–1934, Boston lawyer, partner of Arthur Hill.

134. Elihu Root, Jr., b. 1881, New York lawyer.

134. Thomas Barbour, 1884–1946, naturalist and Director of Harvard University Museum.

134. Roger Bigelow Merriman, 1876–1945, Professor of History, Master of Eliot House.

134. Julian Lowell Coolidge, 1873–1954, Professor of Mathematics, Master of Lowell House.

134. Allston Burr, 1866–1949, businessman and financier.

Page

134. Thomas Nelson Perkins, 1870–1937, lawyer, Fellow of the Harvard Corporation, U.S. member of the Reparations Committee.

140. Illustration of Howe family group, following page 140. Seated, left to right: Mrs. Herbert Howe, Herbert Howe, Bishop Howe, Mrs. Howe, Elizabeth Howe Allen; standing, left to right: Reginald Howe, Mrs. Reginald Howe, Wallis Howe, Mrs. Arthur Howe, Arthur Howe, Mark Howe, Frank Howe, Leighton Howe, George Pomeroy Allen.

Chapter 8. Presences

159. *The Shoulder: Rupture of the Supra Spinatus Tendon and Other Lesions in or about the Subacromial Bursa.* E. A. Codman, M.D., Boston, 1934. Copyright 1934 by E. A. Codman. Thomas Todd Company, Printers, Boston, Massachusetts.

The volume in the Boston Athenaeum was presented by Father. The remarks quoted in part are in his handwriting on the pages left blank for comments from the medical colleagues, for whom Dr. Codman intended the book.

159. Dr. Edward H. Bradford, 1848–1926, was Dean of the Harvard Medical School.

159. Dr. Frederic Augustus Washburn, 1869–1949.

163. Elizabeth Evans, widow of Glendower Evans, was a protégée of Judge and Mrs. Brandeis, and a friend of the William James family.

163. John Greenleaf Whittier's *The Friend's Burial*.

Chapter 9. All the Dear People

170. It was when Harold Laski, on a temporary appointment in political science at Harvard, expressed his sympathy with the strikers in the Boston Police Strike in 1919 that President Lowell spoke up.

171. Arthur Shurcliff, *A Man Walks the Earth, Near and Far in New England*. The Old Corner Book Store, Inc., Boston, 1951.

174. Presumably Arthur Theodore Lyman, 1832–1915.

174. Dr. Henry Pickering Bowditch, 1840–1911, physiologist and Dean of the Harvard Medical School.

174. Walter Lincoln Burrage, 1860–1935, surgeon and gynecologist.

177. Charles Allerton Coolidge, 1858–1936, architect, who, like a "court architect" to Harvard for many years, designed many of its buildings.

177. It is Barrett Wendell's *Literary History of America* which Father quotes in his *Holmes of the Breakfast Table*.

Page

Chapter 10. The Mighty Maidens

185. Leon Edel, *Henry James, The Middle Years*. Philadelphia and New York, 1962.

189. Father's tribute to Miss Curtis appeared in the *Boston Globe* after her death.

223. The book by my brother Mark, to which Cousin Alice refers, was his *Holmes-Pollock Letters* (2 vols.), Cambridge, 1941.

227. F. C. Burnand, an early editor of *Punch*, was author of *Happy Thoughts*.

231. Father's tribute to Cousin Alice appeared in the Fall issue of the *Bryn Mawr Alumnae Bulletin*, 1953.

Chapter 11. Voices

234. The concept of the Boston-Harvard mustache belongs to Elizabeth Hardwick, *A View of My Own*, April 1918.

241. It is Jacques Barzun who speaks of Chapman in *The Selected Writings of John Jay Chapman*, edited by Jacques Barzun, New York, 1957.

246. In a letter from Mencken to Bradford, written January 17, 1919, he says, "In my review [*Portraits of American Women*, Boston, 1919] I want to point out how you invented the Lytton Strachey scheme long before Strachey had ever heard of it." *Letters of H. L. Mencken*, collected and annotated by Guy J. Forque, New York, 1961.

248. Hamlin Garland, 1860–1940, novelist, historian, lecturer.

249. Father quotes in *John Jay Chapman and His Letters* from Chapman's *The Roman Catholic Mind*: Extract from my *Secret Journal*, produced and distributed broadly by Chapman in 1928.

> "Yes, Boston has been conquered and subdued.
>   Her monuments are meaningless;—her dome
> That seems to shine in heaven's solitude,
>   Is but a symbol of the Church of Rome.
> Gone is the race that once embattled stood
>   For Liberty—for conscience, hearth and home,
> The stars and stripes wave on, o'er souls that quail.
>   Take heed my country. 'Tis no fairy-tale."

"To a Roman Catholic Friend" (His sister-in-law, Mrs. Winthrop Chanler)

> "Shall we sit and talk it over?
>   I can tell you what I mean;
> Yet not break the glassy cover—
>   The divide that falls between.

Page

> Any thought I hand or slide you
> In your case, you take and toss
> Towards the priest that stands beside you,
> To appraise for gold or dross."

254. Both Chapman and Wister are quoted in Father's *Semi-Centennial History of the Tavern Club.*
Chapman's son Victor was a member of the Lafayette Escadrille, and was killed in combat at Verdun, June 1916.
The "swan boats" in Boston's Public Garden took wing, on Chapman's fancy, to become "The Lohengrins."

255. Langdon Warner, 1881–1955, archeologist, field Fellow of the Fogg Museum, is quoted in the *Semi-Centennial History of the Tavern Club.*

Chapter 12. Mother—the Principle of Resistance to Boston

262. *The Opal,* anonymous, Boston, Houghton Mifflin, 1905.

262. Henry Adams, *The Education of Henry Adams,* Boston and New York, 1918.

272. *The Notion Counter, A Farrago of Foibles, Notes about Nothing by Nobody.* Boston, 1922; *Small Wares, An Overflow from the Notion Counter,* Boston, 1925.

Chapter 13. The Articulate Quincys

280. Ferris Greenslet, the brilliant "literary adviser" to Houghton Mifflin Company.

282. To explain the Quincy-Adams connection: Abigail Smith, who became the wife of John Adams, was the granddaughter of Colonel John Quincy, 1689–1767 (for whom the town of Quincy was named, and who was first cousin of Colonel Josiah Quincy, 1710–1784). She named her son after her grandfather, John Quincy, on his deathbed. John Quincy Adams himself one day was to say, "It was filial tenderness that gave the name. It was the name of one passing from earth to immortality. These have been among the strongest links of my attachment to the name of Quincy, and have been to me through life a perpetual admonition to do nothing unworthy of it."

293. Geoffrey T. Blodgett, Department of History, Oberlin College, Oberlin, Ohio.

Chapter 14. Cotuit—the Calm of the Oyster Beds

297. George Santayana, *The Last Puritan,* London, New York, 1936.

Page

303. Gardner Jackson, 1897–1965, newspaperman and government official. Co-editor, with Marion Frankfurter, of *Sacco-Vanzetti Letters*.

313. Mark Twain, "How to Tell a Story."

Chapter 15. *Mother and Father—as Mother and Father*

332. Illustration of four Josiah Quincys, following page 332. Seated at left: Josiah Quincy, 1772–1864; standing, Josiah Quincy, 1802–1882; infant in arms, Josiah Quincy, 1859–1919; seated at right, Josiah Phillips Quincy, 1829–1910.

332. Al Capp, quoted in *Art Buchwald in New York,* December 30, 1958, "Don't Be a Pal to Your Son."

341. "Delusion and Reality" appeared in the *Atlantic* for December, 1933.

344. François Fénelon, *Spiritual Letters of Archbishop Fénelon.* Translated by H. L. Lear. Quoted in *The Choice Is Always Ours, An Anthology of the Religious Way,* edited by Dorothy Berkley Phillips. Co-edited by Elizabeth Boyden Howes and Lucille M. Nixon. New York, 1960.

345. I cannot be sure the man whom President Lowell quoted was Macaulay; that is simply my impression.

Chapter 16. *A General Calamity*

373. Alexander James, 1890–1946, artist, was the brother of Billy and son of William James, the philosopher.

381. Father's description of Allston Burr occurs in an introduction to a verse in his *Personae Gratae.*

391. The Zen concept of "realization" is described by Herbert Benoît in his *The Supreme Doctrine,* New York, 1955.

391. Thoreau, *Walden,* Boston, 1854.

392. Blaise de Montluc is quoted in a footnote by F. L. Lucas in his book on *Style,* New York, 1955, 1962.

396. Slater Brown is a writer belonging to the period, and a friend of e. e. cummings.

396. Chiang Yee, *The Silent Traveler in Boston,* New York, 1959.

Chapter 20. *The Old Men*

399. It was the National Institute of Arts and Letters to which Father and William Delano wished to see Ruth Draper elected.

401. The lectures—"The Bill of Rights"—were given in 1958 at the Harvard Law School, published by the Harvard University Press in 1958 and in a paperback edition by Atheneum.

Page

405. Dr. Roger Lee was born in 1881, and is a Fellow of the Harvard Corporation.

406. Henry James is the nephew of the novelist.
This Henry James (Harry, to his friends), 1879–1947, was the son of the philosopher William James, and brother of Billy. He was a great friend of Father's. Among many other interests, they shared an interest in both Harvard and biography which James exemplified when he won the Pulitzer Prize for his biography of Charles William Eliot. He also wrote a biography of Richard Olney, and others.

406. Charles E. Wyzanski, Jr., Judge of U.S. District Court in Boston.

407. "On Listening to Benét's John Brown's Body as Read as a Talking Book for the Blind"—poem, *Saturday Review,* February 16, 1952.

408. The chapter on Sarah Orne Jewett appeared in *Who Lived Here?*

408. Arthur Twining Hadley, 1856–1930, President of Yale from 1899–1921.

410. "Fan" refers to Miss Fanny Curtis.

412. Willard Learoyd Sperry, 1882–1954, Dean of the Harvard Divinity School.

415. Leonard Bacon, 1887–1954, author and writer of verse, was a friend of whom Father was very fond. He lived in Peace Dale, R.I., but came often to Boston.

423. The author of *The Initials,* published in 1892, was Jemima (Montgomery) Freifau von Tautphoes.

425. The "terrible misfortune" which had come upon the nation was President Eisenhower's third major illness while in office.

SOURCES

THESE PERSONAL RECOLLECTIONS, as well as the obvious cases in which I could not have had firsthand knowledge or experience, have been supplemented and reinforced by the following books and articles:

Part I. That Most Engaging Youth—the Gallant and Genial DeWolfe

ADAMS, J. DONALD, *Copey of Harvard*, Boston, 1960.

BROOKS, VAN WYCK, *New England: Indian Summer*, New York, 1940.

CATHER, WILLA, *Not Under Forty*, New York, 1936. (Sketches "148 Charles Street" and "Miss Jewett.")

DAVIS, CHARLES BELMONT, ed., *Adventures and Letters of Richard Harding Davis*, New York, 1917.

HOWE, GEORGE, "Number Eighteen," *American Heritage*, New York, June, 1962.

——, *Mount Hope, A New England Chronicle*, New York, 1959.

HOWE, M. A. DEWOLFE (1808–1895) (Bishop), *Reminiscences of My Life*, privately typed.

HOWE, M. A. DEWOLFE, *Memories of a Hostess*, Boston, 1922.

——, *Holmes of the Breakfast Table*, London, 1939.

——, *A Venture in Remembrance*, Boston, 1941.

——, *Bristol, Rhode Island, A Town Biography*, Cambridge, 1930.

JAMES, HENRY, *The American Scene*, New York and London, 1907.

——, *Notes of a Son and Brother*, New York, 1914.

——, "Mr. and Mrs. James T. Fields," *Atlantic Monthly*, 1915.

MATTHIESSEN, F. O., *Sarah Orne Jewett*, Boston and New York, 1929.

MOSES, MONTROSE J., AND GERSON, VIRGINIA, *Clyde Fitch and His Letters*, Boston, 1924.

Part II. Boston—the Place and the People

DANIELS, WILLIAM P., AND MASON, HENRY LOWELL, *Charles Mills Cabot, Harvard College, Class of 1888*, privately printed.

FORBES, EDWARD WALDO, ed., Edith Webster Gregg, *Naushon Memories.*
The Island Books, selections from unpublished records in the possession
of the Forbes family of Naushon Island.

HOWE, M. A. DEWOLFE, *Semi-Centennial History of the Tavern Club,*
Boston, 1934.

LEE, JOSEPH, *Frances Rollins Morse,* one of a collection of sketches by
friends, privately printed.

MCIVER, ELIZABETH PUTNAM, *Early Days at Putnam Camp,* privately
printed, read at the Annual Meeting of the Keene Valley Historical
Society, September, 1941.

MORISON, S., AND R. RUZIKA, *Recollections of Daniel Berkeley Updike,*
Boston, 1943.

Part III. The Underground Spring That Fed You All

BOWEN, CATHERINE DRINKER, *John Adams and the American Revolution,*
Boston, 1950.

HOWE, M. A. DEWOLFE, *Biographer's Bait,* Proceedings of the Massachusetts Historical Society, Vol. 68.

——, *The Articulate Sisters,* Cambridge, 1946.

——, *Josiah Phillips Quincy,* Proceedings of the Massachusetts Historical Society, Vol. 45.

HOWE, QUINCY, *Reminiscences,* Oral History Research Office, Columbia
University, 1962.

MUNROE, J. P., *The New England Conscience,* 1915.

QUINCY, EDMUND, *Life of Josiah Quincy,* Boston, 1867.

QUINCY, JOSIAH, *Memoir of the Life of Josiah Quincy, Jun. of Massachusetts,* Boston, 1825.

QUINCY, JOSIAH, *Figures of the Past, from the Leaves of Old Journals,*
Boston, 1883.

QUINCY, SAMUEL M., *History of the Second Massachusetts Regiment of
Infantry. A Prisoner's Diary.* Boston, 1882.

Part IV. Old Age Is Like Another Country

HOWE, M. A. DEWOLFE, *Later Years of the Saturday Club,* Boston, 1927.

CHECKLIST OF PUBLISHED BOOKS
BY M. A. DEWOLFE HOWE

THE FOLLOWING CHECKLIST is not a bibliography. It does not include magazine articles, introductions to other books, or any of the countless miscellaneous pieces of writing by my father which were published in his lifetime.

Biographical

American Bookmen. New York: Dodd, Mead & Company, 1898.

Phillips Brooks (in *Beacon Biographies* series). Boston: Small, Maynard & Co., 1899.

Life and Letters of George Bancroft. New York: Charles Scribner's Sons, 1908.

Life and Labors of Bishop Hare, Apostle to the Sioux. New York: Sturgis & Walton Co., 1911.

George von Lengerke Meyer—His Life and Public Services. New York: Dodd, Mead & Co., 1919.

Memories of a Hostess—Boston: Atlantic Monthly Press, 1922.

Barrett Wendell and His Letters. Boston: Atlantic Monthly Press, 1924. (Received Pulitzer Prize for biography.)

Causes and Their Champions. Boston: Little, Brown & Co., 1926.

Classic Shades. Boston: Little, Brown & Co., 1928.

James Ford Rhodes, American Historian. New York and London: D. Appleton & Co., 1929.

Representative Twentieth Century Americans. Chicago: American Library Association, 1930.

Portrait of an Independent—Moorfield Storey, 1845–1929. Boston: Houghton Mifflin Co., 1932.

The Children's Judge—Frederick Pickering Cabot. Boston: Houghton Mifflin Co., 1932.

John Jay Chapman and His Letters. Boston: Houghton Mifflin Co., 1937.
Holmes of the Breakfast Table. London: Oxford University Press, 1939.
A Venture in Remembrance. Boston: Little, Brown & Co., 1941.

Historical

Boston, the Place and the People. New York: The Macmillan Co., London: Macmillan & Co., Ltd., 1903.

Boston Common: Scenes from Four Centuries. Cambridge: Riverside Press, 1910; Boston: Houghton Mifflin Co., 1921.

The Boston Symphony Orchestra. Boston and New York: Houghton Mifflin Co., 1914. Semicentennial ed., with John N. Burk—Boston and New York: Houghton Mifflin Co., 1931.

The Humane Society of the Commonwealth of Massachusetts. Boston: printed for the Humane Society at the Riverside Press, 1918.

The Atlantic Monthly and Its Makers. Boston: Atlantic Monthly Press, 1919.

I'm from Boston—Scenes from the Living Past (illustrated by picture and story). Boston: Atlantic Monthly Press, 1920.

Later Years of the Saturday Club. Boston: Houghton Mifflin Co., 1927.

Bristol, R. I.: a Town Biography. Cambridge: Harvard University Press, 1930.

A Partial and Not Impartial Semi-Centennial History of the Tavern Club. Boston: Houghton Mifflin Co., 1934.

The Tale of Tanglewood. New York: Vanguard Press, 1946.

Boston Landmarks (with photographs by Samuel Chamberlain and reproductions of old prints). New York: Hastings House, 1946.

Who Lived Here? (with photographs by Samuel Chamberlain). Boston: Little, Brown & Co., 1952.

Edited

The Beacon Biographies (31 volumes). Boston: Small, Maynard & Co., 1899–1910.

The Memory of Lincoln, 1899.

Home Letters of General Sherman. New York: Charles Scribner's Sons, 1909.

Lines of Battle (and other poems) by Henry Howard Brownell, 1912.

Letters of Charles Eliot Norton (with Sarah Norton). Boston: Houghton Mifflin Co., 1913.

The Harvard Volunteers in Europe. Cambridge: Harvard University Press, 1916.

A Scholar's Letters to a Young Lady (passages from the later correspondence of Francis James Child). Boston: Atlantic Monthly Press, 1920.

Memoirs of the Harvard Dead in the War Against Germany. Cambridge: Harvard University Press. Vol. I, 1920; Vol. II, 1921; Vol. III, 1922; Vol. IV (with others), 1923; Vol. V (with others), 1924.

A Late Harvest—Writings of C. W. Eliot. Boston: Atlantic Monthly Press, 1924.

Marching with Sherman—Letters and Campaign Diaries of Henry Hitchcock. New Haven: Yale University Press, 1927.

New Letters of James Russell Lowell. New York and London: Harper & Brothers, 1932.

The Articulate Sisters. Cambridge: Harvard University Press, 1946.

The Scholar-Friends: Letters of Francis James Child and James Russell Lowell (with G. W. Cottrell, Jr.). Cambridge: Harvard University Press, 1952.

Verse

Rari Nantes. Privately printed, by the Riverside Press, Cambridge, from designs of D. B. Updike, 1893.

Shadows. Boston: Copeland and Day, 1897.

Harmonies, A Book of Verse. Boston: Houghton Mifflin Co., 1909.

The Known Soldier; and Other Reminders of the War Dead. Boston: McGrath-Sherrill Press, 1924.

Yankee Ballads. Cambridge: Washburn & Thomas, 1930.

Songs of September. Boston: Houghton Mifflin Co., 1934.

Personae Gratae. Boston: Club of Odd Volumes, 1953.

Sundown: Later & Earlier Selected Poems. Boston: Little, Brown & Co., 1955.

INDEX

Adams, Brooks, 294–96
Adams, Charles Francis, 291
Adams, Henry, 262, 277
Adams, J. Donald, 51, 53
Adams, James Truslow, 241, 307–08
Adams, John, 281, 282
Adams, John Quincy, 281, 283
Adams, Samuel, 282
"Afterwards" (Howe), 349–50
Alcott, Bronson, 287
Aldrich, Thomas Bailey, 78, 86, 256
Alexander, F. M., 158
Allen, Alfred Reginald, 236
Allen, Elizabeth Howe, 236
Allen, Frederick Lewis, 258, 395
Allen, Reginald, 10, 11
All His Benefits (Howe), 324
American Bookman, 79
Ames, John Worthington, Jr., 367–68
Ames, Winthrop, 255, 322
Amory, Cleveland, 213
Appleton, William Sumner, 192
Arnold, Matthew, 74, 129, 202
Articulate Sisters, The (Howe, ed.),
  280, 377
Astor, Lady Nancy, 194
Atkinson, Brooks, 235
Atlantic Monthly, 4, 9, 12, 63, 66–67,
  77, 86, 90, 130, 151, 244–45, 253,
  272, 273, 335, 341, 355, 358, 407
Atlantic Monthly and Its Makers, The
  (Howe), 241
Atlantic Monthly Press, 240, 241, 243,
  257, 258
Atlas magazine, 336

Bacon, Leonard, 415
Baker, George P., 45

Baldpate Inn, Georgetown, Massachu-
  setts, 169
Baldwin, James, 30
Bancroft, George, 88
Barbour, Thomas, 134, 372
Barrymore, Ethel, 45
Barrymore, John, 51
Barton, Otis, 302
"Battle Hymn of the Republic," 90–
  91
"Beacon Biographies Series" (Howe,
  ed.), 79, 87–88, 233
Beard, Mary, 163
Beau Brummel (Fitch), 45
Beebe, William, 302
Berenson, Bernard, 42, 140, 427–29
Betty's Finish (Fitch), 46
Binyon, Laurence, 129, 203
"Biographer's Bait" (Howe), 285
Blaine, James Gillespie, 248
Book Buyer, 79
Booth, Edwin, 51, 74
Booth, Edwina, 143
Boott, F., 49
Boston, the Place and the People
  (Howe), 88, 92
Boston Athenaeum, 355–58, 378
Boston *Globe*, 198
Bostonians, The (James), 83
Bostonians, the "Dear People," 164–
  84
Boston Landmarks (Howe), 376
"Boston Letters" (Howe), 79
Boston *Post*, 53
Boston Symphony Orchestra, 107, 108,
  239, 379, 380
Bowditch, Henry P., 174
Bowditch, Nathaniel, 157, 174

ABOUT THE AUTHOR

After writing five novels, Helen Howe has here written her first work of nonfiction. Her novelist's gifts serve her well in this portrait of her father, Mark A. DeWolfe Howe, and the remarkable Bostonians who were his friends and colleagues.

Helen Howe is a member of a distinguished family which includes not only her father, who was the author and editor of more than forty books, and her mother, Fanny Quincy Howe, an essayist, but also two brothers— Quincy Howe, author, radio commentator, and editor of *Atlas* magazine, and Mark DeWolfe Howe, author and professor at Harvard Law School.

Miss Howe's early life was spent in Boston, where she was born and where she attended private schools and Radcliffe College. After teaching for a year, she decided to become an actress, spent a year in dramatic study in Paris, and in New York at the Theatre Guild School. There followed fifteen years during which, as a monologuist, she toured the country, twice appeared at the White House and gave solo recitals in New York and London theaters and supper clubs. She also has lived in Hollywood for three years.

Her first novel, *The Whole Heart,* appeared in 1943 and was followed by *We Happy Few, The Circle of the Day, The Success,* and *Fires of Autumn.*

Helen Howe and her husband, Reginald Allen, Special Assistant to the President and to the General Manager of the Metropolitan Opera, live in New York and also have a home at Mt. Desert, Maine.

Howe.

Gentle Americans.